Hong Kong's
Reunion with China

Hong Kong Becoming China: The Transition to 1997

Ming K. Chan and Gerard A. Postiglione

Series General Editors

Because of Hong Kong's remarkable development under British rule for the past 150 years and its contemporary importance as a world economic and communications center on the Pacific Rim, and due to Hong Kong's future status as a Special Administrative Region of the People's Republic of China from 1997 well into the mid-twenty-first century, M.E. Sharpe has inaugurated this new multi-volume series. Published for an international readership, this series aims at providing both expert analysis and the documentary basis for a more informed understanding of Hong Kong's transition as a free society and capitalist economy toward socialist Chinese sovereignty under the "One Country, Two Systems" formula.

This series explores various crucial dimensions of Hong Kong's current development in this transition process and their implications for the international community. Individual volumes in this series will focus on key areas and issues ranging from China's Basic Law for Hong Kong, education and social change, the existing common law legal system, the historical relationship between Britain, China, and Hong Kong, urban growth and infrastructural development, the control of the media, social movements and popular mobilization, the cultural identity of Hong Kong Chinese, to economic linkages with mainland China, the Beijing–Hong Kong–Taipei triangle, "brain drain" and migration overseas, as well as the internationalization of Hong Kong.

The books in this series so far are: *The Hong Kong Basic Law: Blueprint for "Stability and Prosperity" under Chinese Sovereignty?* edited by Ming K. Chan and David Clark; *Education and Society in Hong Kong: Toward One Country and Two Systems*, edited by Gerard A. Postiglione; *The Common Law System in Chinese Context: Hong Kong in Transition,* by Berry Hsu; *Precarious Balance: Hong Kong between China and Britain, 1842–1992,* edited by Ming K. Chan; *Reluctant Exiles? Migration from Hong Kong and the New Overseas Chinese,* edited by Ronald Skeldon; *The Hong Kong–Guangdong Link: Partnership in Flux,* edited by Reginald Yin-Wang Kwok and Alvin Y. So; *Hong Kong's Reunion with China: The Global Dimensions,* edited by Gerard A. Postiglione and James. T. H. Tang.

Ming K. Chan is a member of the History Department, University of Hong Kong, and Executive Coordinator of the Hong Kong Documentary Archives, Hoover Institution, Stanford University.

Gerard A. Postiglione is a member of the Department of Education, University of Hong Kong, and Director of its Education and National Development Program.

Hong Kong Becoming China:
The Transition to 1997

Hong Kong's Reunion with China

The Global Dimensions

Gerard A. Postiglione
and
James T. H. Tang
editors

An East Gate Book

M.E. Sharpe
Armonk, New York
London, England

H-Y LIB
(W)

DS
796
.H74
H72
1997

An East Gate Book

Library of Congress Cataloging-in-Publication Data

Hong Kong's reunion with China: the global dimensions / Gerard A. Postiglione
and James T.H. Tang, editors.
p. cm.—(Hong Kong becoming China)

"A East gate book."
Includes bibliographical references.
ISBN 0-7656-0155-9 (cloth : alk. paper)
ISBN 0-7656-0156-7 (paper : alk. paper)
1. Hong Kong.   2. Hong Kong—Foreign relations.
3. Hong Kong—Economic conditions.   I. Postiglione, Gerard A., 1951-
II. Tang, James Tuck-Hong, 1957-
III. Series.
DS796.H74G66   1997
951.25   dc21
97-9978
CIP

Printed in the United States of America

The paper used in this publication meets the minimum requirements of
American National Standard for Information Sciences—
Permanence of Paper for Printed Library Materials,
ANSI Z 39.48-1984.

BM (c)   10   9   8   7   6   5   4   3   2   1
BM (p)   10   9   8   7   6   5   4   3   2   1

Contents

Foreword: Chinese Globalism in Hong Kong

Lynn T. White III

Hong Kong people are understandably anxious about their future, as the twentieth century ends. This concern follows an old pattern, however; and they may fare as well in this turn as in the past. The "British Crown Colony" ended some time ago, in popular imagination if not in law. By slow steps and without public fanfare, it was replaced by a more modern, less politically or colorfully described "Territory." In the new "Special Autonomous Region" of China, people wonder whether they can maintain their prosperous growth and diverse lifestyle. They are likely to do so, because Hong Kong has long depended—even in politics— far more on trends inside China than either the colonial government or the city's people have liked to conceive, and the recent spate of PRC conservatism is not dominant over other Chinese trends. The long term, as revolutionary centralization falls to market coordination in China, bodes very well for Hong Kong's future.

The "Pearl of the Orient" has always grown from a synergy between global and national interests—and Chinese influences have usually been most pervasive. Even before the city was built, on a "barren Island with hardly a house upon it" as Palmerston said, for centuries already foreigners and Chinese had found many uses for each other in nearby Macau. Trade and cultural contact started in that smaller place largely because local Chinese officials found that Portuguese were effective marine police against local pirates. Of course, not all initiatives were Chinese, but the context even of foreigners' action was overwhelmingly so.

Mercantile and coercive networks of several nationalities profited, especially after the Opium War and the unequal treaty that ceded Hong Kong Island to Britain. This force, used in the interests of imperialist companies more than of their governments, made Hong Kong a global haven; but few would have stayed there without the China market. Scottish, English, American, Parsi, Bohra, American, Teochiu, Shanghainese, Cantonese, and other merchants all used Hong Kong harbor to trade in diverse goods—of which opium was for several decades the most lucrative, most linked to official and unofficial coercion, and most subject to abolishment. Hong Kong's population grew pell-mell, not just because of the city's detachment from China, but because immigrants seeking modern jobs joined wealthy Chinese who came there. Many sought refuge from Taipings after 1850, from radical nationalists after 1900, from Japanese troops after 1937, and from Communists after 1945.

Many Hong Kong Chinese therefore tended to be conservative and anti-political, not just apolitical. Visitors to the city still marvel at the use of window bars near the tops of residential high rises, not just because Hong Kong robbers are entrepreneurial, but also apparently as a symbol to keep various neo-Taipings and revolutionaries out of family spaces. Some Chinese immigrants to Hong Kong understood politics as violent, more than public. This anti-political climate came out of China, although it was also welcome enough to many in the colonial police and civil service who wanted docile citizens, as well as to business people who wanted docile workers. Explicitly public attitudes, by contrast, were sponsored by several governors: Pope-Hennessey with his Irish Catholic ideas about ethnic equality, MacLehose with his Independent Commission Against Corruption, and Patten with his expanded electorate.

Government initiatives have nonetheless been controversial as a genre in Hong Kong. They tend to require both political decisions and tax revenues. Public projects have largely been limited to those which benefit businesses without choosing between them, by lowering the general price of labor. Cheap housing (after a disastrous fire among squatter huts at Shek Kip Mei in the mid-1950s) became an important government expenditure. Water shortages in the next decade forced the use of public funds for reservoirs at Plover Cove and High Island. Transport bottlenecks, which slowed workers from getting to their jobs, inspired the government to support credit for tunnels and the Mass Transit Railway. As Hong Kong capitalists' manufacturing operations moved increasingly into Guangdong, the government raised its traditionally minimal support for education, to produce the white-collar workers, of whom businesses then needed a greater supply.

Hong Kong's projects remained economic, and they might be described in an historical series of economic styles: British imperialist, American liberal, Japanese mercantilist, and "Greater China" regionalist.[1] In recent decades, the culture underlying these styles in Hong Kong has always remained cosmopolitan with strong Chinese characteristics. The state in Hong Kong, except through its effect on the price of labor, has been less prominent as a direct instigator of economic development than in Japan, South Korea, Taiwan, Singapore, or the PRC. A "negative sovereignty," free from outside interference, has been crucial in constructing the Hong Kong "quasi-state."[2] As a result, this city has risen to economic supremacy in South China. Hong Kong in 1995 had a GDP more than 22 percent of the mainland's, but it had just half of one percent of the PRC's population. This economy depends on China, as much as on Hong Kong's connections with other parts of the world.

It creates a cultural identity that like all other really usable wisdom "will remain ambiguous, as cultural identity is continuously remade by human agents."[3] The result may be neither Chinese nor Western (*"bu Zhong bu xi,"* in the dialect of the North where intellectuals most often disdain it). The main musical product from Hong Kong, for example, is surely "Canto-pop," with audiences that are important overseas and will become so in the mainland as the dialect is adapted. China is a large place. The politically dangerous "Hong Kong wind" (*Gang feng*) that Beijing intellectuals and officials tend to scorn blows strongly in many areas. Within Hong Kong, Cantonese television channels are more popular than Mandarin or English ones.[4]

Global influences have been most evident in the sectors of Hong Kong activity that will most help modern reforms in China. Civil law and tertiary education are prime sectors for internationalization.[5] Communist Chinese conservatives may try to arrange intellectual creativity without academic freedom. Traditionalists may hope for political control, even in efficient modern situations, without control by laws that are standard and specialized. But Hong Kong, as China's richest and most diverse city, will increasingly suggest new "traditions" for many kinds of mainland Chinese.

The Tiananmen tragedy obscured this possibility, by suggesting that the Beijing regime could govern modern China without changing. In response, the British offered Hong Kong a Bill of Rights, as well as a broadened electorate that contrasted with earlier colonial styles, and some "insurance" passports.[6] Democracies such as Australia, Canada, and the United States also had sharp, if somewhat different, responses to the June 4 violence.[7] The crucial results of these actions, however, will come in Hong Kong and in China.

Nostalgic Leninists, who have been important at high ranks in the Chinese Communist Party since 1989 (though reformers were important earlier in that decade), will surely rue the sight of Hong Kong Chinese people rallying to maintain their recent rights. They may blame these politics partly on foreign teachers and lawyers. But the mainland of China now hosts many power networks, many of which are in practice separated from the central state. Hong Kong is not China's only "Trojan horse" of modern diversity and capitalism. Actually, the PRC now has a large and scattered herd of such "Trojan horses." Some will compete with Hong Kong, while also envying and emulating its styles.

Especially as Chinese central politics may become more evenly balanced between conservatives and reformers, calls for more Chinese patriotism among Hong Kong people may have a considerable response. Until recently, half of all Hong Kong families included at least one parent born in China. By no means have all of these people been very fearful of the Chinese government, and not all of them see strong reasons to emigrate.[8] Outward-looking traditions among many South Chinese lineages, not just the interests of foreign merchants, have maintained the cosmopolitan atmosphere.

Reports by the World Bank and the United Nations Development Program indicate that no non-democratic government in the world rules a place with either a higher GDP per capita or higher measurable levels of human development than in Hong Kong.[9] Totalism is very difficult to sustain indefinitely, in a society as varied as Hong Kong's. On Chinese grounds, even if following global patterns, a mix of modern styles in both culture and politics will last for many years. The book in your hands is the best possible introduction to the forces that come into play, as China reunites with its most modern city.

Lynn T. White III is Professor of Politics and International Affairs, Woodrow Wilson School, Princeton University.

Notes

1. This expands on ideas in the chapter below by Lai On-Kwok and Alvin Y So.
2. See the chapter below by Byron Weng, quoting James T.H. Tang.
3. Quoted from Helen Siu in the chapter below by Graham Johnson.
4. Much more on these topics is available below in the chapters by Hoiman Chan and Joseph Man Chan.
5. See the chapters below Roda Mushkat and by Gerard A. Postiglione.
6. The chapter below by Ming K. Chan contains far more on these "salvage measures" and allied matters.
7. See the chapter below by Kim Richard Nossal.
8. See the chapter below by Janet W. Salaff and Wong Siu-lun.
9. See especially U.N. Development Program, *Human Development Report, 1996* (New York: Oxford University Press, 1996), p. 135; and for a slightly less clear accounting (because of Singapore's ranking only), World Bank, *World Development Report, 1996* (New York: Oxford University Press, 1996), p. 189.

Acknowledgments

This project has been many years in the making. It resulted from collaboration between the editors that began after Gerry Postiglione returned to Hong Kong from a sabbatical at the Johns Hopkins University School of Advanced Studies. At that time, James Tang was conducting research on Hong Kong's international status and teaching international relations at the University of Hong Kong. Both editors had a special interest in the implications of Hong Kong's transition for the territory's interactions with the global community. They organized a workshop on the theme: "the Internationalization of Hong Kong," sponsored by the Centre of Asian Studies of the University of Hong Kong in March of 1995. Potential volume contributors were invited to present drafts to a specialist audience, after which their papers were critiqued by designated scholar/specialists in the respective fields. Among the participants were the then Vice-Chancellor of the University of Hong Kong, Professor Wang Gungwu, the then Director of the Centre of Asian Studies Professor Edward Chen, the Honorable Burton Levin, Director of the Asia Society Hong Kong Center and past Consul General of the American Consulate in Hong Kong, Gordon Crovitz, Editor of the *Far East Economic Review,* Margaret Ng, Legislative Councilor, Ian Perkins, chief economist of the Hong Kong General Chamber of Commerce, and a number of prominent scholars from the region, including professors John P. Burns, Ming K. Chan, Chi Hsi-sheng, Chung Yue-Ping, Grant Evans, Lui Tai-lok, Paul Kwong and Elizabeth Sinn. We would like to thank the contributors of the volume for their hard work, patience and cooperation, as well as the workshop participants for their useful and constructive comments. Finally, we thank our research assistants Patrick Lam, Michele Fong, and Roy Man Chi-Kwong for their assistance. Any mistakes are the sole responsibility of the editors.

Contributors

Gerard A. POSTIGLIONE is associate professor in the department of education of the University of Hong Kong. He is the series general editor of Hong Kong Becoming China: The Transition to 1997. He has been a visiting scholar at the Johns Hopkins School of Advanced International Studies in 1988 and a visiting professor at Peking University in 1994. Among his most recent publications are the *Hong Kong Reader: Transfer to Chinese Sovereignty* (with Ming K. Chan, 1996), *Social Change and Educational Development: Mainland China, Taiwan and Hong Kong* (with Lee Wing On, 1995), *Higher Education in East Asia* (with Grace C.L. Mak, 1997), and *The Education of China's National Minorities*, forthcoming.

James T.H. TANG is associate professor, department of politics and public administration, University of Hong Kong. Educated in Hong Kong and the United Kingdom, he studied at the University of Hong Kong and Cambridge University, and obtained his Ph.D. from the London School of Economics and Political Science. His research focuses on international relations in the Asia-Pacific region with special reference to China and Hong Kong. He is the author of *Britain's Encounters with Revolutionary China, 1949–54* (1992), and editor of *Human Rights and International Relations in the Asia-Pacific Region* (1995).

CHAN Hoi Man is a lecturer in sociology at the Chinese University of Hong Kong. His research interest is in the sociology of culture, a field in which he has written much in both English and Chinese. His doctoral dissertation entitled *Theory and Society in the People's Republic of China—Outline of a Perspective on Chinese Socialism,* was completed at the University of Toronto.

Ming K. CHAN is a member of the history department of the University of Hong Kong, and executive coordinator of the Hong Kong Documentary Archives at the Hoover Institution of Stanford University. His recent books include: *The Hong Kong Basic Law: Blueprint for Stability and Prosperity under Chinese*

Sovereignty (1991), *Schools into Fields and Factories: The Anarchists, the Guomindang and the National Labor University in Shanghai 1927–32* (1991), and *Precarious Balance: Hong Kong Between Britain and China 1842–1992* (1994).

Graham JOHNSON is professor of sociology in the department of anthropology and sociology, University of British Columbia. He was a visiting professor of applied social studies at the City University of Hong Kong, 1995–97. He has conducted fieldwork in Hong Kong, in the Pearl River Delta region of Guangdong Province, south China and in Chinese communities in Canada over three decades. He has published widely in these areas, including essays in *Reluctant Exiles* and *The Hong Kong –Guangdong Link* (1995), earlier volumes in the Hong Kong Becoming China series of which this volume is also part.

On-Kwok LAI is lecturer in political science and public policy, the University of Waikato (New Zealand), and currently holds honorary appointments at the University of Hong Kong: lectureship in social work and social administration and research fellowship at the centre of urban planning and environmental management. He received a B.Soc.Sc. from the University of Hong Kong (1983) and Dr.rer.pol. from the University of Bremen (Germany, 1991). His research interests are on the comparative socio-political aspects of public (environmental, social and urban) policies.

Roda MUSHKAT is a professor of law at the University of Hong Kong, where she has been teaching since 1979 the subjects of public international law, jurisprudence, law and society, constitutional and administrative law, and conflict of laws. She has been affiliated as a visiting scholar with some of the world's leading law schools. Dr. Mushkat has published extensively in the areas of international refugee law, international environmental law, international law of war, human rights and legal theory. She is considered to be the principal academic authority on issues pertaining to Hong Kong's international legal status and personality, and has recently published *One Country, Two International Legal Personalities: The Case of Hong Kong* (1996).

Kim Richard NOSSAL is professor and former chair in the department of political science, McMaster University, Hamilton, Canada. He has published extensively on international relations issues. He is the author of a number of works on Canadian and Australian foreign policy, including *Rain Dancing: Sanctions in Canadian and Australian Foreign Policy* (1994) and *The Politics of Canadian Foreign Policy* (1997).

Janet SALAFF is professor of sociology in the University of Toronto. She has been employed since 1970 at the University of Toronto, department of sociology, and cross appointed at the Centre for Urban and Community Studies. She is affiliated with the Joint Centre for Asian Pacific Studies (York University and University of Toronto) and the Centre for Asian Studies, University of Hong Kong. She received her Ph.D. degree in 1972 from the University of California, department of sociology. She researches Chinese society on the Pacific Rim and began the study of Hong Kong through the colony's female factory workers, published as *Working Daughters of Hong Kong* (1981). That volume also sparked her interest in participant and naturalistic observation of Chinese family processes, which is continued in her chapter in this volume.

Alvin Y. SO is professor in sociology at University of Hawaii. He received a B.Soc.Sc. from the Chinese University of Hong Kong in 1975 and Ph.D. from UCLA in 1982. He is interested in studying the socio-political issues relating to Hong Kong, the Chinese mainland-Taiwan-Hong Kong triangle, and East Asia. His recent publications include: *Hong Kong–Guangdong Link: Partnership in Flux* (edited with Reginald Kwok, 1995); *East Asia and the World Economy* (with Stephen Chiu, 1995); *Asia's Environmental Movements in Comparative Perspective* (edited with Yok-shiu Lee, forthcoming); *Hong Kong's Embattled Democracy: A Societal Analysis* (forthcoming).

TING Wai is associate professor in the department of government and international studies of the Hong Kong Baptist University. Formerly a research fellow in the Institute of Southeast Asian Studies, Singapore, he obtained his doctorate in political science from the University of Paris-X. His research interests are Chinese politics and international relations. He has published extensively on domestic politics and foreign policies of China, and China-Hong Kong relations.

Byron S.J. WENG is professor of government and public administration at the Chinese University of Hong Kong. His extensive publications, in both English and Chinese, cover mostly the politics, law and foreign policy of the PRC, Taiwan and Hong Kong. His current research focuses on the international relations among three parts of "the Greater China." He has served, at various times, as a member of the Law Reform Commission and a part-time member of the Central Policy Unit in Hong Kong, and as a research member of the National Unification Council and member of the Advisory Committee of the Mainland Affairs Council in Taiwan.

WONG Siu-lun is professor of sociology and director of the Centre of Asian Studies of the University of Hong Kong. He is Hong Kong Affairs Adviser, and a member of the Selection Committee of the First Special Administrative Region Government of Hong Kong. His publications include: *Emigrant Entrepreneurs: Shanghai Industrialist in Hong Kong* (1988), *Hong Kong and 1997: Strategies for the Future* (co-author, 1985), and *Hong Kong's Transition: A Decade after the Deal* (1995).

Hong Kong's Reunion with China

Introduction

Transforming Hong Kong's Global Identity

Gerard A. Postiglione and James T.H. Tang,
with Ting Wai

Unless it maintains its special international status and global linkages after July 1, 1997, Hong Kong could very well become just another city in South China. For the most part, this status was not bestowed, but rather earned through tough competition with other international players. Hong Kong won a significant slice of world trade, adeptly turned itself into a leading global banking center, and took advantage of its location to become a key communication and transportation hub. As the territory returns to Chinese sovereignty, competitor cities from Seoul, to Shanghai, Singapore, and Sydney are watchful of the "one country, two systems" transition process and prepared to capitalize should Hong Kong falter. Whether by virtue of Beijing's manipulation or by its own hand, Hong Kong could loose its competitive edge after 1997 and gradually slide backward toward international oblivion.

Although already highly international, Hong Kong cannot rest on its laurels if it is to meet the challenges of becoming a successful Special Administrative Region (SAR) of China while at the same time maintaining as well as strengthening its global position. It is still well situated to take advantage of many new opportunities of global networking. Its extensive international experience provides valuable wisdom and skills to do this. With about 1,800 multinational companies, Hong Kong remains one of the most open economies in the world for international business ventures. It is still an economic powerhouse with a global influence that seems far out of proportion to its size. But will it remain so? Part of the answer lies in the economy.

Hong Kong is certain to face novel and formidable economic challenges as its international proxy moves from London to Beijing. As the territory's political master, Britain had an important role in bringing Hong Kong into the international economy. Hong Kong adapted well to its affiliation with the Western world under British sponsorship. However, readaptation will be required as China replaces Britain in this role. The Basic Law defines how to some extent, though gray areas abound. What will happen, for example, if multinational companies with offices and commercial interests in Hong Kong (as well as Beijing) become dissatisfied with their treatment by the SAR government? Will they use a back door to Beijing, where the rule of law greatly differs from that in Hong Kong, to get what they want? If so, this could foster a different form of internationalization, perhaps more like mainland China's, than the kind traditionally at work in Hong Kong.

Hong Kong must exact the competition; continue to attract investments, including those from the increasingly globalized overseas Chinese business community; proceed to restructure its domestic economy; and position itself between East and West, North and South, and China and everywhere. Yet economy is still only one, albeit important, dimension of Hong Kong's global future. Among the other key issues are political changes, the continuation of its legal structures and laws, an international and free media, cultural identity, how knowledge is to be disseminated, as well as migration of Hong Kong people, and relationships with other international actors in the global community.

No other place in the world has been so successful at internationalizing without nationalizing. Even while separated from China during the colonial period, Hong Kong achieved a greater degree of participation in the international community than many other countries of the world. Yet it is questionable whether this will continue under the People's Republic of China's special brand of sovereignty. Operating in the international sphere required that Hong Kong have a great deal of autonomy. While much autonomy has been promised, there are certain to be differences from the form of autonomy practiced in pre-1997 Hong Kong. While this does present the PRC with an exciting task for the actualization of its sovereignty, Hong Kong is not an entirely new challenge. The PRC has shown its ability to permit and contain various levels of regional autonomy since its establishment in 1949. It has many decades of experience with its five autonomous provinces, including Xinjiang and Tibet. In these regions it has shown itself to be extremely uncompromising on the question of sovereignty. The PRC has spared no effort to ensure national unity in a world that has seen the disintegration of many major countries by the hand of separatist movements, including the former Soviet Union and Yugoslavia. There is little doubt that the Chinese government would not hesitate to take tough actions in Hong Kong should it perceive that Chinese sovereignty is at stake.

The aspiration of Hong Kong people for a high degree of autonomy within the global community is not altogether different from that of other groups. The struggles waged by cultural minorities in Quebec and Basque country have consisted of demands for limited autonomy and self-rule or similar status within the boundaries of the larger federal structure—demands that fall short of pursuit of complete autonomy with the status of a full international entity on par with a state. However, different dynamics are at work in Hong Kong. The majority of the people are ethnic Chinese, and their cultural identity is highly problematic and complex.[1] The Hong Kong case has to be understood in the context of its specific historical legacy and the political circumstances of the territory.

Historical Legacy

During more than 150 years of British rule, Hong Kong has remained a largely Chinese society, and though a colonial territory, it has enjoyed a high degree of autonomy. Chinese society managed to prosper there without excessive intervention from the colonial administration. The original goal of the British occupation was to establish a stronghold on the coast of Southern China to protect British military, commercial, and political interests in the Far East with little intention of transforming local social structure into a British community. To a large extent, the British government has maintained "indirect rule" over Hong Kong society.

Traditionally, the governor, as the highest official sent to Hong Kong by London, enjoyed a wide range of power. Until 1985, he appointed all the members of the Legislative Council. Constitutionally speaking, parliamentary acts passed in London imposed restrictions on the colonial legislature; however, in practice the legislation of British Parliament for Hong Kong was limited to a few areas such as defense, aviation, nationality, and treaties.[2] The governor seldom exercised what one would consider dictatorial power, and the colonial administration was known for practicing limited government, especially concerning the matters in Chinese society. British colonial governance has been generally lenient, if discriminatory at times.

The administration's economic policy has been characterized as laissez-faire, and despite trends toward "minimum noninterference" and "selective intervention," the government has avoided excessive intervention in the economic development of Hong Kong. Nevertheless, through land sales and other means, the government has exerted a fair amount of control over the economy. At the same time, colonial administrators have incorporated local Chinese elites, especially business people and professionals, into the establishment. As long as the administration had the support of Hong Kong's Chinese, and refrained from being too intrusive into the local Chinese community, the legitimacy of the colonial regime was not directly challenged.[3]

Since 1949, Hong Kong and China have followed divergent paths. As the mainland turned socialist under the leadership of the Chinese Communist Party, Hong Kong continued with its commercial activities and prospered as a free port. By the 1970s, Hong Kong had undergone economic restructuring and successful industrialization, resulting in its becoming one of the four Asian newly industrializing economies (NIEs), which together led the way for the spectacular economic transformation of East Asia. Since then it has taken the lead in its economic development with little guidance from Britain.

Pragmatic Nationalism

Nationalism has not been a significant element in the social psyche of the Hong Kong Chinese. While they often express a sense of pride over achievements by ethnic Chinese all over the world, they generally choose not to identify with the communist regime in Beijing. Thus, it is not surprising that the political identity of Hong Kong Chinese has been somewhat problematic, as reflected in survey results consistently indicating a strong sense of Hong Kong identity. A 1985 survey reported the proportion of respondents who identified themselves as Hong Kongers rather than Chinese was 60 percent; only 36 percent regarded themselves as Chinese. A 1988 survey found that the proportion of people who identify themselves as primarily Hong Kongers had increased to 63.6 percent, with only 28.8 percent regarding themselves as Chinese.[4] Though without a political entity (nation and state) with which to identify, the sense of belonging to Hong Kong has been surprisingly strong. Nevertheless, few if any would entertain the idea of self-determination. Frustration of circumstance has been accepted along with the notion of a "borrowed place on borrowed time."[5]

Long known for their pragmatism and value system based on "utilitarian familism," only in the decade leading to the return of sovereignty have Hong Kong people shed their characteristic political apathy and sole devotion to creation of wealth. Apart from the generation born and bred in Hong Kong after the Second World War, most Hong Kong citizens were migrants who left or "escaped" from China. For this group, Hong Kong was merely a convenient refuge and therefore their political demands were limited. It is hardly surprising that developing a sense of belonging to a place ruled by foreigners proved to be difficult, and thus they did little to challenge colonial rule. Deprived of national identity, Hong Kong's main attractions were political stability, economic prosperity, and social and cultural freedom. Although there were occasional outbursts of anticolonial feelings, and demonstrations against the government, in general Hong Kong people developed a positive attitude toward the honesty and efficiency of the Hong Kong government, and saw the function of government in an instrumental and pragmatic light.[6] In a society where Chinese nationalism was not politically charged, Hong Kong people operated with flexible identities and integrated more easily with those from other parts of the world. Industrious and willing to face challenges of discrimination in foreign lands, many Hong Kong Chinese succeeded in their adopted land after emigration and could therefore claim to be "global people" who see the world as a "global village." Without a strong sense of national identity, Hong Kong people were left with a sense of political impotence, and disbelief in rewards for political actions. Their views toward the territory's links with the outside world were dominated by pragmatic consideration with a focus on economic rather than political relations. Excellent communication networks and information flows with the rest of the world have not increased Hong Kong people's interest in world affairs or in domestic development of the neighboring Asian countries. During the 1990–91 Gulf War, the main concern was over the economic implications of the conflict for Hong Kong properties prices and other investments, rather than the conflict itself. The international news pages in the Chinese-language newspapers of Hong Kong are dominated by translations of reports from major Western news agencies. Those who work for the international desk are usually translators rather than journalists. In-depth analysis and assessment of current affairs from local perspectives are generally lacking. The outlook of Hong Kong people, therefore, is not necessarily highly international.

Hong Kong Chinese have been said to "participate less in almost all forms of conventional and unconventional participatory actions."[7] Aside from periodic protest action against China since 1989, and voting in district- and territorywide elections, the scope of their political action has been limited. Naturally, there has been a strong sentiment of political powerlessness in efforts to challenge the colonial or Beijing governments.[8] The colonial government generally succeeded in resolving domestic political conflicts, and avoided antagonizing the mainland government across the border. At the same time, the colonial administrators managed to maintain an efficient and clean government, especially since the 1970s. With an often inefficient, and repressive government in China, Hong Kong Chinese seemed contented with a stable and prosperous life even though they were under colonial rule.

Thus, the outlook of the Hong Kong people has been shaped by colonial history, Chinese culture, limited political participation, and the commercial nature of Hong Kong. Since 1949, Hong Kong and China have followed distinctly different paths of development. Although the Chinese government has always insisted that Hong Kong is part of Chinese territory, temporarily administered by the British for historical reasons, the two have not shared a view of common destiny. Since the 1980s, economic changes in China have narrowed the gap between the PRC and Hong Kong as the two economies have become increasingly integrated. Their relationship, however, remains largely one of convenience. Politically and socially they are still poles apart. It is challenging to imagine how the vehemently nationalistic outlook of the PRC government will be harmonized with the more moderate and global/pragmatic outlook of the people of Hong Kong.

Limits on International Participation

Hong Kong entered a turbulent period in the 1980s, when the British and Chinese governments began negotiations on the territory's future. As Hong Kong prospered and a new generation of Hong Kong Chinese born and bred in the territory came of age, the stage was set for the Sino-British negotiations and the subsequent agreement to return sovereignty of Hong Kong to China under the "one country, two systems" formula. After the conclusion of the Joint Declaration in 1984, the population of Hong Kong began to become more concerned about how they should be governed than any time in the territory's political history. The political process gradually became more democratized, which opened up the political establishment and placed pressure on the administration to be more accountable to the public. The legitimacy of the colonial administration become increasingly challenged. The problems of sovereignty transfer also generated heated political debates, and Hong Kong people became more aware of their political rights and obligations. In 1991, direct elections to the Legislative Council were introduced for the first time; in 1995, Hong Kong people saw their first fully elected legislature.[9] Recent studies have suggested that a new political culture is emerging in the territory, and that people are prepared to defy the Chinese and Hong Kong governments during election times.[10]

Some scholars, however, identified ambiguities in the emerging pattern of political attitudes in Hong Kong, arguing that in spite of the demand for democratic reform, public commitment to democracy in Hong Kong was instrumental and partial.[11] As the transfer of sovereignty approached, the Chinese identity among Hong Kong people appears to have become stronger. In a 1995 survey, the proportion of Hong Kong Chinese who identified themselves as Hong Kongers decreased from the 1980s to 53.7 percent, and those identified themselves as Chinese increased to 34.2 percent. Although the Chineseness of Hong Kong is a complicated subject, the people of Hong Kong seem to share an increasingly strong desire for political rights and participation. The 1995 survey indicated that among those who identified themselves as Chinese, attitudes toward questions such as state power and the right to demonstrate were not significantly different from those of the "Hong Kongers."[12] The political adjustment and accommodation during this political transition is clearly not a straightforward process. Yet political activism is rising, and political attitudes of the Hong Kong people have undergone significant, if still ambiguous, change.

Hong Kong also gradually acquired a higher degree of autonomy in the management of its external affairs. Since 1969, Hong Kong was empowered to sign bilateral agreements with foreign countries, and from 1973 onward it could even sign multilateral agreements. At the end of 1974 the Hong Kong government was permitted to freely dispose of (and invest) its currency reserves, which were originally deposited in the form of pounds sterling in Britain. As a result of the 1985 Hong Kong Act, and the Hong Kong (Legislative Powers) Order in Council issues in 1986, the Legislative Council of Hong Kong assumed the authority to amend or repudiate any acts implemented by the British Parliament in relation to Hong Kong, and to pass laws with extraterritorial application on matters such as shipping and aviation. In fact, Hong Kong's relations with London were far from smooth. Britain was party to the imposition of textile quotas on Hong Kong textile and clothing exports as early as the late 1950s, and its positions on international trade matters from the 1960s to the 1980s were often in conflict with those of Hong Kong. The Hong Kong government succeeded in reducing the proportion of its burden for the expenditure of the British Army stationed in the city from 75 percent to 65 percent in 1988. As a nonsovereign international actor, Hong Kong has participated autonomously in a large number of international organizations. In 1986, Hong Kong became a contracting party to the General Agreement on Tariffs and Trade (GATT) and a founding member of the World Trade Organization in 1995. By 1990 it established its own shipping registry. It joined the Asia Pacific Economic Cooperation (APEC) together with Taiwan and mainland China in 1991. By 1992 the territory was a member of 1,573 international organizations, compared to China's 1,729. The number of international organizations that located their headquarters/regional headquarters in the territory was 77, compared to 49 in China (see Appendix 1).[13]

The Beijing government has promised Hong Kong a high degree of autonomy and the right to maintain links with the outside world after the transfer of sovereignty. The principles concerning Hong Kong's external relations as expressed in the Joint Declaration are spelled out in the Basic Law (Articles 150 to 157 are in Chapter 7, on external relations). Accordingly, Hong Kong would enjoy autonomy in the management of its own external relations over economic and cultural matters, but not in national defense and diplomatic relations. Such protection, however, is limited by other provisions in the Basic Law that guarantee the political dominance of the central government over the Special Administrative Region.

According to the Basic Law (Article 23), Hong Kong can use the name "Hong Kong, China," to participate in international organizations and can be a signatory to international treaties. In addition, "the Central People's Government shall, where necessary, facilitate the continued participation of the Hong Kong Special Administrative Region in an appropriate capacity in those international organizations in which Hong Kong is a participant in one capacity or another, but of which the People's Republic of China is not a member." However, in cases where the central government believes participation is "not necessary," Hong Kong will have to withdraw its membership from such organizations. Similarly, "international agreements to which the People's Republic of China is not a party but which are implemented in Hong Kong may continue to be implemented in the Hong Kong Special Administrative Region. The Central People's Government shall, as necessary, authorize or assist the government of the Region to make appropriate arrangements for the application to the Region of other relevant international agreements." Moreover, Beijing can request Hong Kong to enact laws on its own to prohibit foreign political organizations from conducting political activities in the city, and to prohibit local political organizations from establishing ties with foreign groupings.

In April 1997, the Hong Kong SAR's Chief Executive–designate, Tung Chee-wah, proposed legislative changes to the Public Order and Societies ordinances. These changes would prohibit political parties from receiving donations from foreign nationals and grant the police authority to reject applications for public demonstrations on the ground of national security. The proposal, in the form of a consultation document, generated heated debates about political freedom in the territory.

In any case, the Beijing government, under the authority of Article 18 of the Basic Law, can, "in the event that the Standing Committee of the National People's Congress decides to declare a state of war or, by reason of turmoil within the Hong Kong Special Administrative Region which endangers national unity or security and is beyond the control of the government of the Region, decide the Region is in a state of emergency, in which case the Central People's Government may issue an order applying the relevant national laws in the Region."

The Hong Kong SAR's international activities will have to be pursued within the framework set by China's foreign policy priorities and relations with others. Mainland China–Taiwan relations, for example, will possibly impose constraints on the international presence of Hong Kong. It has been suggested that Hong Kong's participation in international organizations, including nongovernmental organizations, should be based on the principle of one China—that is, if a particular international organization accepts the People's Republic of China as a member, then Hong Kong should withdraw its membership.[14]

In fact, the Beijing government seems to have ignored the importance of the changing political attitude of Hong Kong people—rising political expectation and participation with a stronger sense of political inefficacy. The director of the Hong Kong and Macau Affairs Office of the State Council of the PRC, Lu Ping, points out:

> Hong Kong should and must continue to maintain her status as an economic and financial center, international business center, and international transportation center. But, Hong Kong in any case should not become a political center, let alone an international political center. If Hong Kong becomes a field where international political forces confront and enter into rivalry, it will bring disaster to the six million people living there.[15]

The Bill of Rights, passed by the Legislative Council in June 1991, is also a major point of contention. According to Article 39 of the Basic Law, "The provisions of the International Covenant on Civil and Political Rights, the International Covenant on Economic, Social and Cultural Rights, and international labor conventions as applied to Hong Kong shall remain in force and shall be implemented through the laws of the Hong Kong Special Administrative Region." The Bill of Rights passed in 1991 consisted of relevant provisions in the International Covenant on Civil and Political Rights.[16] Beijing has rejected the bill, contending that the protection of rights and freedoms of the Hong Kong people is already provided for in the Basic Law. Chinese officials were also dismayed at what they regarded as the supremacy of the Bill of Rights in Hong Kong laws, as legislation not consistent with the bill had to be modified. In October 1995, Chinese officials declared that those laws inconsistent with the Basic Law have to be repealed after 1997.[17]

Beijing's reaction to the 1990 British Nationality (Hong Kong) Act and the 1991 Bill of Rights demonstrated distrust. In an attempt to restore confidence to post-Tiananmen Hong Kong, the British government decided to grant the right of abode to fifty thousand Hong Kong families. Beijing rejected the scheme as an attempt to extend British colonial influence beyond 1997 and, moreover, declared that ethnic Chinese in Hong Kong who acquire British nationality will continued to be regarded as Chinese nationals if they stay in the SAR, thus denying them British consular access privilege.

Beijing's opposition to Governor Chris Patten's 1992 proposal to introduce a larger element of representation to the Legislative Council resulted in the breakdown of Sino-British talks over constitutional arrangements for Hong Kong. In 1995, the first Legislative Council fully elected by the people of Hong Kong was formed. The Chinese side abolished it in 1997, and replaced it with a "provisional legislature" until the first SAR legislature could be elected. Patten's proposal for political reform was considered part of a Western strategy for fighting against China. With the end of Cold War, the West has come to be seen as using Hong Kong as a pawn in the Sino-American trial of strength, thus placing Hong Kong at the so-called center of struggle in the post–Cold War period.[18] In May 1993, the Department of Propaganda of the Central Committee of Chinese Communist Party delivered a document entitled "On the United States Plan of Confrontation against China," the main theme of which is that Washington intends to infiltrate and subvert China through ideological and economic means. Specifically, the document accuses the United States government of attempting to "intervene in Hong Kong affairs publicly, openly support the changes of British government's policy against China, and intend to turn Hong Kong into a place of international political confrontations and a springboard for Britain and United States against China."[19] The selling of advanced military aircraft to Taiwan by both France and the United States in 1992 is seen as part of this grand strategy. The Chinese leadership is highly suspicious of international interests in the territory.

Many Western countries, however, have expressed a strong concern about Hong Kong's transition. For example, the United States Congress passed a *U.S.– Hong Kong Policy Act* in 1992 which requires the administration to report regularly on developments in Hong Kong (see Appendix 2). In March 1997 the United States House of Representatives passed the *Hong Kong Reversion Act* which links Hong Kong's autonomy to economic rights under American law. Also, the Clinton administration adopted a higher profile on the Hong Kong question in 1997, and placed Hong Kong high on the agenda of Sino-U.S. relations.

Whether or not Hong Kong can successfully maintain its international status and external links depends partly on Beijing's perceptions of the world. The internationalized economy of Hong Kong, however, guarantees global interest in the years to come. This may force China, as a Chinese proverb says, "to spare the rat to save the dishes," and help maintain Hong Kong's international status. Yet China remains concerned about foreign involvement in Hong Kong as a source of instability in Hong Kong as well as in China. Beijing will be watchful of Western actions, and is prepared to defend the principle of mutual nonintervention.

Internationalization at Risk?

The issues surrounding Hong Kong's global position and international links grow complex by the day as the process of Hong Kong's transformation from a British colony to a Chinese unfolds. This volume sets out to address a number of questions relating to this process. How international is Hong Kong? What are its international and global dimensions? How important are these dimensions to its continued success? How will these dimensions change, especially beyond the sphere of economics? Is Hong Kong's internationalization, defined in terms of its willingness to embrace international values and its capacity to maintain its international presence, at risk? The volume addresses these questions as they pertain to the changing situation, relations between mainland China, Taiwan, and Hong Kong; the positions of Australia, Canada, and United States on Hong Kong; internalization of international legal values; Americanization vs. Asianization; linkages to the world through Guangdong; strategies to emigrate overseas; cultural internationalization; media internationalization; and universities within the global academy.

Hong Kong's global situation needs to be understood within the framework of the actions of major international players. For example, the important but unstable relationship between the United States and China may very well be further complicated by the Hong Kong factor. U.S. interests in Hong Kong are substantial, with 1,200 American companies and 36,000 American citizens residing there. Moreover, 10 percent of the work force is employed by American firms in Hong Kong. It can, therefore, be expected to speak on issues of stability, fairness, and rule of law. Aside from having the largest American Chamber of Commerce operating in Hong Kong, the United States has a consulate that hopes to maintain its economic services, as well as cultural and even military activities (sixty-six naval vessel port calls each year, including aircraft carriers and submarines). U.S. policy toward China, including relations with Taiwan, can be expected to have an increasingly strong effect on American interests in Hong Kong, which was much less a possibility under colonial administration. A key factor, as Ming Chan notes in Chapter 1, will be how Hong Kong people will deal with an ongoing, sometimes subtle, sometimes overt, crisis of confidence in their new status, and whether they will takes sides in policy conflicts between the United States and China.

Regardless of how the United States deals with the Hong Kong SAR, there will be increasing limitations of Hong Kong's internationalization. Serious problems remain in the reunification due to obvious differences in size and economic disparity and bureaucratic mentality between the PRC and Hong Kong. Ming Chan astutely argues for "an enlightened, positive, and sensitive global perspective on Hong Kong's status transformation."

Hong Kong's global situation must also be understood from the point of view that it is one among different "Chinese actors" in the international arena. From this perspective, the limitations of its internationalism become clear. In Chapter 2, Byron Weng adeptly contrasts the international images of these three actors and their relationships with one another. Internationalization becomes a process in which both mainland China and Taiwan are attempting to internationalize Hong Kong in their own way. Citing evidence that Hong Kong is arguably a quasi-state, Weng skillfully demonstrates how its international dimensions are bound up with its relationship to the other two Chinese actors (mainland China and Taiwan) and their triangular relationship within the global community. While it is assumed that these dimensions are important to its continued success, it is clear that changes in these dimensions after 1997 will have much to do with the increasing interdependence among the three actors. At risk is not only Hong Kong's internationalism, but also its way of life, to which the international community can lend support by playing a monitoring role. Yet it remains to be seem how much of a role the international community will play in Hong Kong's future. As many countries now find their elections being monitored, the global community may take great interest in assuming a monitoring role in Hong Kong's unfolding democratization. Beijing may very well accept external monitoring as long as it is not interference. What is certain, as Weng predicts, is "greater triangular interdependence." Hong Kong may even play a part in shaping the manner in which China solidifies its position in the family of nations. While Hong Kong is unquestionably international, its global dimensions are inextricably bound up with the polices of three major Western countries: Australia, Canada, and the United States. As Kim Nossal observes in Chapter 3, Hong Kong's continued success is dependent on how the international cards are played by these three countries. Yet involving the international community in its development is a sensitive issue. Should such involvement become significant, there is little question that these countries, key players in their own right, will continue to be major destinations for Hong Kong emigrants. At the same time, these Western countries also have major interests at stake in Hong Kong. Unfortunately, as Nossal notes, their views of China inevitably affect their attitudes toward Hong Kong—attitudes that have swung between taking individual approaches and taking a more galvanized approach. At risk is Hong Kong's global position, which could very easily be lost if the major Western countries, including the Untied States, do not play their cards right.

The United States is by far not free of competition for China's attention. Japan and other countries in the region will become more influential in shaping

Hong Kong's development. In fact, the East Asian region is likely to exert an increasing influence on Hong Kong's development in comparison to Britain or the United States. For Lai On-Kwok and Alvin So, as they argue in Chapter 4, Hong Kong is international insofar as the major economic projects affecting it are international. But the international projects have been sponsored at different times by the United States, Japan, and other Asian newly NIEs, as well as by the emerging economies of the region, including China. These economic projects have extended Hong Kong's global dimensions through forms of capital accumulation, export-led industrialization, and the international division of labor. In short, these dimensions are the basis of Hong Kong's continued success. From this economic standpoint, the internationalization of Hong Kong is hardly at risk; however, that internationalization is now increasingly driven by Asia, rather than United States or Japanese. While the future seems to promise an expansion of this Asianization, there are forces that could slow it down, including divisions in Asia along religious, political, and cultural lines as well as around security issues.

Lai and So trace the process that led colonial Hong Kong to its status as an NIE in the global arena and how that process was brought about through a series of projects backed at different periods of time by different international economic players. From the 1940s to the 1960s, the only significant international sponsor was the United States. Beginning in the late 1970s, they argue, Japan's economic project in the region sponsored a trajectory for Hong Kong's participation in the global economy that differed significantly from U.S. sponsorship. Moreover, by the late 1980s, the larger Asian project including Taiwan, Singapore, and Korea, as well as mainland China and other developing economics in the region further shaped Hong Kong's internationalization. In general, these major economic projects are reflected in a shift away from Americanization and toward Asianization.

The most significant economic project for Hong Kong is the one involving its hinterland, which borders the PRC. This project is important not only because of the major implications of the hinterland for the restructuring of Hong Kong's economy, but also because it is focused on Southern China, the region through which Hong Kong will rejoin China. The implications here are far-reaching, especially in cultural terms, because these southern regions share a common heritage. As Graham Johnson shows in Chapter 5, each side of the border is having a major social and cultural influence on the other. Already a prominent member of the global economy, Hong Kong, as much as Beijing, has become the sponsor for South China. Guangdong is Hong Kong's link into the mainland Chinese economy, and Hong Kong is Guangdong's link into the global economy (with the rest of South China riding its coattails). Since most of Hong Kong's people come from the Pearl River Delta, by far the most dynamic part of southern Guangdong, extensive social networks have developed that span and link the regions.

The social and cultural aspects of this phenomenon cannot be underestimated, for fundamental issues of identity are being brought into question. As Johnson remarks, "Hong Kong constitutes a distinct local variant of Chinese culture. Its distinction reflects, in part, responses to the pressures of world systems." The risk for Hong Kong is that in exerting its strong cultural influence on Guangdong, it has planted seeds for social transformation that Beijing is not prepared to accept. This may necessitate reining in Hong Kong's influence, not at the Shenzhen border, which would be futile given the strength of the cultural bond with the adjoining regions, but rather shielding Hong Kong from the "culturally corrupting" forces of the international community. Thus, a key question concerns the degree to which certain international values have become anchored in Hong Kong.

The rule of law, an independent judiciary, a bill of rights, and other legal provisions are good indications of Hong Kong's international legal personality. It already has a well-developed international legal framework and is a "respectable player in the international arena"; however, the question remains whether or not Hong Kong can maintain its international legal personality. To do so, according to Roda Mushkat in Chapter 6, it must "internalize" existing legal values and legal arrangements. Aside from interference by the PRC through legislative infiltration, another threat to its solid international legal basis is its parochialism. Unless that legal personality can be securely anchored in indigenous values and culture, it will quickly erode. International isolation would certainly spell doom, but even a slight move to cordon off the global community could begin to undermine the integrity of the legal system. Maintaining at least a degree of integration with the key international players is essential.

The cultural problematic of Hong Kong's identity is yet another key dimension in its internationalization. Culture becomes influenced by, and in turn shapes, the economy. Moreover, the economic give-and-take between Hong Kong, its adjacent regions, and the rest of the world is characterized by cultural penetrations with repercussions for sociocultural life in Hong Kong. Rather than selective assimilation, there is a mechanism of cultural indigenization at work in Hong Kong. To better understand this mechanism, Hoiman Chan in Chapter 7 presents two programs for Hong Kong's cultural internationalization, one normative and one partial. These represent two alternative stages upon which Hong Kong's "cultural drama is enacted." The former program is confident as it combines cosmopolitanization and indigenization processes. The latter crumbles under the weight of China's mammoth influence so that Hong Kong can no longer to hold its own in cultural terms.

It appears that the internationalization of Hong Kong culture has until now been ephemeral and incomplete. Interestingly, this is exemplified in the emerging preference of many multinational companies in Hong Kong to hire university graduates from mainland China rather than from Hong Kong, not only because of their superior language skills in Mandarin as well as English, but more importantly for their more international outlook. Thus, some argue that only with strong national sentiments can one come to possess the foundation to develop a meaningfully grounded international perspective. The cosmopolitanism of Hong Kong, then, has been a filter, albeit an incomplete processor, for the creation of a localized culture that is at once global and rooted in indigenous values. The result, however, is cultural disorientation. As Chan notes, "The cultural vision of 'Greater Hong Kong' is fast waning, because the cultural stamina of Hong Kong has failed."

A major ingredient in Hong Kong's cultural internationalization has been the continual emigration flow to other countries, with its accompanying current of return migration. Overseas Chinese will continue to play a key role in Hong Kong's internationalization. Yet the emigration problem is not fully settled. Economic growth rivaling that of most Western countries has resulted in Hong Kong's no longer continuing to be a stepping stone to still healthier economies in the West but rather a terminus. Moreover, the economic growth of South China, from where most immigrants come, outstrips that of Hong Kong, while Hong Kong's economic development now outstrips the West's. While it is virtually impossible to put aside political considerations of 1997 and how they affect emigration in the years ahead, the equation for potential emigrants from Hong Kong is more complex than before. While political change from sovereignty retrocession has brought measurable levels of anxiety, there can never be total certainly about the future. Thus emigration patterns will not only be a barometer of anticipated anxieties, but also a result of actual changes. Moreover, further emigration cannot ignore the role of social class as it enters the analysis of Hong Kong's global migration patterns. As Wong Siu-lun and Janet Salaff note in their detailed studies of families in Hong Kong in Chapter 8, "when people move, they mobilize forms of resources." These resources are not distributed evenly across social groups. Network capacities are influential and network capacities to and through South China to other global destinations are now more valuable than ever before. The risk to internationalism here is only indirectly implied. It is one in which choices to emigrate depend on social networks. Furthermore, those networks that get one in the "back door" for quick approval of emigration applications are the most valuable. In such cases, the internationalization of Hong Kong via emigration could become increasingly regulated.

Two of the most highly internationalized dimensions of Hong Kong are its media and higher education systems, which share a concern for freedom of speech. For the media the issue is press freedom; for universities it is academic freedom. Media internationalization in Hong Kong is ubiquitous. Changing this would alter the essential character of Hong Kong. Moreover, media internationalization is inextricably intertwined with the transfer of economic information essential to Hong Kong's continued success in international competition. Unlike other forms of internationalization, the media easily reaches into the homes of the citizenry not only through newspapers, but now through televisions and computers. The media has not only brought the world to Hong Kong but has also brought Hong Kong to the world. It is perhaps the greatest challenge to Beijing's patience with Hong Kong's freedoms. The risks are self-evident. Even before the transfer of sovereignty, limitations on media freedoms were made known as they apply to reporting on Taiwan and other sensitive national issues. Nevertheless, as Joseph Man Chan asserts in Chapter 9, "As evidenced by the diversity of reports produced by international media in Beijing now, there is no reason to believe that their counterparts in Hong Kong will [uniformly self-censor] in 1997." Strength in numbers could be significant in that some international media will not bend to pressure, and this in turn makes it "easier for the local media to speak their mind." This phenomenon may hold true for the academic world as well.

While the international and local Hong Kong media have been locked in debates about their future freedom to report on events, the same has not been true for Hong Kong's academic community. It is difficult to find a case of a professor's job being threatened because of critical scholarship that either the Hong Kong or Beijing government would not permit. Since 90 percent of the doctorates of the university professoriate were earned outside of the territory, the academy in Hong Kong could be considered China's most international sector. This sector has become increasingly integrated into the global academy through its participation in all forms of academic activity, as well as through the value it places on academic freedom. The degree of academic freedom will certainly be related to the degree to which the academic profession in Hong Kong maintains a viable international dimension. While the composition of the profession is relatively international in character, its potential for maintaining that international dimension is less certain. As Gerard Postiglione notes in Chapter 10, Hong Kong is not at the bottom of the international rankings in measures of academic freedom. Yet given the fact that Hong Kong has long touted its freedom of speech, it is worthy of concern that it ranks below its East Asian neighbors Japan and South Korea on the question posed to its academics of whether academic freedom is strongly protected in its society.

Despite the problematic nature of the territory's transition, as manifested in a multitude of dimensions—political, economic, legal, media, cultural, educational—Hong Kong will continue to be highly international. The global outlook of Hong Kong people will for a long time to come be problematic. That outlook has always been limited by Hong Kong's not being a nation, and this will not change. The aspiration to be different and special, as well as a desire for international recognition, were fully demonstrated when thousands of Hong Kong people rushed to the streets to greet the territory's first Olympic gold medalist, Lee Li San, in the summer of 1996. Yet only a couple of months later, the people of Hong Kong were out in force to protest against the Japanese claim that the Diaoyutai Islands are part of Japanese territory, and to demand that both the Beijing and the Taipei governments take tough actions against Japan.

Nevertheless, it is hard to see how its international participation and saliency in the global arena will remain unchanged now that Hong Kong is part of China rather than Britain. Political dimensions of its international character will be projected through Beijing rather than London, while economic dimensions of its international character are expected to continue largely as before. Yet these two dimensions are inseparable in reality. This volume has set out to achieve the modest aim of highlighting selected aspects of the extensive scope of Hong Kong's international and global dimensions. The volume, however, does not attempt to address the conceptual problem of distinguishing between "internationalization" and "globalization."[20] As the literature on the subject often uses these terms interchangeably, so will the chapter contributors. We recognize, nevertheless, that internationalization is based in processes involving the state, and since Hong Kong is not a state, this places legal limits on its international status. Thus the term "global" seems more suitable for Hong Kong's situation. Still, it becomes impossible to ignore the fact that the bulk of Hong Kong global activities intersect the international system, including state to state relations. Therefore, although Hong Kong is not a sovereign state, it is an international player. If we shift the focus to its society, in which no national identity is institutionally fostered, "global" seems more fitting to describe the disposition of Hong Kong people, even though a large number of people with foreign passports again reinforces its "international" dimension.

As Hong Kong transforms from a colonial dependent territory to a Chinese Special Administrative Region, its international status will be more connected to China's position in the world. The nature of Hong Kong global linkages are shifting as the political identities of Hong Kong people inevitably become more nationalized. But a mix of pragmatic nationalism and globalism is likely to continue to characterize Hong Kong's outlook as the China–Hong Kong reunion takes place. A Hong Kong that is part of China, but with its global linkages intact, could be a great asset to both China and the world. It is therefore not in China's interest to turn the city into just another Chinese city, or to discourage the international community from recognizing the SAR's special international status. In the final analysis, Hong Kong must rise to the enormous challenge the reunion brings.

Notes

1. The reunion of Hong Kong with China as a Special Administrative Region has generated heated discussion in the local intellectual community. See the June, July and August issues of the Chinese-language Hong Kong journal *Ming Pao Monthly* in 1996. See also Gerard Postiglione, "National Minorities and Nationalities Policy in China," in Berch Berberoglu, ed., *The National Question: Nationalism, Ethnic Conflict and Self-Determination in the Twentieth Century* (Philadelphia: Temple University Press, 1995).

2. A brief and succinct summary of the role of the British government in managing Hong Kong affairs can be found in Norman Miners, *Government and Politics of Hong Kong,* 5th ed. (Hong Kong: Oxford University Press, 1991), Chapter 16, pp. 214–225. See also Ting Wai, "The External Relations and International Status of Hong Kong." Occasional Papers/Reprint series in *Contemporary Asian Studies*, University of Maryland School of Law, May 1997.

3. On the question of legitimacy, see, for example, discussions in Ian Scott, *Political Change and the Crisis of Legitimacy in Hong Kong* (Hong Kong: Oxford University Press, 1989), pp. 322–335.

4. See Lau Siu-Kai and Kuan Hsin-Chi, *The Ethos of Hong Kong Chinese* (Hong Kong:

The Chinese University Press, 1988), p. 2; Lau Siu-Kai, Lee Ming-Kwan, Wong Po-san, and Wong Siu-lun, *Indicators of Social Developments: Hong Kong 1988* (Hong Kong: Institute of Asia-Pacific Studies, The Chinese University of Hong Kong, 1991), pp. 177–178.

5. Richard Hughes, *Borrowed Place, Borrowed Time,* 2d ed. (London: Deutsch, 1976).

6. The most serious challenge to the colonial government in recent history were the riots in the 1960s, when pro-Beijing groups demonstrated against the government in Hong Kong. See Lau and Kuan, *Ethos,* pp. 80–93, and Lau et al., *Indicators,* 1991, pp. 186–194, for survey data and analysis of the attitude of Hong Kong people toward government. On Hong Kong's global and local identities, see also Ting Wai, "The External Relations," and James T.H. Tang, "Hong Kong's International Status," *Pacific Review* 6, 3 (1993).

7. See Lau Siu-Kai and Kuan Hsin-Chi, "The Attentive Spectators: Political Participation of the Hong Kong Chinese," *Journal of Northeast Asian Studies* 14, 1 (Spring 1995), p. 4.

8. Ibid., pp. 12, 15.

9. The sixty members of the Legislative Council, however, were elected through three different types of constituencies: geographic constituencies, functional constituencies, and an election committee formed by members of the regional/urban councils and district boards.

10. Tsang Wing-kwong, "A Defiant Electorate: A Study of Electoral Choice in the 1995 Legislative Council Election," paper presented to a conference on the 1995 Legislative Council Election, Chinese University of Hong Kong, May 17–18, 1996.

11. Lau Siu-Kai and Kuan Hsin-Chi, "The Partial Vision of Democracy in Hong Kong: A Survey of Political Opinion," *China Journal,* no. 34 (July 1995), p. 263.

12. Rowena Kwok Yee Fun and Elaine Chan Yee-man, "Political Identity and Participation in the 1995 Legislative Council Elections," paper presented to an international conference on Political Development in Taiwan and Hong Kong, Centre of Asian Studies, University of Hong Kong, February 8–9, 1996.

13. Miners, *Government and Politics of Hong Kong,* pp. 215–223; *Yearbook of International Organizations, 1993/1994,* 11th ed. (Munchen: K.G. Saur, 1993), vol. 2.

14. See Ming Pao, 25 July 1995, p. A4; and *Hong Kong Economic Journal,* 26 July 1995, p. 8.

15. See *Wen Wei Po,* 14 May 1993, p. 2; *Ta Kung Pao,* 14, May 1993, p. 12.

16. *Hong Kong Bill of Rights.*

17. See *Wen Wei Po,* 27 October 1995, p. A12.

18. See Jing Xiao-Ru, "The Sino-British Duel Has International Background," *Ming Pao,* 29 December 1992, p. 41; Tsang Shu-Ki, "Hong Kong Becomes the Center of Struggle of the New Cold War," *Ming Pao,* 2 December 1992, p. 41; Lee Kuan-Yew also has similar arguments, see the interview of Lee Kuan-Yew in *Ming Pao,* 18 December 1992, p. 2; Wen Wei Po, 18 December 1992, p. 6. See also James T.H. Tang, "The International Dimension of Mainland China's Unification Policy: The Case of Hong Kong," in Jaushieh Joseph Wu, ed., *Divided Nations: The Experience of Germany, Korea, and China* (Taipei: Institute of International Relations, National Chengchi University, 1995); and Ting Wai, "External Relations."

19. Quoted from Chen Meng-Bin, "The United States Action of Strategic Containment Against China," *Mirror Monthly,* June 1993, p. 44.

20. Internationalization has been defined in different ways. The *Concise Oxford Dictionary* defines it as, "make international, esp. bring (territory etc.) under combined protection etc. of different nations." But the term has also been used in the context of a world shrinking through the process of economic interdependence, the information revolution, and the greater mobility of people. See Joseph A. Camilleri and Jim Falk, *The End of Sovereignty? The Politics of a Shrinking and Emerging World* (Aldershot: Edward Elgar, 1992). It has also been associated with relatively inward-looking societies seeking to broaden and deepen their consciousness and involvement with international affairs, e.g., Japan. See Chikara Higashi, ed., *The Internationalization of the Japanese Economy* (Boston: Kluwer Press, 1990).

1

Global Implications of Hong Kong's Retrocession to Chinese Sovereignty

Ming K. Chan

Despite Beijing's repeated insistence that Hong Kong's retrocession to Chinese sovereignty on July 1, 1997, after 155 years of British colonial rule, is strictly a "bilateral matter" between the governments of the two sovereign powers—the People's Republic of China (PRC) and the United Kingdom of Great Britain and Northern Ireland (UK)—Hong Kong's current transition toward 1997 is in many respects a serious matter of global concern. In fact, the current life and work, as well as the future prospects, of the six million residents in this highly internationalized, semi-autonomous city-state have already been profoundly shaped by this transitional process, which spans from 1984, when the Sino-British Joint Declaration was signed, to 1997, when Hong Kong will become a Special Administrative Region (SAR) of the PRC. This transitional process and Hong Kong's 1997 SAR status naturally have direct and multifold bearings on the economic and strategic interests of Hong Kong's many global partners.

From a global perspective, Hong Kong's importance comes from its role as the eighth largest world trade entity; as the gateway to mainland China; as the busiest container port and fourth-ranking financial center in the world; as a rising star among the four Little Dragons of Asia; and as the international trade, service, and communications hub strategically located at the heart of the Pacific Rim. Hong Kong is a spectacularly successful example of free trade, market economy, and private enterprise, and an open, pluralistic, and dynamic society worthy of study and emulation by other developing communities and economies.

While maintaining extensive linkages in trade, transportation, communications, finance, investment, migration, tourism, education, cultural exchanges, and other spheres with the outside world, Hong Kong is also becoming increasingly integrated with the Chinese mainland. Hong Kong's capital, entrepreneurial skills, extensive global links, and technological inputs are crucial for China's modernization drive. During the past two decades, Hong Kong has served as a powerful catalyst and even locomotive for the remarkable economic transformation of South China, where over three million Chinese workers are now employed by Hong Kong–owned and -managed enterprises.

As such, Hong Kong's incorporation into the PRC under the "one country, two systems" formula has not only already realigned Hong Kong–PRC relations, but it has also shaped and will continue to influence both Hong Kong's global relations and, to some extent, the PRC's own external orientations, especially its relationship with Hong Kong's major international partners. In a more "local" context, linkages with and examples from the global village have also been important points of reference and stimulants in Hong Kong's political and social development during the transitional era.

This chapter will aim at delineating some of the outstanding features and possible patterns of development in Hong Kong's global linkages and external relations that have already been affected by or will likely be conditioned by Hong Kong's transformation toward 1997 and beyond as part of China. Hopefully, these highlighted features and patterns will enhance the ongoing discourse, both academically and in realpolitik, on the "internationalization" and "international legal and functional status" of Hong Kong, not only as a nonindependent city-state but also as a vibrant economic entity and free society both before and after 1997. After July 1, 1997, the Hong Kong SAR may be caught between the competing claims of Chinese national interests as dictated by the PRC central authorities and the vital functional and other global links of its continuation as a world city. There are potential problems and even conflicts between the PRC's desire to "de-internationalize" Hong Kong as a "political center" and its need to maintain and even further promote Hong Kong as an international "economic center," especially as a bridge between China and the world market. In this sense, the global implications of Hong Kong's reunion with China are far-reaching and of lasting consequence.

Basic International Concerns

Deng Xiaoping's "one country, two systems" formula, which is Beijing's guiding principle both for the December 1984 Sino-British accord settling the status of Hong Kong and the Basic Law of the Hong Kong SAR promulgated in April 1990, has validity beyond Hong Kong. This formula was also applied by Beijing to effect the April 1987 settlement of Macau's future status, with the current Portuguese administration to terminate on December 20, 1999, when Chinese sovereignty will be fully restored.[1] Thus, the end of both colonial Hong Kong, a creation of the first of a century of "unequal treaties" (the 1842 Treaty of Nanking) stemming from modern China's first humiliation by Western imperialism in the Opium War of 1839–42, and colonial Macau, the oldest Western enclave established on the China coast in the 1550s, are regarded as two milestones in China's quest for national reunification and international redemption. As such, one must appreciate the Hong Kong and Macau retrocession to PRC sovereignty before the turn of the twenty-first century as major accomplishments by the current Beijing leadership in both domestic affairs (national reunification) and foreign policy.[2]

The bilateral negotiations leading to the settlement and the more than decade-long transition to Chinese sovereignty of these two European colonies in South China have affected and will continue to shape the PRC's relationship with both the UK and Portugal, with sharp turns and dramatic ups and downs, especially in the Beijing–London link. Of indirect, but no less international significance, is the fact that Beijing has also intended to extend this successful "Hong Kong model" to its long-standing and high-priority attempt at reunification with Taiwan. Several key developments—(1) the preservation of the status quo of Taiwan under Guomindang (GMD) rule, (2) the gradual détente between Beijing and the increasingly localized leadership in Taipei, and (3) the fast expanding intensive and extensive human, cultural, and economic exchanges across the Taiwan Strait—are of strategic concern to the United States, Japan, and their allies. These concerns are also of great consequence to the overall international power alignment in East Asia and the Pacific Rim.

Given the deep mutual mistrust across the Strait, it is unlikely that the GMD authorities, the Democratic Progressive Party elites, and the populace of Taiwan will ever accept the "one country, two systems" formula as the basis for their developing but uneasy relationship with the mainland. Still, Hong Kong's political transition is being monitored closely in Taiwan.[3] Admittedly, the similarities between the Hong Kong–Beijing relationship and the Taipei–Beijing linkage are limited: Taipei enjoys significantly stronger bargaining positions in military, economic, and political terms; and Taiwan is not a foreign colony, but is regarded by both the GMD and the CCP party/state leadership as a province of China. Nonetheless, the Hong Kong–Beijing linkage during the transition-reintegration process is definitely a matter of serious concern for Taipei and its external political and economic partners, many of whom are also Hong Kong's major partners in trade and other functional areas.

As long as Beijing still insists on the applicability of the "one country, two systems" formula to the reunification with Taiwan, Hong Kong's transition by the guidelines of the Basic Law in many senses reflects and reveals the PRC's true intentions and actual handling of the reintegration with a Chinese community and economy hitherto under nonsocialist rule.[4] To varying degrees, the economic and strategic interests in East Asia and the Pacific Rim regions, as well as the world prestige of three members of NATO (the United States, UK, and Portugal) and two members of the European Community, are linked directly and indirectly to Hong Kong's transition. While London, and by extension Lisbon, has shouldered and is still carrying considerable administrative responsibilities and diplomatic obligations over transitional matters, the United States and its many allies have their own less visible but not less vital concern for strategic balance and trade/investment stakes vis-à-vis Hong Kong/Taiwan.

Viewed from a slightly different angle, the PRC's relationship with the UK/Hong Kong governments during the 1984–97 transitional process, to a considerable extent reflects Beijing's approach under the reformist mode to the global capitalism bloc in trade, economic cooperation, technology transfer, investment, migration, educational exchange, and other functional dealings. Of course, Hong Kong's increasingly close ties with China, especially the Guangdong–Hong Kong economic integration, represents a very significant world-scale experiment in socialist–capitalist collaboration (and even absorption) that has much direct relevance to the PRC's ongoing reform and modernization. Such developments directly affect Chinese foreign policy and its external orientation in which trade, technology, and economic matters are crucial components.

On the other hand, the "Hong Kong factor" has also shaped U.S. policy toward the PRC. A notable example in this case is the Bush administration's post-Tiananmen renewal of Most Favored Nation (MFN) status for the PRC in 1990, 1991, and 1992, citing the possible disastrous effects of MFN denial on Hong Kong, which is often hailed as a paragon of free trade and market economy. In the first 1992 presidential election debate on October 12, President Bush defend his September 28, 1992, decision to veto the congressional amendment mandating human rights improvement as a condition for the continuation of the PRC's MFN status, arguing that one should encourage China to move further in the course of reform and opening, and that he did not want to "isolate and ruin Hong Kong."[5]

Just as the Taiwan question has been a major factor and still remains a troubling one in U.S.-PRC relations, the Hong Kong factor has the potential of developing into another important element in the U.S.-PRC relationship as well as other Sino-Western links. Following the March 1996 Taiwan Strait crisis (with the PRC's military demonstration against the Taiwan presidential election and the U.S. naval counterpresence off Taiwan's east coast), the PRC's aggressive manifestation of its "politics of national reunification" has also prompted greater international concern for Hong Kong's changing course after 1997. For instance, in mid-July 1996, U.S. assistant secretary of state Winston Lord pointed out in a congressional hearing that Beijing's decision to install in July 1997 an "SAR provisional legislature" to replace the 1995 fully elected legislature would "complicate" U.S.-PRC relations.[6] This would also affect the promised high degree of autonomy for the SAR, and by extension, international confidence in Beijing's faithful implementation of the "one country, two systems," which should supposedly enable Hong Kong to retain its vitality and functional autonomy.

International Response to Hong Kong's Crisis of Confidence

Since the very beginning of the Hong Kong status negotiations in 1982, there has been a serious crisis of confidence among the local populace. While the 1984 Sino-British Joint Declaration mandated the sovereignty retrocession in 1997 with the PRC's promise of a "high degree of autonomy" for the Hong Kong SAR and the preservation of existing rights and freedoms for its residents for "fifty years without change," serious doubts remain about how these guarantees should be understood and upheld by Beijing after 1997. The PRC's domestic record for the past four decades, often in disregard of the extensive rights and freedoms already guaranteed for Chinese living on the mainland by the PRC's own constitution, is not conducive to confidence among Hong Kong people in this transition to Chinese sovereignty.

Even before the Tiananmen events of June 4, 1989, instead of contributing to Hong Kong's "stability and prosperity," the PRC's undemocratic attitude and behavior during the drafting of the Basic Law undermined much of Hong Kong people's guarded optimism about a post-1997 forced incorporation into an undemocratic Chinese polity under a communist dictatorship. Paralleling and responding to Beijing's increasingly intrusive and visible hand in the affairs of transitional Hong Kong, there has been the obvious British retreat from earlier commitments to pre-1997 democratization and the colonial regime's discernibly diminished will and capacity to administer Hong Kong effectively and democratically until June 30, 1997. This has led to the second crisis of confidence in Hong Kong over British colonial mismanagement and even betrayal of the true interests of Hong Kong people in the countdown to 1997.

This double crisis among Hong Kong people has been manifested in very strong and extensive human and institutional "internationalization" efforts. Resorting to the time-honored practice of "voting with one's feet," the substantial overseas emigration traffic from Hong Kong has reached fever pitch since the mid-1980s.[7]

Massive emigration to Canada, the United States, Australia, New Zealand, and the UK reached a record high of 66,000 émigrés in 1992, more than 1 percent of Hong Kong's total population.[8] This overseas exit traffic definitely accelerated after, but did not start with, the June 4 events. Such a widespread, almost epidemic, search for safe asylum abroad, especially among middle-class and professional families, has already resulted in a keenly felt "brain drain" effect on Hong Kong's government and private sectors. This was echoed by a parallel example of institutional "relocation" of major businesses, such as Jardine & Matheson (to Bermuda) and the Hong Kong and Shanghai Banking Corporation (its headquarters transferred to London). There has also been a significant and continuous outflow of capital and investment (under the "diversification" category). Furthermore, another powerful trend has been the increasing number of Hong Kong students seeking high school and university education abroad, some of them with little intention of returning home upon completion of their studies.

These and other related overseas undertakings are the direct results of Hong Kong people's continuous attempts, some at considerable sacrifice (in monetary, career, and family terms), to purchase some international insurance against the uncertainty of the 1997 China syndrome. Thus, the recent mushrooming of "Hong Kong Towns," if not exactly "Honcouver" in Canada, elsewhere in North America and Australia can be regarded as the direct global by-product of Hong Kong's problematic transition to 1997. Of course, in recent years, many Hong Kong people with foreign passports have returned to work in Hong Kong for better pay, often leaving families behind in the newly adopted country of settlement. This also enhances Hong Kong's global links.

While some Western nations, particularly Canada, the United States, and Australia, have been quite eager (due to self-interest) to enlarge quotas for the acceptance of Hong Kong émigrés and capital into their domains, global governmental concern for Hong Kong's transition and post-1997 prospects did not assume any significance or sense of urgency until after the Tiananmen events. During the mid- to late-1980s, international focus on Hong Kong mainly took the form of media coverage of its Little Dragon economy and its contribution to the South China economic takeoff, and academic proceedings on Hong Kong politics or Hong Kong–Beijing relations as a timely research issue.[9] It was Beijing's brutal suppression of the Tiananmen protesters and the subsequent international alarm over the Chinese communist approach to human rights and political dissent despite its economic reform and external opening, that helped to propel Hong Kong's transition into international headlines and policy agendas.

In this sense, while the June 4 events were tragic for the Chinese nation as a whole, they have had unintended beneficial effects on Hong Kong's democratization, especially in terms of the international support it has since received. The fierce and massive local mobilization backing the Beijing prodemocracy movement provided a windfall opportunity to galvanize popular sentiment that re-energized the faltering democratic lobby in Hong Kong. Meanwhile, the local leftist establishment was nearly ruined and its big business elite allies had to lay low. Externally, along with the Western world's changed perception of the Chinese communist regime, the British government also changed course from appeasement to a firmer stance toward China over Hong Kong issues. Besides unilaterally suspending scheduled meetings of the Sino-British Joint Liaison Group until September 1989, Whitehall finally came to acknowledge Hong Kong's very serious crisis of confidence. As salvage measures, London decided to (1) enact a Hong Kong Bill of Rights (along the lines of the International Covenant of Civil and Political Rights, to which the UK was a signatory but had never extended its application to Hong Kong); (2) grant British nationality with full right of abode in the UK to 50,000 qualified Hong Kong households (or about 225,000 local residents); and (3) speed up the pace of the local democratization process.[10]

It was against the backdrop of global condemnation of the June 4 atrocities, and a newfound overwhelming popular support for direct elections in Hong Kong, that Beijing partially yielded to the British demand for up to one-third of the Hong Kong legislature (20 out of 60 seats) to be directly elected before 1997. Although the Hong Kong people were kept in the dark during the Sino-British secret negotiations in mid-February 1990 that finalized the electoral provisions of the Basic Law for "convergence" between the pre- and post-1997 systems, it was a marked departure from Beijing's repeated assertion of sovereign right over a purely "domestic" law-making exercise that would bear no "foreign interference."[11] This provided a limited but still significant constitutional breakthrough for Hong Kong's historic first-ever legislative direct election in 1991, which turned out to be a wholesale repudiation of pro-Beijing candidates.

However, Beijing did not intend to let London or Hong Kong get away easily with such a post–June 4 concession on representative democracy. On the contrary, in their besieged mentality vis-à-vis the global community, the PRC leadership tried to tighten the screws on other key aspects of the Basic Law final version so as to reassert control, to avenge Hong Kong's open support of the Tiananmen protest, and to counter Hong Kong's highly suspect post–June 4 "internationalization." There are numerous cases illustrating this new PRC approach.

For instance, following Beijing's repeated condemnation of Hong Kong pro-democracy figures and organizations as "subversive and counterrevolutionary," and of Hong Kong itself as a "subversive base against the PRC," in the autumn of 1989, Article 23 of the Basic Law second draft was strengthened to ban "subversion against the Central People's Government." Yet it fails to define the term "subversion," which has no place in the common law but conjures up the worst aspects of the PRC's post–June 4 insecurity and paranoia. Specifically aimed at curtailing Hong Kong's global links that would threaten Beijing's absolute control, the same Article 23 of the Basic Law also isolates local political groups from the international community by banning any ties with foreign political organizations that are not allowed to operate in the SAR.

As part of its strongly negative reaction to the British Nationality Package offered to 225,000 qualified Hong Kong residents and to the overseas emigration fever, which reached crisis proportion by the late 1980s, Article 67 of the Basic Law places strict limits (20 percent of total legislative membership) on eligibility for election into the legislature of foreign passport holders and Hong Kong Chinese with foreign right of abode. Similar restrictions also apply to the top two dozen ranking civil service positions in the future SAR government, as many civil servants are eligible for full British citizenship with right of abode and employment in the UK under the British Nationality Package.

Thus, it seems clear that in the strained relationship with the West after June 4, 1989, especially in its sharp discord with London, the PRC's recent approach to Hong Kong reflects the official emphasis on the "one country"—that is, the absolute sovereignty of the PRC state—rather than the "two systems" and "high degree of autonomy" aspects of the formula that reflect the true spirit of the 1984 Sino-British Joint Declaration. This was obviously the case in the Hong Kong government's June 1991 promulgation of the much toned-down Hong Kong Bill of Rights. Despite Article 39 of the Basic Law (specifying the continued validity in the SAR of the International Covenants on Civil and Political Rights, and on Economic, Social, and Cultural Rights, even though the PRC is not a signatory), the bill has been met with strong criticism from Beijing, which had already decided to abrogate it after 1997.[12]

In 1995, the PRC provoked great local and international alarm when its Hong Kong SAR Preliminary Working Committee (which was Beijing's "second stove," set up in mid-1993 to preempt the British colonial regime in the aftermath of Sino-British discord over 1994–95 electoral reform) proposed to "resurrect" six discarded Hong Kong ordinances, which were amended to comply with the Bill of Rights. If these laws were indeed reinstated after July 1, 1997, the police would have much greater power over public meetings and the government would more easily be able to outlaw organizations and interfere with television and radio broadcast and press freedom. It also called for the de-linking of the Hong Kong Bill of Rights with the International Covenant on Civil and Political Rights, to which the PRC is still not a signatory state.[13]

Another political-legal controversy stemmed from the December 1991 Hong Kong legislature's (now with directly elected elements) rejection of a Sino-British bilateral agreement on the composition of Hong Kong's Court of Final Appeal limiting the number of foreign judges to only one out of five. This Sino-British deal was regarded by many Hong Kong people as a serious retreat from the Basic Law provision (Article 82) allowing for "judges from other common law jurisdictions" to be invited to sit as judges of the Hong Kong Court of Final Appeal.[14] The PRC's extremely narrow interpretation and "minimalist" application of Basic Law provisions in this case can be regarded as another sign of its "counterinternationalization" approach to the political and legal-administrative development in transitional Hong Kong. Then, in June 1995, the PRC and UK governments reached a new agreement on the Court of Final Appeal that would delay its formal establishment until after July 1, 1997. They otherwise retained much of the substance of the earlier (1991) agreement. While the new agreement signaled a gradual improvement in Sino-British relations, with the PRC foreign minister's fall 1995 visit to London as a mark of better, if still limited, bilateral cooperation in Hong Kong's transition matters, it did not enhance international confidence in the SAR's rule of law under an independent and impartial judiciary.[15]

The PRC has derived, and hopes to continue to gain, substantial and much needed material and other benefits from Hong Kong's extensive international functional links, especially in trade, finance, investment, transportation, technology transfer, communications, and other valuable services. For this reason, Beijing's response to the maintenance and future expansion of Hong Kong's global economic ties and business network has generally been positive. One can point, for example, to the near autonomy on international civil aviation and shipping the Hong Kong SAR will enjoy under the Basic Law (Articles 124–135). The economic miracle in Guangdong during the past two decades, which now serves as a national role model for Dengist reform and modernization, has definitely enhanced the PRC leadership's appreciation of Hong Kong's internationalized economic contribution to the mainland. Perhaps it was with such pragmatic considerations in mind that Lu Ping, director of the PRC State Council's Hong Kong and Macau Affairs Office, at one point even suggested that one of the new "functional constituency" seats in the 1995 Hong Kong legislative election could be allotted to a representative from the various foreign chambers of commerce in Hong Kong.[16] The largest among these is the American Chamber of Commerce, which has served aggressively and effectively as a lobbyist for the continuation of the U.S. MFN treatment for PRC products. However, Beijing reacted rather negatively to a particular item of official U.S.–Hong Kong linkage—the 1992 U.S.–Hong Kong Policy Act as an "American conspiracy to internationalize Hong Kong at the expense of Chinese national sovereignty."[17]

Limits to the "Internationalization" of Hong Kong

On September 20, 1991, Senator Mitch McConnell (R–Kentucky) introduced the United States–Hong Kong Policy Act to the U.S. Senate. This Senate bill (S.1731) eventually gathered 29 co-sponsors, 18 Republicans (including then Senate minority leader Senator Robert Dole) and 11 Democrats (including Vice-President, then Senator, Albert Gore). Soon afterward, a similar bill (HR 3522) was also introduced to the U.S. House of Representatives by Representative John Porter (R–Illinois) and it enjoyed wide bipartisan support and sponsorship. Passed by both chambers of the U.S. Congress in mid-September 1992, the US–Hong Kong Policy Act of 1992 became law with President Bush's signature on October 5, 1992, the last day of the congressional session and exactly four weeks before the U.S. presidential election.

This law has the avowed objective "to establish the policy of the United States with respect to Hong Kong after July 1, 1997." Specifically, it sets policy guidelines for each of the nine areas in which Hong Kong is authorized to pursue independent bilateral relations—economic, trade, finance, monetary, shipping, communications, tourism, culture, and sport. It also recognizes Hong Kong's legal status under U.S. law, "ensuring that this status will not be affected by the 1997 transition." Finally, the law requires the secretary of state to report to Congress on all developments affecting U.S. interests in Hong Kong.[18]

In essence, this is special legislation to affirm the official American political and economic commitment to support Hong Kong's continuing status as a free society and capitalistic economy practicing free trade after 1997, when the United States will treat the Hong Kong SAR as a distinct entity from the PRC on such matters as import quotas, traffic links, technology transfer, visas and migration, cultural and educational exchange, transportation, and communications rights. In a more positive light, the US–Hong Kong Policy Act can be interpreted as American encouragement to further economic liberalization and functional internationalization of the South China region with Hong Kong as the dynamic center for reform and development.

In a realpolitik perspective, this is a much toned-down and narrower parallel (no defense–military–arms sales links and no pseudo-diplomatic provisions) to the U.S.-Taiwan Relations Act of 1979 following the "normalization" of U.S.-PRC relations and Washington's formal recognition of Beijing as the sole, legitimate national government of all China.[19] In fact, the U.S.–Hong Kong Policy Act does not challenge the PRC's sovereignty over Hong Kong, but only reaffirms U.S. support for the Sino-British Joint Declaration. The specific wording of the clauses in the law reflects such sensitivity; there are numerous uses of the phrase, "in accordance with applicable laws of the PRC," "with the authorization of the Central Peoples' Government of the PRC," and so forth, in reference to actual U.S.–Hong Kong links in economic and functional matters.

However, in creating and according a special, distinctive status for Hong Kong after 1997, with fully or highly autonomous rights and privileges in bilateral economic and functional relations with the United States, the law provoked Beijing's wrath as "an unwelcome American interference in purely Chinese domestic affairs detrimental to healthy Sino-U.S. relations."[20] Part of the problem behind the PRC's displeasure with the U.S.–Hong Kong Policy Act lies in the act's not-too-well-concealed implications: (1) as demonstrated by the events of June 4, the PRC regime cannot be fully trusted to faithfully honor the letter and spirit of the Joint Declaration and to allow Hong Kong to fully exercise and enjoy the promised "high degree of autonomy"; (2) in the event of a possible future sharp deterioration in U.S.-China relations, the United States can resort to stern measures against the Chinese mainland without any rupture in U.S.–Hong Kong linkages, or without causing serious direct damage to Hong Kong, where the United States and its allies have substantial economic and numerous other vested interests underlining their desire to preserve Hong Kong's internationalized status quo; and/or (3) the United States is offering preferential treatment to Chinese territories not under the direct or active jurisdiction of the centralized Chinese communist system in Beijing (Taiwan since 1949, Hong Kong after 1997). Such U.S. posture has the dangerous potential of encouraging centrifugal separatism or runaway regionalism in the external orientation and developmental path among particular areas or communities within the PRC (such as South China), with the lure of relative economic advantages and other special material incentives that the United States might offer.[21]

American support, even if only unofficial, for exiled Tibetan activists definitely rings Beijing's alarm bell on this third assumption. The still very tense cross-strait situation and the far from unpredictable outcome of the PRC's reunification attempts with Taiwan, which enjoys special ties with the United States, only makes the second and third assumptions unwelcome or even unacceptable to Beijing. The U.S.-Taipei links in fact helped to "tarnish" the PRC's perception of this U.S.–Hong Kong Policy Act. The late 1992 U.S. decision to sell F-16 fighter jets to Taipei's air force and Beijing's retaliatory boycott of international arms control negotiations are clear examples of a long string of unfriendly acts in an already strained relationship. Even though the last-minute February 1995 and June 1996 Sino-American accords on the intellectual property rights issues may have averted a full-scale trade war, on the economic and functional fronts much friction and hostility still remain between these two Pacific powers, which are also Hong Kong's most important economic partners. In such a charged atmosphere, one can hardly expect Beijing to respond positively to the U.S. law on the Hong Kong SAR with all the negative policy implications and dark scenarios.

While the U.S.–Hong Kong Policy Act is undoubtedly a significant governmental breakthrough in Hong Kong's quest for increased international support, multilateral exchange, and global cooperation, it also represents in some sense the fruition or culmination of larger concerns and wider supportive efforts toward Hong Kong over the past decade by some of the Western industrial democracies, notably United States' most intimate ally and largest economic partner, Canada. In this context, the United States is again taking the lead in expressing strong concern for Hong Kong's future under PRC sovereignty. On March 11, 1997, the United States House of Representatives passed 416–1, a Hong Kong Reversion Act, which will link Hong Kong's SAR autonomy with PRC economic rights under American Law.[22] As the leader of the NATO and G-7 block, and as the UK's most powerful ally with still considerable strategic interests, economic capacity, and military strength in the Asia-Pacific region, the United States' official stance on Hong Kong's future status at this critical juncture of its transition is definitely of moral and practical global consequence.

Even though the PRC's Basic Law for Hong Kong recognizes the crucial importance of Hong Kong's extensive global economic network and functional ties and partially allows for maintaining them, Beijing, in its overriding concern for centralized control, national reunification, and absolute state sovereignty, will have little tolerance of Hong Kong's developing any external link that may carry any unwelcome political or diplomatic, not to mention strategic, implication. Both the Joint Declaration and the Basic Law explicitly reserve national defense and foreign affairs concerning the SAR as exclusive prerogatives for the sovereign state in Beijing. Even the SAR's permitted participation in international organizations and conferences is restricted to those "not limited to states," and it must "be using the name of 'Hong Kong, China,' " according to strictly defined parameters set by the Basic Law (Articles 151 and 152).

Thus, it should be clear that despite Hong Kong's proven capacity to function effectively as an "international legal personality" and the global recognition of this, as well as its remarkably successful post–World War II performance as a highly autonomous world economy entity, Beijing in the foreseeable future, will not wish to see the further "internationalization" of Hong Kong toward any status resembling a genuinely autonomous "city-state" that is not closely confined to the PRC's political/diplomatic orbit.[23] Of course, international law and current diplomatic practice are rather vague and even underdeveloped when it comes to universal recognition and ready acceptance of a special category of partially self-governing dependent domains with global strategic or economic significance. Perhaps as one political scientist recently suggested, Hong Kong can be viewed as a "quasi-state" in international affairs with both positive and negative sovereignty restraints on the part of the PRC.[24] Of course, any external attempts at promoting political or diplomatic internationalization to alter Hong Kong's constitutional status are certainly very misguided.

In light of the above, the overt official support with strong policy implications from the United States, and, by extension, other Western (democratic and capitalistic) powers not enjoying cordial relations with Beijing may have the potentially counterproductive effect of turning Hong Kong into an international "hostage" of high economic and human stakes in any Sino-Western ideo-political tug of war. To some extent, the recent mutual threats of trade sanctions and, until now, the annual MFN status renewal controversies between the United States and China have already caught Hong Kong in the middle. While mainland China appreciates and in rational terms needs the economic and other material inputs from and via Hong Kong, the PRC party/state leadership have had a solid record of subordinating economic needs to ideo-political considerations. The recent unresolved Sino-British discord over financial arrangements for the construction of a U.S. $21 billion new airport in Hong Kong, despite both its obvious utility to South China and agreements in the September 1991 Sino-British Memorandum of Understanding, is an acute reminder of the old Maoist dictum, "politics takes command" in Chinese domestic and international affairs.

Indeed, some hard-liners in the PRC often view Hong Kong with mistrust and alarm. In a dark scenario, it may seem that a highly internationalized, freewheeling capitalist and blatantly "pro-West" Hong Kong has the makings of a dangerous Trojan horse not just capturing Guangdong through the pocket book but casting evil spells of Western capitalism/imperialism/neo-colonialism all over the mainland. The unauthorized May 1991 exit through Hong Kong to the United States of Xu Jiatun, former PRC chieftain in Hong Kong, for "tourism and relaxation" only added to the die-hards' suspicion of Hong Kong's accelerating internationalization efforts as trying to achieve political ends with economic means.

While the United States and the Western powers have attempted to use economic pressure and incentive to induce liberal change in the PRC, Beijing is also fully prepared to use trade and other economic countermeasures for domestic political and foreign policy objectives. Just as Hong Kong has worked effectively as China's "softcore" salesman to the Western world on the MFN and World Trade Organization issues, one can expect the SAR's continued service to the motherland in this light. On the other hand, PRC's stance on the SAR's global economic links can be an important international bargaining chip, which, in extreme circumstances, may even become the target of Beijing's blackmail (even though it will also be self-destructive) vis-à-vis a hostile, external world.

In summer 1996, less than a year before the formal sovereignty transfer, there are openly expressed international concerns for Hong Kong's future global vitality and functional capacity in several keys areas of political and economic significance. For instance, as of 1996 Hong Kong hosts ninety-five foreign consular establishments. Of these, thirteen maintain diplomatic relations with Taipei but not Beijing. Up until June 30, 1997, they are all accredited to the UK government. But after July 1, 1997, these thirteen consulates will face a new fate. Either their home governments will have to switch diplomatic recognition from Taipei to Beijing, or their consular representation in the PRC's Hong Kong SAR will cease or will only exist under the guise of "unofficial" trade offices. Among these thirteen affected countries are South Africa and Panama, both important targets of Beijing's diplomatic attempts to isolate Taipei internationally.[25]

Thus, Hong Kong's change of status in 1997 yields Beijing a powerful weapon to pressure Taiwan in the global arena. Likewise, the lack of a shipping agreement between Taiwan and Hong Kong SAR is of growing concern to Taipei, especially in view of the difficulties in establishing mainland–Taiwan direct shipping links due to political and legal problems. However, there is also the other side of the same coin: in using Hong Kong SAR's preexisting global links to pressure Taiwan for the PRC's agenda of national reunification, Beijing can also effectively, internationally or otherwise, "de-internationalize" the Hong Kong SAR's global functional links. It is in a similar light that the American Chamber of Commerce in Hong Kong voiced its alarm over press reports about a draft legislation being prepared by the British colonial regime for the Hong Kong SAR government (which must fully submit to the national government in Beijing in foreign affairs and national defense matters under the Basic Law) making it mandatory to follow Beijing's lead in case of economic sanctions or other trade war measures vis-à-vis any foreign country.[26] If this were to be actualized, it would definitely impair Hong Kong's economic autonomy. And in view of the recent tension in U.S.-PRC economic disputes, this dark scenario is not beyond actualization after 1997. Of course, the situation could be further complicated by the fact that while Hong Kong is a regular member in good standing in the World Trade organization, the PRC has yet to become a member.

If this were to be the case, then Hong Kong would easily tarnish its economic autonomy and global functional vitality, much contrary to the letter and spirit of the "one country, two systems" model. It would also be tragic if despite the goodwill and helping hands of Hong Kong's major international economic partners (such as the 1992 U.S.–Hong Kong Policy Act's treatment of the SAR as distinct from the PRC in trade and other functional matters), Beijing "de-internationalizes" Hong Kong and even kills the goose that lays the golden eggs. Therefore, the people and institutions in Hong Kong should work closely among themselves and with the outside world to safeguard their much cherished functional autonomy and all too crucial global links and international capabilities both to preserve their successful way of life and work and to continue their vital contribution to the Chinese nation.

It is in this line of defense that the Hong Kong public fully supports the government's very firm stance to preserve Hong Kong autonomy in customs matters by rejecting the U.S. customs' attempt in mid-1996 to set up "joint inspection" of Hong Kong garment factories to combat illegal transshipment of items produced in mainland China. It is indeed an ironic twist that of all Hong Kong's major economic partners, it befalls the U.S. government, contradictory to the U.S.–Hong Kong Policy Act's true spirit, to try to extend its "long-arm jurisdiction" into Hong Kong at the expense of the territory's much needed economic and other autonomy at this critical juncture of its transition to 1997.[27] It becomes even more ironic that despite the PRC's tendencies to "de-internationalize" Hong Kong, the PRC's Hong Kong and Macau Affairs Office director Lu Ping recently repeated the official assurance that Beijing is fully determined to prevent official PRC organs at all levels from stretching their long arms to interfere with the Hong Kong SAR after 1997.[28]

Notwithstanding the PRC officialdom and Hong Kong leftist/antidemocratic circles' strong criticism of Hong Kong governor Chris Patten and Democratic Party Chairman Martin Lee's attempts to "internationalize" the Hong Kong issue (by visiting the United States, Canada, and Australia to meet with government leaders, give congressional testimonies, and conduct press meetings), Beijing and its Hong Kong elite allies recently began to realize the importance and hence the necessity of gaining better international understanding of, and confidence in, the SAR. Lu Ping and a delegation of SAR Preliminary Working Committee key members (some of them holders of foreign passports) visited the United States in 1995. In June 1996, Lu Ping visited Japan and Southeast Asia with extensive public exposure and press coverage. The Hong Kong tycoon–funded Better Tomorrow Foundation with its HK$100 million endowment recent undertook extensive public-relations efforts in the United States to win support for their more conservative, pro-Beijing version of post-1997 Hong Kong. Perhaps these efforts reflect their more recent reckoning that the true hinterland of social and economic Hong Kong must incorporate the world community at large as well as the Chinese mainland north of Shenzhen River.

Thus it seems that paralleling Beijing's ultra-nationalistic assertion of "national sovereignty" over Hong Kong issues (expressed as a major achievement in national reunification, as militantly displayed in the Taiwan Strait crisis in March 1996), there is a belated awareness and grudging acceptance of the crucial global implications of Hong Kong's successful reintegration with China. Of course, in this sunset era of British decolonization, not only nationalism or ultra-nationalistic claims can easily color if not really overwhelm Hong Kong's very enriching cosmopolitanism, but local parochialism also rears its head. That might combine with nationalistic fever to mitigate against Hong Kong's pre-1997 gains in the world arena. Indeed, one also cannot entirely rule out the possibility, however remote, of a serious outbreak of ultra-nationalistic, hyper-patriotic or even xenophobic sentiments among Chinese residents in the SAR sometime after 1997, or, for that matter, the SAR's possible systematic discrimination against foreign-educated or foreign passport–holding Hong Kong personnel or those with international professional qualifications in both the public and private sectors.[29]

The continued employment of nonlocal Chinese in the civil service, public organizations, academic institutions, and private concerns is guaranteed by the Basic Law, which only requires the SAR chief executive, senior officials (about two dozen), and the chief justice of the Court of Final Appeal to be local Chinese and also limits non-Chinese SAR citizens to 20 percent of the membership of the legislature. While boosting the populace's own self-esteem in decision making and leadership, there is still the possibility that the current drive toward localization with its clear anticolonial and non-British overtone might, after 1997, when coming under the spell of ultra-nationalistic sentiments, become a parochial and even xenophobic tendency. This will depend very much on the PRC's ideo-cultural lines and its relations with the outside world. Nevertheless, Hong Kong's localization efforts as a necessity in the decolonization process and the foundation building of a genuine high degree of local autonomy could be a healthy and natural development, especially in nurturing political and managerial leadership for the SAR.

While localism might counterbalance cosmopolitanism, it could also help to resist and contain unwarranted central interference in the name of sovereignty and nationalism. The social-cultural gulfs that separate the people of Hong Kong from their mainland compatriots have as contributing factors both Hong Kong–Cantonese inputs as well as exposure and adoption/adaptation of foreign elements. In this social-cultural realm, global influences help to make Hong Kong culture colorful, more pluralistic, and distinct from the mainland Chinese vintage. And because of the proliferation of Hong Kong Chinese communities overseas, Hong Kong culture is also externally linked and sustained. Indeed, in a Hong Kong that is becoming more integrated with China while also trying to maintain and even enhance its global links, the interplay of the forces of localism, nationalism, and cosmopolitanism after 1997 will create interesting dynamics that further transform the territory and its people in the twenty-first century.

Concluding Observations: Beyond 1997

As a parallel development to decolonization, but on the other side of the coin of localization, is the expanding range and growing complexity of Hong Kong's global linkages. With the tremendous growth, outreach, and diversification of its economy, Hong Kong has assumed an increasingly significant functional role and strategic vitality as a world-class commercial, transportation, financial and communication hub on the Pacific Rim.

In its manifold functional capabilities, its economic power projection, and its intermediary role for the Chinese mainland, Hong Kong has been even more highly internationalized since the early 1980s. The gradual fade-out of the British colonial raj with its London-centered orientation, and the absolute decline of British economic hegemony and monopolies, yielded room both for Hong Kong to expand its external ties and for China and many other external interests to come in. The resulting pluralistic international influences have already substantially enriched the economic and cultural lives of Hong Kong people and enlarged their political horizon, especially with the worldwide promotion of democratic values and human rights. Furthermore, the massive overseas exodus of Hong Kong people for education, business, and migration and settlement has enlarged and deepened Hong Kong's very impressive international networks in human terms. The attention and concern for Hong Kong in international media, business, academic, and political circles, especially on the 1997 China–Hong Kong integration issue, also help to strengthen Hong Kong's global linkages and high-profile presence on the world stage. In the context of the world trend toward democratization and human rights awareness, the future SAR's global connections would be of utmost concern for the PRC, which has often regarded with suspicion Hong Kong's relationship with the outside world as potentially dangerous and even undermining Beijing's sovereign prerogatives in security/defense and foreign policy.

As of July 1997, with the PRC government exercising sole control over the defense/security and foreign affairs of the SAR, issues that were previously handled by London on Hong Kong's behalf may be treated very differently by Beijing. For instance, Vietnam boat people have become an issue due to the British-created "first port of asylum" policy. Whether or not these still remain in Hong Kong will depend heavily on the state of Sino-Vietnamese relations. Even if Hong Kong's elected legislature can reflect the populace's collective will on this matter, it will be entirely up to Beijing to set the policy and implement its decision in the manner it sees fit. Also, notwithstanding the Hong Kong people's aversion to the PRC's military presence in their midst, Hong Kong might become a vital Chinese arms sales or purchase conduit, or even the PRC's military base for power projection into the South China Sea, with all the territorial disputes and island claims remaining unsolved on the threshold of the twenty-first century.

Perhaps by then, global politics and economic self-interest as well as the Asia-Pacific power balance will have changed and China will have changed as well. Nonetheless, Hong Kong shall still be an issue of global concern. If the EEC's Maastricht accord is fully put in effect, then the political union aspect of a common European foreign and defense policy might theoretically (though most unlikely in any realistic calculation) involve the entire EEC bloc, on account of one or two of its members (UK and/or Portugal), in a confrontation with China over events in Hong Kong or Macau. As stipulated in the Joint Declaration, the Sino-British Joint Liaison Group will continue to function, until January 1, 2000. By then, there will be some 225,000 UK passport holders who are former colonial Hong Kong residents but entitled to settle and work anywhere within the EEC.

If the EEC link is of any significance in our understanding of transitional Hong Kong, it will probably be in the comparative lesson on the difficulties in achieving political unity and legal/administrative incorporation, even with a considerable foundation in economic integration, among free nations with functioning democratic political systems within the Western Christian civilization and rule of law tradition. The Danish rejection of the Maastricht accord and the British withdrawal from the European Union's monetary linkage are vivid examples of the complexities of collaborative efforts toward economic integration and eventual political union.

The Guangdong–Hong Kong economic integration is indeed one of the most remarkable modern examples of functional collaboration and interdependence transcending legal, administrative, and ideo-political demarcations.[30] Yet it seems far too premature, even among optimists, to talk about the South China political union, at least not before the SAR's supposed termination date of 2047. In this sense, the forthcoming PRC–Hong Kong reunion and integration/incorporation can hardly be expected to take place without considerable or prolonged adjustment pains.

Even in an ideal scenario, in which China is no longer a communist dictatorship with a socialist economy, serious problems would still remain for the Hong Kong–mainland reunion: (1) the imbalance in size, scale, and magnitude between the two parts of the Chinese nation, coupled with the traditional (not just communist) Chinese notion of big brother–little brother relationship as applied to Hong Kong; (2) the great disparity in level of socioeconomic development, income, lifestyle, and mentality/world view, as well as socioeconomic culture, between the Chinese people in these two communities; and (3) the epidemic and historic reach of a large and intrusive Chinese bureaucracy, the extensive red-tape hierarchy, and corruption involving officialdom (see the example of pre-1949 Guomindang, not communist, China) obliterating free trade and fair business vital to Hong Kong's survival. It will require considerable self-restraint, tolerance, and patience on the part of the senior political partner (the mainland central authorities) in their approach to the junior partner, Hong Kong, with its six million cosmopolitan and productive residents, to make this retrocession/integration/absorption process work for the true interests of both partners and the global community.

In closing, perhaps one may still argue for an enlightened, positive, and sensitive global perspective on Hong Kong's status transformation. It is of critical importance for those outside Hong Kong to organically incorporate the "Hong Kong factor" in their multifold official and unofficial exchange and collaboration relationship with the PRC so as to strengthen Hong Kong's world status as both a Chinese and global asset. Indeed, the post-1997 continuation of Hong Kong's vitality as a free port, open society, even as the "Switzerland of Asia" or the "Pearl of the Pacific Rim" with a thriving economy serving China and the world is a global development that shall be treasured by all.

If recent developments in the political/diplomatic arena can be useful indicators for continued global support for Hong Kong's transformation into a successful world city and PRC SAR, then there may be grounds for optimism, even though when compared with Taipei, Hong Kong has no powerful lobby in the United States or elsewhere. In spring 1996, British prime minister John Major announced in his official visit to Hong Kong that the UK will offer visa-free access to future Hong Kong SAR passport holders, thus discharging what little is left of the British "moral responsibility" to the Hong Kong people and also claiming the honor of being the first country in the world to do so. (Major also insisted that London will closely monitor the SAR's developments for the PRC's full compliance with the Sino-British Joint Declaration with the warning of international sanctions for violations.[31]) Soon afterward, Singapore became the second country to offer SAR passports visa-free access. In March 1997, Canada also announced via-free entry for short-term visitors with Hong SAR passports.

In July 1996, both the Canadian and Australian foreign ministers paid official visits to Hong Kong, and besides meeting top government officials, they talked with leaders of the major local political parties.[32] Of course, both Canada and Australia, being advanced industrial democracies in the British Commonwealth, strongly support Hong Kong's democratization efforts under the British sunset regime. But the influx of immigrants and investments from Hong Kong, and trade and other economic interests in and through Hong Kong have helped to make Hong Kong a significant issue of domestic, diplomatic, and economic concern for Ottawa and Canberra. The fact that Raymond Chan, the minister of state for Asia/Pacific at Ottawa's Department of External Affairs, is originally an immigrant from Hong Kong has much symbolic and realpolitik significance.

In August 1996, the Japanese foreign minister visited Hong Kong, which counts Japan as a major economic partner, also the PRC's key Asian economic partner. Japan, like many other countries, places much store in Hong Kong's post-1997 role as an efficient, reliable, and impartial middleman between itself and the Chinese market. However, the Japanese foreign minister's visit to Hong Kong was marred by his insensitive statement asserting Japanese sovereignty over the disputed Diaoyutai Islands. This was followed by an extremely ill advised and totally undiplomatic uttering in early September 1996 by the Japanese consul-general in Hong Kong that the dispute over the islands was a "minor matter" that the local media should not blow out of proportion. This provoked a very strong formal rebuttal by the PRC Foreign Ministry spokesperson and added fuel to the local protest movement.[33] This case illustrates how the supposedly "colonized" Hong Kong Chinese spontaneously rose for a patriotic cause to defend Chinese national interests vis-à-vis foreign encroachment, and in so doing indirectly turned Hong Kong into a frontline, if not the arena, of Chinese international politics.[34] This will of course carry serious implications for the post-1997 era.

From late August 1996, public protests and demonstrations emerged in mainland China, Taiwan, and Hong Kong to assert the Chinese national sovereignty claims over the Islands against a right-wing Japanese attempt to resurrect a lighthouse there. Unhindered by the cautious.and even passive stance of both the Beijing and Taipei regimes, the people of Hong Kong were able to mount a most fierce and spirited campaign against the revival of Japanese militarism and Japanese infringement on Chinese sovereignty over the Diaoyutai Islands. Hong Kong's manifestation of Chinese nationalistic sentiment included an impressive protest march of some twenty thousand participants on September 15, 1996, and a protest statement campaign that collected over 765,000 signatures in four days (September 14–18).[35] Similar to the first Diaoyutai Islands movement a quarter of a century ago, Hong Kong, due to its relative freedom, was able to assert leadership among the worldwide Chinese communities to play the most vocal and high-profile role in this protest movement. In contrast, the PRC government, alarmed by the uncontrollable potential of a rising public anti-Japanese campaign, took high-handed measures to constraint and even demobilize this anti-Japanese outburst on the mainland. The Beijing officialdom probably did not wish to see the private collective actions of its citizens disturb its rather delicate official diplomatic and economic relations with Japan, and it also could not tolerate any massive public demonstration over such an emotional issue that was not under its sponsorship and could easily escalate and be transformed into an anti-government movement. Thus, while the Beijing authorities reiterated their "understanding" of Hong Kong's very vocal demonstration, which saw the pro-democracy lobby joined hand with the local leftist front, the PRC officialdom was less much tolerant toward domestic anti-Japanese activists.[36]

If the September 1996 popular anti-Japanese mobilization in Hong Kong is not an isolated case, then there is the possibility that after 1997 private undertakings in the SAR may create problems for the PRC central authorities in the conduct of foreign policy. Thus, the prospect of the PRC officialdom's tolerance of any such patriotic popular mobilization against a foreign target in the SAR might become problematic, especially in view of the Basic Law's very clear delineation of foreign relations being the prerogatives of the central government. In other words, public activities by private individuals or grassroots organizations in the SAR with international repercussions might not enjoy the same freedom and nongovernment interference as in the 1990s under the British colonial sunset regime.[37] Indeed, this might become another potential area of Hong Kong SAR's "de-internationalization" for the sake of serving the national interest of China as interpreted by the Beijing central authorities.

While all the world seems to be coming to Hong Kong in the critical final hours of its transition to Chinese sovereignty, Hong Kong also claims a breakthrough by winning its historic first-ever Olympic medal, a gold medal, in women's windsurfing at the 1996 Atlanta Olympic Games—the last time Hong Kong will compete as Hong Kong. After 1997, Hong Kong's participation in the Olympic Games will be under the title of "Hong Kong, China." Yet Hong Kong SAR will dispatch a separate team from the PRC national team.

If this gold medal symbolizes Hong Kong's truly becoming a mature, respected, and successful player in the world of sports right before the dawn of its reunion with China, it is indeed a most timely and profoundly appreciated morale-boosting victory for all of Hong Kong. Both the colonial government and the PRC local organs participated fully in the public celebrations of the gold medal winner's triumphal homecoming.[38] Perhaps, a Hong Kong that gains the applause of the world will also gain the much deserved recognition, welcome, and trust of the Chinese nation long after the celebratory fireworks ends on July 1, 1997.

With the helping hand of the outside world, and buttressed by informed and careful policy toward China with a built-in "Hong Kong factor" on the part of Hong Kong's global partners in many fields, Hong Kong may be able to retain its best for China and the world to enjoy beyond 1997.

Notes

1. See Shiu-hing Lo, *Political Development in Macau* (Hong Kong: Chinese University Press, 1995), Chapter 1, for Macau's retrocession to China.

2. A good example of official PRC expression of such sentiment is the April 7, 1990, *People's Daily* editorial, "The Hong Kong Basic Law: A Creative Masterpiece." This item and two other pieces from the *Beijing Review* on the Basic Law and the Hong Kong settlement as a great victory and triumph of world significance for the PRC can be found in Ming K. Chan and David J. Clark, eds., *The Hong Kong Basic Law: Blueprint for "Stability and Prosperity" under Chinese Sovereignty?* (Armonk, NY: M.E. Sharpe, and Hong Kong: Hong Kong University Press, 1991), pp. 235–245.

3. Taipei's concern for Hong Kong's transition to 1997 is reflected in various official measures, such as the addition of a new "Mainland China and Hong Kong Affairs" chapter (pp. 137–144) in the official *Republic of China Yearbook, 1991–92*, and the establishment of a Special Hong Kong Affairs Task Force in the Executive Yuan in 1983. This task force in January 1991 became the Hong Kong and Macau Department of the Mainland Affairs Council of the Executive Yuan.

4. William H. Overholt, "Hong Kong and China after 1997: The Real Issues," in Frank J. Macchiavola and Robert B. Oxnam, eds., *The China Challenge: American Policies in East Asia* (New York: In conjunction with the Asia Society, 1991, *Proceedings of the Academy of Political Science,* v. 38, no. 2), p. 34, argues that the "one country, two systems" strategy is working toward Taiwan, despite Tiananmen, in broad functional terms of Taiwan tourism to, investment in, and trade with the mainland. Also see Ming K. Chan, "Hong Kong's Imperfect Transition to 1997: Implications for Chinese Mainland–Taiwan Relations," paper presented at the international conference "Taiwan on the Move," Chung-li, Taiwan, April 1996.

5. The verbatim script of this debate is reported in full in the *New York Times,* October 12, 1992.

6. *Sing Tao Daily,* (U.S. edition), July 25, 1996.

7. On Hong Kong migration, see Ronald Skeldon, ed., *Reluctant Exiles: Migration from Hong Kong and the New Overseas Chinese* (Armonk, NY: M.E. Sharpe, and Hong

Kong: Hong Kong University Press, 1994).

8. This figure is from the Hong Kong government's official yearbook, *Hong Kong 1994: A Review of 1993* (Hong Kong: Government Information Services, 1994), p. 412.

9. For instance, as early as 1987–88 there were several Hong Kong–focused panels in major international academic conferences, including the first-ever Hong Kong subject double panel at the annual meeting of the Association for Asian Studies in San Francisco, March 1988. In successive AAS annual meetings in 1990 and 1996 there were also Hong Kong subject round tables or double panels. Hong Kong–focused articles have appeared with considerable frequency in major scholarly journals like *Asian Survey, China Quarterly,* and *Pacific Affairs* since the mid-1980s. The same is true for academic monographs and anthologies on Hong Kong. See Ming K. Chan, *The British Sunset in Hong Kong: Historical Challenge in the Wilsonian Era of Transition* (Hong Kong: Hong Kong Economic Journal, 1989), pp. 154–159, 171–175.

10. On the June 4 event's positive fallout effect on Hong Kong democratization and the changed British policy toward Hong Kong and Beijing, see Chan, "Democracy Derailed," in Chan and Clark, eds., pp. 17–21 and also pp. 246–255.

11. With the Basic Law constitutional provisions settled by this Sino-British secret deal, eighteen seats, instead of the ten promised in the 1988 Hong Kong Government's *White Paper,* were to be directly elected in the 1991 first-ever legislative direct election, and the number will be increased to twenty in the 1995 election, the last to be held in Hong Kong under British administration. See Ming K. Chan, "Democracy Derailed," in Chan and Clark, eds., *The Hong Kong Basic Law,* pp. 25–29.

12. See *South China Morning Post,* June 6, 7, 1991; and also Nihal Jayawickrama, "Interpreting the Hong Kong Bill of Rights," paper presented at Canada and Hong Kong: Legal Issues Workshop, York University, Toronto, October 2, 1992.

13. Bruce Bueno de Mesquita, David Newman, and Alvin Rabushka, *Red Flag over Hong Kong* (Chatham, NJ: Chatham House, 1996), p. 126.

14. On the historic legislative veto of a British and Hong Kong government decision, see *South China Morning Post,* December 5, 1991, and editorial, November 1, 1991; and *Hong Kong Economic Journal,* December 5, 1991.

15. Bueno de Mesquita et al., pp. 62–64.

16. *Sing Tao Jih Pao,* July 17, 1992.

17. For an example of Beijing's opposition to the U.S.–Hong Kong Policy Act of 1992, see *Sing Tao Jih Pao,* September 23, 1992.

18. The rationale and explanation for this bill were given in a June 4, 1992, speech by its original sponsor, Mitch McConnell, in "Hong Kong and the Future of China Three Years after the Tiananmen Square Massacre," *Heritage Lectures,* No. 385 (Washington, DC: Heritage Foundation, 1992).

19. On the Taiwan Relations Act and the U.S.–Taipei link since 1979, see Ramon H. Myers, ed., *A Unique Relationship: The United States and the Republic of China under the Taiwan Relations Act* (Stanford, CA: Hoover Institution Press, 1989).

20. *Hong Kong Economic Journal,* April 6, 22, 23, 24, 1992; *South China Morning Post,* April 10, 1992, column by Frank Ching.

21. A senior-level U.S. official statement expressing strong hope for Guangdong's economy says that its "large market-oriented sector now exceeds the state sector. This engagement has led to the integration of China's coastal provinces with Hong Kong, Taiwan and the global economy." See Secretary of State James Baker III's essay "America in Asia: Emerging Architecture for a Pacific Community," *Foreign Affairs* (winter 1991/92), p. 16. This may not be fully in accord with Beijing's grand strategy for national development.

22. On the Hong Kong Reversion Act, see *South China Morning Post,* March 13, 1997, and *Asia Week,* March 28, 1997, p. 25.

23. On Hong Kong's capacity for being an "international personality," see Roda Mushkat, "Hong Kong's International Personality: Issues and Implications," in William Angus, ed., *Canada–Hong Kong: Some Legal Considerations* (Toronto: Joint Centre for Asia Pacific Studies, University of Toronto/York University, 1992) [Canada and Hong Kong Papers, No. 2], pp.14–30.

24. On the international legal and political status of Hong Kong as a "quasi-state," see James T.H. Tang, "Hong Kong and the New International Order: Problems of a Dependent Polity in a Changing World," unpublished September 1992 conference paper, and his "Hong Kong's International Status," *Pacific Review* 6, 3 (1993), pp. 209–211.

25. *Sing Tao Daily,* August 19, 1996.

26. *South China Morning Post,* August 18, 1996, especially the editorial, p. 10.

27. *Yazhou Zhoukan,* July 7, 1996, pp. 36–37.

28. *Yazhou Zhoukan,* July 7, 1996, pp. 21–23.

29. This would be, ironically, a reversal of the long, deliberate, and pervasive British colonial discrimination against non-British-style education and qualifications as late as the late 1980s and even into the early 1990s. See Chan, *The British Sunset in Hong Kong,* pp. 42–51. The Hong Kong Bar Association's opposition to allowing American lawyers into local practice is another often-cited example.

30. A detailed historical and contemporary analysis is Ming K. Chan, "All in the Family: Hong Kong–Guangdong Linkages in Historical Perspective, 1842–1992," in Alvin So and Reginald Kwok, eds., *The Hong Kong–Guangdong Link: Partnership in Flux* (Armonk, NY: M.E. Sharpe, and Hong Kong: Hong Kong University Press, 1995).

31. *South China Morning Post* and *Sing Tao Jih Pao,* both March 7, 1996.

32. *Far Eastern Economic Review,* August 8, 1996, p. 12, reports that Governor Patten gave Canadian external affairs minister Lloyd Axwathy a list of PRC dissidents living in Hong Kong now who needed to be relocated by 1997 when the two met on July 22, 1996. Also see *South China Morning Post* and *Ming Pao Daily,* both July 23, 1996, and *Sing Tao Daily,* July 25, 1996.

33. *South China Morning Post,* August 29, 1996; and *Oriental Daily News* September 6, 1996.

34. The historical tradition of Hong Kong Chinese serving as China's frontline of defense against foreign imperialism can be traced back to the mid-nineteenth century and has a very glorious record during the 1920s. See Ming K. Chan, ed., *Precarious Balance: Hong Kong Between China and Britain 1842–1992* (Armonk, NY: M.E. Sharpe, and Hong Kong: Hong Kong University Press, 1994), Chapters 1–5; and Jung-Fang Tsai, *Hong Kong in Chinese History: Community and Social Unrest in the British Colony 1842–1913* (New York: Columbia University Press, 1993), Chapters 5–8.

35. *South China Morning Post,* September 16, 1996; *Oriental Daily News* 12–16; 1996 and *Ta Kung Pao,* September 19, 1996.

36. *South China Morning Post* and *Oriental Daily News,* both September 16, 1996.

37. In the earlier period, the British colonial regime was not so tolerant and civilized toward popular mobilization. One should note that in the 1971 Diaoyutai Islands movement, the Hong Kong police resorted to very stern repression measures against the local protesters, many of them high school and university students. These victims of Hong Kong police brutality were severely beaten, arrested, jailed, and even subsequently black listed. Of course, this was in the era before the Bill of Rights, which covers freedom of assembly and speech. For the most recent Hong Kong publication on the Diaoyutai issue with contributions from the earlier generation of Diaoyutai movement activists, see *Ming Pao* ed., *Daioyutai: Zhongguodi lingtu* (The Diaoyutai Islands: China's Territory) (Hong Kong: Ming Pao Publishing, 1996).

38. *South China Morning Post,* August 8, 1996.

2

Mainland China, Taiwan, and Hong Kong as International Actors

Byron S.J. Weng

The internationalization of Hong Kong is, by nature, a subject about which Beijing will have much to say. It is also a matter that requires participation from other members of the international community and, to some extent, cooperation from Taiwan. Taiwan is relevant by virtue of her status as a competing successor to the pre-1949 China, which makes her "the other Chinese international actor."

In this chapter, we shall examine the three Chinese international actors, which consists of mainland China, Taiwan, and Hong Kong; discuss the evolving relationships among these three; and assess the U.S.–Hong Kong Policy Act 1992 as an example of international reaction to the Hong Kong transition. Hopefully, such discussions will shed some light on the possibilities and limitations of Hong Kong's internationalization.

Multiple Chinese International Actors

In terms of the law of the sovereign state system, one would have to say that there are four "Chinese" international actors. They are (1) the People's Republic of China (PRC), whose government claims to be and is recognized in many diplomatic communiqués as "the sole representative" of both mainland China and Taiwan; (2) the Republic of China (ROC) on Taiwan, whose government effectively and exclusively rules the Taiwan, Penghu, Jinmen, and Mazu region and is recognized as an equal by some thirty largely insignificant sovereign governments, or as a de facto government of said region for nonpolitical purposes by over 140 others; (3) Hong Kong, where the existing British colonial government is recognizeded by practically every other government in the world except that of the PRC; and (4) in a similar position, the Portuguese colony of Macau.

Technically, before July 1, 1997, and December 20, 1999, respectively, Hong Kong and Macau are not yet parts of China. However, because Beijing insists that these two territories have always been Chinese, one is forced to consider them as Chinese in that sense.

Of the four, the PRC is a bona fide sovereign actor. The ROC on Taiwan is a controversial de facto sovereign actor with a nebulous status. And Hong Kong and Macau are quasi-states with a subsovereign status. The picture is a blurred and complicated one. In international perspectives, the key question for the PRC is what role she will play as a political superstate. For Taiwan, the question is one of recognition, both from Beijing and from other national capitals. As to Hong Kong and Macau, determining the extent of authorization (or autonomy) from their future sovereign, China, will be more than half of the game.

Since Macau is relatively insignificant and its status similar to that of Hong Kong, the remainder of this chapter shall not deal with Macau, except to note briefly her specific features as a quasi-state. We shall refer to three rather than four Chinese actors after this.

The PRC as a Superstate

Three international images of the PRC stand out today, namely, a new yellow peril in the making, a dynamic economic force with a gigantic market, and a defiant challenger on the world scene.

By population, territory, history and culture, economic viability, government effectiveness, or her potential overall capabilities, China is a country no one can afford to take lightly. The world will benefit or suffer greatly not only from what China does but also from what China simply is. China can become an overbearing actor, outweighing most if not all others if successfully modernized, or become an unbearable burden for the rest of the world should she fail to develop or turn out to be intransigent. One may say with some justification that, by taking good care of her own population, Beijing makes a real contribution to world peace.

If waves of Chinese refugees were to land in the neighboring countries, like the Vietnamese did after 1975, the problems would be mind-boggling. If Beijing were to open the gates so that Chinese people could freely emigrate, the impact on the more advanced parts of the world would become a very real concern. Countries with thriving Chinatowns in their cities would no doubt feel the pressure in very substantial ways. Witness the Hong Kong experiences over the past half a century. Whenever Beijing or Guangdong authorities encouraged the people of the mainland to cross the borders, or ceased to cooperate in border control, the British Hong Kong government always became rather nervous. The demands on jobs, housing, schools, and public services that multitudes of refugees put on a community with lesser resources could be back-breaking. If Beijing decided to really overwhelm Hong Kong with refugees or "illegal immigrants," it would be hard to imagine what effective countermeasures the British Hong Kong government could possibly come up with.

Thus, the dictatorial and patriarchal rulers of China are in a position to make decisions that will have far-reaching effects on the world as well as on China and the Chinese people. Their influence is therefore enormous, and means of checking them need to be found. At times like the 1989 Tiananmen incident, or whenever a member of international society is made to react to situations such as the smuggling of large numbers of Chinese illegal immigrants, the above-mentioned image of China may well surface in the minds of many, especially those who have to deal with the Chinese.

A Dynamic Economic Force with a Gigantic Market Potential

China is also seen as an enormously attractive market since Deng Xiaoping started the reform and open-door policy. A population of 1.2 billion and a decade of a sustained double-digit growth rate are a formidable combination that many traders and investors find almost irresistible.

However, it is one thing to say that the Deng reforms have been successful and quite another to say that China is already an open, functioning international market. Similarly, it is one thing to say that Beijing is not likely to reverse its course, but quite another to say that the capitalist ways of the free world are here to stay.[1] As of spring 1996, Deng Xiaoping's Four Cardinal Principles are still upheld and the regime stands firm on the platform that the socialist idea of public ownership will continue to be the rule. Keynesian macroeconomic mechanisms are not too effective because the market is at best only half open in China. The rule of law is not at all reliable yet. Overall economic growth may be impressive, but rural–urban and coastal–inland contradictions seem to be quite pronounced. There are serious center–region conflicts of interest that threaten political instability in the post-Deng period.

Material life may have improved for many, but quality of life is becoming worse for all. Social costs in terms of environmental pollution, the breakdown of the moral fabric, and new class differences have been extremely high. The flows of migrant labor are getting bigger as the reform of public enterprises gets under way. Too many people are still dependent on the "big pot of rice." The armed forces are torn between business concerns and defense duties and their reliability is sometimes questioned. Bureaucratic corruption is rampant and widely condemned, but persistent. Political reforms are lagging far behind. Various kinds of crisis, including divisions in the CPC, are still expected. Indeed, Beijing is faced with very difficult problems in the years ahead.

This is not to say that the China market is not big or not enticing. It is important to note, however, that the statement, "China is an attractive market," is a simplistic description of the situation and can lead to inaccurate and risky conclusions.

A Defiant Challenger

The defiant challenger image of China is likewise a half-truth. One is reminded of the ups and downs of the status of Chinese immigrants in the United States and the stereotypes about them. Depending on who is speaking and when, the Chinese are either the most hard-working, unassuming, gentle citizens, or the most cunning, clannish, opium-smoking group of people.

Yes, China probably has an axe or two to grind psychologically, for she has been a frustrated giant for over a century. At different times in the past, especially under Mao, Beijing had expressed revolutionary world views and championed wars of national liberation. However, since 1979, Beijing has pursued an independent foreign policy and engaged in diplomacy mainly for China's normal national interests, that is, modernization.[2]

True, Beijing has tended to assert its own peculiar if not erroneous views regarding such established concepts as sovereignty, domestic jurisdiction, democracy, and human rights. The unilateral introduction of the "one country, two systems" scheme is highly unorthodox and makes considerable demands for adjustments on other members of the international system.[3] The self-serving claim that Hong Kong and Macau are not non-self-governing territories[4] is presumptuous and arbitrary. The advancement of the idea that, for developing nations, human rights can only mean, or have to be defined as, the right of collective survival and development[5] is not only unfortunate but, in the final analysis, diametrically opposed to the very idea of human rights.

Such a posture, coupled with the aforementioned image of a potential superpower, have produced in the Western press suggestions that there is a looming "Chinese threat" and that an international "containment of China" may be necessary. Beijing, in turn, has published many rebuttals and counterattacks.[6]

On the other hand, the way in which negotiations with the United States over the Most Favored Nation (MFN) clause and the intellectual property protection issues have transpired in recent years must have been frustrating to Beijing. China's struggle to enter the GATT must have made some Chinese leaders lose sleep; they might even view these as new experiences of national humiliation, whether in fact they are or not. No Chinese leader, least of all Deng Xiaoping, wants to be regarded as "Li Hongzhang No. 2."[7]

The PRC today may be a big power politically but she is a newly industrializing country economically and a regional power at best militarily. Using a different basis of calculation and ranking, the IMF declared in 1993 that the PRC was actually the third largest economy in the world. Beijing immediately rejected the honor, saying that China is still a poor, developing nation. In mid-February 1995, General Chi Haotian, China's defense minister, repeated that same point to the visiting Japanese chief of the general staff. In his words, "China is a big power but she is also a poor country. In terms of economic strength and of modernization of armed forces, there is a large discrepancy when compared to Japan. To catch up with Japan, efforts of several generations will be required."[8]

Taiwan, a Nebulous International Actor

By normal assessment, Taiwan today is a middle power in the Asia-Pacific region. That Taiwan is a territory with 21 million people, supported by a sizable military force capable of self-defense, few dispute. She had the world's twenty-first largest GNP and was the fourteenth largest trading nation, with the second largest foreign exchange reserve in 1995. However, Taiwan has been denied normal international recognition and deprived of the legal capacity to play an active role like other sovereign states.

Before 1986, it was said sometimes that Taiwan was a rather insignificant land of dictatorship, a source of cheap goods, a tourist pass-by. Since 1987, however, she seems to have acquired a new identity.[9] Having produced an economic miracle, she is in the process of creating a viable democracy. Now, according to her governmental spokesman, Taiwan would like to be an independent and influential contributor to the world, especially to international peace and development in the Asia-Pacific region. But she has been not much more than a pawn in the global chess game. She continues to be an international outcast.

Three obstacles are in her way: the self-imposed one-China policy of the ROC government, the problematic principles of sovereignty, and the hostile policy of the PRC government in Beijing.

The Self-imposed One-China Policy

The self-imposed one-China policy has three components. The first was the rigid civil war position, before 1987, of the regimes of Chiang Kai-shek and his son Chiang Ching-kuo, that "Hans (loyal Chinese) and bandits do not coexist."[10] Under the Chiangs, the ROC pursued a foreign policy that denied recognition to the PRC and Beijing. It insisted that there was only one China—the ROC and opposed "one China, one Taiwan" or "two Chinas" just as Beijing does today. The second component is the "three no's policy" (no contact, no negotiation, no compromise) initiated by Chiang Ching-kuo in response to Beijing's 1979 "Message to Taiwan Compatriots."[11] This is still maintained today though only as a formality. The third is the *Guidelines for National Unification* adopted by President Lee Teng-hui's advisory National Unification Council (NUC) in February 1991,[12] which declares Taipei's intention "to establish a democratic, free and equitably prosperous China," and says "both the mainland and Taiwan areas are parts of Chinese territory." In essence, it is a "one China, two governments" formulation.

Although the third component is already a far cry from the first, Lee's one-China policy is still attacked inside Taiwan by the advocates of Taiwan independence as a no-win, self-defeating position. It has been the contention of the Democratic Progressive Party (DPP)[13] that no one outside of Taiwan is likely to think of one China as anything other than the mainland under Beijing's control. Taiwan can have no separate identity as long as it subscribes to the one-China principle.

In order to remove this obstacle or ease its impact, the NUC went to the trouble of adopting a formal resolution entitled "The Meaning of 'One China' " in August 1992. Pointing out the different interpretations given to "one China" by the two sides of the Taiwan Strait, it says that both the PRC on the mainland and the ROC on Taiwan are parts of China. "The ROC, however, currently has jurisdiction only over Taiwan, Penghu, Jinmen, and Mazu," it concedes. Nonetheless, it goes on to assert that "Since 1949, China has been temporarily divided, and each side of the Taiwan Strait is administered by a separate political entity. This is an objective reality that no proposal for China's unification can overlook."

Later, Taipei further clarified its position, saying that "one China" refers to the past and the future after unification, but at the present, China is temporarily divided. And the government of Taiwan will not abandon the one-China principle or declare Taiwan's independence.

Had Taipei adopted such a position before it was driven out of the UN in 1971, one wonders what the situation might have been at present. Unfortunately, that was not the case. Today, the world might be sympathetic to Taiwan, but countries' hands have been tied by developments since 1971.

The Shackle of Sovereign Principles

In Taipei today, one prevailing school of thought argues that China and Taiwan are in the thick of the quagmire that the sovereign state system created. No one can come up with a clear conceptual explanation of "China" as an international actor that students on both sides of the Taiwan Strait, theoreticians or practitioners, are ready to accept as accurate and appropriate.[14]

Just as Taipei did before 1971, Beijing now says that Taiwan is a part of China and that therefore matters relating to Taiwan are in the category of China's domestic affairs in which other countries should not interfere. On this basis, Beijing adopts the position that no government should extend diplomatic recognition to either the ROC or her government in Taipei and that Taiwan is not qualified for membership in intergovernmental international organizations. What Taipei earlier dealt to Beijing, Taipei is now forced to receive.

Because the PRC is a potential superpower and because Beijing insists on its position of "one China, the PRC," most countries yield to Beijing's terms in order to establish formal diplomatic relations with it. However, most of them then turn around and conclude unofficial agreements with Taipei. Thus, many governments maintain double standards in such engagements. Like it or not, such acts are often justified in terms of the cold reality of international politics. Experts on international politics are prone to say that the present international society is one wherein the strong rule and there is little room for morality or justice. When, after severing relations with Taiwan in 1979, the United States adopted a Taiwan Relations Act, she added in effect a new practice in international law through domestic legislation. It was a rare remedial move to accord Taiwan a kind of status by a country that had severed formal relations with the ROC. The flexibility thus introduced was welcomed by Taipei, but it was inadequate.[15]

On the question of international organization membership, the situation is also unsatisfactory. The former Soviet Union was a federal state made up of fifteen republics, but Moscow had clear control over all of them until the USSR fell apart in 1991. Before 1991, the Soviet Union had three memberships in the United Nations—the USSR, Byelorussia and Ukraine. Once it disintegrated, the fifteen republics all became independent, full members of the UN. Today, Moscow controls only one membership, Russia.

In contrast, China is a unitary state in which the central government of the PRC has not been able to exert effective control over all the component parts it claims. While the ROC government was once in control of the mainland, the PRC government has never governed Taiwan at all. Beijing was excluded from the UN before November 1971, and Taipei since then, because the two competing successors chose not to recognize each other and insisted that there could be only one China. In recent years, Taipei has changed its stance. It is ready to pursue a "temporary two-Chinas" course, but Beijing will not relent on its strictly "one-China" position. Hence, China continues to have only one membership in the UN, even though the rest of the world appears to be ready to support two.

In the Asian Development Bank (ADB) and the Asia-Pacific Economic Cooperation (APEC) forum, not only China and Taiwan but Hong Kong is also a full member. The key difference between the UN and these two international organizations, according to Beijing, is not that the former is universal and the latter regional, but that the former is political and the latter nonpolitical.

The rigid doctrine of sovereignty is at least partially responsible for making Taiwan (and the PRC before 1971) a second-class international actor and its people second-class international citizens. Who can say that things are normal and satisfactory when President Lee Teng-hui's plane could not land in Hawaii for refueling, or, when President Lee was granted a visa to make a "private" visit to his alma mater it became an international crisis, even though Washington and Taipei have a friendly relationship. Citizens of Taiwan are often subjected to extortion at customs checks or forced to pay higher costs for services because they come from a country whose status is not recognized or is unclear. Thus, they are somehow not deserving of equal respect or dignity.

As I have argued elsewhere,[16] unless the world comes to grips with the reality of divided nations, not only will many people be condemned unfairly to endure an abnormal international life indefinitely, but all (including, in the case of China, not only Taipei and Beijing but also third countries) will be paying unnecessary costs, tangible and intangible, because of the distorted situation. When the division of nations is extensive, it is problematic to treat it as tempo- rary. When the problem is blatant, it is foolish to play ostrich. Serious inconsis- tency and arbitrariness should not continue to be acceptable. The people of divided nations, typically mainland Chinese before 1971 and Taiwan residents since then, have little choice but to live with a prolonged, unnecessary situation of injustice. To them, this is clearly one of the unsatisfactory aspects of the prevailing sovereign state system. Had the world been organized by principles other than those dictated by a rigid sovereign doctrine, both China before 1971 and Taiwan since then might have had other choices.

Modifications of the doctrine of sovereignty have been suggested. It is argued that this traditional concept is inadequate for dealing with international relations involving divided nations.[17] Since divided nations, prior to their division, are defined by an "absolute and indivisible" sovereignty, a division necessarily calls up the question of relocation of that sovereignty. Each of the two entities result- ing from the division is compelled to claim exclusive successor status. It is, therefore, not possible to settle the problem unless both contenders agree to a permanent partition or one contender conquers the other.

As remedies, it is argued that dual and cross recognitions should be made not only possible but normal where divided nations are concerned. Admission of the competing successors into international organizations and conferences should be simple and automatic. Alternately, there have been suggestions that sovereignty should be redefined as "divisible" under certain conditions, or that international society should accept the concept of multisystem nation and modify international law accordingly.[18] The case is a strong one, but it is not in fact heeded. Unfortu- nately, the time is not yet ripe for such a change.

Thus far, the third parties are neither willing nor able to tackle the problem head on. They seem to prefer to exploit the weaknesses of the divided nations and leave the world with fluid, incoherent, and contradictory answers to relevant questions. So Taiwan suffers on.

Hong Kong's Quasi-State Status

Hong Kong, the crown colony of the United Kingdom since 1842, shall be returned to the Chinese authorities in Beijing come July 1, 1997. Technically, London could have claimed that it was entitled to hold on to Hong Kong Island and Kowloon which were ceded to the British in perpetuity. Only the New Territories, leased to the British for ninety-nine years, was due to revert. This was for a short while the professed position of Prime Minister Margaret Thatcher. However, Beijing would not hear of any such suggestion as it insisted that the three unequal treaties were neither fair nor valid and that China would want the whole of the Hong Kong colony back in 1997. At any rate, China's views have prevailed.

The right of self-determination commonly practiced by former colonies[19] has been denied the peoples of Hong Kong and Macau. They have no choice but to accept the "one country, two systems" arrangement offered by Beijing. It is a clear Beijing position that Hong Kong and Macau affairs should not be on the agenda of any international conference or organization. Furthermore, China will not tolerate any effort by any other member of the international community to monitor the autonomy process of the future HK SAR (HKSAR) and Macau SAR.

"The story of Hong Kong 1997," or "the 1997 transition," is a phenomenon that carries with it certain extraordinary meanings. First, to Hong Kong and its residents, it means the end of a colonial era. A new era in Hong Kong's history is unfolding. Some residents, especially the pro-PRC elements, will no doubt rejoice over this historic change. But, more than a half of the population are refugees or children of refugees from the communist government of China. They will be forced to face their unwelcome masters again. Except for a small minority who have the means and the opportunity to emigrate to other countries, most of them have little choice but to make the necessary adjustments.

Second, to China, 1997 signifies the restoration of sovereignty over the territory after 155 years. The Chinese nation, which suffered and endured humiliation for that period, shall experience the satisfaction of ending the colonial occupation of a Chinese territory. Deng Xiaoping and his colleagues will no doubt get credit for managing to retake this Pearl of the Orient for China and have it so recorded in the annals of history.

Third, to the people of Macau and, more significantly, Taiwan, it can be a formula or a model of their own future. Taiwan cannot but afford to observe the development of Hong Kong in this connection with careful attention.

Fourth, to all patriotic Chinese around the globe, the possibility that Hong Kong may intensify its role as a locomotive for China's economic modernization is a potential source of pride. This process has been gaining momentum with time, and Chinese people have cause to hope that their motherland will grow stronger and that all Chinese will receive greater respect from other peoples in other lands.

Fifth, to the ASEAN nations and other countries of the Asia-Pacific region, the Hong Kong transition spells something uncertain but important. With "Hong Kong, Inc." in the lead, they welcome the fact that China has become more economically oriented and more business-minded. That means less support to revolutionary elements in the ASEAN countries from Beijing and more opportunities for exchange and cooperation, which should bring mutual benefits. On the other hand, there is a distinct possibility that a new, stronger, and therefore more threatening China may rise out of this transition. Be it a limited South China Economic Community or a more extensive Greater China, the prospects are worrisome to some of China's smaller neighbors.

Sixth, to the world at large, it may mean the emergence, under the formula of "one country, two systems," of a new type of international actor. The future Hong Kong SAR may turn out to be significantly different from any other quasi-state, an entity not known before. Such an actor may well be a challenge to the notion of the sovereign state under traditional international law. It is to be noted that Chinese commentators have suggested that the one country, two systems formula is potentially useful for the settlement not only of the Taiwan question, but also of disputes of a similar nature in other countries.

Finally, to many people of the free world, the 1997 transition is tantamount to the delivery of six million people to a communist government by a democratic government, with the approval, overt or tacit, of the other governments of the world. To them, this is a very unfortunate event and a highly unsatisfactory prospect. Justified or not, some historians may say the history of Hong Kong started with one infamous deed, the Opium War, and ended with another, a betrayal of trust—both by the British government.

Many interesting questions need attention from politicians and scholars alike. In this chapter, our question is: What will be the HKSAR's international status? In this context, Roda Mushkat of the University of Hong Kong has examined the theory of autonomy in international law.[20] Using Hurst Hannum and Richard B. Lillich's notion of the "minimum governmental powers,"[21] she defines a territory as autonomous and self-governing when it possesses governmental powers comprising a locally elected legislative body capable of independent decision making on local matters, excluding matters of foreign relations and defense; a locally chosen chief executive with powers of administration and execution; and an independent local judiciary. By this set of criteria, the British colony of Hong Kong is not autonomous since the governor has never been locally elected and the election of the Legislative Council (Legco) members began only in 1991 and only partially.

Mushkat expresses doubts also with regard to the future SAR legislature's independent law-making capability and the true autonomy of the chief executive under the Basic Law. She saw some shadows over the future judiciary in spite of the many provisions that seem to suggest judicial independence. She concludes that complex factors other than formal international legal agreements will affect Hong Kong's future, including its international status.

In contrast, another scholar, James Tang, appears more optimistic.[22] He approached the question through an examination of the concepts of sovereignty and state. Wading through the "conceptual quagmire" of these terms, Tang landed on Robert H. Jackson's ideas of negative and positive sovereignty and quasi-states.[23] Political entities are said to have negative sovereignty "when the international society has conferred upon them a formal-legal entitlement for constitutional independence and freedom from outside interference." They are said to have positive sovereignty when their governments "can provide political goods for their citizens and are capable of collaborating with other governments in international arrangements and reciprocating in international commerce and finance." The former refers to a formal condition while the latter refers to a substantive condition. Jackson uses the term *quasi-states* to denote those entities that possess no negative sovereignty.

Tang finds the future Hong Kong worthy of quasi-state status. It will be an autonomous entity possessing considerable powers of positive sovereignty. In his words, "the degree of its capacity to act is seldom accorded to other contemporary sub-state units. . . . Under the Basic Law, Hong Kong is to enjoy a high degree of autonomy in terms of its internal political authority, power of governance, control of natural resources, and the management of the economy."

Pointing to the U.S.–Hong Kong Policy Act of 1992, discussed later, Tang observes that Hong Kong enjoys a greater degree of international recognition of its special status than most other autonomous entities. Indeed, Hong Kong's formal authority to conduct its external economic, cultural, and social relations and to take part in international organizations is unparalleled. It should be seen as a key player in regional affairs in its own right in the form of a reversed Jacksonian "quasi-state."

This writer agrees with both Mushkat's assessment and Tang's interpretation of the future HKSAR's international status. Mushkat is sound in judging the reality. The future HKSAR can be truly autonomous only to the extent that Beijing authorizes. Loading all the expectations of the Hong Kong people and of the other international players on the Joint Declaration and the Basic Law will undoubtedly be problematic. Yet Tang's interpretation is at least technically correct, and until Beijing decides to do away with the autonomous arrangement, the HKSAR may prove to be unique and substantial as an autonomous entity.

If the "one country, two systems" formula is adhered to, the HKSAR's autonomy will be considerable as a substate unit. For instance, it will continue to have its own currency and passports. It will be a separate customs area and a member of World Trade Organization (WTO). As an economic entity, it is already a member of a number of international organizations and will be qualified for membership in others. It will still be a favored corporate regional headquarters. And it will serve, in diplomacy or in commerce, as an arena for international bargaining, espionage, and intrigue.

This becomes even clearer as we look later into the ways by which some provisions of the Joint Declaration and the Basic Law are translated into actionable laws by an influential country such as the United States.

Macau Rides Along with Hong Kong

The tiny Portuguese-administered trading port of Macau will be returned to China on December 20, 1999. A Sino-Portuguese Joint Declaration was signed on March 26, 1987, and a Basic Law of the Macau SAR was adopted by the National People's Congress (NPC) of the PRC on March 31, 1993. With some necessary modifications, the two documents essentially duplicate the transition arrangements worked out for Hong Kong.

Like Hong Kong, Macau will become the Macau SAR with a quasi-state status. There are probably only two significant differences between the two Joint Declarations. Unlike the UK, Portugal did not contest China's assertion that Macau "is Chinese territory." "The interests of residents of Portuguese descent in Macau" are specifically given protection. The other important difference stems from the fact that, unlike the UK's convoluted and discriminatory nationality policy, Portugal's law recognizes only one type of nationality. All residents in Macau enjoy full Portuguese citizenship and right of abode in Portugal. Hence, they will be able to move to the European Union countries much more easily than the residents of Hong Kong.[24]

Mainland China–Taiwan–Hong Kong Relations

At any given time, international perspectives of the three Chinese actors are understandably conditioned by the relations among them. Any of the three actors can unilaterally or through mutual interactions alter aspects of her foreign relations.[25] Other international actors have to respond to changes in such relations.

The three sides of the Chinese triangle are different and unequal. All are complicated and changing. Mainland–Taiwan relations were those between competing successors to the pre-1949 China until Taipei abandoned the contention in 1991. Now they are two regions of a divided nation playing a unique on-off game of unification. Mainland–Hong Kong relations are a mixture of Sino-British diplomacy and central–local relations within the larger China context. They will become a matter of the HKSAR's autonomy come 1997. Taiwan–Hong Kong relations have always been overshadowed by the other two sides. Relations were largely suppressed, informal, and abnormally low-key before 1987. Although improving, the clouds overhead are still thick and dark. Whether the clouds will dissipate depends largely on decisions made in Beijing.

Needless to say, the three sides are intertwined and interactive. Betterment in mainland–Taiwan relations will almost instantly improve Taiwan–Hong Kong relations. Worsened mainland–Hong Kong relations will most likely signal a warning to Taipei about such things as the "one country, two systems" policy and adversely affect mainland–Taiwan relations. Likewise, Taiwan–Hong Kong accords arrived at without Beijing's approval may be taken as a challenge and cause Beijing to react.

Mainland China–Taiwan Relations

Theoretically, it is possible to identify the key variables determining the relations between the PRC and the ROC as the two competing successors of pre-1949 China. They include the attitudes and policies of the competitors toward each other; the relative merits of their respective systems; the example set by, and the lessons to be drawn from, the Hong Kong experience in "one country, two systems"; and developments in the international environment, especially the Asia-Pacific region. The evolutionary patterns of their relationship and the eventual alternative outcomes can also be projected. Their relationship may go through several stages, for example, hostility, stalemate, competition, cooperation, negotiation, settlement. The possible outcomes include unification by conquest or negotiations into a unitary or federal state or a confederacy, or separation into two states.[26]

In reality, over the past forty-five years the relationship between the PRC and the ROC has undergone six stages of development. Briefly, these are:[27]

1. tense cold war, 1949–58;
2. relaxed, stalemated cold war, 1959–71;
3. closed competition in a state of nominal cold war, 1971–78;
4. Beijing's unilateral overtures for negotiation and open competition, 1979–87;
5. open competition and partial cooperation, 1987–present;
6. informal negotiations, 1991–present.

As mentioned earlier, before 1971, the ROC was upheld as the sole representative of China in the UN and other capitals, with the blessing of the United States. In November that year, the PRC replaced the ROC in the UN and fortune turned for the two contenders.

The next significant development thereafter occurred on New Year's Day 1979, when Beijing made the first of its détente overtures and invitations to unification talks. Although Taipei initially responded with a "no contact, no negotiation, no compromise" policy, in November 1987, the late ROC president, Chiang Ching-kuo, saw fit to open the door for mainland visitation by separated families. Since then, the "three links and four exchanges"[28] proposed by Beijing have taken place very substantially.

Beijing's formula for national unification, beginning probably in 1979 and most certainly since 1984, has been "one country, two systems." "One country" means there is only one China, the PRC, and that Taiwan is a part of China. Anything to the contrary—two Chinas; one China, one Taiwan; Taiwan independence—is not acceptable. "Two systems" means socialism in the mainland and capitalism in Taiwan, but it does not mean equal status for the two systems or regions. Rather, Beijing is the central government while Taipei, like Hong Kong, can only be a SAR, that is, a local government. There have been changes in strategy and tactics, but this basic position has never been altered.

To this, Taipei has countered with a "one country, two governments" proposal as stipulated in its 1991 Guidelines for National Unification. The Guidelines succinctly and authoritatively spell out the goal, principles, and three-stage process of Taiwan's mainland policy. Taipei implies its willingness to recognize

Beijing on condition of reciprocity. However, to build a China of democracy, freedom, and equitable prosperity, unification can only be conditional and done in stages. Taipei would have official communications, exchange official visits with Beijing, and permit official postal, commercial, and communication/transport services with the mainland only when the parties are no longer (1) posing a threat to each other's security, (2) denying the other's existence as an "equal political entity," and (3) excluding the other side from international relations. Consultation for unification can be realistic only after there is mutual trust.

Taipei's concession, however, was not good enough and the conditions remain unacceptable to Beijing. Cross-strait relations are still in a stalemate, though on a different plateau. In the meantime, Taipei promulgated in July 1991 a special law, entitled Regulations on Relations between the Peoples of the Taiwan Region and the Mainland Region,[29] to stabilize the people-to-people relations across the Taiwan Strait.

Both Beijing and Taipei have their institutions for cross-strait affairs in place. In 1990, Taipei established a presidential National Unification Council (NUC) for setting policy guidelines, a Mainland Affairs Council (MAC) for implementation of the government's mainland policy, and a Straits Exchange Foundation (SEF) as the private, government-authorized intermediary organization for contact and negotiations with the mainland.

Beijing had already set up in 1989 its CPC Leadership Group on Taiwan Affairs for policymaking and a State Council Office on Taiwan Affairs. Another body, the Association for Relations Across the Taiwan Strait (ARATS), was set up as the counterpart of Taipei's SEF in 1991.[30]

Using the SEF-ARATS set up, the two sides have since met for unofficial negotiations, culminating in the Koo-Wang Talks of April 1993 in Singapore.[31] In recent years, Taipei's policy of "three no's" has become something like "no contact unless it is unofficial and approved first, no compromise unless it is judged harmless and profitable, and no negotiation except when necessary for settling an urgent problem through unofficial channels."

On August 31, 1993, Beijing issued a white paper, The Taiwan Question and Unification of China,[32] and on 5 July 1994, Taipei issued its own, An Explanation of Relations between the Two Sides of the Taiwan Strait.[33] In each case, the opposing side criticized the other's document as hostile and rigid. In between, in late March 1994, there was an unfortunate incident at Qiandao Lake in Zejiang Province where a group of Taiwan tourists were robbed and murdered. Insensitive handling of the incident by PRC officials caused quite a protest from Taiwan, and relations between mainland China and Taiwan suffered a serious setback. For its part, Taipei also contributed grist to Beijing's mills. In January 1994, Lee Teng-hui granted an interview to a famous Japanese writer, Ryotaro Siba,[34] in which Lee was reported to have said a number of things echoing Taiwanese separatist sentiments. Beijing's propaganda machines took Lee to task in no uncertain terms. Lee was labeled a *dutai* leader who speaks about unification but supports independence.

Perhaps to arrest the downturn of relations, on January 30, 1995, Beijing issued a statement now commonly referred to as "Jiang's 8 Points."[35] In addition to repeating the key points of some previous statements, notably "Ye's 9 Points" of 1981[36] and "Deng's 6 Points" of 1983,[37] it said:

1. The principle of one China must be upheld. China's sovereignty cannot be divided. Any act or talk of Taiwan independence shall be opposed.

2. Beijing will not object to the development of economic and cultural relations between Taiwan and other countries, but will oppose any move for "expanding international living space" with "two Chinas" or "one China, one Taiwan" as its goal. Only after unification could Taiwanese compatriots, along with other people of all nationalities in our country, enjoy dignity and honor internationally.

3. On the one-China premise, Beijing will negotiate with Taipei authorities over any topic of their concern. Individuals representing various groups, factions, and parties can be absorbed into the negotiation delegations. As the first step, the two sides can talk over formal termination of hostility. The nomenclature, venue, and form of political negotiations acceptable to both sides can be found if only we proceed to consultation on an equal basis soon.

4. Chinese do not attack Chinese. The use of force will be aimed not at Taiwan compatriots but at interfering foreign forces and those who contemplate *(tumou)* Taiwan's independence.

5. Taiwanese business interests will be protected. Cross-strait economic cooperation should be greatly promoted. Beijing is ready to endorse unofficial agreements about the protection of Taiwanese investments. The "three links" should be realized soon.

6. Chinese culture is the spiritual bond of all Chinese people. It can serve as an important basis for peaceful unification.

7. The Taiwanese way of life and Taiwan compatriots' wishes to rule themselves shall be fully respected. Their interests and concerns shall be catered to by all departments of the party and the government, including missions abroad. All are welcome to visit the mainland.

8. Leading persons of the Taiwan authorities are welcome to visit Beijing "in their appropriate capacities." We are ready to accept similar invitations. We can exchange views, but it should not be necessary to do so in an international venue.

On first impression, the statement contains more carrots than sticks. But, it is clear that no real concession is given. First, Jiang has nothing to say about "Taiwan as a political entity." Although Jiang spoke of "consultation on an equal basis," all commentators believe that he meant something like "party-to-party," not "government-to-government," negotiations. To Beijing, negotiations are for setting the terms of Taiwan's reintegration into China—that is, surrender—not terms of mutual recognition or partition.

Second, Beijing still maintains the threat of force. To say "Chinese do not attack Chinese" is easy. That is what was said before the massacre of June 4,

1989. Beijing repeats often that, in principle, unification will be accomplished by peaceful means, unless (a) Taipei declares independence; (b) Taiwan is invaded by foreign power(s); (c) Taiwan falls into disorder; or (d) Taipei refuses unification for a long time.[38] There is no evidence that this position has changed. Whether it is an outright attack (by air or sea), a blockade (by warship, airplane, or missile), or harassment (by air raid, naval bombardment, etc.), or any other conceivable means of Beijing's threat,[39] Taiwan cannot afford to be complacent about this. Sober thinkers, including those inside the Democratic People's Party (DPP), all say that Taipei will be sorry if it fails to take seriously Beijing's threat to use force.[40]

Third, Beijing still denies Taiwan's sovereign status and intends to isolate Taiwan from any international arena that is political in nature, however remotely. In an internal document issued only weeks before Jiang's 8 points, Chinese cadres and bureaucrats were instructed in detail how not to use language that may convey any meaning of two Chinas or one China, one Taiwan.

In response to the Jiang overture, Taipei decided that replies should be given in stages by officials of different levels and only on key points. On 21 February, Premier Lien Chan said in his oral report to the Legislative Yuan that in the present stage, the two sides of the Taiwan Strait are better advised to "face the reality, increase exchanges, respect each other, and work toward unification." What prevents mainland–Taiwan unification, he said, are the differences in political-economic systems and standard of living between the two regions, not the so-called "Taiwan independence" movement. Just the same, he said that relations between the two shores have entered into an era of consultation.[41] Reportedly, Lien's response was well received in Beijing.[42]

On April 8, President Lee Teng-hui convened the reorganized NUC and issued a six-point statement. Lee's statement reiterated the key principles of the Guidelines for National Unification and stipulated the following:[43]

1. Since 1949, Taiwan and the mainland have been ruled by two separate political entities that do not come under each other's jurisdiction. That is the origin of China's unification question. Only by respecting this historical fact can we realistically pursue China's unification.

2. Based on Chinese culture, the two shores can and should cultivate national sentiment and brotherly feelings, and strengthen information, academic, scientific-technological, and sports exchanges and cooperation.

3. The two shores should develop their complementary economic and trade relations. Taiwan will supply her own skills and experiences to help improve the mainland's agriculture, and contribute to the mainland's prosperity through investment and trade. The exchange of views about commerce and navigation/aviation can take place when conditions mature.

4. Leaders of the two sides can meet naturally at international conferences of economic and sports organizations of which both are members, and thereby reduce enmity and increase mutual trust.

5. All disputes between the two shores should be settled by peaceful means. Refusing to pledge not to use force against Taiwan on the grounds of "Taiwan independence forces" or "foreign interference" is a distortion and a neglect of the spirit and policy of the Republic of China, and can only lead to deeper suspicion and obstruct mutual trust. The relevant departments of our government are studying matters relating to the question of the termination of hostility. When Beijing formally announces no use of force on Taiwan, Penghu, Jinmen, and Mazu, we shall engage in a preparatory consultation with it about pertinent negotiations at the most opportune time.

6. The two shores are duty-bound to jointly maintain the prosperity of, and promote democracy in, Hong Kong and Macau. The government of the ROC shall continue to participate in Hong Kong–Macau affairs and actively serve our compatriots therein after 1997 and 1999, respectively.

Lee's statement politely and effectively touched upon all of Jiang's points. The tone was conciliatory, although, in substance, it kept Jiang's approach at a distance. One should note the precondition Lee put on any negotiation for terminating hostility and his suggestion that a Lee–Jiang meeting should be "natural" and in an international setting.

Unfortunately, the situation deteriorated quickly when President Lee was granted a visa to make a "private" visit to Cornell University in June 1995. The New China News Agency (NCNA) and *People's Daily* issued a series of invectives aimed at President Lee, and the People's Liberation Army (PLA) carried out massive military exercises intended to intimidate Taipei. All talks between the two shores were suspended indefinitely.[44] The first-ever presidential election by popular suffrage in Taiwan scheduled for March 23, 1996 and the mandate Lee was likely to get from that election were apparently of concern to Beijing. The dark clouds over the Taiwan Strait were so thick that the United States government found it necessary to set up a special unit to monitor the situation. For months, the concerned parties were kept guessing as to Washington's possible reaction should Beijing resort to force over the Taiwan question. On February 20, 1996, Winston Lord, assistant secretary of state for Far Eastern affairs, announced that the United States would respond in accordance with the Taiwan Relations Act. This was taken by many commentators as a clear warning to Beijing.[45]

Tensions across the Taiwan Strait were eased somewhat in 1996, but major differences remain.

Mainland–Hong Kong Relations

As alluded to earlier, mainland–Hong Kong relations are matters of autonomy between Beijing and the HKSAR come 1997. Since this book has a chapter dealing with this, our discussion here shall be very brief.

Through Sino-British negotiations, Beijing secured a British promise to return

Hong Kong.[46] By the Basic Law, Beijing disclosed its designs for the future HKSAR. Hong Kong's autonomy is based on the authorization from the central government in Beijing in accordance with Article 31 of the 1982 PRC constitution. By law, the NPC can take away what it authorizes. The binding power of the Sino-British Joint Declaration will have very little impact in reality. Whether Beijing would be willing to pay the political, social and economic costs of rescinding autonomy is another matter.

Many in Hong Kong who worry about life under a communist government and wish to secure the HKSAR's autonomy are endeavoring to make the territory as democratic and as open as possible before the fated date arrives. For its part, Beijing has taken many steps to forestall "undesirable" developments in Hong Kong such as democratization, expansion of human rights, and internationalization of the transition issues. Beijing has declared that it will never allow Hong Kong to become a "subversive base" for "anti-China" activities.

It is important to remember what Deng Xiaoping said on April 16, 1987, when he granted an audience to the Hong Kong members of the Basic Law Drafting Committee in the Great Hall of the People in Beijing:

> Do not think that everything will be rosy if only all Hong Kong affairs are left to the Hong Kong people. . . . If something endangering the vital interests of the nation occurred in Hong Kong, or if something damaging to Hong Kong's basic interests appeared, could Beijing not inquire about it? One cannot presume that there will be no destructive forces in Hong Kong. . . . if they take action and turn Hong Kong into a bastion for opposing the mainland under the guise of democracy, that . . . calls for interference.[47]

This statement quite effectively dispels any misconception that Beijing will not interfere in Hong Kong affairs after 1997.

As 1997 approaches, Hong Kong's dependence on the mainland continues to expand in the economic field and beyond. In April 1993, in the middle of Beijing's hostile campaign against him, Patten traveled to Washington to lobby the American government not to deny the PRC the MFN status. Behind him, the Hong Kong press reported that should the PRC lose that status, the Hong Kong economy would suffer a loss of no less than U.S.$16.6 billion and 70,000 Hong Kong jobs would be affected. This was so even though Hong Kong's manufacturing sector had already moved to Guangdong in a massive way. During the 1994–95 Sino-American intellectual property rights talks, Hong Kong again braced itself for the expected negative impact from U.S. sanctions under Clause 301 should the talks fail (Taiwan did so, too). After all, Hong Kong has always been dependent on the mainland for water, food, and raw materials. Now, one must add to the list land, labor, and government support. It cannot be long before Guangdong officials say that Hong Kong is at the mercy of China. Indeed, China's good will is becoming more and more important to Hong Kong.

There is no question that the Hong Kong transition was seriously and adversely affected by the Tiananmen incident of June 4, 1989. Instead of converging, Beijing and the British Hong Kong government went their separate ways. Governor Patten introduced a democratization package, and Hong Kong had its most democratic (though still limited) elections in history. And Beijing scrapped the "through train" for the deputies of all three tiers of representative bodies.

Several undertakings by the British Hong Kong government were challenged by Beijing sources. Among them were the new airport and port development projects, the Right of Abode Bill, the Hong Kong Human Rights Act of 1991, and amendments of certain laws based on the new Human Rights Act. Concurrently, a Preliminary Working Committee (PWC) of the Preparatory Committee of the HKSAR appointed by Beijing[48] reviewed the laws of Hong Kong and made recommendations about the organization of the first HKSAR government and other relevant matters, including the agenda for a provisional HKSAR legislature, terms of continuing service for the civil service, and methods of selecting the first chief executive. In early 1996, the Preparatory Committee was established. The transition was moving toward its final stage. In due course and even before July 1, 1997, there will be a Provisional Legislature to carry out "midnight legislation," a chief executive designate functioning along with a lame-duck governor, and a PLA contingent to be stationed in Hong Kong.

Already, more and more local people and groups are switching their primary attention and their allegiance from London to Beijing. Just by the strategic appointment of pro-Beijing individuals to such newly important posts, Beijing seems to be gaining control over Hong Kong. Hundreds of individuals have been given the honor and privileges of membership in the People's Congresses and the Chinese People's Political Consultative Conference (CPPCC) at both national and provincial levels, or have been made Hong Kong affairs advisers, and district affairs advisers. Apparently the old united front strategy still works wonders.

Hong Kong will probably keep its "many-splendored" romantic image as well as its economic vitality. Many of Hong Kong's favorable attributes (beautiful hills and harbors, modern and efficient infrastructure, banking network, utilitarian familism, industriousness, hedonism, and so on) will not so easily disappear. But the PRC's impact on press freedom, rule of law, and government efficiency, among other things, has already been felt by many.[49] It will no doubt get stronger after 1997.

For Hong Kong, the reform in the PRC is all-important. If it continues and is successful, Hong Kong people should be able to look forward to a bright future. Otherwise, hard times may be unavoidable.

Taiwan–Hong Kong Relations

Although the British government recognized the PRC regime as early as January 8, 1950, the Hong Kong government did not immediately ban Kuomintang (KMT) activities in the territory.[50] In the 1950's, Hong Kong was a battleground for the continuing CPC-KMT civil war. In May 1950, the British government impounded some seventy airplanes in a controversial case involving the new PRC government and the Nationalist regime and validated a convenient sale of the disputed airplanes to the Civil Aviation Transport Corporation of General Clare Chennault.

Every year, on the national days of the two competing Chinese states, October 1 (PRC) and October 10 (ROC), the representative organs of the two sides organize celebration ceremonies, while the people of Hong Kong show their allegiance to either the PRC or the ROC by flying the respective national flags. The Hong Kong government has always tolerated such peaceful displays of political attitudes.

However, in 1955, the KMT elements in Hong Kong were blamed for the mid-air explosion of an Indian carrier, *Kashmir Princess,* which killed many members of the Chinese delegation to the Bandung Conference.[51] In 1956, on October 10, an overly zealous mob attacked the pro-Beijing labor union, shops, and schools. Reportedly, Premier Zhou Enlai then laid down three conditions as the basis for mainland China–Hong Kong relations: first, Hong Kong must not be used as an international anti-PRC military base; second, no activities aimed at undermining the PRC authorities are to be permitted; and third, PRC personnel must be protected.[52] These conditions have effectively suppressed the political activities of pro-Taiwan elements in Hong Kong ever since. From the mid-1950s to 1987, Taiwan–Hong Kong relations were largely limited to tourism and trade. The two governments did not deal with each other much, and people from each place generally avoided political associations involving elements from the other.

Since November 1987, with Taipei's visitation policy in effect, Hong Kong has become a middle point for some 1 to 1.5 million travelers from Taiwan to mainland China every year. This has meant lucrative business not only for China Airlines and Cathay Pacific Airways but also numerous other businesses in Hong Kong. Of all the tourists to Hong Kong, Taiwanese are the loosest with their purses, spending on average more than U.S.$900 a trip in 1991.

In 1993, Taiwan–Hong Kong trade totaled U.S.$ 20,183 million, of which $18,454 million were Taiwan exports and $1,728 million were Taiwan imports. More than $8,500 million of that trade was actually indirect trade between Taiwan and mainland China, which also made Hong Kong a broker growing fat on her profits. Hong Kong's role as a market for China was partially overshadowed by its new role as an entrepôt port.

During the past few years, Hong Kong has, for the first time since 1956, warmed up to Taiwan somewhat. Under Governor Chris Patten, the Hong Kong government seems to be seeking ways to respond to Taiwan's friendly gestures. It has relaxed its entry controls over Taiwan residents and ROC officials, and has permitted the registration of organizations such as the Taiwan Chamber of Commerce, the Hong Kong–Macau Taiwanese Association,[53] and the Taiwan Businessmen's Association (HK). The Hong Kong General Chamber of Commerce and the ROC Federation of Industrial Unions have come to jointly sponsor a rotating yearly meeting for the purpose of discussing matters of mutual concern. Hsu Sheng-fa, the head of the ROC Federation of Industrial Unions and a member of the Executive Committee of the KMT Central Committee, was received by Governor Patten in his office in 1992, a gesture that would have been inconceivable in earlier times. That small breakthrough did not escape a mild protest from Beijing, and was loudly applauded in both Taiwan and Hong Kong.

Perhaps Hong Kong people are awakening to the reality that Taiwan is a partner in their own effort to meet the "one country, two systems" challenge. It is often pointed out that the very presence of the Taiwan question is helpful to Hong Kong. However, weary of Beijing's pressure, Hong Kong is still more cautious than Taiwan in their bilateral relations. In 1994, "the double tenth" celebration at the Hong Kong Cultural center was done without a display of the ROC flag due to pressure from the Hong Kong government. The reason behind this was a strong protest from the NCNA–Hong Kong that the permit for the rental of a government-owned venue to the ROC bodies was unwarranted.

Despite the obstacles and setbacks, Taipei keenly wants to build positive bilateral relations with Hong Kong. A Taipei Trade center (Hong Kong) came into being in April 1991 to service Taiwan merchants. A Hong Kong–Macau Association was established in Taipei in May 1992 to facilitate unofficial interchanges of all kinds. Many influential Hong Kong personalities have been invited to visit Taiwan, and several Taiwanese commercial banks have set up branches in Hong Kong.

With regard to the 1997 transition, Taiwan has many concerns that require urgent attention. Three sets of questions come to mind. The first pertains to the legal status of the HKSAR in ROC laws. Since the HKSAR will become a part of China, is it a part of the ROC? If so, will the citizens of Hong Kong have the same rights and obligations of ROC citizens elsewhere? On the other hand, if it is defined as a part of the PRC, will the Regulations on Relations between the Peoples of the Taiwan Region and the Mainland Region apply? How is conflict of laws to be settled? Can Hong Kong remain a "third place" between the mainland and Taiwan? Should it be given a separate status? These are questions with far-reaching implications.

The second set of questions is about Taipei's more concrete policy choices in response to the Hong Kong transition. How can the ROC deal with open and clandestine communist penetration of Taiwan through the HKSAR? Should there be differentiated treatment for individuals, groups, and corporations with PRC qualifications and those with HKSAR qualifications with regard to entry, residence, employment, investment, public service, and so forth? If so, how can PRC persons, natural or legal, and PRC capital be recognized and separated? Should the ROC–HKSAR relations be basically reciprocal, conditional, or open?

The third set of questions is about matters that cannot be settled without cooperation from Beijing. For instance, under the provisions of the Basic Law, will Taipei be able to continue to maintain its unofficial official agencies? Article 23 of the Basic Law specifically requires the HKSAR government to enact laws to prohibit acts of "treason, secession, sedition, subversion against the Central People's Government, or theft of state secrets." The same article also prohibits political ties with foreign political organizations or bodies. How will Taiwan and KMT-related groups be classified under such laws? Will the Chung Hwa Travel Service, which handles visas to Taiwan, be allowed to operate? Will China Airlines be permitted to carry on with its business? What will be the fate of the educational institutions, student organizations, labor unions, and newspapers either affiliated with, or sympathetic to, the ROC?

Besides these questions, Taipei also must consider the ultimate possibility, however remote, of the application of the Hong Kong model to Taiwan. In this context, monitoring the actual development of the Hong Kong model is a must.

In April 1984, the former head of Beijing's Hong Kong–Macau Office, Ji Pengfei, said openly that Taiwan elements will be welcome in Hong Kong as long as they obey the law of the HKSAR and engage in no disruptive activities; that existing economic and cultural ties will continue; and that Taiwan organs in Hong Kong should make positive contributions to the smooth transition of Hong Kong. This was reaffirmed by Deng Xiaoping on October 3, 1984. In Deng's words,[54]

> After 1997, Taiwan's organs in Hong Kong may still stay. They can propagate "the three principles of the people," and they can curse the CPC. We are not afraid of their curses; the CPC cannot be downed by curses. But, in actual behavior, they must take care not to create chaos in Hong Kong or do "two China" things. They are all Chinese. We believe they will hold to the position of our nation and safeguard the larger picture, the dignity, of our nation.

On the basis of such policy statements, Taipei decided that, in principle, the Hong Kong ties will continue and the semigovernmental organs will not be withdrawn. But Taipei clearly prefers not having to go to Beijing about Hong Kong affairs. If the future HKSAR can be substantively autonomous, Taiwan–Hong Kong relations may be more agreeable and productive.

Taiwan's current policy is to plan to stay in Hong Kong and to expand her presence in a manner that will be seen as conducive to Hong Kong's stability and prosperity. The MAC has already adopted a Hong Kong–Macau Relations Act,[55] which deals with most of the first two sets of questions raised above. This unilateral endeavor may not be well received or sufficient, however. On June 22, 1995, Qian Qichen, in his capacity as the chairman of the PWC, disclosed a policy of the Central People's Government regarding post-1997 Hong Kong questions involving Taiwan.[56] It contained seven basic principles, as follows:

1. The various unofficial relations presently existing between Hong Kong and Taiwan, including economic and cultural exchanges and personal contacts, shall remain basically unchanged.

2. Investment, trade, and other business activities of Taiwan residents, and Taiwanese capital of various kinds in and with Hong Kong are encouraged and wel-

come. Their legitimate rights and benefits in Hong Kong shall be protected by law.

3. Air and sea routes between the HKSAR and the Taiwan region shall be managed as "special regional routes" in accordance with the principle of "one China." Air and sea navigation and transportation between the two regions shall be conducted under the principle of two-way reciprocity.

4. Taiwan residents may enter and leave the Hong Kong region, attend schools, be employed, or set up residence in accordance with the law of the HKSAR. The Central People's Government (CPG) shall make arrangements regarding questions of documents held, and so forth, to facilitate Taiwan residents entering or departing Hong Kong.

5. The civic groups and religious organizations of the HKSAR pertaining to education, science, technology, culture, arts, sports, professions, medicine and hygiene, labor, social welfare, social work, and so on may, under the principle of nonsubordination, noninterference, and mutual respect, maintain and develop relations with their counterparts in the Taiwan region.

6. Official contacts, negotiations, signing of agreements, and establishment of organs between the HKSAR and the Taiwan region carried out in whatever names shall be reported to the CPG for approval or, with concrete authorization of the CPG, be approved by the SAR chief executive.

7. The existing Taiwan organs and personnel in Hong Kong may continue to stay, but they must strictly observe the Basic Law of the HKSAR of the PRC, must not violate the "one-China" principle, and must not engage in activities that cause damage to Hong Kong's stability and prosperity or activities inconsistent in nature with those for which they are registered.

It is to be noted that Qian's statement was disclosed soon after President Lee Teng-hui's Cornell visit and after Beijing had suspended contacts between the two shores. One probable reason was that Beijing wanted all Hong Kong elements to know what to do when the Taiwan factor came up. The basic tenet is clear: Beijing will take charge where Taiwan is involved. Of the seven points, what alarmed Taipei most was point seven, which would undoubtedly tie the hands of Taipei representatives in Hong Kong after 1997. Therein lies a seed of future friction among Beijing, Taipei, and Hong Kong, and between Beijing and Hong Kong too, for the interests of the two are often not the same.

Whether the core ROC agencies and organizations will really be tolerated in Hong Kong come 1997 remains to be seen. In any case, some form of negotiations with Beijing over Taiwan–Hong Kong relations is likely to take place in the near future simply because there is no practical way to get around it.

International Reaction to the Hong Kong 1997 Transition:
The United States–Hong Kong Policy Act of 1992

There is no question that the triangular relations among the three Chinese international actors are also influenced by developments in the larger international environment, especially the Asia-Pacific region. In turn, the attitudes of the international community are affected by mainland China–Taiwan–Hong Kong relations. As a matter of common sense, we can anticipate that any third country will weigh the three Chinese actors and evaluate their respective importance in terms of its own national interests. It is only natural that each capital will have its own consideration of relations with the PRC and Taiwan when it makes decisions about Hong Kong.

Since the subject matter of this book is the internationalization of Hong Kong, I shall provide here an overview of the most significant response from the international community with regard to the Hong Kong transition—the response of the United States. The United States is the only country that has actually enacted a special and comprehensive law in response to the Hong Kong situation. Without doubt, the U.S.–Hong Kong Policy Act of 1992 represents the most straightforward and significant response of the international community so far. It certainly deserves the attention of anyone interested in the question of Hong Kong's future international status and role. A brief examination of that act will reveal the nature of Washington's key concerns about the Hong Kong situation. Such concerns include the HKSAR's international status, its future business prospects, the specter of human rights violations and their impact on immigration policy, and the implications of a "greater China."

For the United States, Hong Kong has always been an attractive city. During the Cold War, Hong Kong was a key China-watching station and the most welcome stop for navy ships. Now, it is a major trade partner and investment attraction. In the words of former consul-general Richard Williams,

> No doubt about it, the U.S. wants Hong Kong to remain stable and prosperous after its reversion to China in 1997, by retaining its liberties and system of laws. No doubt about it, the success or failure of this effort will have a major effect on U.S. policy toward China.[57]

Well-informed U.S. officials like Williams see Hong Kong as a city whose economic philosophy and temperament are similar to those of the United States, and a place that "serves as economic stimulus and example for Southern China." They understand the sentiment of "the one million demonstrators in the streets of Hong Kong" during China's democracy movement in 1989 and the reasons for the brain drain from Hong Kong due to the 1997 transition. They offer support to Hong Kong and call themselves "prudent optimists" about Hong Kong's future.

Testifying before the U.S. Congress, the 1992 governor of the American Chamber of Commerce in Hong Kong, William H. Overholt, said that his organization was the largest American Chamber of Commerce in the world outside the continental United States, with more than 1,000 corporate members. Over 250 American firms had their regional headquarters located in Hong Kong. Pointing out that Hong Kong was the headquarters location of 51 percent of all multinational corporations with regional headquarters in Asia, Overholt spoke enthusiastically of Hong Kong's confidence and vitality. In his view, the foundation stones of the post-1997 period were in place and the Hong Kong and Chinese economies had already achieved a high level of integration. Deng Xiaoping had advocated that China create more Hong Kongs, he stressed.[58] Overholt represents those who think "the tail will wag the dog."

Over the years, the United States has been involved directly in such issues as the Vietnamese refugees in Hong Kong and the brain drain problems, and indirectly in Hong Kong's constitutional development and human rights issues. In the latter half of 1990, the United States altered its immigration policy to allow for a delayed entry form of citizenship for employees of American firms. That move was hailed by the Hong Kong governor as a positive step toward helping Hong Kong maintain its stability and prosperity.

In a further step, the U.S. Congress passed the U.S.–Hong Kong Policy Act of 1992 in August 1992.[59] This most unusual act found in the Sino-British Joint Declaration a number of desirable provisions and declared that the U.S. Congress wished to see full implementation of those provisions. Through the act, the U.S. Congress proposes as U.S. policy, among other things, the following (my summary; italics added):

First, in bilateral relations with Hong Kong, the United States should, in consultation with the PRC government where required by law,

1. Play an active role before, on, and after July 1, 1997, in maintaining Hong Kong's confidence and prosperity, Hong Kong's role as an international financial center, and mutually beneficial ties between the two peoples;
2. Maintain the U.S. Consulate-General and other agencies such as the USIA American Library in Hong Kong, and *invite Hong Kong to maintain its official and semi-official missions in the United States after June 30, 1997;*
3. *Recognize Hong Kong's passports and treat Hong Kong as a separate territory for purposes of issuing entry visas to the United States after June 30, 1997;*
4. *Treat Hong Kong as a separate territory with regard to commercial matters* such as import quotas, certificates of origin, Most Favored Nation status, and *negotiate directly with Hong Kong* to conclude bilateral economic agreements;
5. Recognize Hong Kong's ships and airplanes registered in Hong Kong and negotiate directly with Hong Kong to conclude air service agreements;
6. Maintain and expand exchanges in culture, education, science, and academic research with Hong Kong.

Second, in multilateral relations, the United States should:

1. *Support Hong Kong's participation in all appropriate multilateral conferences, agreements, and organizations in which Hong Kong is eligible to participate;*

2. Continue to fulfill its obligations to Hong Kong under international agreements, so long as Hong Kong reciprocates, *regardless of whether the PRC is a party* to the particular international agreement;
3. Respect Hong Kong's status as a separate customs territory, and a contracting party to the GATT/WTO, whether or not the PRC participates in the latter organization.

Third, with respect to Hong Kong's status in U.S. law,

1. *The U.S. laws shall continue to apply to Hong Kong after July 1, 1997, as before.*
2. *On or after July 1, 1997, whenever the president determines that Hong Kong is not sufficiently autonomous, the president may issue an Executive Order suspending the treatment of Hong Kong as autonomous from the PRC.*

Fourth, with regard to reporting requirements,

1. The secretary of state shall transmit to the speaker of the House and the chairman of the Senate Foreign Relations Committee a report on conditions in Hong Kong of interest to the United States no later than March 31 of the following years: 1993, 1995, 1997, 1998, 1999, and 2000.
2. Such a report shall include, among other things, a description of *the development of democratic institutions* in Hong Kong and the nature and extent of Hong Kong's participation in multilateral forums.

The reader can probably sense the reason why I took pains to give the act such a careful summary. Short of the recognition normally accorded a sovereign state, Hong Kong cannot ask for more support from any country. Taking Beijing's "one country, two systems" seriously, Washington has put it in black and white that it is extending to Hong Kong all it can for a quasi-state in the form of an SAR.

A reading of the act leaves little doubt as to Hong Kong's future international status. Washington will engage directly in bilateral relations with the HKSAR to the extent that the latter enjoys autonomy. The HKSAR's power to issue passports and conclude agreements of an economic and cultural nature is recognized. Hong Kong will be treated as a territory separate from mainland China for passport, visa, immigration and commercial purposes. In multilateral relations, the United States is ready to support Hong Kong's rights, as a separate customs territory, to participate in the activities of the GATT (WTO) as a full member, "regardless of whether the PRC is a party."

Without specifically saying so, the act expresses American concern about the specter of future human rights violations in Hong Kong. The secretary of state is required to transmit periodic reports to Congress, which must include "a description of the development of democratic institutions in Hong Kong and the nature and extent of Hong Kong's participation in multilateral forums." Implications are that democracy and participation in multilateral forums will give the Hong Kong people opportunities to air their feelings and views regarding happenings in the HKSAR, including violations of human rights. Furthermore, the president of the United States is empowered to "issue an Executive Order suspending the treatment of Hong Kong as autonomous from the PRC" at his discretion. Presumably, Beijing will have to pay a price if it fails to respect the HKSAR's autonomy. And effective autonomy, by implication, will be more conducive to human rights protection.

The act also says "the U.S. laws shall continue to apply to Hong Kong after July 1, 1997, as before." This means, among other things, that Hong Kong will continue to have its immigration quota in the United States, which was increased from 5,000 to 20,000 per year after 1989.

As to Hong Kong's future business prospects, the act says the United States shall continue to play an active role "in maintaining Hong Kong's confidence and prosperity and Hong Kong's role as an international financial center." For such purposes, Washington intends to maintain official and semi-official missions in the HKSAR and will invite Hong Kong to do the same in the United States. Hong Kong will enjoy its own import quotas, certificates of origin, Most Favored Nation status, and will be able to conclude bilateral economic agreements where the United States is concerned. Washington will also continue to recognize Hong Kong's ships and airplanes registered in Hong Kong and negotiate directly with Hong Kong to conclude air service agreements. Furthermore, "mutually beneficial ties between the two peoples," such as exchanges in culture, education, science, and academic research with Hong Kong will be maintained and expanded.

The Act could not escape Beijing's protest. In fact, Beijing accused Washington of "interference" and made its indignation public. This was duly noted by the State Department in its first Report to Congress on Conditions in Hong Kong, March 31, 1993.[60] However, Beijing's protest could only go so far. For one thing, the act is a piece of domestic legislation purporting to be protecting American interests. A state is entitled to make her own decision in external as well as internal policies. China may have interests in other countries that she needs to protect some day. Then, the fact that the United States treats Hong Kong as an autonomous territory may work to Beijing's advantage. The Most Favored Nation status extended to both the PRC and Hong Kong is a case in point.

In the 1993 Report to Congress just mentioned, the State Department of the U.S. government reiterated American interests in Hong Kong. These include: (1) assuring a smooth transition from British to Chinese sovereignty; (2) continuing Hong Kong's admirable record of protection of human rights; (3) ensuring steady advances in democratic development; and (4) strengthening relations between the United States and Hong Kong.[61] The report also referred to roughly 200 multilateral agreements in force in Hong Kong and gave a list of 42 international organizations and associations in which Hong Kong participated. Considerable detail was given about the Sino-British disputes over Governor Patten's proposal for extending democracy within the Basic Law, and about the airport and Container Terminal Nine projects. It also reported the Chinese threat to cancel contracts not approved by the Chinese government after 1997.[62] In conclusion, the report stressed that "the United States believes the Governor's proposals are constructive and hopes they will receive careful attention and discussion by all concerned parties."

The second report required by the U.S.–Hong Kong Policy Act of 1992 was submitted to U.S. Congress on March 31, 1995.[63] It highlighted several significant developments in U.S.–Hong Kong relations, including agreements signed with regard to extradition, mutual legal assistance, air services, and investment. The tone is optimistic about economic and commercial matters. It pointed out that over 1,800 foreign companies maintain regional headquarters or offices in Hong Kong, including some 370 American firms. Referring to the fifth (1994) annual Hong Kong American Chamber of Commerce business confidence survey, it reported that most of the 446 respondents planned either to maintain or expand their investments, although those viewing their prospects as "good" declined from 72 percent in 1993 to 56 percent, primarily because of rising costs. Factors enticing U.S. firms to Hong Kong mentioned were: (1) excellent telecommunications and port infrastructure, (2) the sanctity of contracts and respect for rule of law, (3) high quality of life for executives' families, (4) the use of English in commerce and government, and (5) the unsurpassed expertise of Hong Kong entrepreneurs in assessing the mainland market.

However, in other developments affecting U.S. interests in and relations with Hong Kong, and the development of democratic institutions, the report was less optimistic. China's repeated reference to Hong Kong as a "base of subversion," the indication that a provisional legislature might be set up, the limited cooperation in the Joint Liaison Group (JLG), uncertainties in the legal system after 1997 as manifested in the disputes over the Court of Final Appeal arrangement, adverse developments about freedom of expression, slow progress in settling problems related to HKSAR passport issuance, delay in the Container Terminal Nine project, declining civil service morale, and so forth were cited as causes for anxiety. China's threat to dismantle elected bodies come 1997 was deemed as "having a most deleterious impact upon confidence in Hong Kong."

I suggested earlier that when the United States adopted the Taiwan Relations Act she added in effect a new practice in international law through domestic legislation. This is also true with regard to the U.S.–Hong Kong Policy Act of 1992. In the case of Taiwan, there are no official diplomatic ties between Washington and Taipei, and Taiwan is considered a de facto sovereign state. In the case of Hong Kong, there will be official ties between Washington and Hong Kong, although Washington acknowledges fully that Hong Kong will be an SAR under the PRC. In both cases, Beijing lodged its protest against Washington for interference in domestic affairs. However, Beijing had little choice but to acquiesce in Washington's fait accompli actions. In other words, the questions of Taiwan's and Hong Kong's international status and to some extent developments inside Taiwan and Hong Kong that are considered material to the United States, have become internationalized by virtue of Washington's domestic legislation.

There remains the Greater China notion for us to investigate. The question is this: Will the incorporation of Hong Kong (and later Macau, and possibly also Taiwan) lead to the formation of a Greater China economically and politically? If so, how should the international community take it?

The prestigious *China Quarterly* held a workshop in Hong Kong on just this subject in January 1993 and released a special issue later that year.[64] Earlier, the American Enterprise Institute had organized an international conference entitled "The Chinese and Their Future" in January 1991.[65] In April 1994, the CSIS-Pacific Forum organized a special conference, also in Hong Kong, to discuss the "natural economic territory" of China. The Institute on Global Conflict and Cooperation of the University of California system also sponsored an international conference on "the China Circle" in 1994. It seems the Americans have been quite sensitized by this Greater China notion.

At the twenty-second Sino-American Conference hosted jointly by the Center for Strategic and International Studies (Washington, D.C.) and the Institute of International Relations (Taipei) and held in Washington, D.C., in June 1993, I ventured the view that the emergence of the Greater China thesis has to do with a number of developments in recent years. Most of them are events or trends involving mainland China–Taiwan–Hong Kong relations. They include: (1) the impressive economic performance of mainland China, Taiwan, Hong Kong, and Singapore amid worldwide recession; (2) the projected return of Hong Kong to China in 1997; (3) Taiwan's much publicized U.S.$301 billion "Six-Year Plan for National Construction"; (4) the rapid expansion in mainland China–Taiwan interactions; (5) the accelerating interdependence of the South China–Hong Kong economies; (6) the many open suggestions for the formation of various forms of regional groupings or spheres with Chinese communities as key members; and (7) the special attention given to China by the United States over MFN status and other questions. All these are factors that conjure up images in the minds of perceptive people.[66] There has also been no lack of talk about the "smart Chinese" and the special intercontinental networks of Chinese overseas. Outsiders may see in a Greater China the shadow of the "yellow peril in the making" image. Ironically, Beijing sometimes feeds that image by its words and deeds. Its leading role in the 1993 Bangkok Declaration on Human Rights is a case in point.

In truth, the factors listed above are all too often exaggerated. It has been observed that the Chinese people tend to excel when not under Chinese rule. Unlike the Japanese, they have a lot of difficulty working together; they are too often engaged in endless feuds among themselves. Sun Yat-sen complained, for instance, that Chinese people are incapable of true unity, just like a pail of sand. Continuing altercations between mainland China and Taiwan and serious difficulties between Beijing and Hong Kong occupy the headlines of the free press in Taiwan and Hong Kong. The differences and difficulties among the potential components of a Greater China are very pronounced indeed. The idea of a Southern China economic market consisting of Guangdong, Fujian, Hong Kong, and Taiwan is indeed promising. It is certainly more plausible than the Asia-Pacific Basin Community, which caught the imagination of many a commentator in the 1980s. There is also a potential Tumen River Delta economic area in the north, but that involves Japan and Korea. However, the Greater China as conceived by American and Chinese observers is, all told, rather contrived.

Conclusion

To speak of the internationalization of Hong Kong is to speak of the need to enlist the assistance of the international community for Hong Kong. Such assistance may serve two purposes: helping Hong Kong develop in a healthy way and checking mainland China from leading Hong Kong astray. Hong Kong's transition from a British colony to a Chinese SAR is a historically unprecedented venture that involves systemic change as well as international transactions. Hong Kong is a small quasi-state not equipped to deal with such a task; it needs assistance of all kinds. It is also an important regional center for various international transactions; it necessarily invites international concern and attention. The PRC may be large and powerful, but she is inexperienced in the business of the kind of transition that Hong Kong is going through. And because it has a questionable past performance record, Beijing will be wise not to reject international assistance. Beijing, too, needs international assistance as a learner.

Hong Kong, like Taiwan, needs to facilitate the internationalization of its own status problem, if for no other reason than to buy time. The international community, especially the supporters of human rights and democracy, must and can afford to monitor the autonomy process of the HKSAR. Measured but unequivocal international involvement does not necessarily constitute interference in China's domestic affairs. It will help not only Hong Kong but also Taiwan and mainland China on their way to democracy and better protection of human rights. It should not be swept aside because of Beijing's objections. It is my belief that independent thinkers and, in due course, far-sighted political leaders inside mainland China will find good reasons to support this view. Like it or not, mainland China cannot prevent her own peaceful evolution.

Elsewhere, I have opined that all three parties suffer a degree of insecurity. Beijing is afraid of "peaceful evolution" and Taiwan independence; it feels a threat against its power to rule from the outside world and a threat against its territorial integrity from the separatists. Taipei is concerned that it may lose status as a sovereign equal of Beijing; it sees a threat against Taiwan's "national security" from the mainland. And Hong Kong is wary of losing its promised autonomy and its free way of life; it sees a threat against its right to self-rule from the central government and a threat against its capitalist system from the socialist north.[67]

Nonetheless, greater triangular interdependence is predictable. The call for more interaction as well as closer cooperation among the three Chinese international actors is heard everywhere. In the economic field, Taiwan and Hong Kong have helped in accelerating the mainland's development and reform. In the future, the mainland's economic impact on the two will probably prove to be the greater. In the cultural sphere too, the three parties have become busily engaged in numerous ways.

Ultimately, the future well-being of all three territories and any idea of a greater China depend on the nature of the Beijing authority. A more open, liberal regime in Beijing would no doubt be a centripetal force conducive to national integration. Conversely, a closed, oppressive Beijing regime would prove centrifugal and cause separatist movements to become active. Unfortunately, the great majority of people on the mainland, elite and masses alike, are still democratically illiterate. At the present stage, liberalization beyond a degree may only mean chaos in China. To expect that leaders like Jiang Zemin and Li Peng can soon function in a democracy is unrealistic; one might have to wait until the Western-trained generation rises to the power center. China is a big country that can only be moved or changed slowly. A little help from outside can do a lot of good.

The people of Hong Kong, together with their fellow capitalists in Taiwan and elsewhere, are in a race against the communist hard-liners of Beijing to transform the great earth of China by their respective preferred formulas. Hopefully, they will not inadvertently gamble away their own democratic future in exchange for some short-term material gains. While a genuinely liberal democratic regime in mainland China is out of the question, if there is steady progress toward better protection of human rights and a higher standard of living for the common men and women of China, neither Taiwan nor Hong Kong will oppose national integration or resist central rule.

Taiwan is now targeted by Beijing as the next to be taken over. But, precisely for that reason, Taiwan may well play a significant role in Hong Kong's internationalization. The people and government of Taiwan have been doing what they can to enlist international assistance for their cause. What she does, if nothing else, might help us identify some ways and means of internationalization that could prove either beneficial or harmful for the parties concerned.

Global and regional changes in international relations have been phenomenal. Already the rules of the Cold War have become obsolete just like the rules of classical European balance of power. Challenges to the notion of sovereignty are increasing as the nations become more interdependent. The UN has broadened in function and the idea of regionalism is taking on new meanings. A later generation will have a very different game to play altogether. We need a new vision to meet new challenges. The Hong Kong transition may well be fertile ground for just that. It can be the first step to help make a market-oriented China more ready to join the family of nations and contribute its share to world peace.

Notes

1. A balanced view about the state of China's reform and its prospects can be gained by consulting these recent publications: Susan L. Shirk, *The Political Logic of Economic Reform in China* (Berkeley and LA: University of California Press, 1993); Richard Baum, *Burying Mao: Chinese Politics in the Age of Deng Xiaoping* (Princeton, NJ: Princeton University Press, 1994); Joseph Fewsmith, *Dilemmas of Reform in China: Economic Debate and Political Conflict* (Armonk, NY: M.E. Sharpe, 1994); and Willy Wo-lap Lam, *China after Deng Xiaoping: The Power Struggle in Beijing since Tiananmen* (Hong Kong: Professional Consultants, Inc., 1995).

2. See pertinent discussions in David Shambaugh and Thomas W. Robinson, eds., *Chinese Foreign Policy* (Oxford: Clarendon, 1994); John W. Garver, *Foreign Relations of the PRC* (Englewood Cliffs, NJ: Prentice-Hall, 1993); and Han Nian-lung, *Diplomacy of Contemporary China* (Hong Kong: New Horizon Press, 1990).

3. See Weng Songran (Byron S.J. Weng), " 'Yiguo liangzhe' chulun: gainian, xingzhi, zhangai han qianjing (A Rustic Theory on 'One Country, Two Systems': Concept, Nature, Content, Obstacles and Prospects)," in F.Q. Quo and Zhao Fusan, eds., *"Taiwan zhi Jianglai" Dierci Xueshu Taolunhui Lunwenji* (Papers Presented at the Second Symposium on 'Taiwan's Future') (Beijing: Friendship Publishing Co., 1985), pp. 349–384.

4. On March 10, 1972, only a few months after entering the UN, Huang Hua, then ambassador of the PRC, sent a letter to the General Assembly's Special Committee on Colonialism. It said the question of Hong Kong and Macau is "entirely within China's sovereign right and does not at all fall under the ordinary category of colonial territories."

5. See State Council Information Office, *Zhongguo de Renquan Zhuangkuang* (Human Rights in China), (Beijing: Zhongyang Wenxian Chubanshe, 1991).

6. See articles by Weng Songran, Wu Guoguang, and Liu Jinghua on relevant topics in the April 1996 issue of *Ershiyi Shiji* (Twenty-First Century Bimonthly).

7. Li Hongzhang was the Chinese ambassador sent by the Qing court to sign the humiliating Treaty of Guandao (Shimanoseki) ceding Taiwan to Japan in 1895. His name, somewhat unfairly, has come to be associated with a sense of national shame in China.

8. See *Yazhou Zhoukan,* March 5, 1995, p. 15.

9. See Gary Klintworth, *New Taiwan, New China: Taiwan's Changing Role in the Asia-Pacific* (New York: St. Martin's Press, 1995).

10. See Michael Kau, "The ROC's Diplomatic Impasse and New Policy Initiatives," in Chu Yun-han, ed., *The Role of Taiwan in International Economic Organizations* (Taipei: INPR, 1990), pp. 1–26.

11. See Byron S.J. Weng, "Taiwan's International Status Today," *China Quarterly,* no. 99 (September 1984), pp. 462–480.

12. The Guidelines for National Unification was passed by the presidential National Unification Council on February 23, 1991, and adopted by the Executive Yuan on March 14, 1991. This short document is still the single most important statement on Taiwan's mainland policy.

13. The First Section of the Basic Platform of the DPP adopted at its 5th Party

Congress in June 1993 and amended at its 6th Party Congress on May 1, 1994 is entitled "Establishing an Independent and Self-Ruling Sovereign Republic of Taiwan."

14. The explanation on the meaning of "one China" was adopted by the National Unification Council on August 1, 1992, in order to quell a confusing debate within Taiwan. It is not readily acceptable to Beijing, however, and the debate continues. See discussion later in this chapter.

15. Fifteen years on, Washington made a minor adjustment in early 1995. It now permits direct contact between U.S. diplomatic officials and their Taipei counterparts. It was not much more than another patchwork measure, however. See *Zhongguo Shibao*, January 1995.

16. See Byron S.J. Weng, "Sovereignty Split-Toward a Theory of Divided Nations," *Chinese University Bulletin, Supplement 32*, 1995, pp. 21–37. Also see Byron S.J. Weng, "The Evolution of a Divided China," in Lin Zhiling and Thomas W. Robinson, eds., *The Chinese and Their Future: Beijing, Taipei and Hong Kong* (Washington, DC: AEI Press, 1994), pp. 345–385.

17. The Bodin notion of absolute and indivisible sovereignty is clearly no longer adequate in meeting the actual needs of our time. The world has changed in too many ways. Instead of an era of nation-states operating in a classical balance-of-power system, ours is an age of such new things as superpowers and ministates, international organizations and multinational corporations. The globe is shrinking due to fiber-optic communications and space shuttles. It is being redefined because of virtual reality and satellite wars. Almost all aspects of our life are affected. How can the doctrine of sovereignty alone resist adaptation to new situations?

18. Be that as it may, states and nations are still living under the doctrine of sovereignty. The possibility of the world's being organized under some other principles seems too remote to receive general attention. We are forced, therefore, to continue our deliberations on international affairs around the notion of absolute sovereignty. But is it not conceivable that, for different reasons, the peoples of Kurdistan, Chechnya, and so forth would want to modify the doctrines of sovereignty? See R.B.J. Walker and Saul H. Mendlovitz, eds., *Contending Sovereignties: Redefining Political Community* (Boulder and London: Lynne Rienner, 1990), especially the concluding essay by R.B.J. Walker, "Sovereignty, Identity, Community: Reflections on the Horizons of Contemporary Political Practice."

19. See Chiu Hungdah and Robert Downen, eds., *Multi-system Nations and International Law: The International Status of Germany, Korea and China*, proceedings of a Regional Conference of American Society of International Law (University of Maryland Law School, OPRSCAS, 1981), No. 8. Also Gregory Henderson, Richard Ned Lebow, and John G. Stoessinger, *Divided Nations in a Divided World* (New York: David McKay, 1974).

20. See Michal Pomerance, *Self-Determination in Law and Practice: The New Doctrine in the United Nations* (The Hague, Boston, and London: Martinus Nijhoff, 1982).

21. Roda Mushkat, "The International Legal Status of Hong Kong under Post-transitional Rule," *Houston Journal of International Law* 10, 1 (autumn 1987), pp. 1–24.

22. Hurst Hannum and Richard B. Lillich, "The Concept of Autonomy in International Law," in Yoram Dinstein, ed., *Models of Autonomy* (New Brunswick, NJ: Transaction Books, 1981), pp. 232–236.

23. James Tang, "Hong Kong's International Status," *Pacific Review* 6, 3 (1993), pp. 205–215.

24. Robert H. Jackson, *Quasi-States: Sovereignty, International Relations, and the Third World* (Cambridge: Cambridge University Press, 1990).

25. See Susan Henders, *Building Macau's Autonomy under China's Rule* (M. Phil

Thesis, The Chinese University of Hong Kong, 1991), pp. 79–80.

26. The impact of internal changes on the relations among the Chinese actors is examined closely from different perspectives in Lin and Robinson, eds., *The Chinese and Their Future.* See also, Byron S.J. Weng, "Economic Interactions and Political Altercations: Prospects for Mainland–Taiwan–Hong Kong Relations," in Gerrit W. Gong and Lin Bih-jaw, eds., *Sino-American Relations at a Time of Change* (Washington, DC: CSIS, 1994), pp. 181–198.

27. See Byron S.J. Weng, "Sovereignty Split—Toward a Theory of Divided Nation."

28. See Weng Songran, "A Preliminary Study on the Relationships Between the Two Sides Across the Taiwan Straits in the Coming Ten Years," *Jiushi Niandai,* no. 193 (February, 1986), pp. 24–31.

29. First proposed by the late Ye Jianying, then chairman of the National People's Congress in 1981, the three links refer to direct links for postal service, commerce, and transport and communication, and the four exchanges refer to exchanges in the fields of academics, culture, sports, and science and technology. *Taiwan Diqu yu Dalu Diqu Renmin Guanxi Tiaoli* (Regulations on Relations Between the Peoples of the Taiwan Region and the Mainland Region), promulgated by the President, July 31, 1992, and effective from September 18, 1992. Also its *Shixing Xize* (Implementation Bylaws) issued by the Executive Yuan, September 16, 1992.

30. More specifically, the PRC's institutions on Taiwan work actually include the following: (1) the CPC Central Leading Group on Taiwan Work, and under its direction, the Provincial Taiwan Work Groups and Taiwan Work Offices to county level; (2) the CPC United Front Department, which has under its jurisdiction, (a) the Association for Relations Across the Taiwan Straits (ARATS), (b) the All-China Taiwanese Association, (c) the Taiwan Democratic Self-Government League, (d) the KMT Revolutionary Committee, (e) the Chinese Committee for the Promotion of Peaceful Unification, (f) the Committee for National Unification, CPPCC, etc.; (3) the Taiwan Affairs Office, State Council, with Taiwan Affairs Offices to county level; and (4) the Taiwan Affairs Office, Foreign Ministry.

31. Koo Chenfu and Wang Daohan are, respectively, head of Taipei's Straits Exchange Foundation (SEF) and head of Beijing's Association for Relations Across the Taiwan Straits (ARATS). Their May 1993 talks, supposedly on nonpolitical matters, signaled a breakthrough in mainland–Taiwan relations.

32. Office of Taiwan Affairs and Office of Information, State Council, *Taiwan Wenti yu Zhongguo Tongyi* (The Taiwan Question and China's Unification), August 31, 1993. Full text in *Renmin Ribao,* September 1, 1993.

33. *Taihai Liangan Guanxi Shuomingshu* (An Explanation of Relations between the Two Sides of the Taiwan Straits), (Taipei: MAC, July 1994).

34. Sima Liaotailang (Siba Ryotaro), *Taiwan Kiko* (Taiwan Journal), serialized in *Siukan Asahi* (Asahi Weekly), May 1994. See also, Chen Hua-kan, "Sima Liaotailang Had a Good Grasp of Japanese Sympathy for Taiwan," *Xinxinwen* (The Journalist Weekly) nos. 467–468, February 18–March 2, 1996, pp. 31–33.

35. Full text in *Lianhebao,* February 5, 1995, p. 3.

36. Ye Jianying, "Further Explanations of the Policy Line on Taiwan's Return to the Motherland and the Realization of Peaceful Unification," September 30, 1981. Full text in various newspapers on October 1, 1981. Also, *Zhonggong DuiTai Gongzuo Yanxi yu Wenjian Huibian* (A Compendium of Analyses and Documents on the CPC's Taiwan Work), (Taipei: Fawubu Diaocaju [Bureau of Investigation, Ministry of Justice], 1984), pp. 67–69.

37. Deng Xiaoping spoke to Winston Yang of Seton Hall University on June 26, 1983. The tenet of the conversation was reported by Yang in the August issue of *Qishi*

Niandai, and by Beijing in Deng Xiaoping, *Jianshe you Zhongguo Tese de Shehuizhuyi* (Building Socialism with Chinese Characteristics). The official version is reproduced in *Zhonggong DuiTai Gongzuo Yanxi yu Wenjian Huibian* (A Compendium of Analyses and Documents on the CPC's Taiwan Work), (Taipei: Fawubu Diaocaju [Bureau of Investigation, Ministry of Justice], 1984), pp. 70–72.

38. This last condition was aired by Professor Qian Weichang, now head of Zhongguo Tongyi Cujinhui (the Association for the Promotion of China's Unification) and the spokesman on Taiwan affairs in the united front organ, the CPPCC. Before President Lee's visit to Cornell University in June 1995, neither the top leaders such as Deng Xiaoping, Jiang Zemin, Li Peng, nor those in direct charge of the Taiwan question such as Qian Qichen, Wang Zhaoguo, Wang Daohan, and Tang Shubei had publicly made any such statement.

39. Conceivable mainland threats against Taiwan may include the following: (1) a *military campaign* against Taiwan, e.g., an outright attack (by air or sea), a blockade (by warship, airplane, or missile), or acts of harassment (by air raid, naval bombardment); (2) a *diplomatic tightening* aimed at squeezing Taiwan out of international arena and denying Taiwan diplomatic relations with other countries; (3) a *border relaxation* to flood Taiwan with mainland refugees; (4) a *strategic commercial plan* designed to lure and to trap Taiwan's businessmen in trade and investment; (5) a *coastal smuggling operation* to put guns and drugs onto the island via fishing boats; and (6) a *clandestine sabotage operation* to incapacitate Taiwan's infrastructure or to incite internal strife between different economic strata or language groups.

40. See Byron S.J. Weng, "Taiwan's Mainland Policy Before and After June 4," in George Hicks, ed., *Broken Mirror: China after Tiananmen* (Essex: Longman, 1990), p. 261.

41. *Zhongguo Shibao,* February 22, 1995, p. 1; Ziyou Shibao, February 22, 1995, p. 124.

42. *Zhongguo Shibao,* February 24, 1995, p. 1.

43. Full text in *Zhongguo Shibao,* April 8, pp. 1–2.

44. For a more detailed discussion of the events surrounding President Lee's Cornell University visit, see Byron S.J. Weng, "Beijing's Taiwan Policy: Continuity and Change," Hung-Mao Tien, ed., *Cross Strait Relations and Their Policy Implication for the Asia-Pacific Region* (Armonk, NY: M.E. Sharpe, forthcoming).

45. Keeping Beijing and Taipei guessing had the merit of not only discouraging Beijing from the use of force, but also preventing Taiwan from issuing an independence declaration. The American preference was, of course, not having to become militarily involved. See, e.g., *Yazhou Zhoukan,* week of February 25–March 3, 1996, p. 7.

46. For discussions on the importance of Hong Kong to China, see Sung Yun-wing, "Hong Kong's Economic Value to China," in Sung Yun-wing and Lee Ming-kwan, eds., *The Other Hong Kong Report 1991* (Hong Kong: Chinese University Press, 1991), Chapter 23; and Byron S.J. Weng, "The Integration of Outlying Areas: The Case of Hong Kong," in Harish Kapur, ed., *The End of an Isolation: China after Mao* (The Hague: Martinus Nijhoff, 1985), pp. 308–361.

47. See *Wenhui Bao,* April 17, 1987, p. 2, and reports in other Hong Kong papers.

48. Until early 1995, Governor Patten refused to recognize the PWC as a legitimate organ with which the government of Hong Kong should deal directly. He said the proper channel for communication with the Chinese authorities should be the Sino-British Joint Liaison Group. This is reminiscent of Beijing's refusal to recognize the Legislative Council under the British Hong Kong government. However, beginning in February, there are signs that Patten may have relented some.

49. The press has been exercising self-censorship in Hong Kong for some time. See Weng Songran, "1997 yu Xianggang Xinwen Ziyou (1997 and Freedom of the Press in Hong Kong)," (The 8th [1993] Wu Shunwen Journalism Lecture, Taipei: Wu Shunwen

Xinwen Jiangzhu Jijinhui), (Vivian Wu Journalism Award Foundation).

50. See Byron S.J. Weng, "The Integration of Outlying Areas: The Case of Hong Kong," pp. 308–361; and Li Kwok-sing, "The Past, Present and Future of the CPC's Hong Kong Policy," *Yazhou Zhoukan,* no. 9 (July 1994), pp. 27–69.

51. See *Zhongguo Gongchandang Zhizheng Sishinian* (The Communist Party of China in Power 40 Years), (Beijing: Zhonggong Dangshi Ziliao Chubanshe, 1989), p. 95.

52. See Jerome A. Cohen and Hungdah Chiu, *People's China and International Law: A Documentary Study* (Princeton, NJ: Princeton University Press, 1974), pp. 176–180; and Li Kwok-sing, "The Past, Present and Future of the CPC's Hong Kong Policy," p. 34.

53. Created only in 1989, this relatively insignificant civic group is already an arena of power struggle. Individuals with clear leftist ties have used extraordinary means to try to take over its leadership and failing that have created a rival association. The NCNA's Department of Taiwan Affairs has also interfered in its operation and not very subtly so.

54. What Ji Pengfei told a group of Hong Kong dignitaries on April 21, 1984 became known as the Three Ji Principles of Taiwan–HKSAR relations. See *Wenhui Bao,* April 22, 1984. On October 3, 1984, Deng Xiaoping reaffirmed the gist of those principles. See *Deng Xiaoping Wenxuan* (Selected Works of Deng Xiaoping), vol. 3 (Beijing: Renmin Chubanshe, 1993), pp. 72–76.

55. This author was a co-convener, together with Professor Tsai Ying-wen of the National Cheng Chi University in Taipei, of a team of seven scholars who prepared, under a contract with the Mainland Affairs Council, the first draft of Draft Hong Kong–Macau Relations Act, with fifty-eight articles. It was published as a consultative draft in March 1994 by the MAC. It was passed in March 1997. The concept of the law is reminiscent of Washington's Taiwan Relations Act of 1979. Parts of its contents resemble the 1992 Regulations on Relations Between the Peoples of the Taiwan Region and the Mainland Region of the ROC. Special attention is paid to the different conditions and needs of Hong Kong after 1997, and of Macau after 1999.

56. Full text in *Ming Bao,* June 23, 1995.

57. Richard L. Williams, "The Importance of Hong Kong to the United States," a speech given at the Columbia University Hong Kong Week Conference, November 13, 1990. USIS-HK News Release, 20 November 1990.

58. William H. Overholt, "U.S. Relations with Hong Kong," (Testimony to the Subcommittee on Asian and Pacific Affairs, Foreign Relations Committee, U.S. Senate, regarding S. 1731, a bill to establish policy of the United States with respect to Hong Kong after July 1, 1997), April 2, 1992.

59. The U.S.–Hong Kong Policy Act of 1992 was introduced by Senator Mitch McConnell and amended in the nature of a substitute put together by Representative John Porter and three House Foreign Affairs subcommittees. In was adopted by both houses of Congress in August and signed into law by President Bush on October 5, 1992. Full text was released by the USIS-HK. See *Foreign Policy Backgrounder,* October 16, 1992.

60. See "A Report to Congress on Conditions in Hong Kong as of 03/31/93 as Required by Sec. 301 of the United States–Hong Kong Policy Act of 1992," USIS-HK, *Foreign Policy Backgrounder,* April 6, 1993.

61. Ibid. The report also entailed significant developments and exchanges, including the establishment on April 27, 1993, of a Center for Hong Kong–American Educational Exchange (later renamed the Hong Kong–America center) at the Chinese University of Hong Kong to promote academic links between the United States and Hong Kong.

62. On November 30, 1992, the Hong Kong and Macau Affairs Office of the PRC State Council announced that, except for certain land leases, "other contracts, leases and agreements signed and ratified by the Hong Kong British government but not approved by the Chinese will be invalid after June 30, 1997." However, the PRC government contin-

ued to welcome investments in Hong Kong and would take a "positive attitude" in examining and approving contracts, leases, and agreements after June 30, 1997, on behalf of the future HKSAR.

63. "A Report to Congress on Conditions in Hong Kong as of March 31, 1995 as required by Sec. 301 of the United States–Hong Kong Policy Act of 1992." 16 pp.

64. *China Quarterly,* no. 136 (December 1993).

65. See Lin and Robinson, eds., *The Chinese and Their Future: Beijing, Taipei, and Hong Kong.*

66. See Weng, "Economic Interactions and Political Altercations . . . ," pp. 193–194. In my view, a northeast Asian economic sphere made up of Jilin, Liaoning, Tianjin, Shandong, South Korea, and Japan is also plausible. More grandiose ideas such as a Greater Chinese Economic Community composed of mainland China, Hong Kong, Taiwan, and Singapore are just wishful thinking. Functionally, a Greater China is still a figment of the imagination today.

67. See Weng, "Economic Interactions and Political Altercations . . . " The conclusion of that paper remains valid today.

3

Playing the International Card?
The View from Australia, Canada,
and the United States

Kim Richard Nossal

Given the delicacy and complexity of Hong Kong's return to the sovereignty of the People's Republic of China (PRC) in 1997, perhaps it is not surprising that a specialized language has emerged to frame the discourse of "Hong Kong becoming China." Some phrases in this lexicon may be completely unintelligible to a non-Chinese outsider, their etymology and meaning knowable only to the cognoscenti: "second stove," "two ups and two downs," "three-legged stool," "astronauts," "through train."[1] Some are words or phrases that might be superficially understandable but have a special (and often highly contested) coded meaning in the context of Hong Kong reversion to China in 1997: "a question left over from the past," "one country, two systems," "a high degree of autonomy," "convergence," "insurance policy," "stability and prosperity," "compatriots," "Hong Kong people ruling Hong Kong," "those who love the motherland," "an economic city rather than a political city," and, in the context of international relations, "internationalization" and "playing the international card."

In the normal discourse of international politics, "internationalization" is generally unproblematic when used in most contexts: internationalizing an issue merely means involving the international community—normally other governments—in the resolution of that issue. In the context of Hong Kong's return to China in 1997, however, the political meaning of this term depends on who is using it and how it is being used. As the editors of this volume note, internationalization in a Hong Kong context has a number of facets, including both an internal and an external dimension. The focus of this chapter is on aspects of the external dimension and the meaning of internationalization in contemporary Hong Kong politics.

It is true that those writing about Hong Kong have given internationalization a range of meanings. For example, one usage implies that "international" and "internationalization" are synonymous: internationalizing Hong Kong means keeping the territory as *international* as possible in the post-1997 era—in other words, while recognizing that it will return to Chinese sovereignty, seeking to retain as many of the attributes that in the post-1945 era made Hong Kong a dynamic and wealthy economy and a unique political community: an openness to global flows of capital, goods, and services unfettered by state interference and intervention; private and public sectors that are outward-looking and open to the processes of globalization, willing to import, adapt, and use global trends, technologies, and practices; and a work force that is, relatively speaking, cosmopolitan, multinational, and internationally oriented.[2]

A related meaning fixes on movement. Danny Lam, for example, examines the efforts of some Hong Kong people to internationalize their wealth, not by selling their assets and moving capital out of Hong Kong, but by borrowing against their Hong Kong assets in order to acquire substantial holdings in other countries.[3] And, as used by Ronald Skeldon, the term fixes on the effects of the large-scale migration of people since the early 1980s: Hong Kong, Skeldon suggests, has been internationalized by virtue of the tens of thousands of Hong Kong people who have migrated to Canada, Australia, the United States, Britain, Singapore, and other destinations—and back again,[4] creating a web of people-to-people linkages between the territory and the international system.

A variant of these meanings focuses on efforts to maintain Hong Kong as an international actor after 1997: this is the meaning attached to the term by James T.H. Tang in his exploration of Hong Kong's international status.[5] In the pre-1997 period, the Hong Kong government enjoyed a range of international relations equaled by no other noncentral government in the contemporary international system.[6] In the post-1997 regime promised by the Joint Declaration of December 19, 1984, and the Basic Law of April 4, 1990, the new Hong Kong Special Administrative Region (HKSAR) government would have the authority to conduct a comparable range of international relationships. Thus, the internationalization of Hong Kong can refer to efforts both by the Hong Kong government itself[7] and by other states in the international system to entrench the territory as firmly as possible as an international actor in the years up to 1997—as a way of ensuring that it will be easier for the HKSAR government to continue to operate in the international system as an actor separate if not autonomous from the central government in Beijing. This, it is hoped, will help keep Hong Kong as an international city, and ultimately ensure that the "one country, two systems" formula works successfully.

However, the most common meaning of internationalization in the context of Hong Kong politics is its normal international politics meaning: in other words, efforts to involve the international community in the transition to Chinese sovereignty, by, for example, involving other governments directly in Hong Kong affairs or raising the Hong Kong issue at international meetings. Such a definition of internationalization can have a positive or negative connotation, depending of course on one's perspective. For some in Hong Kong and in some foreign countries, involving the international community in the transition is a largely positive development, and to be welcomed.[8] In this view, the internationalization of Hong Kong—by involving the international community and keeping international attention focused on what happens in Hong Kong—will help to smooth the transition in 1997; maintain confidence in Hong Kong itself; and thus ensure that the "one country, two systems" formula works.

By contrast, there are others, especially in China, who regard attempts by members of the international community to involve themselves in Hong Kong affairs as most unwelcome. In this view, such efforts are little more than interference by other countries in what will be after July 1, 1997, properly domestic Chinese affairs. In their eyes, the internationalization of the Hong Kong question has a distinctly negative connotation.

Related to internationalization in this usage is the idea of "playing the international card." This is a phrase used almost exclusively by the Central People's Government (CPG) in Beijing.[9] It is drawn from diplomatic parlance, where "playing a card" merely indicates the common practice of one state using friendly relations with another government to bolster its power against a third (and usually unfriendly) state—as when the United States was said to have "played the China card" in the 1970s by seeking to use a de facto alliance with China against the Soviet Union. In the context of Hong Kong's reversion to China, "playing the international card" refers to efforts by some—usually the British government or the last British governor of Hong Kong, Chris Patten—to involve other members of the international community in the Hong Kong issue.

Three members of the international community are usually implicated in such efforts at internationalization: Canada, Australia, and the United States. It is easy to see why the PRC would charge these countries with internationalization and "playing the international card," for there can be little doubt that the governments in Canberra, Ottawa, and Washington involved themselves in the Hong Kong issue, particularly since the "crisis of confidence" that seized the territory after the events of June 4, 1989. This is an involvement that they readily admit flows from their deeply rooted interests in ensuring that the transfer of sovereignty in 1997 and thereafter is pacific and conflict-free.

Some of the interests are economic, reflecting not only the importance of the dynamic economy of what some have called "Greater China" for American, Australian, and to a lesser extent Canadian trade, but also a common concern in Washington, Canberra, and Ottawa for a continuation of business as usual in the

Asia-Pacific after 1997.[10] Some of these interests are politico-diplomatic: a concern to ensure that the transition to "one country, two systems" is smooth and unproblematic. And some of the interest stems from the patterns of immigration from Hong Kong since the Sino-British agreement, the Joint Declaration of December 19, 1984, to return Hong Kong to Chinese sovereignty in 1997—patterns that have favored Canada and Australia, and, to a lesser extent, the United States.[11]

But how accurate is the characterization that Australia, Canada, and the United States have sought to internationalize the Hong Kong question? This chapter looks at the policies of these three countries toward Hong Kong after 1989, and concludes that it was neither the purpose nor the consequence of the policies of these countries to internationalize the Hong Kong question. Rather, after 1989 the three governments took particular steps to boost confidence in Hong Kong in the post-1997 period, but in each case the policy fell squarely within the bounds of the Joint Declaration of 1984, and came nowhere close to the kind of internationalization of the Hong Kong question so feared by the central authorities in Beijing.

Australia, Canada, and the United States

Australia, Canada, and the United States are the three countries besides Britain and China that have the closest interest in Hong Kong. In part this is because of the migration patterns of Hong Kong people since the Sino-British negotiations of the early 1980s. Those Hong Kong people who sought to provide themselves with exit options from the territory demonstrated an overwhelming preference to locate in the United States, Canada, or Australia; for their part, these three countries—each of them having been built on successive waves of immigrants from disasters and troubles—consistently demonstrated a willingness to welcome Hong Kong people as the latest wave.[12] This mutual attraction resulted in large numbers of Hong Kong people settling in American, Australian, and Canadian cities in the decade after the Joint Declaration.

But one also looks naturally to Australia, Canada, and the United States when the internationalization of Hong Kong is mentioned because, unlike the governments of virtually all other states in the international system, the governments in Canberra, Ottawa, and Washington developed their Hong Kong policies after the events of June 4, 1989 in a way that was designed to protect what they saw as their parochial interests in Hong Kong's future.

It should be noted that prior to June 1989, the "Hong Kong policy" of each of these countries was largely limited to declaratory policy. To be sure, some, like Gerald Segal, would disagree with such an assertion; they would suggest that the immigration policies of Australia, Canada, and the United States were critical aspects of the approaches of these states toward Hong Kong. However, I will argue below that immigration policy only became an important component of the Hong Kong policies of these countries after 1989.

Between 1984 and 1989, declaratory policy for policymakers of all three governments consisted of a "mantra" with several components. First, the mantra expressed satisfaction in the imaginative compromise of "one country, two systems" that would return Hong Kong to Chinese sovereignty while providing Hong Kong people a "high degree of autonomy" to enjoy their unique political and economic system for at least fifty years after the reversion to Chinese sovereignty. Second, the mantra expressed confidence that the CPG in Beijing would carry out the obligations it had embraced in the Joint Declaration. Third, in order to maintain confidence in Hong Kong in the period prior to the transition, policy would be aimed at "providing assistance" to the two states explicitly recognized as being the only ones that should be legitimately involved in Hong Kong affairs—Britain and the PRC.[13]

This declaratory mantra stemmed from a common belief among Western countries during this period that alternative policy options, or alternative perspectives on the Sino-British agreement, would be too costly, or ineffective, or simply inappropriate. Given that other options, such as maintaining the status quo or declaring independence, were simply not in the cards, the "one country, two systems" formula embraced by the Chinese and British governments *was* an ingenious solution to what was always a thorny problem.

Likewise, the opportunities for other countries, even close friends of Britain, to interpose themselves in the process, either during the negotiations or immediately after the Joint Declaration was signed, were always limited. To be sure, Chalmers Johnson implicated the United States government in what he called the "mousetrapping" of Hong Kong;[14] and Gerald Segal has declared that it was "curious" that the United States was the "inactive superpower" during this period.[15] But the evolution of American policy toward the Hong Kong issue in the early 1980s is hardly surprising. There was much to be gained if the Sino-British arrangement worked, but a great deal to be lost if attempts at involvement backfired and merely aroused antagonism in Beijing and a unilateral reassertion of Chinese sovereignty over Hong Kong. In short, in the United States, and even more so in smaller and weaker countries like Australia and Canada, a complacent policy had considerable attractions.

Finally, when considering the policy approaches of Western countries to the Hong Kong question in the mid-1980s, it should be remembered that the Joint Declaration was signed at a time when relations between China and the countries of the West such as Australia, Canada, and the United States were at their warmest point in the Open Door era; confidence in the Chinese government was high. To have expressed negative views in 1984—for example, publicly doubting China's willingness to abide by the terms of the Joint Declaration—would have been widely seen in policy circles in Western capitals as unfriendly and therefore inappropriate. (It is true that after June 1989 there was some recantation of such friendliness: for example, the former Australian ambassador to Beijing, Stephen FitzGerald, ruefully characterized Australian policy toward

China during the 1980s as an "Alice in Wonderland approach."[16] But it should be noted that these were views in retrospect: made in a speech in November 1989, FitzGerald's recantation was, in light of the events of June 4, 1989, fashionable and popular; but it bears noting that such a view would have been distinctly unfashionable in the autumn of 1984.

The events of June 4, 1989 brought the relatively complacent approach of the governments of Australia, Canada, and the United States to an end. Policymakers in Canberra, Ottawa, and Washington—no less than anyone else—understood full well the implications for Hong Kong of the large-scale use of force by the Chinese government to suppress domestic political protest. They knew that the events of June 4, 1989 would shake the confidence of many Hong Kong people about the future and deepen their doubts about the willingness of the government in Beijing to live up to the promises of the Joint Declaration.

But it can be argued that it was not just the confidence of Hong Kong people that was shaken. The highly visible role of some Hong Kong people in the prodemocracy protest movement in China, the huge (and unprecedented) street demonstrations in the territory in the spring of 1989, and the role of some Hong Kong people in such schemes as Operation Yellowbird[17] all seem to have underscored the fears of officials in Beijing that Hong Kong did indeed have the potential to be a "political city" rather than the purely "economic city" that the PRC had assumed it was getting. This, in turn, prompted the government in Beijing to resort to threats against the expression of such political views, thereby violating the spirit, if not the letter, of the commitment of the Joint Declaration and the Basic Law to maintaining a "high degree of autonomy" for Hong Kong, and confirming the fears of many Hong Kong people about what a "high degree of autonomy" would mean in practice. In short, the Beijing massacre had considerable implications for confidence in the "one country, two systems" formula.

The most immediate and concrete manifestation of the crisis of confidence came in an acceleration of emigration from the territory. Official Hong Kong government estimates of total emigration from the territory show that there was little change in patterns of emigration between 1980 (two years before the Sino-British negotiations that began in 1982) and 1986 (two years after the Joint Declaration): in those six years, approximately 20,000 people emigrated from Hong Kong each year. Then, beginning in 1987, the number of people emigrating took an upward turn, from 19,000 in 1986, to 30,000 in 1987, to 45,000 in 1988. And after the events of June 4, emigration from Hong Kong sharply increased, rising to 62,000 in 1990 and 66,000 by 1992.[18]

As Table 3.1 shows, Hong Kong people had been seeking to emigrate to the prime destinations of Australia, Canada, and the United States in slowly increasing numbers over the course of the 1980s. Immigration policy in both Australia and Canada not only favored well-educated and highly skilled immigrants, but also actively encouraged immigrants with capital to invest; and indeed, as Table 3.1 shows, changes in Canadian policy in the mid-1980s that created new oppor-

Table 3.1

Immigrants to Major Destinations Whose Last Place of Previous Residence was Hong Kong, 1960–1992

	Australia	Canada	United States
1960	—	1,146	
1961	n.a.	710	
1962	n.a.	426	
1963	n.a.	1,008	
1964	n.a.	2,490	
1965	n.a.	4,155	75,007 (1961–70)
1966	n.a.	3,710	
1967	n.a.	5,767	
1968	n.a.	7,594	
1969	n.a.	7,306	
1970	n.a.	4,509	9,720
1971	n.a.	5,009	7,960
1972	715	6,297	10,916
1973	734	14,661	10,300
1974	1,130	12,704	10,700
1975	1,593	11,132	12,547
1976	1,302	10,725	16,950*
1977	1,633	6,371	12,272
1978	2,313	4,740	11,145
1979	1,836	5,966	16,838
1980	2,822	6,309	n.a.
1981	1,960	6,451	n.a.
1982	2,414	6,542	11,908
1983	2,756	6,710	12,525
1984	3,691	7,696	12,290
1985	5,136	7,380	10,975
1986	4,912	5,893	9,930
1987	5,140	16,170	8,785
1988	7,942	23,281	11,817
1989	9,998	19,994	12,236
1990	11,538	28,825	12,853
1991	16,747	22,340	15,564
1992	15,656	38,841	16,741

Sources:
Australia: Department of Immigration and Ethnic Affairs, Australian Immigration, Canberra, Consolidated Statistics, No. 13, 1982; Department of Immigration, Local Government and Ethnic Affairs, Canberra, Statistical Note 36: Asian Immigration, 1988; Bureau of Immigration Research, Immigration Update, several issues.
Canada: Employment and Immigration Canada, Ottawa, Annual Immigration Statistics.
United States: U.S. Department of Justice, Washington, D.C., Statistical Yearbooks of the Immigration and Naturalization Service.
Notes:
1. Australia: settler arrivals for the financial year 1 July –30 June, with 1992 referring to settler arrivals 1991–92, etc.
2. Canada: landed immigrants in calendar year.
3. United States: immigrants admitted in fiscal year, 1 July –30 June from 1970 to 1975 and from 1 October–30 September from 1977 to 1992. The 1989, 1990, 1991, and 1992 figures exclude the intake under the Immigration Reform and Control Act (IRCA), which allowed people who had been resident unlawfully since 1 January 1982 to become residents during these years. The data for 1980 and 1981 have been "lost" at source.
*Includes transition quarter June to September in realigned year.

tunities for very wealthy would-be immigrants opened the door to an increasing number of applicants from Hong Kong. But, as Table 3.1 also demonstrates, it was not until the Beijing massacre in 1989 that there was a sharp acceleration in the number of people leaving Hong Kong for Australia, Canada, and the United States.

Officials in Canberra, Ottawa, and Washington were well aware that their immigration policies were contributing to the crisis of confidence sparked by the events of June 4, 1989: in the same way as a run on a bank is accelerated by the mere sight of people crowding about the bank's doors trying to withdraw their money, so confidence in Hong Kong was further eroded not only by the actual departure of increasing numbers of skilled, educated, and wealthy Hong Kong people, but also by the *appearance* of the haste and eagerness to leave in the crowded line-ups at the Canadian Commission and the Australian and American consulates.

In the aftermath of the Beijing massacre, therefore, the American, Australian, and Canadian governments embarked on a conscious effort to bolster confidence in Hong Kong. But despite the close political, diplomatic, economic, and cultural links between and among these three countries, Australia, Canada, and the United States never constituted a special bloc on the Hong Kong issue. While the three governments had coordinated their responses to the events of June 4, 1989, along with other Western countries,[19] no comparable efforts were undertaken in developing a coordinated policy toward Hong Kong in the years after 1989. For example, there were many occasions when the leaders of the three countries met each other during this period: all three of them at the Asia-Pacific Economic Cooperation (APEC) forum; the Canadian and Australian prime ministers at the biennial Commonwealth Heads of Government Meeting; the American president and Canadian prime minister at the G-7 annual summit or their bilateral summits. But Hong Kong was never an agenda item for summit-level coordination.

Instead, the Hong Kong policy in each of these countries remained primarily a lower-level concern. Officials from the three countries, particularly those posted in Hong Kong itself, compared notes on their countries' respective policy approaches, and exchanged views on appropriate responses to local developments. However, there was a clear reluctance to "coordinate" their policies on Hong Kong too closely—for fear that the government in Beijing would interpret such coordination as the Western countries "ganging up" on China. As a result, because each country defined its interests rather differently, those differences were purposely allowed to manifest themselves in the confidence-building policies pursued by Canberra, Ottawa, and Washington instead of being coordinated into a homogenized "Western" policy (as so frequently occurs in other areas).

Likewise, it should be noted that officials of these three countries persistently denied, in public and in private, that the "i-word"—internationalization—was an appropriate way to describe their policies.

Canada

Of the three countries, Canada took the most aggressive approach toward Hong Kong. Developed in the months after the Beijing massacre, Canada's policy consisted of three main elements.

The first was confidence-building: seeking to persuade Hong Kong people that the transition was going to work. The Canadian government began by rejecting an assumption common among other countries, in particular Britain, that the way to inspire confidence in Hong Kong was to provide as many Hong Kong people as possible with an "insurance policy"—formal immigrant status, or citizenship, or the right of abode in a "safe" Western country, but without the usual requirement that the immigrant use the visa immediately. Armed with the right of entry in the future, the argument ran, Hong Kong people would choose to remain where they were needed most: in Hong Kong. Thus, governments of countries most eagerly sought after by Hong Kong people—notably Canada—were urged to issue deferred immigrant status for Hong Kong people.

It is true that Canadian officials were becoming increasingly concerned that they were acquiring a reputation for being, in Segal's words, little more than "narrow-minded poachers of people from Hong Kong,"[20] particularly with its "investor" and "entrepreneur" programs, which provided Canadian landed immigrant status to people for a price. However, the Canadian government rejected the "insurance policy" proposal as a means of bolstering confidence in the territory. Policymakers in Ottawa had never been fond of the idea of allowing deferred immigrant status prior to 1989; their opposition hardened after 1989, even when the United States embraced the scheme in the 1990 amendments to its Immigration Act, discussed in more detail below.

The Canadian government offered various arguments against the "insurance policy" scheme. First, since the 1960s, Canadian immigration policy had operated on the basis of universality, and to tamper with it in particular cases such as Hong Kong's would set a dangerous precedent that might well lead to the dismantling of the universal nature of the program. Second, the universality of immigration policy commanded widespread political support in Canada; to introduce "special consideration" in the case of some countries and not others would fracture that support. Third, Canada had spent the better part of the 1970s and 1980s pressing in different international fora for the free flow of peoples internationally, and such schemes would contradict such a position. Finally, Canadian officials argued privately that such schemes, while they might provide some individuals with greater security, were unlikely to build confidence in the territory as a whole. Confidence-building, they argued, had to come from other sources.

While the Canadian government took a hard line in rejecting such schemes after 1989, it should be noted that Ottawa did introduce what one Canadian official privately and euphemistically termed "a certain flexibility" into the administration of immigrant visas issued to Hong Kong people. In other words, the Canadian government continued to demand that those issued with Canadian visas take up residence in Canada immediately. However, Hong Kong immigrants to Canada found that they could return to Hong Kong to work for short periods of time, returning to Canada periodically to maintain a formal presence in the country, giving rise to the phenomenon of Hong Kong "astronauts" (so-called because of the amount of time they have to spend in the air satisfying the residency requirements of their new home and meeting the requirements of their businesses in Hong Kong[21]). While not as open as the deferred immigration schemes being proposed by Britain, the more "flexible" administration of Canadian immigration policy after 1989 did provide a small Canadian contribution to confidence-building through immigration.

But Canada's main efforts at confidence-building focused on organizing high-profile events that kept the international spotlight on Hong Kong. Mirroring the Hong Kong government's own strategy, a key component of the Canadian policy was high-level visits by Canadian politicians to Hong Kong. From 1990 onward, a succession of Canadian federal and provincial ministers, including two prime ministers and numerous provincial premiers, visited the territory, giving speeches that stressed the importance to Canada and the international community of Hong Kong's future after 1997. Of particular importance was the visit by Prime Minister Brian Mulroney in May 1991: the prime minister spent five days in Hong Kong, an unusually long time for the prime minister to spend at one destination abroad; moreover, in a calculated signal of the importance that his government attached to Hong Kong, Mulroney purposely did not visit China on that trip.

Likewise, the Canadian government sponsored a series of high-profile visits of Hong Kong governors to Canada, beginning with Sir David Wilson, who visited Canada in May 1990. Both Sir David and Chris Patten were received by the Canadian government with the same diplomatic protocol accorded a senior member of a friendly Western government. The Canadian government also took a number of diplomatic initiatives to raise Hong Kong's visibility in the diplomatic firmament: the Canadian government granted "senior official" status to the Hong Kong Economic and Trade Office in Toronto; Ottawa joined in the multinational efforts to secure admission for the Hong Kong government in the APEC forum, which was granted in November 1991; and Canada put the Hong Kong issue on the agenda of bilateral meetings with counterparts in both London and Beijing.

The second component of Canadian policy was bridge-building: trying to put into place formal agreements and linkages with the Hong Kong government and administration that would, it was hoped, extend beyond the reversion in 1997. Examples of such bridge building are the development of the Canada–Hong Kong Parliamentary Friendship Group in 1992 or the Civil Service Cooperation Agreement of 1991, a scheme of staff exchanges, study programs, and high-level visits of public service managers to promote greater interaction between Hong Kong's civil service and Canada's. Included in this bridge-building effort were attempts to formalize bilateral ties between Hong Kong and Canada by negotiating and signing a number of international agreements, including treaties on air services, narcotics control, film co-production, extradition, foreign investment, environmental cooperation, and economic cooperation.

Bridge-building also included the development of people-to-people linkages between Canada and Hong Kong. The most visible of these was the holding of reciprocal festivals: in June 1991, the Canadian government organized a festival in Hong Kong, and in the autumn of 1992, Hong Kong held a month-long series of festivals in five Canadian cities.[22] (This was followed by a "Metro Toronto Week" in Hong Kong in the fall of 1993, organized by the city of Toronto.)

The third component of Canada's policy was institution-building—providing active and vocal Canadian support for the building and strengthening of democratic institutions in Hong Kong. Some parts of this policy were relatively uncontroversial, such as the seconding of a Federal Court judge to Hong Kong in 1990 to provide advice on the drafting of a Bill of Rights; or providing Canadian bureaucratic expertise in running elections and preparing access to information legislation. Likewise, Canadian support for civil service exchanges was designed to assist in the process of transition from the colonial administration to the new HKSAR government. Rather more controversial, however, was the Canadian government's overt support for the reform package introduced by the governor of Hong Kong, Chris Patten, in October 1992. Patten's view that greater democratization in the territory was consistent with the Joint Declaration and with the maintenance of a distinct "way of life" for Hong Kong after 1997 was of course hotly contested by Beijing. Nonetheless, the government in Ottawa left little doubt that it agreed with Patten rather than China.[23]

The United States

The response of the United States to the crisis of confidence in Hong Kong caused by the Beijing massacre took a markedly different tone. Hong Kong never became a high-profile issue for either the Republican George Bush or his Democratic successor, Bill Clinton. Indeed, there were some, like the Heritage Foundation in Washington, who criticized the Bush administration for its "hands-off" approach.[24] The importance of Hong Kong for American interests may have been readily acknowledged by American officials, but neither president saw fit to pay an official visit to the territory (though Bush, no longer in office, did visit Hong Kong in November 1993); and although American diplomats in Hong Kong were outspoken in efforts to boost confidence in the territory after 1989,[25] and although Washington offered support for the Patten reforms,[26] the United States government did not embrace the kind of coordinated and overt policy of confidence-building pursued by the Canadian government.

This does not mean, however, that Washington ignored the issue of confidence and the risks to American interests in Hong Kong after the events of June 4, 1989. On the contrary, confidence-building measures were embraced by the Bush administration and took several forms.

First, the question of confidence in Hong Kong became intertwined with what became an annual ritual political battle between the Congress and the executive over the Most Favored Nation (MFN) status of the People's Republic of China.[27] When members of Congress first bruited the idea of punishing Beijing for the events of June 4, 1989 by revoking China's MFN status, the Bush administration proved very receptive to the attempts of both the British and the Hong Kong governments to stall such efforts. Not only was this in keeping with Bush's broader commitment to engage rather than isolate the PRC,[28] but it also reflected a growing sensitivity to Hong Kong's peculiar interests stemming from its relationship to the economy of Southern China[29]—and an equally solid understanding of the huge economic damage that would be inflicted on the Hong Kong economy were the MFN initiative to succeed.[30] To be sure, some, like William McGurn, argue that the Bush administration used Hong Kong as a "convenient out"—Bush wanted to avoid sanctions against China and saw Hong Kong as "a nice way around it."[31] But there can be no denying that the willingness of first the Bush administration, and then the Clinton administration in 1993 and afterward, to withstand the political pressures from Congress for a harsher approach to China can be seen as part of a broader concern about confidence in Hong Kong. This concern had a direct impact on the deeply entrenched American economic interests in the territory.

A second strand in the efforts of the United States to bolster confidence in Hong Kong after June 1989 was to change the U.S. approach to immigration from Hong Kong. Unlike Canada (and, as we will see below, Australia), by 1990 the U.S. government had agreed to embrace the "insurance policy" approach to immigration being pressed on Western countries by Britain in an effort to staunch the flow of emigrants from the territory. Amendments to the United States Immigration Act of 1990 doubled the annual immigrant visa quota from 5,000 to 10,000; it also provided for the creation of a special immigrant category for those employed by American firms in Hong Kong: 12,000 visas per year in 1991–92 and 1992–93, with immediate family members also issued visas and not counted in the 12,000 quota.

Most important of all, instead of demanding that those issued with immigrant visas to the United States use them within four months, the new legislation gave recipients until January 1, 2002, to use their visas.[32] By extending the deadline for the use of the visa into the next century and well after the reversion of Hong Kong to Chinese sovereignty, the United States government hoped to create what one American official called a "safety net."[33] And, it was hoped, the several hundred thousand Hong Kong people who might be recipients of these U.S. visas (either as applicants or family members) would feel secure enough with this safety net under them to stay in Hong Kong until and beyond 1997, knowing that, if things went wrong, their fall would be cushioned.

A third strand of the confidence-building measures was the support of the Bush administration for the U.S.–Hong Kong Policy Act of 1992. Introduced as legislation by Senator Mitch McConnell (R–Kentucky) in September 1991, Senate Bill S.1731 sought to address a thorny legal problem that will arise from the transfer of sovereignty from Britain to China. Until 1997, American law will treat Hong Kong for legal purposes as part of Britain. That means that Americans dealing with Hong Kong are able to take advantage of the friendly relations between the United States and Britain. However, when Hong Kong reverts to Chinese sovereignty, American citizens dealing with Hong Kong will have to operate under the considerable legal restrictions of United States law that cover relations with China, particularly in areas of trade, technology transfer, tourism, and other matters.

The idea behind the McConnell Bill was to amend American law in a way that would essentially exempt Hong Kong from whatever legal restrictions there might be on American citizens dealing with China. The essence of S.1731 was to propose that under American law, Hong Kong be treated as a "nonsovereign entity," which would be distinct from the rest of China for the purposes of American law. Mirroring the areas specified in the Joint Declaration of 1984 in which the HKSAR was promised "a high degree of autonomy"—economic, trade, financial, monetary, aviation, shipping and communications, tourism, cultural, and sport—the McConnell bill creates the possibility of separate treatment for Hong Kong under American law.

But S.1731 was not simply an arcane exercise in reshaping international law. On the contrary, McConnell himself made it quite plain that part of the purpose of his bill was political: to increase the linkages between the United States and Hong Kong prior to 1997 in the hope not only that the ties would remain in place after 1997, but that the very act of increasing ties would boost confidence and decrease emigration.[34] However, the bill also contained a key measure designed to keep international attention fixed on Hong Kong throughout the 1990s, and after 1997: under its provisions, the U.S. secretary of state would be required to report regularly until the year 2000 to Congress on the progress of transition to Chinese sovereignty; moreover, one section of this report would have to discuss the development of democratic institutions in Hong Kong.

The Bush administration's response to the McConnell Bill was largely, but not totally, positive. On the one hand, the administration clearly welcomed the bill's intent to carve out a separate status for Hong Kong under American law and its efforts to bolster confidence in the territory. On the other hand, Bush administration officials had considerable reservations about the bill's reporting requirements, seeing them as unnecessarily provocative.[35]

These reporting requirements, however, were seen by many as the way in which China could be held more accountable for developments in Hong Kong after 1997. For this reason, both Martin Chu-ming Lee, chairman of the Hong Kong Democratic Party, and Chris Patten stressed the importance of the McConnell Act during their official visits to Washington in April and May 1996. Partly as a result of their lobbying, an amendment to the McConnell Act was introduced into the House of Representatives in June 1996. Attached to an appropriations bill for foreign operations, the amendment replaced the vague reporting features of the original act with specific provisions requiring the president to report to Congress on the CPG's plans for a new legislature, progress in implementing the Basic Law, the selection process for the chief executive, the treatment of political parties, the independence of the judiciary, and the implementation of the Bill of Rights.[36]

A fourth element of American policy mirrored the efforts of other countries to keep Hong Kong plugged into the international community. However, the focus of this confidence-building activity was more one-way than in the case of either Australia or Canada. For example, after 1989, high-level visits increased considerably, but they consisted mainly of numerous Hong Kong officials and personages visiting the United States. By contrast, there were relatively few high-level visits to Hong Kong by administration officials, and when such a visit did occur, it tended to be as part of a visit to China, such as Commerce Secretary Ron Brown's visit in August and September 1994. However, visits to the territory by members of Congress steadily rose over the early 1990s: in 1993, for example, approximately twenty-five members of Congress visited Hong Kong.[37] While neither Bush nor Clinton visited Hong Kong as president, Clinton did receive Patten at the White House in May 1993 and expressed general support for Patten's 1992 electoral reform package. Vice-President Al Gore met with Hong Kong's chief secretary, Anson Chan, in April 1994. And in April 1996, Gore, together with the National Security Adviser Anthony Lake, hosted Martin Chu-ming Lee, chairman of the Hong Kong Democratic Party. But the Clinton administration adopted a more high-profile approach to the Hong Kong question—following the president's reelection in 1996. Senior officials including both Gore and Secretary of State Madeleine Albright made sure that the Hong Kong issue was discussed in their meetings with senior Chinese leaders during their visits to China in 1997.

Some aspects of American policy mirrored the approaches of the two middle powers, while others did not. For example, the U.S. government did join with Australia and Canada in giving support for Hong Kong membership in international organizations. By contrast, when the Hong Kong government launched a Hong Kong–USA '94 festival in the United States in October 1994 following the success of the festivals with Canada, the government in Washington did not demonstrate the kind of enthusiasm that Ottawa had shown for this people-to-people tool of statecraft. On the other hand, while both the Australian and Canadian governments tended to be muted in their responses to saber-rattling by China, the Clinton administration was not hesitant to express its concern when the CPG exerted pressure, as it did in April 1996 by bruiting the possibility that civil servants would be required to take loyalty oaths.[38]

Australia

Like Canada and the United States, Australia was also galvanized into embracing a more activist policy toward Hong Kong after June 4, 1989. Australian links with the territory were also considerable: by the early 1990s, two-way trade was running at approximately AUD$2 billion;[39] approximately thirteen thousand Australian citizens were living in Hong Kong; there was a large immigrant population from Hong Kong in Australia; and Australia was a growing center for both tourists and fees-paying secondary and tertiary students from the territory. Thus, like Canada and the United States, the Australian government had good reason to embrace confidence-building measures in the years after 1989. However, the approach taken by Australia was closer to that of Canada than that of the United States.

One of the similarities between the Australian and Canadian approaches was that Canberra refused to use Australian immigration policy as a confidence-building measure. To be sure, Australia, like Canada, was such a popular destination for Hong Kong people that the Australian government could not avoid the problem of the "brain drain." And, like Canada, Australia was being pressed by Britain into accepting a deferred passport scheme as a means of inducing people to remain in Hong Kong. However, policymakers in Canberra rejected the idea of changing Australian immigration policy to establish an "insurance policy" for Hong Kong people. And so, like Canada, the Australian government decided on a balancing act. On the one hand, it would reject any change to Australia's "global nondiscriminatory" immigration policy; as Minister for Foreign Affairs Gareth Evans put it in a speech in April 1991, Canberra had spent twenty years trying to overcome the legacy of its previously discriminatory "White Australia" policies: "we are not about to tar ourselves with that brush again." On the other hand, Evans noted that the Australian government would be "sensitive to the situation of Hong Kong residents."[40]

As it turned out, Australian immigration rules already in place in 1989 provided such "sensitivity." First, Australia allowed its immigrants considerable flexibility. Like Canada and the United States, Australian immigration rules require that immigrants, or "settlers," take up their immigrant visas immediately; unlike Canada or the United States, however, new settlers, once landed, are allowed to leave immediately: they are given a multiple re-entry visa, allowing them to leave Australia for a maximum of three years. Only after three years must they return to Australia for a full twelve months before qualifying for another multiple re-entry visa.

Second, Australian immigration rules permit employees of Australian firms abroad who obtain permanent residence in Australia to continue to reside in their country of origin (as long as they remain employed by that firm). To retain the right to take up permanent residence in Australia, such individuals need only spend one day in Australia in the first three years, and one day in Australia in the next five years. Moreover, these resident-return rights were also available to family members of Australian citizens: that is, if one member of the family secured citizenship by spending the requisite two years in Australia, the right to take up permanent residence under the one-day rule described above was extended to all members of the family.

As will be clear, Australian rules provided a form of "insurance policy," and this diminished somewhat the pressure on Canberra to implement a deferred immigration or passport scheme. As Kee and Skeldon note, these rules allowed entire families to "settle" in Australia, but then immediately move back to Hong Kong.[41]

Another similarity between Australia's policy toward Hong Kong after 1989 and both the Canadian and American approaches was the shared concern for bolstering confidence in Hong Kong by "plugging" Hong Kong into the international community. For example, Canberra took the lead in promoting Hong Kong's membership in the Pacific Economic Cooperation Committee (PECC), and facilitating Hong Kong's participation in the Asia-Pacific Economic Cooperation (APEC) process.[42]

The Australians, like the Canadians, also embraced the idea of high-profile visits as a means of bolstering confidence. On a number of occasions, Gareth Evans, who had been Australia's minister for foreign affairs since 1988, visited Hong Kong, giving speeches that sought to encourage confidence in the territory beyond 1997. Likewise, Hong Kong governors have been invited on official visits to Australia, the most recent of these by Chris Patten in February 1994. And, as in the Canadian and American cases, legislative links have been encouraged: for example, an Australian parliamentary delegation visited Hong Kong in July 1994, holding talks with their Legco (Legislative Council) counterparts.[43]

However, Australian policy toward Hong Kong took a divergent twist on one issue: Patten's reform package, introduced in October 1992. While Patten's plan to expand democratic institutions in Hong Kong was greeted by wholehearted support by the Canadian government and somewhat more moderate support by the Clinton administration, the Australian government was clearly divided on the question. For his part, Evans had declared himself to be firmly in favor of the Patten reforms from the outset. In part this reflected his belief, shared with his Canadian counterparts, that building democratic institutions in Hong Kong prior to 1997 would make the implementation of the "one country, two systems" formula easier after 1997. And in part, it reflected a former law professor's attachment to the ideals of human rights and the rule of law, a perspective that manifested itself in a broader Australian push for human rights in Asia.

By contrast, the Australian prime minister, Paul Keating, was not at all as sure. According to a leaked transcript of a meeting with Chinese premier Li Peng in June 1993, Keating said that he was concerned about "stability and prosperity" in the territory—a barely disguised code used by those opposed to the Patten reforms. Moreover, Keating went so far as to allow that he was "not particularly impressed with Patten's modus operandi or his taking an interest in Hong Kong's political system so late in the piece."[44] And despite Australian efforts to promote high-profile visits as a way of boosting confidence in the territory, room could not be found in Keating's schedule to allow him to visit Hong Kong on his way to Beijing in June 1993.

This difference of opinion was most clearly evident during Patten's trip to Australia in 1994. In a speech on February 16 welcoming the governor to Australia, and in television interviews later, Evans took the opportunity to again endorse the reform proposals, saying that he had "admiration" for Patten's pro-democracy efforts, claiming that they were "eminently worth taking."[45] By contrast, following a meeting with Patten, Keating remained totally silent on the question of reform.

The Internationalization of Hong Kong?

There is little doubt that some would interpret the approaches of the Australian, Canadian, and U.S. governments that have been described in this chapter as efforts to internationalize the Hong Kong question. Certainly pro-PRC voices and the government in Beijing itself have always been quick to denounce inappropriate interference by other countries in Hong Kong affairs. For example, a pro-PRC paper, *Wen Wei Po*, suggested that the U.S.–Hong Kong Policy Act created "an appendage of the United States and an independent state in disguised form, which will be at the United States' beck and call."[46] Likewise, when the Australian minister for foreign affairs and trade, Gareth Evans, expressed "admiration" for Patten's reform proposals, he was roundly criticized in the Chinese press for making "irresponsible comments and indiscreet remarks" and was told that no third country has the right to speak on Hong Kong matters.[47] And there was a tendency in Beijing to see policy toward Hong Kong as part of a "conspiracy" by Western powers to interfere with the return of Hong Kong to China.[48]

But how accurate is such a depiction? If we take internationalization to mean a coordinated attempt by some countries to make Hong Kong an "international" question, then it can be argued that in fact we did not see internationalization at work in the run-up to 1997. First, internationalization requires the coordination of policy by foreign governments—in order for an issue to reach the international agenda. As we have seen, the governments in Canberra, Ottawa, and Washington did not seek to coordinate their approaches to Hong Kong. More importantly, as the account here should make clear, it is unlikely that they would have been unable to even if they had tried: there is simply too much disagreement among the three governments on the best way to approach the Hong Kong issue. The divergence over using immigration as a confidence-building mechanism provides one clear demonstration of this: an attempt *was* made—by Britain—to coordinate such an approach, and it failed.

The Americans obliged, but the Australians and Canadians did not, pursuing their own equally divergent paths.

And on other issues, it is clear that there was little agreement among the three governments on the "right" approach. For example, all three countries trod divergent paths on the issue of confidence-building. A further measure of the lack of coordination was the degree to which policymakers were quite prepared to be privately critical of some of the approaches toward Hong Kong of the other two countries (frequently couching their criticism in terms of friendship, as in "If the government of X were a true friend of Hong Kong, it would do [or not do] Y").

Second, for an issue to be internationalized, governments have to try to move an issue to an international forum, and out of the ambit of the sovereign control of bilateral relations. But on the Hong Kong question, the governments examined in this chapter have all been scrupulous in their attachment to the precepts of the 1984 Joint Declaration, even after 1989. Publicly, confidence continued to be expressed in the ability of the "one country, two systems" formula to work.[49] And actions generally matched those words: for example, efforts were not made to alter the basic conditions for the return of Hong Kong to Chinese sovereignty agreed to by Britain and the PRC in the early 1980s. For example, no government encouraged the growth of an independence movement in Hong Kong, or called for an international conference on the Hong Kong question, or even raised the Hong Kong question in such bodies as the United Nations, APEC, or the Commonwealth.

And even on the issue of democratization, where the PRC could with more justification complain that they will be inheriting a political community in 1997 very much unlike the one they signed on in 1984, one would be hard-pressed to conclude that there was coordinated international pressure behind the Patten reforms. The account in this chapter makes clear that Australia, Canada, and the United States had very different views about democratization, ranging from the enthusiasm of the Mulroney government in 1992 and 1993, to the more qualified and muted views of the Clinton administration, to the sharp contrast in Australia between the enthusiasm of the foreign minister and the stony silence of the prime minister.

What we have seen, I would argue, are three governments that to a greater or lesser extent were prodded into action after the events of June 4, 1989, to try and avert the likelihood of significant damage to their interests if the transition went awry. The steps that they took in the early 1990s sought to bolster levels of confidence in Hong Kong itself and to demonstrate, by working to plug Hong Kong as much as possible into the international system, that "a high degree of autonomy" for the new HKSAR government could work. And, perhaps most importantly, these steps were intended to signal to China that how it dealt with Hong Kong mattered, though Australia and Canada tended to be less confrontational than the United States.

In short, the insistence of policymakers in Canberra, Ottawa, and Washington that the "i-word" does not accurately describe their policies is not just bland diplomatese. On the contrary, it reflects a recognition that the internationalization of the Hong Kong issue was not possible in the early and mid-1990s.

Conclusion: The Way Ahead

Such a conclusion also has implications for the post-1997 period. We should begin by noting that government officials in Canberra, Ottawa, and Washington will continue to be concerned after 1997 with political and economic conditions in the HKSAR. It is highly unlikely that these governments will lose interest in the success of the "one country, two systems" experiment, if only because too many Australian, Canadian, and American citizens have deep ties to the new HKSAR.

But the policy behavior of these three governments prior to 1997 suggests that it is unlikely that they will abandon the essential aversion to the internationalization of the Hong Kong question after reversion. Both the Australian and Canadian governments already had begun the process of incorporating their Hong Kong policies into their broader China policies in the mid-1990s,[50] and it is likely that this process will continue after July 1, 1997. For its part, the United States is likely to pursue a divergent path, in large measure because of the division in powers between a human-rights-minded Congress and a White House which, whether occupied by a Democrat or a Republican, will tend to want to put American policy toward China—and the HKSAR—into a broader perspective.

This means that each of these countries will continue to monitor the transition—the Australians and Canadians informally, the Americans more formally because of the requirements of the Hong Kong Policy Act of 1992. And if the reversion goes awry, it is highly unlikely that any of these countries will sit back and watch impassively from afar.[51] On the contrary, it is likely that all three governments will seek to engage China, though it will depend on the correlation of domestic forces within each country whether the approach adopted is one marked by hectoring, lecturing, and sanctions, or, as Michel Oksenberg has advocated, one that is marked by a constructive and cooperative policy designed to engage China.[52]

But whichever approach the Australians, Canadians, and Americans take in the post-1997 period, the analysis in this chapter suggests that it is unlikely that these governments will have either the interest or the ability to internationalize the Hong Kong issue. Their dealings with China on Hong Kong issues will be strictly bilateral.

In short, whether or not internationalization is at risk depends on how the term is defined. If internationalization is simply keeping Hong Kong as plugged in to the international community as possible after 1997, then internationalization is not at risk. The eyes, and the attention, of the international community will remain fixed on Hong Kong after 1997. But if internationalization is defined as a process by which foreign governments actively seek to make the implementation of the Joint Declaration an international issue, over the objections of the PRC, then the analysis in this chapter suggests that the prospects that internationalization will be used as a tool to influence CPG behavior are low. Foreign countries like Australia, Canada, and the United States will try hard to ensure that the "one country, two systems" formula works. But those policies will fall far short of internationalization.

Notes

1. The "second stove" refers to a rival authority to the British-appointed Hong Kong government. Such a body, appointed in advance of 1997 by the Central People's Government in Beijing, comprising both Hong Kong people and some from the People's Republic of China, would hold consultations and elections prior to 1997. "Two ups and two downs" refers to the procedure for approving the Basic Law for Hong Kong: there were two rounds of drafting, handed "down" twice by the Basic Law Drafting Commission for consultation and discussion and then "up" to the National People's Congress Standing Committee. The "three-legged stool" refers to the idea of tripartite talks between the governments of China, Britain, and Hong Kong; the Central People's Government has persistently rejected such talks, insisting on talks solely between the two sovereign governments in London and Beijing. "Astronauts," discussed in more detail below, are Hong Kong people who have emigrated and maintain a residence abroad but continue to work in Hong Kong. The "through train" is the idea that it would be good for confidence in the territory if as much of Hong Kong's government as possible were to "straddle" 1997. It has been used in particular in reference to the 1995 Legislative Council (Legco) elections, which will see some legislators hold office until 1999.

2. Including a large number of Hong Kong students studying overseas: for example, between 1992 and 1994, over forty-four thousand student visas were issued for Hong Kong students by Australia, Britain, Canada, and the United States. See *Hong Kong 1995* (Hong Kong: Government Information Services, 1995), Appendix 30, p. 504.

3. For a discussion of this phenomenon, see Danny Kin-Kong Lam, "Hongkong Chinese Emigration and Investment Patterns in Response to the 1997 Problem," *Journal of Northeast Asian Studies* 9 (Spring 1990), pp. 63–65.

4. Ronald Skeldon, "Migration from Hong Kong: Current Trends and Future Agendas," in Ronald Skeldon, ed., *Reluctant Exiles? Migration from Hong Kong and the New Overseas Chinese* (Armonk, NY: M.E. Sharpe and Hong Kong: Hong Kong University Press, 1994), p. 327.

5. James T.H. Tang, "Hong Kong's International Status," *Pacific Review* 6 (1993), pp. 205–206.

6. Kim Richard Nossal, "A High Degree of Ambiguity: Hong Kong as an International Actor after 1997," *Pacific Review* 10, no. 1 (1996), pp. 4–103. Also Tang, "Hong Kong's International Status," pp. 205–215; and Roda Mushkat, "Hong Kong as an International Legal Person," *Emory International Law Review* 6 (1992), pp. 105–170.

7. By the autumn of 1989, the government of Hong Kong had developed a comprehensive strategy to boost local and international confidence in Hong Kong: *Hong Kong Standard,* August 12, 1989; *South China Morning Post,* October 15, 1990. The chief secretary, Sir David Ford, outlined this strategy to Legco in May 1990, noting that it included high-level visits by Hong Kong government officials, including the governor, to "target" countries, inviting "influential persons" from abroad, participating in interna-

tional conferences, and holding conferences in Hong Kong. Hong Kong, Legislative Council, *Reports of the Meetings,* vol. 3, 1989–90, May 23, 1990, pp. 1629–1630.

8. For example, when he visited Washington, DC in May 1990, Martin Lee Chuming, member of the Hong Kong Legislative Council (Legco) and leader of the United Democrats of Hong Kong (later the Democratic Party) publicly urged the United States government to "internationalize" the Hong Kong question: *South China Morning Post,* May 3, 1990.

9. For example, "Internationalization of Hong Kong question gets nowhere," *Beijing Review,* December 11, 1989, pp. 14–15, quoted in Tang, "Hong Kong's International Status," p. 205; "Editorial Says 'Internationalization' Will Bring Disaster to Hong Kong," Foreign Broadcasting Information Service (hereafter FBIS), December 14, 1992, quoted in Christopher K. Costa, "One Country, Two Foreign Policies: United States Relations with Hong Kong after July 1, 1997," *Villanova Law Review* 38 (1993), p. 847.

10. See, for example, the argument in David M. Lampton, "Hong Kong and the Rise of 'Greater China': Policy Issues for the United States," in John P. Burns et al., *Hong Kong and China in Transition,* Canada and Hong Kong Papers No. 3 (Toronto: Joint Centre for Asia-Pacific Studies, 1994), pp. 73–84.

11. The most comprehensive examination of the migration of Hong Kong people after the 1984 agreement can be found in Skeldon, ed., *Reluctant Exiles?*

12. This is not to suggest that there was *equal* willingness on the part of these states: as Table 3.1 below shows, Canada was the most open to Hong Kong immigration, the United States relatively more closed, with a relatively small immigrant quota from Hong Kong until the early 1990s. For a comparative discussion, see Gerald Segal, *The Fate of Hong Kong* (London: Simon and Schuster, 1993), chaps. 7–9.

13. For the reactions of the United States government to the 1984 Joint Declaration, see Chiu Hungdah, "The Hong Kong Agreement and U.S. Foreign Policy," in Jürgen Domes and Yu-ming Shaw, eds., *Hong Kong: A Chinese and International Concern* (Boulder, CO: Westview Press, 1988), pp. 183–195; for the text of the statement of the Australian prime minister, Bob Hawke, in response to the initialing of the agreement, see Australia, Department of Foreign Affairs, *Australian Foreign Affairs Record* 55 (September 1984), p. 1029; also, M.D. Copithorne, "The Canada–Hong Kong Relationship," *Transactions of the Royal Society of Canada,* 6th series, vol. 1 (1990), pp. 241–248.

14. Chalmers Johnson, "The Mouse Trapping of Hong Kong: A Game in Which Nobody Wins," *Asian Survey* 9 (September 1984), pp. 887–909.

15. Segal, *Fate of Hong Kong,* p. 116.

16. Stephen FitzGerald, "Australia's China," *Australian Journal of Chinese Affairs* 24 (1990), pp. 315–335.

17. Operation Yellowbird was a scheme organized by Hong Kong people in the wake of June 4, 1989, to smuggle dissidents out of China to asylum abroad via Hong Kong, *Newsweek,* April 1, 1996, pp. 44–45.

18. See Ronald Skeldon, "Hong Kong in an International Migration System," in Skeldon, ed., *Reluctant Exiles?,* p. 28, Table 2.1.

19. Ann Kent, *Between Freedom and Subsistence: China and Human Rights* (Hong Kong: Oxford University Press, 1993), pp. 213–230; Kim Richard Nossal, *Rain Dancing: Sanctions in Canadian and Australian Foreign Policy* (Toronto: University of Toronto Press, 1994), chaps. 8 and 10; and Kim Richard Nossal, *The Beijing Massacre: Australian Responses,* Australian Foreign Policy Papers (Canberra: Department of International Relations, Australian National University, 1993).

20. Segal, *Fate of Hong Kong,* p. 139.

21. As Skeldon notes, the Chinese for astronaut, *tai kong ren,* "felicitously combines the English meaning of a person who spends time in space, that is, an airplane, with a

Cantonese play on words around 'empty wife,' 'home without a wife' (in Hong Kong), or 'house without a husband' (at the destination)." Skeldon, "Reluctant Exiles or Bold Pioneers: An Introduction to Migration from Hong Kong," in Skeldon, ed., *Reluctant Exiles?*, p. 11.

22. For an account, see *Canada and Hong Kong Update* 8 (Fall 1992), pp. 5–7.

23. External Affairs and International Trade Canada, *Press Release* no. 200, October 9, 1992.

24. *Far Eastern Economic Review*, June 13, 1991, p. 11.

25. Notably the U.S. consul-general, Richard Williams, who in May 1991 gave an uncharacteristically blunt speech urging a resolution to issues between China and Hong Kong: see *Far Eastern Economic Review*, June 13, 1991, p. 11.

26. The official U.S. State Department reaction to the Patten proposals came on November 16, 1992: "[They] represent a constructive approach to the goal of democratization in Hong Kong, a goal which the U.S. strongly supports." Quoted in *Canada and Hong Kong Update* 8 (Fall 1992), p. 3.

27. For an excellent account, see Harry Harding, *A Fragile Relationship: The United States and China since 1972* (Washington, DC: Brookings Institution, 1992).

28. See William J. Barnds, "Human Rights and U.S. Policy Towards Asia," in James T.H. Tang, ed., *Human Rights and International Relations in the Asia Pacific* (London/New York: Pinter, 1995), pp. 71–82.

29. For a discussion, see Sung Yun-wing, *The Economic Integration of Hong Kong with China in the 1990s: The Impact on Hong Kong*, Research Papers no. 1, Canada and Hong King Project (Toronto: Joint Centre for Asia Pacific Studies, 1992).

30. In the early 1990s, there was considerable fear about the effects of a major conflict over trade: a common estimate by the Hong Kong government at the time of the 1990 revocation initiative was that removing China's MFN status would cost Hong Kong approximately U.S.$10 billion in business and twenty thousand jobs. By 1995, a more sanguine view prevailed: the Hong Kong government was estimating that a full-fledged Sino-American trade war could trim the territory's gross domestic product by only 0.1 percentage points, and cost a mere $47 million of the re-exports from China to the United States: Reuters, February 3, 1995.

31. William McGurn, *Perfidious Albion: The Abandonment of Hong Kong 1997* (Lanham, MD: Ethics and Public Policy Center, 1992), p. 118.

32. United States, Congress, *Congressional Record*, 136th Congress, November 2, 1990, E3704; *Far Eastern Economic Review*, February 14, 1991, pp. 28–29; Segal, *Fate of Hong Kong*, pp. 124–125.

33. Assistant Secretary of State for East Asia/Pacific Affairs, testifying before the Senate Foreign Relations Committee, Subcommittee on East Asia/Pacific Affairs, April 2, 1992: USIS, American Consulate-General, Hong Kong, *Foreign Policy Backgrounder*, April 3, 1992, p. 7.

34. United States, Congress, Senate, *Congressional Record*, 137th Congress, September 20, 1991, S13412–13.

35. See Solomon's testimony before the Senate Foreign Relations panel, suggesting that congressional reports should focus solely on the impact of the transition on American interests: *Backgrounder*, 9.

36. Reuters, June 12, 1996.

37. Reuters Australasian Briefing, August 21, 1993.

38. Reuters, April 23, 1996.

39. For a survey of Australian economic links with Hong Kong and Southern China in the early 1990s, see Australia, Department of Foreign Affairs and Trade, East Asia Analytical Unit, *Southern China in Transition: The New Regionalism and Australia* (Canberra, 1992).

40. Australia, Department of Foreign Affairs and International Trade, *Australian Foreign Affairs: The Monthly Record,* April 1991, p. 134.

41. Kee Pookong and Ronald Skeldon, "The Migration and Settlement of Hong Kong Chinese in Australia," in Skeldon, ed., *Reluctant Exiles?* p. 190.

42. Gareth Evans and Bruce Grant, *Australia's Foreign Relations in the World of the 1990s* (Carlton, Vic.: Melbourne University Press, 1991), p. 237.

43. For the report of the delegation, see Australia, Parliament, *Commonwealth Parliamentary Debates,* Senate, November 10, 1994, pp. 2927–2930.

44. See, for example, Reuters, February 16, 1994; *Sydney Morning Herald,* January 25, 1995.

45. *South China Morning Post,* February 17, 1994; *The Age,* Melbourne, February 21, 1994.

46. Quoted in Costa, "One Country, Two Foreign Policies," p. 859, *fn* 225.

47. Zhang Junsheng, deputy director of the Hong Kong branch of the Xinhua News Agency, in a statement to journalists: *Sydney Morning Herald,* February 19, 1994.

48. For a good discussion of the PRC's views, see Joseph Y.S. Cheng, "Sino-British Negotiations on Hong Kong during Chris Patten's Governorship," *Australian Journal of International Affairs* 48 (November 1994), pp. 229–245.

49. It is true that when they speak privately, policymakers are prone to be as unsure about the future as Hong Kong people themselves: one finds both pessimists and optimists in their ranks.

50. For discussions of the evolving China policy of these two middle powers, see Jeremy R. Paltiel, "Negotiating Human Rights with China," in Maxwell A. Cameron and Maureen Appel Molot, eds., *Canada among Nations, 1995: Democracy and Foreign Policy* (Ottawa: Carleton University Press, 1995), pp. 165–86; Stuart Harris, "Australia–China Political Relations: From Fear to Friendly Relations?" *Australian Journal of International Affairs* 49 (November 1995), pp. 237–248.

51. It should be noted that according to the forecasting model applied to the Hong Kong situation by Bruce Bueno de Mesquita and his associates, active international interest is predicted for the post-1997 period, but with mixed results: see Bruce Bueno de Mesquita, David Newman, and Alvin Rabushka, *Red Flag over Hong Kong* (Chatham, NJ: Chatham House, 1996), pp. 100–119.

52. Michel Oksenberg, "What Kind of China Do We Want?" *Newsweek,* April 1, 1996.

4

Hong Kong and the Newly Industrializing Economies: From Americanization to Asianization

Lai On-Kwok and Alvin Y. So

In the literature on development, Hong Kong, Singapore, South Korea, and Taiwan are commonly dubbed the East Asian NIEs (newly industrializing economies). This is because Hong Kong, like the other East Asian NIEs, exhibited an impressive economic track record of nearly 10 percent growth in GDP over the past three decades. In addition, Hong Kong shared the East Asia NIEs' pattern of export-oriented industrialization, under which manufactured goods accounted for the lion's share of the total merchandise exports. Moreover, the exports of the East Asian NIEs were not confined to low-tech, labor-intensive products. There has been substantial technological upgrading, economic diversification, and movement of capital and professionals in their economies and the region itself. Furthermore, whereas foreign companies largely constituted the ownership of Latin American NIEs, indigenous firms owned the labor-intensive industries of the East Asian NIEs. Finally, by the 1990s, the East Asian NIEs (leading other Asian economies) have become a powerhouse to propel the world economy forward.

Why were the NIEs able to transform themselves from backward economies in the mid-twentieth century into economic powerhouses of the world economy at the turn of the twentieth century? Or more specifically, what were the conditions that led Hong Kong, Singapore, South Korea, and Taiwan to adopt export-led industrialization during the 1950s and the 1960s? What explains their upgrading to the status of NIEs despite the downward turn of the world economy in the 1970s? And what are the future prospects for the NIEs as the center of capital accumulation in the world economy in the twentieth century?

In the literature on development, there are three general explanations for East Asian NIEs.[1] First, the culturalists contend that Confucianism provides the key to understanding the economic success of East Asia.[2] It is argued that Confucianism encouraged investment in human capital, promoted family entrepreneurship, and endorsed a new pattern of personalistic corporate management. Second, from the viewpoint of neoclassical economists, Bela Balassa argues that limited government intervention and reliance on the private sector accounts for the high GDP growth rates of the East Asian states.[3] Third, with regard to the statist literature,[4] it is contended that since the East Asian states experienced both bureaucratic autonomy and public–private cooperation, the strong states in East Asia not only were able to formulate strategic developmental goals, but were also able to put them into effective policy action to promote rapid industrialization. On the other hand, the focus of the literature on Hong Kong is on the Chinese factor. Hong Kong's pattern of development is attributed to its special linkages with Guangdong,[5] with mainland China,[6] or with the Chinese triangle of Hong Kong–mainland–Taiwan.[7]

Although Confucian culture, market and private enterprises, the developmental state, and the China dimension are important factors, the literature has not paid sufficient attention to the regional context that gave rise to the peculiar pattern of East Asian development.[8] As Bruce Cumings points out, "an understanding of the Northeast Asian political economy can only emerge from an approach that posits the systemic interaction of each country with the others, and of the region with the world at large."[9]

The aim of this paper, therefore, is to offer an alternative *regional* explanation of Hong Kong and other East Asian NIEs' development. We will discuss four regional projects (the American, the Japanese, the Chinese, and the Asianization projects) in Asia in the second half of the twentieth century. We focus on these four projects because they provided a regional interface through which internationalization took place. Since Hong Kong has been a British colony and engaged in entrepôt trade since 1942, it has never ceased undergoing the process of internationalization. However, Hong Kong's pattern of internationalization varies from one phase to another because of the changing Asian regional context. During the second half of the twentieth century, in particular, Hong Kong's internationalization through the Asian regional interface has gradually shifted from "Britainization" to Americanization, Japanization, Sinification, and then more recently to Asianization. In what follows, we will show that the four regional projects have promoted export-led industrialization in Hong Kong, Singapore, South Korea, and Taiwan in the 1950s and 1960s; upgraded them to the NIEs in the 1970s; diversified their economies in the 1980s; and turned them into an economic powerhouse in the 1990s.

Aside from regionalization of international dynamics, there is also the nationalization of the regional projects, as the latter worked through national structure and became internalized in domestic political economy.

Although the main focus of this chapter is on the regionalization of international dynamics, it should be pointed out that the four regional projects have provoked divergent sociopolitical and institutional responses from the NIEs, resulting in their different patterns of state structure, economic policy, and corporate power. Thus, Hong Kong has experienced, to a certain extent, a somewhat different developmental trajectory from the other East Asian NIEs in the late twentieth century.[10]

Finally, since this is a volume on Hong Kong's internationalization, the Hong Kong case will be given prominence in this chapter. For example, it will be shown that the Chinese national reunification project has exerted more impact on Hong Kong than on other East Asian NIEs.

To begin our discussion, let us focus on the American project in the post–World War II period.

Americanization from the Late 1940s to 1960s

The American Project

After World War II, the United States replaced Great Britain as the new hegemonic power of the world and assumed supremacy in the realms of the military, finance, commerce, industry, and ideology. Under American leadership, the postwar world economy thus became much more liberal, multilateral, and interdependent. In addition, in the United States and other Western core countries, a new "fordist" relationship emerged between capital and labor, in which Keynesianism, the welfare state, and wage settlement between organized labor and capital combined to create a fast-growing demand for consumer goods. Subsequently, this new "fordist" relationship under U.S. hegemony led to an unprecedented expansion (the upward phase) of the capitalist world economy.

In response to the Chinese communist revolution and the spread of working-class and peasant movements in Korea and Japan, the United States developed a regional polarization project in the late 1940s. East Asia was divided into two opposing spheres: a communist bloc composed of mainland China, North Korea, and the Soviet Union; and a capitalist bloc that included Japan, the "free China" of Taiwan, and South Korea. The capitalist bloc was constructed within the framework of U.S. strategic supremacy, and it was used to encircle and isolate the communist bloc in East Asia.[11]

The United States tried its best to contain the spread of communism from China to other East Asian states. The United States sent warships to protect the defeated Nationalist Party (Guomindang, or GMD) in Taiwan, sent soldiers to fight against the communists in Korea, supported counterrevolutionary activities in China, froze mainland Chinese assets in the United States, imposed an economic embargo on mainland Chinese products, prevented mainland China from gaining a seat in the United Nations, and waged ideological attacks on Chinese "communist totalitarianism" in the mass media.

Since the United States could expect little military or political support from its European allies, which had become exhausted and dispirited during World War II, it designated Japan as a bulwark to be built up against the spread of communism in Asia and as a critical element in a U.S.-led East Asian order. George Kennan, who played the key role in pushing for this Japanese ally policy, explains that the change of geopolitical situation in the East Asian region called for "the economic rehabilitation of Japan and the restoration of her ability to contribute constructively to the stability and prosperity of the Far Eastern region."[12] Later, in the Korean War, South Korea and Taiwan were included in this U.S.-led anticommunist front as well.

In this respect, geopolitical concerns, not corporate profitability, were at the heart of the U.S. regional polarization project. In order to build up a strong anticommunist bloc in the Pacific Rim, the United States provided economic aid, loans, industrial contracts, and opened its domestic markets to its East Asian allies, while tolerating their continued discrimination against dollar imports. The U.S. patronage of capitalist allies and its assault on communist foes in East Asia had a profound impact on the contour of development in this region.

Export Industrialization

Hong Kong, Singapore, South Korea, and Taiwan experienced a turbulent period shortly after World War II, as they were confronted with serious economic and political problems. However, these states were also blessed by the United States' project of regional polarization and endowed with very favorable developmental conditions.

More distinctive in the case of Hong Kong, vis-à-vis other Asian NIEs, the Chinese communist revolution prompted a large number of Shanghainese textile firms to divert their production to the colony.[13] In addition, the massive inflow of refugees from China, many of whom had industrial employment experience, created a pool of potential entrepreneurs willing to work hard and take the risk of setting up manufacturing firms. This particular conjuncture of refugee capital, refugee labor, and pre-existing entrepôt trading networks provided the impetus for Hong Kong's export-oriented industrialization in the early 1950s. Intense conflict between socialist China and the capitalist power bloc also explained the lack of political unrest in Hong Kong in the 1950s. As immigrants fleeing from communist rule, the new Chinese capitalists and working class in Hong Kong tolerated the British monopoly of the state machinery in order to prevent any political instability that would threaten the business environment. Moreover, unions tended to be small and ideologically divided between pro–communist China and pro-Taiwan factions. The favorable world market situation and lack of domestic class struggle help to explain the liberal, noninterventionist policy of the Hong Kong state. Different from the authoritarian states of Taiwan and South Korea, the Hong Kong state did not need to militarize itself or promote an anticommunism ideology to justify its colonial rule, nor did it need to involve itself in the promotion of export industrialization because the Chinese capitalists had already gained a head start in exports in the 1950s.[14]

Taiwan and South Korea, too, benefited from the Cold War geopolitical environment. Foreign economic assistance carried great weight in alleviating huge government budget deficits, financing investment, and paying for imports. Nearly all U.S. aid before 1964 was provided on a grant basis, thus making it possible for South Korea and Taiwan to begin their export-led growth in the 1960s without a backlog of debt.[15] Although Hong Kong and Singapore did not receive a large-scale inflow of American aid, the Cold War order also brought a large increase of their exports through the American military and related procurement during the Vietnam War period. The development of the electronics industry in Hong Kong and Singapore, for example, has always been attributed to the increased demand for military-related electronic equipment during the Vietnam War.[16] Furthermore, the Vietnam War brought a large number of GIs to Hong Kong and Singapore, which gave birth to the booming tourist industry in both economies.

In addition, the United States was willing to open its own market to the NIEs while tolerating their continued discrimination against dollar exports. The U.S. market was critical to the NIEs' economic growth because it was their largest single market throughout the 1960s and 1970s. Furthermore, the United States took an active role to induce the South Korean and Taiwanese states to adopt an outward-looking economy. For instance, after making it clear that U.S. aid would not be continued by the mid-1960s, the USAID mission in Taiwan prodded the Taiwanese state to liberalize its trade regime and adopt the strategy of export industrialization.[17]

Finally, the U.S. polarization project helped build up a strong authoritarian state in Taiwan and Korea. Military tensions in the East Asian region justified the actions of the Taiwanese and Korean states in building up the military, banning labor unions and strikes, and suspending democratic elections. Moreover, U.S. aid not only helped solve their economic problems in the 1950s, it also presented the states with powerful tools with which to intervene in the economy, enforce compliance in the private sector, and build up a strong military for defense. Furthermore, the Chinese communist revolution and the Korean War helped establish anticommunism as a hegemonic ideology to control the civil society.[18]

In sum, the Cold War, U.S. aid and markets, and U.S. pressure helped induce Hong Kong, Taiwan, and South Korea in different ways to pursue the strategy of export-led industrialization. Nevertheless, their industries in the 1960s were the type of what Gary Gereffi calls "export-platform," consisting of foreign-owned, low value-added, and labor-intensive assembly of manufactured goods in export-processing zones.[19] Their industries used imported raw materials; they had no direct access to foreign markets; and they were dependent on U.S. transnationals for finance, export, and marketing. Thus researchers in the dependency tradition stressed the constraints of this type of low-valued production on their development possibilities.[20] What then explains the upgrading of Hong Kong, Taiwan, and South Korea to NIE status in the 1970s?

The Japanese Project from the 1970s to the Late 1980s

The Japanese Project

By the early 1970s, the U.S. regional polarization project had run its course. Mark Selden uses 1970 as the approximate time of transition in the political economy of East Asia.[21] There was the end of the radical phase of China's Cultural Revolution; the beginning of U.S. withdrawal from Indochina; and the U.S.–China diplomatic breakthrough that transformed the lines of regional power, paving the way for China's full re-entry to the capitalist world economy. As the Cold War started to fade away, geopolitics also began to play a much smaller role in U.S. policy toward East Asia than before.

At the same time, the golden era of postwar economic expansion came to an end in the early 1970s. Burdened by a huge military, humiliated by defeat in the Vietnam War, unable to carry out its welfare promises to its citizens, and plagued by growing budget deficits, the United States gradually turned into a declining hegemon. Its industrial, commercial, and financial supremacy was increasingly challenged by rival core powers. There was also the decline of the U.S. dollar and the end of its convertability into gold.

On the other hand, there was an explosive growth of Japanese exports to the United States—tripling between 1964 and the 1970s, with a consequent transformation of the previous trade surplus with Japan into a $1.4 billion deficit.[22] Subsequently, there was the emergence of "value-added" politics in the United States, with American corporations trying to hold onto their share of higher value-added activities through protecting the U.S. domestic market, condemning unfair trade practices of their competitors, and pushing other industrial powers to raise their currency values.

Many developing countries—including many Latin American NIEs—slipped into recession by the end of the 1970s due to the downward turn of the world economy and the closing of the U.S. market. What, then, explains the continual economic growth of the East Asian states?

Charles Oman points to the "new forms of investment" (NFI) through which the Japanese investors do not hold a controlling interest via equity participation.[23] Similarly, Richard Hill and Yong Joo Lee suggest that the Japanese adopted a new regional project of global localization, which implies that core manufacturing is governed by a global outlook but that attention is also paid to growth of the host economy.[24] To maintain global competitiveness, Japanese corporations retained high value-added production processes at home, and they developed technology that dramatically increased productivity in their domestic plants. However, unlike the American corporations, Japanese corporations transferred not only routine, low value-added production but also some medium value-added production to host countries. Japanese corporations have been found to be more willing than U.S. firms to accept minority equity restrictions, engage in technological cooperation, make loans, and invest in ways compatible with the industrial strategies of the East Asian states.[25]

As Stephen Bunker and Denis O'Hearn explain, NFI and global localism were implemented by the Japanese to exploit a different set of contradictions as they began their ascent to industrial hegemony.[26] In the beginning, Japanese firms were reluctant transnationals due to the character of their production system, characterized by flexible specialization, spatial agglomeration, and just-in-time delivery logistics achieved through cooperation between managers and workers on the one hand and between parent firms and subcontractors on the other.[27] From the Japanese perspective, overseas production reduced competitiveness, efficiency, and quality while raising costs. Close links between parent companies, a skilled and flexible work force, and high-quality parts firms were difficult to find outside of Japan.

However, as Japan's market strength grew during the 1970s, so did her trade surplus with the rest of the world. Japan's trading partners reacted with protective measures, including import restrictions (quotas and tariffs) and foreign exchange balancing policies (forcing Japan to raise its yen value). Developing countries raised local content requirements.[28] To circumvent trade restrictions, Japanese corporations upgraded their subsidiaries, expanded their production facilities, and encouraged more of their suppliers to go offshore. Besides, the Japanese flexible production system predisposed Japanese corporations to transplant their integrated production systems abroad once exports gave way to direct foreign investment.

In addition, as a result of rapid economic growth, intense interenterprise competition, and rising wages, Japan's wages were no longer cheap by the standard of advanced industrial countries. The oil shock and the sharp rise of the yen in the 1970s and 1980s further led to a rapid increase in the costs of production in Japan. These economic pressures prompted Japanese corporations to engage in a transborder expansion into the developing countries.[29] What was the impact of this Japanese regional integration project on Hong Kong, Singapore, Taiwan, and South Korea?

Upgrading to the NIEs

Arrighi et al. report that only fifty-four investment projects in the NIEs were authorized by the Japanese government through 1964. But in the early 1970s, a total of 1,171 projects were authorized: 581 for South Korea, 400 for Taiwan, 111 for Singapore, and 79 for Hong Kong.[30] What Japanese capital was seeking were locations close at hand with efficient, cheap, flexible labor supplies, and with maximally privileged access to the United States and other core markets. From this viewpoint, Japan's former colonies of South Korea and Taiwan, which had as privileged access to the U.S. domestic market as did Japan, and the city-states of Singapore and Hong Kong, were good locations.[31]

The first wave of the Japanese transborder expansion in the 1970s consisted of mostly traditional, labor-intensive industries (like textiles, apparel, and footwear) that relied on low wages and an unskilled work force in the export processing zones. However, Gereffi observes that there was a very pronounced shift in the 1980s toward an upgraded, skill-intensive version of export-led industrialization in the East Asian NIEs.[32] These new export industries included higher value-added items that employed sophisticated technology and required a more extensively developed, tightly integrated local industrial base. Products ranged from computers and semiconductors to numerically controlled machine tools, automobiles, televisions, videocassette recorders, and sporting goods. This export dynamism in East Asia did not derive solely from introducing new products, but also from continuously upgrading traditional ones. The upgrading of the East Asian NIEs can be seen in the case of Hyundai, the automaker of South Korea. Hyundai, after forming an alliance with Japan's Mitsubishi Motors, was able to manufacture the Pony Excel and the Sonata with core components imported or licensed from Mitsubishi, and Hyundai exports both cars to the U.S. market.[33]

What explains the transfer of some medium value-added production processes from Japan to the NIEs? Why, unlike the U.S. transnationals, which demanded monopolies and oligopolies, are the Japanese corporations willing to make some class compromises with the East Asian corporations? First of all, while the U.S. corporations could draw upon the geopolitical patronage of their state and entered the developing states in a monopologistic fashion, the Japanese corporations could not follow the same pattern. This is because control over the geopolitics in East Asia was, to a certain extent, out of reach for the Japanese corporations and state. East Asia still falls under U.S. political hegemony and under a unilateral U.S. security network. Japan lacks a strong military, and lingering suspicions remain from World War II such that other Asian states view the prospects of Japanese regional political dominance with alarm. As a representative of a Japanese transnational corporation explains, "We don't have military power. There is no way for Japanese businessmen to influence policy decisions of other countries."[34]

Subsequently, Japanese corporations had to engage in hard bargaining with the strong states and corporations in the East Asian NIEs. For example, Taiwan and South Korea set ceilings on foreign ownership; demanded local production for domestic markets, technology transfer, and research and development sharing through joint ventures; and improved coordination between Japanese manufacturers and indigenous firms. Competition among Japanese and U.S. corporations, saturated demand and surplus capacity in the United States, growing trade barriers in the core states, and the rising incomes of East Asian states made East

Asian markets highly attractive to Japanese corporations. For instance, Hyundai's 14 percent equity relationship with Mitsubishi came after the Korean firm rejected offers from Volkswagen, Renault, and Ford. In order to obtain access to the growing South Korean market, Mitsubishi offered lower royalty payments and became the only foreign corporation not to demand managerial participation in Hyundai. The agreement even allowed Hyundai to compete directly in Mitsubishi's own markets and to import technology and parts from Mitsubishi's competitors.[35]

What resulted was the formation of an East Asian regional production network based not just on product cycles but also on a value-added hierarchy. Technology tie-ups between Japan, South Korea, and Taiwan are becoming more common; local sourcing of components are more frequent due to the high value of the yen; and Japanese auto assemblers and suppliers have been yielding market-entry niches to South Korea and Taiwan.

Since Hong Kong's manufacturing firms were small and locally owned, they did not have the financial capacity to invest in advanced technology and capital equipment, nor did they possess strong bargaining power with transnational corporations. Fortunately, the "demonstration effect" of Japan and the NIEs had lured mainland China to open its door to foreign investment in the 1980s, thus providing a golden opportunity for Hong Kong firms to enhance their competitive power in the world economy.

The Chinese Project in the 1980s

The Chinese Project

While the East Asian NIEs experienced robust economic development in the 1970s, socialist China experienced economic stagnation and serious unemployment problems. Consequently, when the United States terminated its polarization project and welcomed China back to the capitalist world economy, and when the old revolutionary generation passed away in the mid-1970s, the leaders in the Chinese Communist Party (CCP) replaced revolutionary Maoism with market socialism and open the door to foreign investment.

The CCP developed an open-door policy toward foreign investment through the establishment of special economic zones (SEZs) and the opening of coastal cities and delta areas. Following the path of the East Asian NIEs, the CCP wanted to attract large-scale, high-tech, capital investment from U.S. and Japanese corporations. The preferred form of the operation was the "joint venture" between the mainland Chinese government and the transnationals, so that Chinese managers could acquire advanced technology, Western management know-how, and information about world market conditions from their foreign partners. It was hoped that these joint venture projects would invigorate aging state enterprises, raise industrial production to levels comparable to those of core states, help Chinese industries to break into the world-market, and earn the needed foreign currency through export industrialization.

In order to attract foreign investment, mainland China tried hard to improve the investment climate. Over 200 pieces of joint venture legislation were passed; the socialist state spent enormous amounts of capital in infrastructure construction; and special privileges such as cheap factory sites, low rates of taxation, low wages, and tariff exemptions were granted to the transnationals.[36]

Nevertheless, these Chinese concessions failed to impress the transnationals. There were frequent complaints about unnecessary regulations and numerous layers of required permits from the Chinese bureaucracy; about operational problems, including rigid labor laws, difficulties in getting reliable supplies of high-quality raw materials, lack of enterprise autonomy, and inability to remit foreign currency profits out of China; and about the closed Chinese market. In this respect, the open-door policy failed to achieve its goal of attracting high-tech capital investment from the transnational corporations. In the arena of value-added politics, while socialist China wanted to be treated like an East Asian NIE and move up the value-hierarchy, U.S. and the Japanese corporations saw China merely as a backward peripheral state and were unwilling to transform their medium value-added production processes to it.

Since the open-door policy could not achieve its goal, mainland China proposed a national reunification project to encourage Hong Kong and Taiwanese investment in Guangdong, Fujian, and other coastal provinces. The Chinese open door policy *cum* national unification project marks a major distinction between Hong Kong (and to a lesser extent Taiwan) and other NIEs in this phase of development. In 1988, the CCP put forward a coastal development strategy, guaranteeing that Hong Kongese and Taiwanese establishments would not be nationalized, that exported goods from them would be free from export tariffs, and that their management would have complete autonomy in running their firms in mainland China. The coastal development strategy had the following characteristics.[37] First, instead of appealing to U.S. and Japanese investors, the coastal-development strategy was targeted at the patriotic investors from Taiwan and Hong Kong. Second, instead of aiming to attract large-scale investments from the transnationals, the strategy was targeted at small investment projects from the small and medium-sized firms in Taiwan and Hong Kong. Third, instead of demanding high-tech, capital-intensive investment and the utilization of local materials, the strategy allowed investment in labor-intensive industries, which relied solely on raw material imports. Assembly-line industries would help solve the serious unemployment problem, and foreign raw-material imports would help ease the shortage of raw materials in mainland markets. Fourth, instead of encouraging joint venture contracts, the present strategy preferred wholly owned foreign investment because of capital shortages.[38] In short, through the coastal development strategy, mainland China declared that it was willing to enter the regional production network at the low value-added level.

Economic Diversification

Hong Kong corporations were the first group to respond to the Chinese project. By 1990, Hong Kong had invested an estimated U.S.$ 26 billion in mainland China. As over 60 percent of all FDI in mainland China were from Hong Kong, the latter became the largest foreign investor in China.[39] Hong Kong investment was concentrated in the nearby Guangdong Province in the Pearl River Delta and took the form of "outward processing."[40] Outward processing involves a partnership between Hong Kong and Chinese capital. The Hong Kong investor supplies the machinery, material, technology, product design, and marketing services; the Chinese partner provides the plant, labor, water, electricity, and other basic facilities, and assembles the product according to the Hong Kong design. The Hong Kong investor pays the Chinese partner a "processing fee," which covers workers' wages and the above-mentioned expenses incurred on the Chinese side. Maruya Toyhhirou estimates that by June 1991 there were twenty thousand Hong Kong garment, plastic, textile, and electronic firms conducting outward processing in Guangdong.[41] These Hong Kong firms employed more than three million workers in Guangdong, about six times more than these firms employed in the colony itself.

What is more, Hong Kong has been turned into a service center for mainland China. Hong Kong was developed as a facilitator or intermediary for mainland trades and investment, providing valuable channels of information to China, "serving as a contact point for China's trade, financing China's modernization, acting as a conduit for technology transfer, and providing a training ground where China can learn and practice capitalist skills in a market environment."[42] The growing importance of Hong Kong as a service center is evident from its re-emergence as an entrepôt and transshipment center for trade with China and the East Asian region. Sung Yun-wing estimates that China's total exports and imports consumed, re-exported, transshipped, and intermediated by Hong Kong were 56 percent and 49 percent respectively.[43]

In the late 1980s, Taiwan's mainland investment also increased rapidly from U.S.$100 million in 1987 to U.S.$2 billion in 1990. By mid-1992, investment by Taiwanese companies in China was estimated at U.S.$4 billion.[44] Similar to Hong Kong's investment, Taiwan's mainland investment exhibited the following characteristics. First, with respect to locale, most Taiwanese investment has been in Guangdong and Fujian—the two mainland provinces closest to Taiwan. Second, with respect to the investors, they came mostly from small and medium enterprises (SMEs). The average investment scale of mainland operation was U.S.$650,000, and the average number of workers employed on the mainland was 312 (about 1.5 times the number employed by the parent firms in Taiwan). Third, with respect to ownership, it is estimated that 70 percent of Taiwanese investment in Guangdong and Fujian provinces were sole-ownership enterprises rather than joint ventures with mainland companies. Finally, with respect to the nature of investment, most is in such labor-intensive industries as shoe-making, plastic products, and textiles.[45] Mainland investment enhanced the economic competitiveness of Taiwanese corporations in the global market because it provided them with cheap labor, resources, and investment opportunities.

The significance of the Chinese project for Hong Kong and Taiwan is that it helps to diversify their economies. For example, the relocation of labor-intensive manufacture industries has released pressure on labor and land resources, which are both short in Hong Kong, allowing Hong Kong to concentrate its energy on technological upgrading and the service sector. At the macroeconomic level, the ratio of manufacturing industries to GDP and employment in Hong Kong has been decreasing steadily since the 1980s, and the share of service sectors (such as commerce and trade, transport and communication, and finance) has been increasing instead. At the firm level, Hong Kong manufacturers began to concentrate on trading. Thus the Hong Kong corporations are gradually transformed into a modern trading house focusing on marketing, product design, quality control, inventory control, management, and financial arrangement.[46] The Hong Kong economy, in turn, has diversified itself to become the financier, investor, supplier, designer, promoter, exporter, middleman, and technical consultant of the Chinese mainland economy.

Nevertheless, economic diversification and restructuring in Hong Kong (to a lesser extent in Taiwan) have also led to certain problems. The obvious case is the structural unemployment of the work force and the formation of an underclass in Hong Kong.[47] In addition, the Chinese project has resulted in the formation of a dualistic societal structure with fault lines along the urban-rural and industrial-agricultural sectors in mainland China.[48] In spite of their hypereconomic growth rates, the Chinese triangle of mainland–Taiwan–Hong Kong is thus vulnerable to social problems and political unrest because of their dualistic societal structure.

The Asianization Project Since the Late 1980s

By the late 1980s, the Japanese East Asian project had run its course. As Hong Kong, Singapore, South Korea, and Taiwan were upgraded to the status of NIEs with different niches in development, they gradually lost their geopolitical privileges with the United States. The NIEs, too, had to face the trade restrictions (tariffs, quotas, rising foreign currency value) that the United States had imposed upon Japan earlier. In addition, as a result of the NIEs' economic successes, there were labor shortages, increasing labor disputes, escalating land prices, and the emergence of environmental protests—all of which served to raise the cost of production in the East Asian NIEs. Furthermore, after three decades of development, the NIEs' corporations have acquired both the ability and the need to expand their scope and scale of business. With the domestic market becoming increasingly saturated, looking outward is the logical step.

The Chinese national reunification project, too, has intensified competition in the world economy. The infusion of Hong Kong know-how and capital into Guangdong has led to what Sung calls "the economic take-off of Guangdong."[49] In the reform era (1978 to 1990) Guangdong's real per capita GDP grew at the average annual rate of 11 percent per year, a performance exceeding that of the East Asian NIEs at the time of their economic take-off. Xu et al. further point out that after the exposure to Hong Kong consumption patterns through visitors and the mass media, mainland Chinese are looking forward to owning their own consumer durables.[50] Sensing this vast domestic market, Guangdong thus embarked on import substitution production. By assimilating Hong Kong investment and domestic market information, Guangdong quickly developed light industries such as household electronics, garment, food, and beverages, to capture the mainland market. In the early 1990s, after being nurtured by domestic markets for almost a decade, and after improving the quality and styling of consumer products, Guangdong began to export increasingly into the international market. Since Guangdong has become one of the international centers for manufacture and export of shoes, toys, and bicycles, its exports will soon be in keen competition with the NIEs' products in the world economy.[51]

In order to secure a stable supply of cheap docile labor, raw materials, and a larger market share, Japan and the East Asian NIEs have developed a new Asianization project since the 1980s. Nevertheless, aside from economic impetus, there are also political forces inducing NIE's investment to new territories. For example, the Chinese national unification project, especially after the June 4, 1989, incident in Beijing, had pushed those Hong Kongese and Taiwanese entrepreneurs who were afraid of the communist regime to invest in Southeast Asia.[52]

Therefore, instead of focusing on East Asia, the new Asian regional project since the late 1980s is extended to the ASEAN states (Thailand, the Philippines, Indonesia, and Malaysia). On the other hand, the ASEAN states have adopted a liberal strategy, including relaxation of government control over foreign exchange and investment, to attract direct foreign investment (FDI) into their designated development areas. In the late 1980s, this Asian project was further facilitated by the appreciation of the Japanese yen, the Taiwanese dollar, the Korean won, and the Singaporean dollar against the depreciation of the Indonesian rupiah, the Malaysian ringgit, and the Thai baht. The result was a complicated division of labor of technology, management, marketing, trade, production, and investment across different states in East Asia and Southeast Asia.

The Asianization of the Asian economy can be observed from the following indicators. First, the NIEs formed "growth triangles" with their neighboring states. The origins of growth triangles, according to their proponents, are based on economic complementarity and geographical proximity.[53] Following the successful path of Hong Kong–Guangdong integration, Singapore formed the Johor–Singapore–Riau triangle and South Korea invested heavily in China's Yellow Sea Economic Zone.[54] There was also a northern growth triangle involving Indonesia–Malaysia–Thailand, centered around Penang, Medan, and Surat Thani. The areas for cooperation included tourism promotion, electricity generation, food processing, shipping, and so forth. In the Asian context, it is considered "politically and culturally correct" in the growth triangle to help your neighbors, namely, to promote development through Asian states rather than subject your nation to the hegemonic domination of the United States.

Second, after the NIEs became net exporters of foreign investment in the late 1980s, there was observed an increasing tendency for the NIEs to invest outside of their regions. For example, mainland China has become the hottest spot for Singaporean investors. As *ASEAN Digest* reported, the Singapore–Suzhou Township Project under construction is being developed by a joint venture between a Singaporean corporation and state enterprises in Suzhou and Jiangsu, followed by seventeen Asian corporations with an investment total of up to U.S.$30 billion. When completed, this Suzhou project will provide housing for 600,000 people and employment for 360,000.[55] Moreover, after Hong Kong–based finance and service companies formulated a regional strategy in the late 1980s, they invested in almost every ASEAN state. In the 1990s, Hong Kong's investment was 11.2 percent of Thailand's FDI total, 8.1 percent of Indonesia's, 6.7 percent of Singapore's, 6.3 percent of the Philippines', and 3.8 percent Malaysia's.[56] In fact, by the 1990s, the East Asian NIEs had surpassed both the United States and Japan as the biggest foreign investors in China, Indonesia, Malaysia, and Thailand.[57]

Third, aside from the Asianization of Asian FDI, there is also the Asianization of Asian trade. For ASEAN trade flows in 1990, 17 percent was intra-ASEAN, 34 percent was with East Asia, while only 18 percent was with NAFTA, 15 percent with the EC, and 15 percent with the rest of the world.[58] K. Kozul-Wright reports that the volume of intraregional trade among the developing Asian economies was even higher than that among the EC economies.[59] In 1991, Asia surpassed the United States as Japan's largest export destination, and two years later Japan's trade surplus with the region surpassed its trade surplus with the United States.[60]

Fourth, there is the Asianization of production network, as can be seen in the case of Jinbao, a calculator factory in Thailand.[61] In Jinbao, the innovation behind the product, the brand name, and the marketing are Japanese. All key components for the calculators are also imported from Japan. All procurement and administration are controlled from Taipei, and the management of the plant is Taiwanese. The labor is Thai. Output from the plant is exclusively for export. In international trade data Jinbao's production is recorded as Thai exports of electronic goods. To purchasers at the other end the products appear to be Japanese. The direct foreign investment statistics indicate a Taiwanese investment.

Finally, there is the Asianization of migration streams.[62] Intraregional mobility and migration of skilled labors, entrepreneurs, and business people, coupled with the increased volume of tourism, have become part of the Asianization process in the 1990s. This process is further reinforced by the political uncertainty over the unresolved national unification projects of China and Korea, as well as the high income profile of the NIEs, which enables more middle-class people (in the name of the next generation's future) to opt for migration to Asia-Pacific countries.

To recapitulate, the emerging configuration in Asia in the 1990s is a single economic region characterized by growth triangles, dense intraregional trade, financial transactions, investment, production networks, and migration streams predicated on full engagement in the world economy.

Economic Powerhouse and Political Rivalry

It was through the above dynamics that Asia has become a new epicenter of capital accumulation in the world economy at the end of the twentieth century. In 1980, trans-Pacific trade began to surpass trans-Atlantic trade in value. By the end of the decade, it was 1.5 times greater. At the same time, trade among countries on the Asian side of the Pacific Rim was about to surpass in value trade across the Pacific.[63] Over the past thirty years, real GNP multiplied twelve times in the NIEs, eleven times in Japan, and six times in China as well as in ASEAN. By comparison, the U.S. economy expanded 2.5 times and the world economy three times.[64]

One by one, East Asian states came out of the U.S. shadow and began to assert their own economic, political, and cultural initiatives. In the 1990s, Japan gradually emerged from a regional to a global economic power, challenging the hegemony of the United States. Technologically, Japan's high-tech sectors were closing the gap with the United States, while Japanese manufacturers outsold their American competitors. As a result, Japan accumulated a sizable trade surplus and became the largest creditor of the world. Japan also started to play a leadership role in global affairs, and its "flying geese" model of development began to attract followers from the periphery.[65] By the late 1980s, Hong Kong became the third largest financial center in the world after London and New York in terms of foreign banks represented. Taiwan, for its part, "specialized" in accumulating foreign cash reserves. By March 1992, it held $82.5 billion in official reserves, topping the international ranking by a good margin over Japan, which came in second with $70.9 billion.[66] South Korea, too, not only paid off its debts but also experienced an explosive growth in the inflow of direct foreign investment to $625 million in 1987.[67]

In order to slow down hegemonic decline and to arrest the trend toward the Asianization of Asian economy, the United States set up the APEC (Asia Pacific Economic Cooperation) forum. With the United States as the leader, APEC includes non-Asian states such as Canada, Chile, Mexico, Australia, New Zealand, Papua–New Guinea as well as Asian states (Japan, China, Hong Kong, Singapore, South Korea, Taiwan, Indonesia, Malaysia, the Philippines, Thailand,

and Brunei). The formation of APEC enabled the United States to address major economic issues and disputes in the Asia-Pacific region. In 1993, the United States tried to transform APEC into an Asia-Pacific economic community to foster free trade and to forge close trade and investment ties in the region.[68]

However, some Asian states have reservations regarding the transformation of APEC from a consultative forum to a regional trade bloc that would discriminate against third countries. Mahathir Mohamad, prime minister of Malaysia, was particularly vocal about the APEC: "We don't want APEC to become a structure community and we don't want it to become a trade bloc. We don't want APEC to overshadow ASEAN nor do we want to see APEC being dominated by powerful members. Everyone should be equal."[69]

The APEC forum in Seattle in 1993, in fact, triggered a new epoch of Asian solidarity between China and ASEAN via-à-vis the challenge from the United States. As an alternative to the United States APEC, there was support for the formation of an alternative organization—EAEC (East Asian Economic Caucus). Qian Qichen, China's foreign minister, explains: "East Asian countries are confronted with certain challenges and problems. It is therefore useful for them to conduct dialogue, consultation, and coordination on questions of common concern."[70]

In addition, the AFTA (ASEAN Free Trade Area) was launched and a common effective preferential tariff agreement among ASEAN economies was adopted. As Singapore's prime minister, Goh Chok Tong, points out, "there was a critical difference between de-facto integration that had occurred in Asia and that which was being pursued in the EU and NAFTA; the private sector, not governments, drove the integration of Asia."[71]

Conclusion

In the literature on Hong Kong, the focus is on the China factor. Hong Kong's pattern of development is attributed to its special linkages with Guangdong and mainland China. However, from a regional perspective, the Chinese factor is only one of the four regional projects that have exercised a profound impact on the development of Hong Kong, Singapore, South Korea, and Taiwan.

During the Cold War era, the United States provided aid and procurement contracts in addition to opening its domestic market to its allies in East Asia. Blessed by U.S. patronage, Hong Kong, Singapore, South Korea, and Taiwan started export-led industrialization during the 1950s and 1960s. In the 1970s, the Japanese corporations transferred some medium value-added production processes to Japan's East Asian neighbors, enhancing the industrial upgrading of Hong Kong, Singapore, South Korea, and Taiwan, and elevating them into NIEs. In the 1980s, the Chinese national reunification project provided the opportunity for Hong Kong and Taiwan to diversify their economies from manufacture to trade, finance, and service. Finally, in the 1990s, growth triangles, dense intraregional trade, transnational production network, Japan's and the NIEs' investment in ASEAN states, and regional migration streams resulted in the Asianization of Asian economies, transforming Asia into a new epicenter of capital accumulation in the world economy.

Two questions remain: What is the future of the Asianization project? And how will this Asianization project affect Hong Kong?

On the one hand, the future prospects of the Asianization project seem to be promising. This is because there is still enormous room for expansion. So far, the Asianization project is centered upon the integration of East Asia and Southeast Asia. This project can spread to South Asian states (India, Bangladesh, and Pakistan) as well as economies linked to Asian countries (eastern Russia, Australia, and New Zealand). On the other hand, there are powerful forces to slow down the scope of Asianization. Asian states are deeply divided along religious lines (Confucianism, Buddhism, Hinduism, and Islam), political ideologies (democracy, authoritarianism, and market socialism), colonial heritages (British, Japanese, and American), boundary disputes (between China and the Philippines, and between South Korea and Japan), and security tensions (Chinese military exercise in the Taiwan Strait, and North Korean military alert along the South Korea border). There are always institutional attempts to divide Asian states into different trading blocs, such as the AFTA (ASEAN Free Trade Area) and the inaugural Asia–Europe Meeting (ASEM—the seven-member ASEAN plus China, Japan, and South Korea with fifteen-member European Union). Subsequently, although the prospect for Asianization is bright, it will not be an unproblematic expansion. Most likely, the Asian economies will be gradually integrated in the midst of conflict and rivalry among the Asian states.

How, then, will this Asianization project affect Hong Kong? Hong Kong is at the forefront of the Asianization of the Asian economy. Hong Kong corporations have invested in Singapore for more than a decade, and they are the major contributors of FDI in Thailand, Indonesia, and the Philippines. Subsequently, Hong Kong's economy will benefit if the ASEAN economies are on the rise and the Asianization process is continued at the turn of the twenty-first century.

In this respect, the contribution to Hong Kong studies of adopting a regional perspective is that it shows Hong Kong's development is shaped not just by its linkages with mainland China but is also influenced by other Asian regional dynamics initiated by the United States, Japan, the NIEs, and the ASEAN states. Although the 1997 transition and the Chinese national reunification project may be the most crucial factor in the determination of Hong Kong's development, this Chinese project overall is embedded in the context of the Asian region and is mediated through other regional dynamics. For example, as significant as the resumption of Hong Kong's sovereignty by the Beijing government in 1997, and as problematic as Hong Kong's democratization in the 1990s,[72] these political processes happened side by side and interacted with other regional dynamics such as industrial upgrading, economic diversification, the Asianization of Asian economies, and the military tension in the Taiwan Strait.

Unfortunately, the Asianization project and the Chinese project had a contradictory effect on the nature of the Hong Kong state. On the one hand, the Chinese national reunification project will weaken the Hong Kong state after 1997. Transforming into a local government under close Beijing supervision, unable to satisfy the middle class's demands for democracy, and incapable of solving the working class's quest for full employment, the Hong Kong state will have less autonomy, legitimacy, and capacity in the post-1997 administration than before. On the other hand, the Asianization project calls for a strong Hong Kong state that promotes technological upgrading, stimulates local economy, and bargains with other Asian states. Asianization will enhance the capacity and legitimacy of the Hong Kong state by making it less dependent on the mainland Chinese economy, enriching its economic resources through ASEAN investment and trade, and upgrading its status in the interstate system. As such, it will be interesting to see whether the possible bright prospect of the Asianization project can strengthen the Hong Kong state so much that it may provide the needed cushion effect to carry Hong Kong through the political drama of the 1997 transition.

Notes

1. See Alvin Y. So and Stephen W.K. Chiu, *East Asia and the World-Economy* (Newbury Park, CA: Sage, 1995).

2. For example, see Gilbert Rozman, "The Confucian Faces of Capitalism," in Mark Borthwick, ed., *Pacific Century* (Boulder, CO: Westview Press, 1992), pp. 310–318.

3. Bela Balassa, "The Lessons of East Asian Development: An Overview," *Economic Development and Cultural Change* 36, 3rd supplement (1988), S273–S290.

4. See Alice Amsden, *Asia's Next Giant: South Korea and Late Industrialization* (New York: Oxford University Press, 1989).

5. Reginald Y.W. Kwok and Alvin Y. So, eds., *The Hong Kong–Guangdong Link: Partnership in Flux* (Armonk, NY: M.E. Sharpe, and Hong Kong: Hong Kong University Press, 1995).

6. Sung Yun-wing, *The China–Hong Kong Connection* (Cambridge: Cambridge University Press, 1992).

7. Michael Hsing-Huang Hsiao and Alvin Y. So, "Accent Through National Integration: The Chinese Triangle of Mainland–Taiwan–Hong Kong," in Ravi A. Palat, ed., *Asia-Pacific and the Future of World-System* (Westport, CT: Greenwood, 1993), pp. 133–147.

8. Alvin Y. So and Stephen W.K. Chiu, "Modern East Asia in World-Systems Analysis," *Sociological Enquiry* 66 (1996), pp. 471–485.

9. Bruce Cumings, "The Origins and Development of the Northeast Asian Political Economy: Industrial Sectors, Product Cycles, and Political Consequences," in Frederic Deyo, ed., *The Political Economy of the New Asian Industrialism* (Ithaca, NY: Cornell University Press, 1987), p. 47.

10. See Stephen W.K. Chiu, C.K. Ho, and Lui Tai-lok, *Economic Restructuring in Hong Kong and Singapore* (Boulder: Westview Press, 1996); Alvin Y. So and Stephen W.K. Chiu, "The Hong Kong Mode of Development: An Exception to the NIEs?" Paper

presented to the Annual Meeting of the American Sociological Association, New York, August 1996.

11. Mark Selden, "China, Japan, and the Regional Political Economy of East Asia, 1945–1995," paper presented to the Japan in Asia Workshop, Cornell University, March 31–April 2, 1995.

12. Quoted in Jon Halliday, *A Political History of Japanese Capitalism* (New York: Pantheon Books, 1975), pp. 187–188.

13. See Wong Siu-lun, *Emigrant Entrepreneurs* (Hong Kong: Oxford University Press, 1988).

14. Alvin Y. So, "The Economic Success of Hong Kong: Insights from a World-System Perspective," *Sociological Perspectives* 29 (1986), pp. 241–258; Alvin Y. So and Stephen W.K. Chiu, "The Hong Kong Mode of Development: An Exception to the NIEs?"

15. Carter J. Eckert, "Korea's Economic Development in Historical Perspective, 1945–1990," in Mark Borthwick, ed., *Pacific Century,* pp. 289–308.

16. Stephen W.K. Chiu, "The Changing World Order and the East Asian Newly Industrializing Countries," in David Jacobson, ed., *Old Nations, New World* (Boulder, CO: Westview Press, 1994), pp. 75–114.

17. Lin Ching-yuan, *Industrialization in Taiwan, 1946–72* (New York: Praeger, 1973), p. 83.

18. Thomas B. Gold, *State and Society in the Taiwan Miracle* (Armonk, NY: M.E. Sharpe, 1986); Hagen Koo, "Strong State and Contentious Society," in Hagen Koo, ed., *State and Society in Contemporary Korea* (Ithaca, NY: Cornell University Press, 1993), pp. 231–249.

19. Gary Gereffi, "New Realities of Industrial Development in East Asia and Latin America: Global, Regional, and National Trends," in Richard Appelbaum and Jeffrey Henderson, eds., *State and Development in the Asian-Pacific Rim* (Newbury Park, CA: Sage, 1992), pp. 85–112.

20. Walden Bello and Stephanie Rosenfeld, "Dragons in Distress: The Crisis of the NICs," *World Policy Journal* 7 (1990), pp. 431–468; Andre Gunder Frank, "Asia's Exclusive Models," *Far Eastern Economic Review,* June 25, 1982, pp. 22–23.

21. Mark Selden, "China, Japan, and the Regional Political Economy of East Asia."

22. Giovanni Arrighi, "The Rise of East Asia: World-System and Regional Aspects," paper prepared for the conference "L'economia mondiale in transformazione," Rome, October 6–8, 1994, p. 15.

23. Charles Oman, *New Forms of Investment in Developing Countries* (Paris: OECD, 1989).

24. Richard Child Hill and Yong Joo Lee, "Japanese Multinationals and East Asian Development," in Leslie Sklair, ed., *Capitalism and Development* (London: Routledge, 1994), pp. 289–315.

25. Kuniko Fujita and Richard Child Hill, "Global Toyotaism and Local Development," *International Journal of Urban and Regional Research* 19 (1995), pp. 1–22.

26. Stephen Bunker and Denis O'Hearn, "Strategies of Economic Ascendants for Access to Raw Materials: A Comparison of the United States and Japan," in Ravi A. Palat, ed., *Pacific-Asia and the Future of the World-System,* pp. 83–102.

27. Richard Child Hill and Yong Joo Lee, "Japanese Multinationals and East Asian Development."

28. Ibid.

29. Thomas Andersson, "The Role of Japanese Foreign Direct Investment," in Lars Oxelheim, ed., *The Global Race for Foreign Direct Investment* (Berlin: Springer-Verlag, 1993), pp. 205–231.

30. Giovanni Arrighi, Satoshi Ikeda, and Alex Irwan, "The Rise of East Asia: One Miracle or Many?" in Ravi A. Palat, ed., *Pacific-Asia and the Future of the World-System,* pp. 41–65.

31. Bruce Cumings, "The Origins and Development of the Northeast Asian Political Economy: Industrial Sectors, Product Cycles, and Political Consequences," pp. 44–83.

32. Gary Gereffi, "New Realities of Industrial Development in East Asia and Latin America: Global, Regional, and National Trends," in Richard Appelbaum and Jeffrey Henderson, eds., *State and Development in the Asian-Pacific Rim* (Newbury Park, CA: Sage, 1992), pp. 85–112.

33. Richard Child Hill and Yong Joo Lee, "Japanese Multinationals and East Asian Development."

34. Johnathan Friedland, "The Regional Challenge," *Far Eastern Economic Review,* June 9, 1994, p. 42.

35. Richard Child Hill and Yong Joo Lee, "Japanese Multinationals and East Asian Development."

36. Dennis F. Simon, "The Economic Activities of Western Nations in Mainland China," paper presented to the conference on Trade and Investment in the Mainland, Taipei, June 23–24, 1990.

37. See D. Yang, "China Adjusts to the World Economy: The Political Economy of China's Coastal Development Strategy," *Pacific Affairs* 64 (1991), pp. 42–64.

38. Andrew Nathan, *China's Crisis* (New York: Columbia University Press, 1990).

39. Alvin Y. So, "Political Determinants of Direct Investment in Mainland China," in Sumner La Croix, Michael Plummer, and Keun Lee, eds., *Emerging Patterns of East Asian Investment in China* (Armonk, NY: M.E. Sharpe, 1995), pp. 95–112.

40. Victor F.S. Sit, "Industrial Out-Processing—Hong Kong's New Relationship with the Pearl River Delta," *Asian Profile* 17 (1989), pp. 1–13.

41. Maruya Toyojiro, "Economic Relations Between Hong Kong and Guangdong Province," in T. Maruya, ed., *Guangdong* (Hong Kong: Centre of Asian Studies, the University of Hong Kong, 1992), pp. 126–147.

42. Sung Yun-wing, "The Role of Hong Kong and Macau in China's Export Drive," working paper No. 85/11. (Australian National University: National Center for Development Studies, 1985), p. iii.

43. Sung Yun-wing, *The China–Hong Kong Connection* (Cambridge: Cambridge University Press, 1992), p. 25.

44. *Far Eastern Economic Review,* September 19, 1992, p. 12.

45. Michael Hsing-Huang Hsiao and Alvin Y. So, "Taiwan–Mainland Economic Nexus: Socio-Political Origins, State-Society Impacts, and Future Prospects," *Bulletin of Concerned Asian Scholars* 28, no. 1 (1996), pp. 3–12.

46. Victor F.S. Sit, "Industrial Outprocessing."

47. See Stephen W.K. Chiu, On-Kwok Lai and Ching-Kwan Lee, *A Study of the Impact of Industrial Restructuring on Women Workers* (Hong Kong: Federation of Women, 1996), unpublished; Tai-Lok Lui and Wong Hung, *Disempowerment and Empowerment: An Exploratory Study on Low-Income Households in Hong Kong* (Hong Kong: Oxfam Hong Kong, 1995).

48. Chan Kam-wing, "Post-Mao China: A Two Class Urban Society in the Making," *International Journal of Urban and Regional Research* 20 (1996), 20(1), pp. 134–150.

49. Sung Yun-wing, "Economic Integration of Hong Kong and Guangdong in the 1990s," in Reginald Kwok and Alvin Y. So, eds., *Hong Kong–Guangdong Link,* pp. 224–250.

50. Xu Xueqiang, Reginald Kwok, Lixun Li, and Xiaopei Yan, "Production Change in Guangdong," in Reginald Kwok and Alvin Y. So, eds., *Hong Kong–Guangdong Link,* pp. 135–162.

51. X.M. Wang, "Guangdong: Economic Growth and Structural Changes in the 1980s," in Maruya Toyojiro, ed., pp. 18–48.

52. Henry W.C. Yeung, "The Geography of Hong Kong Transnational Corporations in the ASEAN Region," *Area* 27 (1995), pp. 318–334.

53. Min Tang and Myo That, *Growth Triangles: Conceptual Issues and Operational Problems.* Economic Staff Paper No. 54, Asian Development Bank, Manila, 1994.

54. K.C. Ho and Alvin Y. So, "Semi-Periphery and Borderland Integration: Singapore and Hong Kong Experiences," *Political Geography* 16 (1997), pp. 241–259.

55. *ASEAN Digest,* December 95/January 96, p. 6.

56. Henry W.C. Yeung, "The Geography of Hong Kong Transnational Corporations in the ASEAN Region,", p. 321.

57. World Bank, *The East Asian Miracle* (Oxford: Oxford University Press, 1993), pp. 52–54.

58. Mohamed Ariff, "The Prospects for an ASEAN Free Trade Area," *The World Economy* 17 (1995), p. 54.

59. K. Kozul-Wright, "Transnational Corporations and the Nation State," in J. Michie and J.G. Smith, eds., *Managing the Global Economy* (Oxford: Oxford University Press, 1995), p. 144.

60. Terutomo Ozawa, "Foreign Direct Investment and Structural Transformation: Japan as a Recycler of Market and Industry," *Business and the Contemporary World* 5 (1993), pp. 129–130.

61. Mitchell Bernard and John Ravenhill, "Beyond Product Cycles and Flying Geese: Regionalization, Hierarchy, and the Industrialization of East Asia," *World Politics* 47 (1995), 171–209.

62. See Ronald Skeldon, ed., *Reluctant Exiles* (Armonk, NY: M.E. Sharpe, and Hong Kong: Hong Kong University Press, 1994); Ronald Skeldon, "Immigration and Population Issues" in Stephen Y.L. Cheung and Stephen M.H. Sze, eds., *The Other Hong Kong Report 1995* (Hong Kong: Chinese University of Hong Kong Press, 1995).

63. See Terutomo Ozawa, "Foreign Direct Investment and Structural Transformation: Japan as a Recycler of Market and Industry"; Johnathan Friedland, "The Regional Challenge," *Far Eastern Economic Review,* June 9, 1994, pp. 40–42.

64. Mark Selden, "China, Japan, and the Regional Political Economy of East Asia, 1945–1995," paper presented to the Japan in Asia Workshop, Cornell University, March 31–April 2, 1995. pp. 8–9.

65. Stephen W.K. Chiu and Alvin Y. So, "Will Japan Become the Next Hegemon in the World Economy?" *Contemporary Development Analysis* 1 (1996), pp. 27–51.

66. *The Washington Post,* June 29, 1992, p. A1.

67. George E. Ogle, *South Korea: Dissent Within the Economic Miracle* (London: Zed Books, 1990), p. 37.

68. Mohamed Ariff, "The Role of APEC: An Asian Perspective," *Journal of Japanese Trade and Industry* 13 (1994), pp. 46–49.

69. *The Australian,* September 19, 1994, p. 2.

70. *ASEAN Digest,* January/February 1994, p. 13.

71. Ibid., April/May 1995, pp. 5–6.

72. See Alvin Y. So, "New Middle Class Politics in Hong Kong: 1997 and Democratization," *Asiatische Studien Etudes Asiatiques* (Swiss Asian Studies) 49 (1995), pp. 91–109; Sum Ngai-Ling, "More than a 'War of Words': Identity, Politics and the Struggles for Dominance During the Recent 'Political Reform' Period in Hong Kong," *Economy and Society* 24 (1995), pp. 67–100.

5

Links to and Through South China: Local, Regional, and Global Connections

Graham E. Johnson

Hong Kong's relationships to both China and the global economy have changed since the end of the Pacific war and the establishment of the People's Republic of China, lending a distinctive international character to Hong Kong. The establishment of the People's Republic of China was simultaneous with the beginnings of adjustment in the form of the global economy. These were major factors in the structural transformation of the Hong Kong economy, which were to be important for significant social changes in a British colony that was to survive the "winds of change" and the end of empire.

Hong Kong's relationship to China shifted as the People's Republic of China struggled to create new political and economic forms over the course of its first three decades. The intimate relationship with Guangdong Province and its Pearl River Delta hinterland, so central to the economic and social character of Hong Kong in the century after the British assumption of political control,[1] was compromised as a Soviet-driven developmental model became dominant in China and marginalized Guangdong Province. A dynamic manufacturing economy with a major international presence was fashioned beginning in the 1950s as a response to shifts in the global economy; the movement of capital, entrepreneurial skill, and labor power to Hong Kong from China as the result of political change; and a redefinition of the economic relationships between China, Hong Kong, and China's role in the world economy.

By both accident and design, a Hong Kong identity was created in the 1970s. It was built upon the vibrant manufacturing economy that was created in the

1950s and the 1960s, an important feature of which was that it constantly recast itself. The newly fashioned Hong Kong identity became apparent as major policy changes in China began shortly after the death of Mao Zedong in 1976. The mechanisms of economic control, modeled on Soviet practices, were dramatically altered.[2] The decentralization of authority to the provinces and away from the central state, efforts to incorporate market principles, a cautious opening to the forces of the global economy, and the search for innovative principles of economic organization were all part of the extensive reform of a system that had been in place for more than a quarter-century. Those measures, yet again, began to redefine the economy of Hong Kong, and had major political, social, and cultural consequences.

The shifts in China's relationship to the world were increasingly channeled through Hong Kong and gave to Hong Kong and the practitioners of Hong Kong's economic success a major opportunity to influence the direction of economic change in the Guangdong hinterland and beyond. China, especially Southern China, became increasingly integrated into the global economy. Hong Kong was the major point of access for China to the global economic system. Policy reform gave rise to dramatic, if uneven, development in China, especially in the southern coastal regions. It also brought enormous economic opportunities to Hong Kong in the 1980s that have continued into the 1990s. It created a political—and cultural—challenge, as China sought to restore its sovereignty over Hong Kong and erase, at last, one of the most potent symbols of the indignities that were suffered from the end of the first Opium War and the subsequent humiliations that followed the first "unequal treaty," which saw Hong Kong ceded "in perpetuity" to the British crown.

Hong Kong's relationships to the world and to China have always been central issues in the nature of Hong Kong's economic and political character as well as its social and cultural possibilities. It was China trade, and a dispute as to how British merchants should conduct it, which led to Hong Kong's foundation as a British colony in 1841, and which provided its raison d'être in the century that followed. It was the inward direction that Chinese policy assumed in the three decades after 1949 that cut Hong Kong adrift from a dependence on the entrepôt trade and fostered a new set of relationships in a changing global economy, having wide-ranging social consequences for Hong Kong itself. It has been the China factor, along with continued structural shifts in the global economy, that has further defined the character of Hong Kong since the late 1970s.

This chapter addresses some of the changes in Hong Kong's domestic characteristics over the past forty years and how they have been brought about by Hong Kong's links with the world as a whole. It also addresses the nature of change in Hong Kong in the recent past partly in terms of its relationship with China. Since the 1970s, Hong Kong has experienced major social shifts. Since 1979, as Hong Kong has assumed a new role in China's economic future, its social and cultural impact on China, and especially on its immediate hinterland, has been considerable. Since the signing in 1984 of the Sino-British Joint Agreement on the Future of Hong Kong between Britain and China, and the efforts to deal with the transition to Chinese sovereignty, politics within Hong Kong has changed.[3] All these changes have contributed to a new complexion for Hong Kong since the early 1980s. Its distinctive international character, built on its own variant of "Chineseness," has not merely had consequences for the increasingly affluent residents of Hong Kong, but has also had a major impact on the region of China immediately proximate to the territory, especially in the Pearl River Delta region, which has undergone major transformation.

Reactions to the political events in China in the spring of 1989 were one measure of the internal changes within Hong Kong. The events of June 4, 1989, were traumatic and produced an unprecedented reaction on the part of a substantial segment of the Hong Kong population. They also resulted in short-term pessimism and dismay. Continued involvement in the burgeoning economy of China, and particularly Guangdong Province, however, quickly dispelled some of the gloom. Despite feelings of uncertainty and ambivalence, which remain a source of concern, there is nonetheless a buoyancy that derives from a sense of satisfaction and accomplishment in the place that Hong Kong has become. There is a broad perception that the influence of Hong Kong extends beyond its formal administrative boundaries to China and to the world in which it has assumed a major presence. This has allowed residents of the territory to look forward with some confidence to an enhanced *regional* status after 1997. It derives in part from a sense of an augmented international presence.

I will outline some of the features that have made Hong Kong distinctive in a global and international setting over the past twenty-five years. I will further draw attention to the role that Hong Kong has come to play in the transformation of South China and Guangdong Province in particular. Hong Kong's fractured links with its hinterland in the period before 1979 had a pronounced effect on its own economic performance in a global context. The links to China have changed significantly since China's period of economic reform began in 1979. This has had internal consequences and may affect the future of the territory.

Hong Kong's economic interests have been a major element in the transformation of its Pearl River Delta hinterland. Hong Kong connections have been intense in all parts of the Pearl River Delta region, and have extended significantly beyond the physical bounds of the delta. There has been major structural change as local production systems in some parts of the Pearl River Delta have become incorporated into the global economy. Entrepreneurial activities with Hong Kong partners were a key to economic transformation, especially in the early phases, and have continued into the 1990s.[4]

Yet it would be erroneous to imagine that the entire Pearl River Delta represents a unitary phenomenon. There are different emphases in the experience of economic and social development strategy within the hinterland. In the eastern delta region, an intense relationship with economic interests from Hong Kong,

Taiwan, and elsewhere has most firmly linked the area to global forces. In the central delta area, historically the most commercialized and wealthiest region of the entire Pearl River Delta, partnerships with entrepreneurs from Hong Kong and elsewhere were, and are, only one aspect of the process of economic transformation. In the western delta region, the major links are with overseas Chinese (*huaqiao*), rather than with Hong Kong and Taiwanese "compatriots" (*tongbao*). The impact of these connections, which are typically channeled through Hong Kong, is substantial, especially for the social infrastructure. They are, however, qualitatively different and have not resulted in the fundamental economic restructuring that has characterized the eastern and central delta regions.

Hong Kong can be seen in terms of the administrative boundaries that the territory has possessed since 1898, which will form the Special Administrative Region after 1997. Hong Kong can also be viewed as a much wider entity that extends well beyond its formal administrative bounds. Its economic activity is no longer contained by borders dating from the colonial period. Its cultural impact is wider and more powerful than it was earlier in its history. A regional structure of great strength has been created by forces that are a consequence of newly fashioned links to China, built on transformed links to the world.

From Entrepôt to Entrepreneur: Some Consequences of Economic Transformation

The expansion of European capitalism into East Asia in the mid-nineteenth century forcibly opened China to the full force of economic processes. China reluctantly became a part of the "world system," and Hong Kong played a role in Chinese economic history in the century that followed, along with a set of "Treaty Ports" that were created in the wake of the Anglo-Chinese conflict that ceded Hong Kong "in perpetuity" to the British.[5]

In 1945, when the Japanese occupation ended, Hong Kong's role in the world economy was poised to undergo a major transformation. The immediate consequence of civil war in China in the late 1940s, and the formation of the People's Republic of China in 1949, was the flight of capital and entrepreneurial skill to Hong Kong. There was also a massive in-migration of people from throughout China to Hong Kong, especially from its Pearl River Delta hinterland. Chinese capital and entrepreneurial skill and ample supplies of cheap and hard-working labor contributed to the economic system that emerged in the 1950s and the 1960s.

From the early 1950s, China, by contrast, moved in a distinctive "socialist" direction and became significantly insulated from the global economy for the succeeding thirty years.[6] Hong Kong's economic relationship to China changed. Ezra Vogel has suggested that Hong Kong "lost" its hinterland in 1950 in the wake of the formation of the People's Republic of China.[7] The entrepôt trade with China, which had been Hong Kong's raison d'être from its beginnings as

British colony, was compromised by China's domestic policies and by American foreign policy dictates after 1950.

In the years immediately following the formation of the People's Republic of China, despite the economic difficulties that cessation of the China trade created, an efficient and prosperous manufacturing economy was formed that assumed an increasingly important role in a global economy, itself undergoing a major restructuring. Its developmental path was later paralleled by those of Taiwan, South Korea, and Singapore (the Asian "NIEs") and was marked by rapid economic growth.[8] By 1980, Hong Kong had a per capita GNP on par with some southern European economies and was second only to Japan in Asia (with the exception of oil-rich Brunei).

Hong Kong's development performance from the 1950s on was based on manufacturing. It began with textiles—a consequence of the relocation of Shanghai interests in the late 1940s.[9] That performance was assisted by domestic policies of the Hong Kong government, the most strategic of which was the system of subsidized public housing, which had major consequences for wage rates and allowed Hong Kong to become competitive in the global economy. The interventionist role of the Hong Kong government in creating the social infrastructure that assisted the efforts of Hong Kong entrepreneurs to respond creatively to a rapidly changing global economy has often been overlooked in accounting for the economic success of "Adam Smith's other island."[10]

Up to the mid-1960s, textiles were dominant both in terms of industrial employment and as the major commodity for Hong Kong's domestic export performance. There was a gradual shift from textiles to garments and clothing accessories beginning in the mid-1960s, and by the mid-1980s Hong Kong was one of the major global producers of fashionable clothing. Other technological possibilities were rapidly incorporated. Plastics made their appearance in the late 1960s, and in the late 1970s electronics products (including digital clocks and watches) were added to a very substantial electrical goods industry.

Manufacturing is still one of the largest components of GDP and employment. Its share, however, has been declining since the early 1970s. It comprised fully 40 percent of GDP in 1965, declined to 31 percent in 1971, was a little over 20 percent throughout the 1980s, and by 1994 was less that 12 percent. Its share of the labor force had declined to 26 percent in 1991[11] and has been declining by an average of 14 percent annually since then. It was less than 19 percent in 1994. In 1984, the manufacturing sector employed 898,947. By 1994, this figure had declined by more than 50 percent to 423,015.[12]

Hong Kong's economy has changed, both as a consequence of global forces and, since 1979, changing economic relations with an outward-looking China. Hong Kong has become increasingly integrated with parts of its rapidly changing Pearl River Delta hinterland, which has become an important location for much of the industrial capacity that was central to Hong Kong's own economic history from the 1950s up until the late 1970s.

Hong Kong became a major financial center in the 1970s. This was in part due to changes in the nature of the global economy, which saw the production of key manufactured goods shift away from Europe and North America to East and Southeast Asia. The tertiary sector in Hong Kong had assumed major proportions as early as 1970. Transport, storage and communications, finance, insurance, real estate and business services and the growing tourist industry became increasingly important in the 1970s, and total employment in these areas grew from about 40 percent in 1970 to almost 50 percent in 1980. With reform in China, these sectors continued to expand and their employment share was 72 percent in 1994. Over 60 percent of Hong Kong's GDP derived from finance and banking, trade, and transport service in 1994.[13]

Trade has always been a key component for Hong Kong, but until the late 1970s the entrepôt trade with China was minuscule. After 1950, China remained an important source of Hong Kong's imports, but Hong Kong's domestic exporters sought other markets and forged an international economic presence. Hong Kong's trade performance was good throughout the 1970s. The entrepôt trade continued to be of only modest proportions until the late 1970s. After 1980, with China's "open-door" reform policies having a major impact in Southern China, the entrepôt trade was reborn. The volume of Hong Kong's trade increased dramatically in the 1980s as the composition of Hong Kong's trading partners also changed. China became Hong Kong's largest trading partner but, equally, Hong Kong became China's largest trading partner.[14] China's domestic export trade grew dramatically to reach U.S.$120.95 billion in 1994, of which 24 percent was conducted with Hong Kong.[15]

The dramatic growth rates that the Hong Kong economy began to enjoy in the 1980s were due to a renewed relationship with China, especially its Guangdong hinterland. Hong Kong's GNP had experienced steady growth through the 1960s and into the 1970s. It was U.S.$750 million in 1960 and grew from U.S.$2.5 billion in 1965 to U.S.$11.74 billion in 1977. It reached U.S.$38.56 billion in 1986, U.S.$63.99 billion in 1989, and U.S.$132.30 billion in 1994. Per capita GDP increased from U.S.$6,971 in 1986 to U.S.$21,827 in 1994.[16] As one consequence, substantial investible funds have been generated. Hong Kong entrepreneurs have become global in their activities and, like other entrepreneurs in East Asia, have begun to have an impact on economies where they hitherto had little involvement.

Hong Kong entrepreneurs are, however, culturally most comfortable in China and most familiar with their largely Cantonese-speaking hinterland in the Pearl River Delta region. While the internal character of Hong Kong's economy changed, Hong Kong entrepreneurs did not relinquish control over profitable production lines whose output was in great demand in the affluent societies of the First World. During the 1980s, the conditions of production changed for Hong Kong, and high wage rates compromised Hong Kong's ability to efficiently produce commodities that demanded large amounts of labor. Plastics and textiles diminished in importance for the Hong Kong economy and labor force. Hong Kong entrepreneurs increasingly shifted certain product lines out of Hong Kong. Some went to Malaysia, Thailand, and other parts of Southeast Asia, a few to Africa, but most went to China. Some were relocated to the new Shenzhen Special Economic Zone, which was built in Hong Kong's image and resembles the new towns of the Hong Kong New Territories, although it is much bigger than any of them.[17] Most, however, went beyond the zone to the Pearl River Delta itself. Hong Kong entrepreneurs became central to the economic well-being of localities within its hinterland to which they were often connected by ties of kinship and sentiment.

Social, Political, and Cultural Change

Less precise to document than economic changes are the social, political, and cultural dimensions of change. These are clearly related to the substantial economic performance over the period since the late 1960s. Government intervention, especially through housing policies, was clearly crucial for economic performance. Low levels of taxation and the implicit subsidization of wage rates contributed to Hong Kong's burgeoning prosperity. Government revenue was nonetheless substantial and grew along with the economy. It stood at HK$1.8 billion in 1967 and had reached HK$175 billion in 1994. Public expenditure grew in a similar fashion. The government commits proportionally more to health, education and social welfare than it did in 1967, although social welfare expenditures still represent only a relatively modest commitment on the part of government.[18] Such expenditures are destined to increase through 1997.[19] The government has always committed substantial sums to physical infrastructure, although some major infrastructural projects have been completed by the private sector. It is the increased *volume* of public expenditures that has had dramatic effect.

Housing is an obvious example of government intervention with welfare consequences. Both the stock and the quality of public housing have improved. Older first- and second-generation housing projects have been torn down and replaced by larger and less utilitarian structures than those that first appeared in the 1950s and early 1960s.[20]

New housing has gone hand in hand with infrastructural improvement. One major program that began in earnest in the early 1970s was new town development. It has had a major role not only in redefining the character of the New Territories, but also in areas of Hong Kong that were once remote from the centers of commercial and industrial activity. The New Territories had begun to change in the 1950s, when the formerly rural areas of North Kowloon and Tsuen Wan became highly industrialized. There were extensive areas under cultivation, both in rice and vegetables, until the early 1970s, when the old market towns of Tuen Mun, Yuen Long, Sha Tin, Tai Po, Fanling, and Sheung Shui became centers for development, following a British planning model. There has therefore been a major dispersion of population and significant reductions of density in the older centers of population concentration.[21] The formerly rural areas of the New Territories have undergone significant urbanization, and the agricultural way of life, which was still clearly discernible a quarter-century ago, has disappeared.

Expansion of the market towns occurred in a context in which Hong Kong was still largely a manufacturing economy, and China was insulated from the global economy. During the 1980s, Hong Kong's industrial character was transformed as much of its industrial capacity moved north across the China border. The logic of new town development has therefore been compromised as Hong Kong entrepreneurs have assumed a greater international role, and have shifted their investments to China and elsewhere. Urban planning decisions went hand in hand with major infrastructural investment, especially in transportation.[22] Until 1969, a single road ran around the New Territories. The journey from Tsuen Wan, on the south shore of the New Territories, to Shau Kei Wan, at the eastern end of Hong Kong island, was a monumental operation that required the better part of a frustrating day to make the round trip. It can now be completed in forty minutes. It is possible to commute from Sai Kung or outlying islands to Central District. In the 1960s, such undertakings involved uncomfortable (and sometimes terrifying) journeys in battered buses and picturesque but painfully slow ferry rides. In the 1990s, transportation has become speedy, cheap, efficient, and, while crowded, reasonably comfortable. An effective subway system and an upgraded railway move large numbers of commuters speedily and efficiently. Bus routes have increased in number, and many buses are air-conditioned. They are supplemented by an array of privately owned minibuses that ply well-defined routes. Taxis are omnipresent and exist in Yuen Long, Tai Po and Tsuen Wan, where they were to be only rarely found a quarter-century ago. Hong Kong is thus an easier place to move around than it once was.

Perhaps the most dramatic infrastructural project is that focused on a new airport development. The issue of a new airport to replace Kai Tak, which has been in operation since the 1920s, has been the subject of numerous reports over the years. Kai Tak's capacity is limited, given the increases in air traffic during the 1980s and into the 1990s. The decision to build a new airport at Chek Lap Kok, on Lantao Island (Dai Yu Shan), can be seen as one boost to confidence in the months after the trauma of June 4, 1989. It is an enormously expensive undertaking, and has resulted in some spectacular disagreements with the government of China, which has strongly questioned the commitment of such a large sum on the eve of retrocession. The project involves the construction of an airport and the associated facilities, such as mass transit, roads, and bridges, to move people and freight to and from the new airport. It is also the outgrowth of a strategy for the comprehensive development of port facilities, and road connections—the so-called Port and Airport Development Strategy (PADS)—which was presented in 1988. The strategy argues for a comprehensive approach to all forms of transportation, including the movement of goods and people within Hong Kong, across the border into China, and to the world as a whole.[23] There is a strong sense that Hong Kong is both a global city with massive international connections (to China and the world) and the dominant transportation hub in the South China region. The PADS strategy is centered upon a perception of Hong Kong's role in the region, and in the international system.[24] It has resulted in major infrastructural work, which will be fully complete only after China assumes sovereignty over Hong Kong.

Cultural Identity

The improvement in Hong Kong's physical space is a reflection of its increasing affluence. Many of its former "Third World" characteristics have largely disappeared from public view, and the population as a whole has shared in the benefits of wealth creation. With this has come a sense of Hong Kong cultural identity that was not apparent until the 1970s.[25]

In the late 1960s, Hong Kong experienced a major economic transformation and its population had begun to enjoy some of the benefits of an improved standard of living. The majority of the population was still predominantly China-born.[26] By 1991, almost 60 percent of the population was Hong Kong–born and the China-born proportion stood at 35 percent.[27] This demographic shift is important. In the late 1960s, the population was predominantly a migrant population. The trauma of relocation from China to Hong Kong in the late 1940s and 1950s was a central theme for much of the adult population.[28] Hong Kong was a refuge and place to remake lives disrupted by revolution and political change. It was not a place to which the bulk of the adult population was linked by close emotional bonds. Their sentiments were likely still attached to homeland locations, however compromised by the social and political changes of the 1950s and 1960s. The links had become fractured and were charged with ambivalence. There were limited opportunities to return to ancestral places of origin, and a reluctance on the part of many to return to scenes of flight. The older generation was often silent as to the reasons for out-migration, and critical cultural knowledge about ancestral localities was not always transmitted. The links with the ancestral homeland were re-established in the 1980s. For the younger generation, however, the emotional impact was blunted by the unwillingness of senior generations to be fully open about the past.

The younger generation, which came to maturity in the 1970s and 1980s, did not carry the emotional baggage of their elders. A sense of Hong Kong identity was established by the young Hong Kong–born population, which saw a growing cultural gulf between the experience of growing up in an affluent and largely apolitical Hong Kong, with its increasing links to the international system, and the China alternative.

There seems little doubt that China, particularly Guangdong Province, had exerted a dominant cultural influence over Hong Kong for the great bulk of

Hong Kong's history. That cultural dominance receded after the establishment of the People's Republic of China. This was in part a consequence of the tight central control that was maintained over all of China's provinces after 1949. This control was especially marked when it came to the complicated provinces of the coastal southeast. Regional cultures were in general overwhelmed by an effort to create national cultural forms with a "socialist" character. The expression of Cantonese culture, cuisine aside, was compromised, as were the other local cultures of Guangdong. The hinterland was "lost" in terms of its economic significance in the first thirty years after 1949. Equally, its potency as a cultural influence was severely limited by national initiatives. Hong Kong was therefore able to create a distinctive version of local culture significantly independent of forces from China itself. This had a major effect on the younger generation in Hong Kong and contributed to the emergence of a sense of Hong Kong identity that the adult China-born population of Hong Kong could not fully share.

Hong Kong's creation of cultural forms that the younger generation began to absorb occurred in a context of major change in the technology of mass communications not the least of which was television. As Hong Kong became increasingly integrated into the global economy and began to share in some potent internationalized cultural forms, it became culturally disassociated from a China that, from the middle 1960s, adopted a "revolutionary" cultural form with little appeal to increasingly affluent Hong Kong youth. Despite the impact of Western popular music and other influences, Hong Kong was, like Taiwan, nonetheless still very much a Chinese cultural context. It began to experiment with popular cultural forms within the context of the Cantonese language. This had become the lingua franca of the Hong Kong population as regional versions of Chinese began to attenuate, particularly under the impact of the education system, film, and television. From a variety of sources, therefore, some global, some indigenous, some broadly Chinese, Hong Kong began to create a distinctive identity.

The politics of China created a strident expressive culture, especially after 1966, that meant little to the Hong Kong–born generation that was barely attached to the political rhetoric of China itself. The attenuation of the economic links from the 1950s cut Hong Kong adrift, and the brashness of the economic structure that Hong Kong carved out was reflected in the cultural forms that were created.

It is important to distinguish cultural expressions at a variety of levels. Stephen Sze distinguishes among (a) elite cultural expressions, (b) those that "document" cultural life, and (c) "mass" culture, which is often driven by commercial interests.[29] All three have developed considerably over the past two decades and have affected the broader cultural life within Hong Kong. Their development has been closely related to affluence and has been driven by the overall values that have emerged within Hong Kong during the period since 1949.

Both the public and private sectors have been involved in the creation of distinctively Hong Kong cultural expressions. Government involvement has grown over time in a variety of ways. A quarter of a century ago, Hong Kong's city hall was virtually the only permanent venue for the performing arts, which were poorly represented and poorly funded. Facilities have expanded enormously since 1970. There is a facility dedicated for the performing arts, but the dispersion of the population has also seen the creation of space in new towns for performances of all kinds. Orthodox "high" culture (with a bias towards Western cultural forms) is vigorous and, as Sze suggests, "practically free from financial troubles."[30] Government-subsidized spaces are also increasingly important for the Chinese and non-Western performing arts. Cantonese opera and other Chinese regional art forms have most recently experienced a revival, in part due to the availability of public performance space.[31]

A recent development of great significance is the marked expansion of a substantial variety of museums. There are now some spectacular museum complexes (such as the Museum of Art, the Science Museum, and the Space Museum), and lesser ones such as the Sam Tung Uk Museum in Tsuen Wan, housed in one of the old Hakka compound villages, and the Museum of Transportation, housed in the old Tai Po Market railway station.

The performing arts and museums require enormous resources from government, although the private sector is also involved. These expenditures are part of a statement about the cultural character of the place that Hong Kong has become. The year 1970 saw the conversion of a former barracks in the tourist area of Kowloon into Kowloon Park, which is also the site of the Museum of History. It was the beginning of a process that has seen large tracts of land set aside for public use. Many of the outlying areas of the territory have been designated as "country parks," which are fully utilized on weekends and public holidays. Clearly, one of the issues that prompts such expenditures is the problem of leisure, a corollary of affluence. There are, however, implications for an emerging Hong Kong cultural identity.

The development of orthodox high culture reflects a process of embourgeoisement of the Hong Kong population, or a segment of it. Museums, and to a lesser degree country parks, attempt to create a sense of heritage preservation. Hong Kong was created to meet commercial needs. A sense of historical heritage has been largely lacking in Hong Kong. The commercial drive that it has exhibited over time has overwhelmed its sense of the past. Little of Hong Kong's architectural past remains, and the formerly rural New Territories have become thoroughly urban in form. The educational system, driven by colonial interests and conscious of the problematic nature of historical interpretation, has tended to de-emphasize history in the school curriculum. Somewhat late in the day, an effort has been made to create an account of the past. The population has responded with an increased sense of identification with a territory that has created some distinctiveness and is different from what can be found north of the border. Indeed, in a headlong rush to wealth and prosperity, Hong Kong's northern neighbors are rapidly transforming the delta landscape and replicating some of the Hong Kong experience, often in partnership with Hong Kong entrepreneurs.

Mass Culture: McDonaldization

Government support of orthodox high culture generally benefits a minority. The majority of the population may benefit from access to government-supported parks and beaches. Government support of orthodox high culture generally benefits only a minority of the population, although a large segment may benefit from access to government-supported museums, parks, and beaches. The population as a whole is, however, subject to private sector as consumers of a distinctive form of mass culture with a particular set of values. In the first phase of Hong Kong's economic transformation, the largely immigrant population was most concerned with meeting the needs for food, shelter, and clothing. In the second phase, especially since the end of the 1970s, in which disposable income has grown at virtually all social levels, a different set of consumption values has come to predominate. Mass media of all kinds—electronic and print—foster the new values of consumption. There is a laissez-faire attitude toward the promotion of these values, with little resistance from the public sector. Television, which is omnipresent, has become a vehicle for advertising items of luxury consumption. Programming is dominated by soap operas, movies, and variety shows. Advertising is disproportionately for travel, real estate, entertainment equipment, watches, brandy, fashionable clothing, credit cards, and food. The other aspect of Hong Kong culture, therefore, is that of excessive consumption to a backdrop of Canto-pop. It is a version that is private sector–driven and reflects an aspect of Hong Kong that is highly visible and readily exported, both across the border to China and with recent migrants to such places as Canada.[32] It is an aspect of the culture that is often negatively evaluated but it is part of Hong Kong's identity in the contemporary period.

This aspect of Hong Kong culture is not, however, distinctive to Hong Kong. It can also be seen as a reflection of certain internationalized values driven by global transformation. The process has been termed by one critic of contemporary development as "the McDonaldization of Society," which he describes as "the process by which principles of the fast-food restaurant are coming to dominate more and more sectors of American society as well as the rest of the world."[33] The cultural issues in Hong Kong's overall transformation are not separate from broader global issues. They also relate to Hong Kong's immediate past, that is, the ties of its people, who are predominantly of Chinese origin, to the Chinese cultural complex. Stevan Harrell and Huang Chun-chieh have recently discussed the issues of cultural change in postwar Taiwan, which, like Hong Kong, has been on the periphery of the Chinese political and cultural system for some decades and has undergone a major economic transformation in a relatively short period of time. They argue that there are tensions along three axes—tradition/modernity, native/foreign, local/cosmopolitan—and that these tensions affect outcomes in situations where "culture is more autonomous than ever before but it is at the same time more uncertain."[34] It is a comment that is wholly appropriate for Hong Kong in the late twentieth century. Culture writ small (the prescriptions for everyday behavior) is the focus of the Harrell's comments about contemporary Taiwan. Change, as in Hong Kong, has brought wealth, the growth of an urban life-style, internationalization, and environmental decline. It has also brought leisure, heightened nostalgia, and the search for tranquil rural alternatives. These are found in the Ta-pao Valley, close to Taipei, in which, Harrell argues, an *invented* bucolic tradition—a rural theme park—appears as a diversion to traffic jams and American-style fast food.[35] Similar phenomena are to be found in Hong Kong and just across the Hong Kong border in Shenzhen, where Hong Kong people can find in an array of theme parks the minorities of China, the Eiffel Tower, the Great Wall of China, the Egyptian pyramids, and other attractions, conveniently packaged, relatively cheap, close at hand, and quickly and efficiently consumed—most appropriate for the fast-paced and time-constrained life of the citizens of the "global village," like the hamburger from a (Western-style) fast-food restaurant. That there is a perfectly fine fast-food tradition in Chinese cuisine is beside the point. The popular culture of contemporary Hong Kong (Taiwan, China, Japan, or Canada) is in part a reflection of a process of internationalization.[36]

Clearly, the kinds of tensions that Harrell and Huang suggest, crucial for an understanding of cultural identity in Taiwan, are not merely appropriate for the Hong Kong case but give rise to competing claims of identity, as Helen Siu has noted.[37] Hong Kong constitutes a distinct local variant of Chinese culture. Its distinctiveness reflects, in part, responses to the pressures of a world system. Hong Kong people have a sense that they are part of a larger Chinese cultural complex. As a consequence of an array of political events that extend to 1841, if not before, there is, however, a further sense of estrangement, even exclusion, from cultural processes within China itself. "Being Chinese" is a complex, even troublesome, problem.[38] As Myron Cohen remarks, ". . . being Chinese is culturally much easier today than it ever was in the past, for this identification no longer involves commonly accepted standards of behavior or belief. Existentially, however, being Chinese is far more problematic, for it is now as much a quest as it is a condition."[39] Siu echoes the comments of Cohen for Chinese in Hong Kong when she states, "Hong Kong as an historical space encompasses vastly different cultural affiliations, social, and political fortunes . . . Who the 'Hong Kong *an* [people]' are will remain ambiguous, as cultural identity is continuously remade by human agents who move across social, cultural, and political boundaries set by historical events quite beyond anyone's prediction."[40]

Political Culture

A recent, and contentious, aspect of Hong Kong's emerging cultural identity relates to political values and their expression in terms of political behavior. It is contentious because it is new and driven by a number of factors, one of the more significant of these being the changed system of administration that will become apparent after 1997. Political behavior, as with other forms of social behavior, has been conditioned by the changes of the past two decades.

Politics in Hong Kong, for much of its history, was constrained by the assumption of colonial policy. Government was colonial government and its expatriate members were dominant figures. Consultation processes occurred and selected members of the population were incorporated into the political process. The great majority of the population had no formal input into the work of government. Only in the New Territories, in the postwar period, was a system of "representative" consultation developed.[41] The agreement for the resumption of Chinese sovereignty over Hong Kong in 1997 set in motion a series of changes. Even before the Anglo-Chinese agreement, the Hong Kong government had recognized the importance of broadening the consultative base. During the 1980s the principle of directly electing representatives to sit on various bodies (e.g., district boards, the Regional Council, the Legislative Council) or indirectly electing them through "functional constituencies" was put into effect.[42]

Elections to the Legislative Council (Legco) were held in 1985, 1988, and 1995. They represent a process that reached a new beginning in September 1991, when 18 members were elected directly to Legco and a further 21 members were elected indirectly through functional constituencies. The significance of the 1991 elections was that, for the first time, a majority of the seats were no longer held by government appointees. Of equal significance is that political parties contested the elections, and those who won seats were, in the main, social activists either critical of government or who had taken a major role in Hong Kong's public protests of the heavy-handed role of the Chinese central government during the political protests in China during the spring of 1989. The 1995 election only furthered the beginnings of 1991.

Enormous public sympathy had been expressed in Hong Kong for the political protests in China from April until their bloody ending on June 3 and 4 of 1989. Hundreds of thousands of people had taken to the streets of Hong Kong in May. This signaled not merely support for many of the apparent aims of the political protesters in China but also reservations about policy attitudes expressed by the Chinese government during discussions about the transition to Chinese rule and implications for the political fate of Hong Kong after 1997.

After June 4, no protests of the scale that had occurred before materialized although perhaps 100,000 people participated in a commemorative meeting on June 4, 1990. The immediate effects of the Hong Kong protests in the spring of 1989 was to encourage the Hong Kong government to increase the number of seats that woulbe directly elected in the 1991 elections to Legco. Another effect was to give the budding politicians of Hong Kong a forum to explore political possibilities in Hong Kong. The year 1989 represents a significant moment in Hong Kong's domestic political history both in terms of the vast numbers that were prepared to take to the streets and as a boost to the political organization of a new breed of political leaders who enjoyed some success in the elections of 1991[43] and again in 1995. It is important to note, however, that the degree of political participation was low. Those who registered an intention to vote were less than half of those eligible to vote. On voting day itself, only about one-third of registered voters actually voted. There appears to be a considerable degree of skepticism about the political process. The results in 1991 and especially 1995 also caused a clear reaction from the authorities in China. There was unhappiness with Hong Kong's reaction to the events in China in the spring of 1989. There was a fundamental objection to the electoral processes that were instituted, especially under the administration of Governor Patten, the last British-appointed governor. There have been many points of contention since Mr. Patten replaced Sir David Wilson (now Lord). The issue of political representation has been among the most thorny.[44]

Political attitudes are, however, volatile and complex. It is clear, as the protests of 1989 indicated, that concerns about the Chinese government and its attitudes toward a post-1997 form are substantial. It is also clear that levels of confidence—especially about economic issues—remain high.[45] The essentially conservative (even Confucian) values of a substantial majority of Hong Kongers appear to reject a confrontational approach in dealing with representatives of the Chinese government on the subject of postcolonial Hong Kong under Chinese rule. Political behavior is dramatically different in an era that sees British mandarins assuming fewer high-level administrative roles in government and in which Hong Kong Chinese businessmen have taken over an economic domination once reserved for the British elite. It also differs quite substantially with respect to age, education, and social class.[46]

As a Hong Kong–born generation has come to maturity, knowledge of the China past of parents and grandparents has receded. This China has not, however, been forgotten, although it has changed. After 1978, the China homeland became the locus to extend the business practices of thirty years of Hong Kong's distinctive approaches to development. The China backdrop was also rediscovered in terms of cultural origins and one source of the identity that had been created in the years of separation.

Hong Kong and the Internationalization of Guangdong and the Pearl River Delta Region

As China's "southern gate," Guangdong has consistently attracted the bulk of China's foreign investment since the reform period began.[47] This has had consequences for the province as a whole, but especially for the Pearl River Delta region. Overall economic growth rates have been rapid since the middle of the 1980s, and contrast with earlier periods, especially in the decade and a half after the beginning of the Cultural Revolution (1965–79). At the beginning of the reform period, the Guangdong provincial economy ranked fifth or sixth in terms of the overall value of production. By the early 1990s, Guangdong ranked first. Its agriculture and industry had forged ahead, and the tertiary sector (construction, transportation, and commerce) was second to none.[48]

A mere twenty years ago, the Pearl River Delta region, the economic core of Guangdong, was a well defined rural area, dominated by double cropping rice, although with a substantial degree of commercialization. Its development through the late 1970s reflected a national strategy, which, in the almost thirty years after the incorporation of Guangdong into the People's Republic of China, gave an agricultural focus to the province as a whole. In the mid-1990s, the region is in the midst of an industrial revolution with distinctive characteristics that was sparked by a set of reform policies dating to late 1978, but has been dramatically facilitated by its proximity to Hong Kong. The transformation is partly locational. It is also a consequence of critical social and cultural links.

Industrialization has occurred throughout much of the Pearl River Delta region. Growth has been especially strong in the eastern region, in the corridor between Guangzhou and Hong Kong. It is also prominent in the central corridor between Guangzhou and Macao. In these parts of the delta, paddy fields, sugar cane, mulberries, and other cash crops have given way to factories and commercial development. An infrastructural transformation has seen bridges, highways, and even railroads replace the ferries and the riverine transport that had dominated the delta region for centuries. There has been a dramatic expansion and changed economic character of market towns, especially in the eastern and central delta region. Increases in rural living standards have resulted in the widespread renewal of village housing. In the western delta region, the historic point of migration of Chinese to Southeast Asia and, especially, North America, the changes have been less marked.

The greater the degree of incorporation into the global economy, the greater the effect on the local economy. The consequences for change have been greatest in the eastern delta. A particular economic strategy was created there, in part as a response to its proximity to Hong Kong and to the opportunities to encourage the proportionally large number of Hong Kong–based émigrés to invest in the area. The effects in the eastern delta can be readily contrasted with other parts of the delta. While change has been substantial in Guangzhou and the central delta areas, the impact of émigré investment has been muted by local characteristics. The western delta region, where the proportion of Overseas Chinese households (those with family members/relatives who migrated to North America and Southeast Asia) is largest, is least incorporated into the global economy. Local economic transformation is therefore least marked.

Dongguan, in the eastern delta region, took full advantage of new policy options after 1979. On the eve of reform, Dongguan was predominantly an agricultural economy. It was insulated from Hong Kong by Bao'an *xian*, which was marginal and neglected throughout the first thirty years of the People's Republic of China. Its road connections, north to Guangzhou and south to Hong Kong, were poor. While its plains were extremely productive, although focused largely on grain production, its hilly regions were poor, especially in the east and south. It changed dramatically, and rapidly, after 1979.[49] The volume of production increases, and other indicators in the 1980s, suggest massive economic change, which has continued in the 1990s. This was based on a particular strategy of close cooperation with entrepreneurs from Hong Kong and elsewhere. In the thirteen years after 1979, U.S.$1.375 billion was invested by outside (mostly Hong Kong) interests. In 1978 there were 377 enterprises, with a total work force of 55,000. At the end of 1992, there were over 25,000 with a work force of at least 750,000.[50] There were 8,000 enterprises that were capitalized from external sources. Many were small, but 338 contributed 64 percent of the total value of industrial production. Ten enterprises had an annual production in excess of 100 million yuan. They include the largest processed coffee manufactory in Asia, a joint venture with a Swiss multinational. The internationalized character of Dongguan's economic activity is clear. Hong Kong had a major role in its creation.

Dongguan is fully open to the world and exhibits an internationalized character, not merely in its production structure but also, through the Hong Kong prism, in aspects of its culture. Some of the consumption values are reflective of those in Hong Kong. It has night clubs, karaoke bars, theme parks—even McDonald's. It is, however, much closer to its agricultural past. Much of the population is still a village population, and while migrants make up an enormous portion, they are close to their rural origins, speaking Putonghua rather than Cantonese, and are only partially integrated into local communities. The impact of Hong Kong as a global and international presence is, however, notable.

The consequences in the western delta region have been markedly different, although Hong Kong is also a potent internationalizing force, the channel for the cultural and economic flows into the area. The funds that flow into the western delta region, substantial though they are, are not put primarily into economic enterprises. Their impact is, nonetheless, significant. The public facilities in the overseas Chinese areas are of high quality. In the overseas Chinese areas there has been major investment in social infrastructure such as roads, schools, hospitals, and public buildings. Schools in particular are superior to those in any other rural region in Guangdong (and possibly China as a whole).

The great majority of families in the western delta have relatives overseas and many households are critically dependent on remittances. Close kinship bonds typically result in substantial remittances, either in cash or in kind. Close kinship ties also increase the possibility of obtaining an immigration visa through family reunification programs, and of leaving the region permanently. Out-migration is the dream of households in the western delta region. There is an "overseas Chinese mentality" characterized by an obsession with the possibilities of a life abroad. The people still believe that the "golden mountain" exists to improve the life chances for themselves and their descendants. It has major consequences for the patterns of development in the western delta region. In the western delta, Hong Kong–based natives of the region, along with their kinfolk and fellow countrymen in the overseas Chinese areas of the world (particularly North America), have resumed with great intensity a set of contacts with the homeland that was compromised by government policy toward overseas Chinese dependents (*qiaojuan*) in the years after the land reform of the early 1950s.

The Pearl River Delta region has been transformed since economic reform was initiated in China in 1979. Rapid economic growth in the region has been fueled by industrial and tertiary sector growth in which outside investment, entrepreneurial skill, and management expertise have been extensively utilized. No region of China has developed as rapidly as the delta has, especially after the mid-1980s. The major stimulus for growth, initially, was Hong Kong. The territory and the practitioners of its economic success, primarily drawn from the Pearl River Delta region, assumed a key role in the innovative policies that were formulated in Guangdong as a result of loosening of central state control, beginning in 1979. Hong Kong was the catalyst that drew the Guangdong provincial economy into the global economy after 1979. In the process, the region was shaped by an array of internationalized values arriving through the Hong Kong window of opportunity.

The characteristics of particular local economies and the nature of the local state evoke distinct responses to the potentiality of reform policies. It is a process in which market forces have assumed an increasingly important role. It is not, however, a process that is independent of the institutional structures that were created in thirty years of state socialism and are underpinned by cultural forms that are much older. The interaction between the market and an array of local forces has given rise to the transformation in the Pearl River Delta region. Institutional clusters have given rise to a set of distinctive and varied responses in a small, but intensely rich, region of South China.

Hong Kong and the practitioners of its economic success, primarily drawn from the Pearl River Delta region, assumed a key role in innovative policies that were formulated in Guangdong beginning in 1979. The economic, political and cultural links between Hong Kong and its hinterland have been critical since the nineteenth century. In the aftermath of the formation of the People's Republic of China they were charged with ambiguity and regarded with suspicion by the central authorities. In the aftermath of reform they have been one key to the economic and political transformation of Guangdong which has seen its firm incorporation into the global economy.

No region of China has developed as rapidly as the delta, especially after the middle of the 1980s. The major stimulus has been Hong Kong. The key figures are Hong Kong–based expatriates who, having left in anticipation of, or shortly after, the formation of the People's Republic of China, responded to calls to return to their native places after the reform initiatives. Their sense of identity with ancestral areas is strong even after a three-decade sojourn in Hong Kong. Equally, however, the appeals from their home areas presented economic opportunity as the global economy continued its restructuring and as Hong Kong's economy underwent change. The eastern delta region, which includes the Special Economic Zone of Shenzhen, has benefited most dramatically from the activities of Hong Kong émigrés. It is in this corridor of development that Hong Kong's influence has been, and will remain, the greatest.

The economic effects of the Hong Kong connection for the overseas Chinese areas are less immediately obvious. In the overseas Chinese areas there has been major investment in social infrastructure such as roads, schools, hospitals, and public buildings. They continue a tradition begun in the nineteenth century when natives of the western delta began to migrate in large numbers to Southeast Asia and North America. This was a tradition disrupted, first, by the Japanese occupation of the homeland and then by government policy after 1950.

Conclusion

Hong Kong and its hinterland have changed dramatically since reform was proposed in 1979. Hong Kong has continued to prosper as it has assisted in and benefited from the transformation of the Pearl River Delta of which it is economically and culturally a part and to which it will be administratively firmly linked in an as yet somewhat uncertain fashion after 1997.

There is little question that the older cultural ties have been strengthened by increasing economic integration throughout the 1980s. Hong Kong has greater economic strength relative to Guangdong than it had in the past. Hong Kong is no longer under the cultural shadow of Guangzhou and Guangdong as it was until 1949. The separate developmental trajectories of Hong Kong and its delta hinterland (including Guangzhou) after 1950 have had major consequences in the 1980s and the 1990s and will likely remain even after the formal resumption of Chinese sovereignty.

A regional economy that is now emerging, energized initially by Hong Kong's enormous entrepreneurial capacities, is split across distinct administrative and political systems. After 1997 the political and administrative barriers will be diminished, although it is unlikely that Hong Kong's economic dominance will lessen. There is clearly an important cultural distinctiveness between Hong Kong and its hinterland that became heightened in the thirty years after 1950, but may have lessened substantially since 1980 as Hong Kong and its hinterland became increasingly integrated. Reservations about the fate of Hong Kong's political structures after 1997 remain. Hong Kong's economic domination of its hinterland will, nonetheless, likely remain well beyond 1997. Hong Kong, as a global city, will continue to link this region of China, if not the entire Chinese economy, to the world.

Notes

1. See, for example, the following chapters in Ming K. Chan, ed., with John D. young, *Precarious Balance: Hong Kong Between China and Britain, 1842–1992* (Armonk, NY: M.E. Sharpe, and Hong Kong: Hong Kong University Press, 1994): Ming K. Chan, "Hong Kong in Sino-British Conflict: Mass Mobilization and the Crisis of Legitimacy, 1912–26," pp. 27–58; Tsai Jung-fang, "From Anti-foreignism to Popular Nationalism: Hong Kong Between China and Britain, 1839–1911," pp. 9–26; and Norman Miners, "From Nationalistic Confrontation to Regional Collaboration: China–Hong Kong–Britain, 1926–1941," pp. 59–70.

2. Joseph Fewsmith, *Dilemmas of Reform in China: Political Conflict and Economic Debate* (Armonk, NY: M.E. Sharpe, 1994), pp. 3–18, 19–55.

3. *A Draft Agreement Between the Government of the United Kingdom and Britain and Northern Island and the Government of the People's Republic of China on the Future of Hong Kong* (Hong Kong: Government Printer, 1984) specifies the broad mechanisms. A set of annexes that deal with China's policy toward Hong Kong, the nature of the Sino-British liaison group, and land leases, plus the exchange of memoranda between the British and Chinese governments, can be found in Frank Ching, *Hong Kong and China: For Better or Worse* (New York: China Council of the Asia Society and the Foreign Policy Association, 1985). The Basic Law was approved by the National People's Congress in April 1990 in an atmosphere changed significantly by the events in China during the spring of 1989 and reaction to them in Hong Kong. A draft of the Basic Law with commentary appears in William McGurn, *Basic Law, Basic Questions* (Hong Kong: Review Publishing Company, 1988). See also George Hicks, *Hong Kong Countdown* (Hong Kong: Writers and Publishers Cooperative, 1989) for views written before June 1989. The perception from Taipei is expressed in Jurgen Domes and Shaw Yu-ming, *Hong Kong: A Chinese and International Concern* (Boulder: Westview Press, 1989). A Canadian view is expressed in Jules Nadeau, *Hong Kong 1997: Dans la Gueule du Dragon Rouge* (Montreal: Editions Quebec/Amerique, 1990). See the comments in James T.H. Tang and Frank Ching, "The MacLehose-Youde Years: Balancing the Three-legged Stool, 1971–86" in M.K. Chan, ed., *Precarious Balance,* pp. 131–148; Frank Ching, "Toward Colonial Sunset: the Wilson Regime, 1987–92," in *Hong Kong and China,* pp. 173–198; Michael DeGolyer, "Politics, Politicians and Political Parties," in Donald H. McMillan and Man Si-wai, eds., *The Other Hong Report: 1994* (Hong Kong: Chinese University Press, 1994), pp. 75–102; and K.K. Leung, "The Basic Law and the Problem of Political Transition," in Stephen Y.S. Cheung and Stephen M.H. Sze, eds., *The Other Hong Kong Report: 1995* (Hong Kong: Chinese University Press, 1995), pp. 33–50.

4. See my "Continuity and Transformation in the Pearl River Delta: Hong Kong's Impact on its Hinterland," in Reginald Y.W. Kwok and Alvin So, eds., *The Hong Kong–Guangdong Link: Partnership in Flux* (Armonk, NY: M.E. Sharpe, and Hong Kong: Hong Kong University Press, 1995), pp. 64–86.

5. For a popular account of the early period, see M. Collis, *Foreign Mud* (London: Faber and Faber, 1946). The most thorough scholarly analysis is still John King Fairbank, *Trade and Diplomacy on the South China Coast* (Cambridge, MA: Harvard University Press, 1953). See also Fred Wakeman, *Strangers at the Gates* (Berkeley: University of California Press, 1967).

6. Carl Riskin, *China's Political Economy: The Quest for Development since 1949* (New York: Oxford University Press, 1987).

7. Ezra Vogel, *One Step Ahead in China: Guangdong under Reform* (Cambridge, MA: Harvard University Press, 1989), pp. 44–47.

8. For a broad account of some of the issues in a global context, see Joyce Kolko, *Restructuring the World Economy* (New York: Pantheon, 1988). On the issues for the NICs see Michael A. Bienefeld, "The International Context for National Development Strategies and Opportunities in a Changing World," in M.E. Bienefeld and M. Godfrey, eds., *The Struggle for Development: National Strategies in an International Context* (Chichester, New York, Brisbane, Toronto, Singapore: John Wiley, 1982), pp. 49–53; also see Peter L. Berger and Hsiao Hsin-huang, *In Search of an East Asian Developmental Model* (New Brunswick, NJ: Transaction Books, 1988).

9. Wong Siu-lun, *Emigrant Entrepreneurs: Shanghai Industrialists in Hong Kong* (Hong Kong: Oxford University Press, 1988).

10. There are some who have argued that Hong Kong represents the vindication of a classical laissez-faire approach to economic growth, the first statement of which was H. Smith, *John Stuart Mill's Other Island: A Study of the Economic Development of Hong Kong* (London: Institute of Economic Affairs, 1966). An extension of the argument can be found in Alvin Rabushka, *Hong Kong: A Study in Economic Freedom* (Chicago: Chicago University Press, 1979). Such arguments are critically analyzed in M. Castells, L. Goh, and R.Y.W. Kwok, *The Shek Kip Mei Syndrome: Economic Development and Public Housing in Hong Kong and Singapore* (London: Pion Press, 1990), pp. 58–117.

11. Ho Lok-sang, "Labour and Employment," in Joseph Y.S. Cheng and Paul C.K. Kwong, *The Other Hong Report: 1992* (Hong Kong: Chinese University Press, 1992), pp. 197–212.

12. Wing Suen, "Labor and Employment," in McMillan and Man, eds., *The Other Hong Kong Report: 1994*, pp. 149–164; and Wong Yiu-tim, "Labor and Unemployment," in Cheung and Sze, eds., *The Other Hong Kong Report: 1995*, pp. 287–302.

13. Census and Statistics Department, *Hong Kong Annual Digest of Statistics: 1995 Edition* (Hong Kong: Census and Statistics Department, 1955), p. 16.

14. Sung Yun-wing, *The China–Hong Kong Connection: The Key to China's Open-Door Policy* (Cambridge: Cambridge University Press, 1991), pp. 104–163.

15. State Statistical Bureau, *Zhongguo Tongji Nianjian, 1995* (Statistical Yearbook of China, 1995) (Beijing: State Statistical Bureau, 1995), pp. 537, 543.

16. *Hong Kong Annual Digest of Statistics: 1995 Edition*, p. x.

17. See my "1997 and After: Will Hong Kong Survive? A Personal View," *Pacific Affairs* 59, 2 (summer 1986), pp. 237–254.

18. Ng Shui-lai, "Social Welfare," in Sung Yun-wing and Lee Ming-kwan, eds., *The Other Hong Report: 1991* (Hong Kong: Chinese University Press, 1991), pp. 329–342; "Social Welfare" in Cheng and Kwong, eds., *The Other Hong Kong Report: 1992*, pp. 297–308.

19. Joe B. Leung, "Social Welfare," in Cheung and Sze, eds., *The Other Hong Kong Report: 1995*, p. 362.

20. Castells, Goh and Kwok, *The Shek Kip Mei Syndrome*, pp. 8–57; Lau Kwok-yu, "Housing," in Sung and Lee, eds., *The Other Hong Report: 1991* (Hong Kong: Chinese University Press, 1991), pp. 343–388; Richard Y.C. Wong and Stanley Staley, "Housing and Land," in Cheng and Kwong, eds., *The Other Hong Kong Report: 1992*, pp. 308–350; Lau Kwok-yu, "Public Housing," in McMillan and Man, eds., *The Other Hong Kong Report: 1994*, pp. 265–296.

21. Norman Y.T. Ng, "Population: Growth, Profile, and Redistribution," in Cheng and Kwong, ibid., pp. 229–234.

22. Leung Chi-keung, "Transportation," in Richard Y.C. Wong and Joseph Y.S.

Cheng, eds., *The Other Hong Report: 1990* (Hong Kong: Chinese University Press, 1990), pp. 459–490.

23. Chu Kim-yee, "Transportation," in Sung and Lee, *The Other Hong Kong Report: 1991*, pp. 389–402.

24. The PADS documents were complemented with Metroplan—a strategic land use and transport development plan for the metropolitan area of Hong Kong. See Lands and Works Branch, *Metroplan: The Aims* (Hong Kong: Government Printer, 1988), and Lands and Works Branch, *Metroplan: The Selected Strategy, an Overview* (Hong Kong: Government Printer, 1988). Metroplan followed on from PADS by assuming that Hong Kong's position as an international business and financial center, a center for light manufacturing industry, and a major destination for international tourism should be augmented. It argued for infrastructural developments to reflect Hong Kong's international character and its regional dominance, which, the planners saw, had only grown with the developments of the South China regional economy and greater global linkages in the 1980s. Both PADS and Metroplan began with the territorial boundaries that had been created in 1898. Metroplan did not fully appreciate the extent of development with the Pearl River Delta hinterland, or the need to integrate planning in Hong Kong with the adjacent regions of China. See "Urban and Regional Planning," in Joseph Y.S. Cheng and Sonny S.H. Lo, *From Colony to SAR: Hong Kong's Challenge Ahead* (Shatin: Chinese University Press, 1995), pp. 227–261.

25. Joseph Y.S. Cheng, "Values and Attitudes of the Hong Kong Community" in Paul Chun-Kuen Kwong, *Hong Kong Trends 1989–92: Index to the Other Hong Kong Report* (Hong Kong: Chinese University Press, 1992), pp. 17–46; Lee Ming-kwan, "Community and Identity in Transition in Hong Kong," in Reginald Y.W. Kwok and Alvin So, eds., *The Hong Kong–Guangdong Link*, pp. 119–134.

26. Census and Statistics Department Hong Kong *Hong Kong Statistics, 1947–67* (Hong Kong: Census and Statistics Department,1969), p. 22.

27. Census and Statistics Department Hong Kong, *Hong Kong 1991 Population Census: Summary Results* (Hong Kong: Census and Statistics Department, 1992), p. 40.

28. There was a significant part of the Hong Kong population that traced its ancestry to the pre-Convention inhabitants of the New Territories and Hong Kong waters; they were not, therefore, part of the migrant population. Substantial numbers had become out-migrants to Britain and elsewhere beginning in the 1950s. There was also a smaller, but nonetheless significant, group of Chinese (and Eurasian) families with a residence of some generations in, and commitment to, Hong Kong. Many of these families were oriented to business or commerce, often in a highly internationalized context, but with a focus on the former Treaty Ports. Perhaps the Kwok family, the founders of Wing On, who operated in Hong Kong, Guangzhou, Shanghai, and in Australia, or the Li family, founders of the Bank of East Asia, are typical examples.

29. Stephen M.H. Sze, "Cultural Life in Hong Kong," in Joseph Y.S. Cheng and Paul C.K. Kwong, eds., *The Other Hong Kong Report: 1992*, pp. 447–462.

30. Ibid, p. 448.

31. This statement should be qualified. There were and are a set of vibrant cultural expressions, many of which are closely linked to ritual occasions. The rich and varied Chinese folk religious culture, which was dramatically augmented by migration, has a significant performance aspect. Operas are held at annual religious celebrations throughout the territory. They typically occur within matsheds erected for the duration of the religious observances. Operatic and musical performances are also held independently of ritual performances. Their development was constrained by the "loss" of the hinterland. See Sau Y. Chan, *Improvisation in a Ritual Context: The Music of Cantonese Opera* (Hong Kong: Chinese University Press, 1991), and Gregory E. Guldin, "Toward A Greater

Guangdong: Hong Kong's Socio-cultural Impact on the Pearl River Delta and Beyond," in Reginald Y.W. Kwok and Alvin So, eds., *The Hong Kong–Guangdong Link,* pp. 89–118.

32. Out-migration has been an important feature of Hong Kong since its early days as a British colony. It was a funnel for substantial numbers of rural migrants, especially from the Pearl River Delta region, as they went to labor in the mines, on the plantations, and on the railroads of Southeast Asia, the West Indies, and the Americas, until well into the twentieth century. See Elizabeth Sinn, "Emigration from Hong Kong Before 1941: General Trends," in Ronald Skeldon, ed., *Emigration from Hong Kong* (Hong Kong: The Chinese University Press, 1995), pp. 11–34. Out-migration from the late 1960s, especially to Australia, Canada, New Zealand, and the United States—countries that had imposed severe restriction on Chinese immigration—has been an important aspect of modern Hong Kong. It furthers the internationalized character of the Hong Kong population, more so given a degree of return migration in which foreign passport holders of Chinese origin have returned to Hong Kong to work, sometimes leaving family members behind in the countries of migration (the "astronaut" phenomenon). There are some important class issues involved in this process. See Ronald Skeldon, ed., *Reluctant Exiles: Migration from Hong Kong and the New Overseas Chinese* (Armonk, NY: M.E. Sharpe and Hong Kong: Hong Kong University Press, 1994). Note the analysis in Janet Salaff and Wong Siu-lun, "Exiting Hong Kong: Social Class Experiences and the Adjustment to 1997," in Lau Siu-kai, Lee Ming-kwan, Wan Po-san, and Wong Siu-lun, *Inequalities and Development: Social Stratification in Chinese Societies* (Hong Kong: Hong Kong Institute of Asia-Pacific Studies, 1994), pp. 205–250. Also see Paul C.K. Kwong, "Internationalization of Population and Globalization of Families," in Choi Po-king and Ho Lok-sang, *The Other Hong Report: 1993* (Hong Kong: Chinese University Press, 1993), pp. 147–174.

33. George Ritzer, *The McDonaldization of Society: An Investigation into the Changing Character of Contemporary Social Life* (Newbury Park, CA: Pine Forge Press, 1993), p. 1.

34. Stevan Harrell and Huang Chun-chieh, "Introduction: Change and Contention in Taiwan's Cultural Scene," in Stevan Harrell and Huang Chun-chieh, eds., *Cultural Change in Postwar Taiwan* (Boulder, CO: Westview, 1994), p. 4.

35. Stevan Harrell, "Playing in the Valley: A Metonym of Modernization in Taiwan," in ibid, pp. 161–183. See also Chan Man-hoi, "Culture and Identity," in McMillan and Man, eds., *The Other Hong Kong Report: 1994,* pp. 443–468.

36. It is only underscored by the enormous apparent proclivity of the Hong Kong population to travel. There are few statistics available on the amount of travel that residents of Hong Kong make. Much of the tourism to China (about 88 percent) consists of visitors from Hong Kong, Macao, and Taiwan, with Hong Kong visitors the most numerous. Travel to other world venues, often by packaged tours, is a profitable business. Impressionistically, it involves all social classes and all ages. Familiarity with the non-Chinese world is substantial. Partly, such travel is to visit relatives who have moved abroad, but tourism to those parts of the world that have few Chinese immigrants appears to be considerable.

37. Helen F. Siu, "Remade in Hong Kong: Weaving into the Chinese Cultural Tapestry," in Tao Tao Liu and David Faure, eds., *Unity and Diversity: Local Cultures and Identities in China* (Hong Kong: Hong Kong University Press, 1996), p. 178.

38. Tu Wei-ming, "Preface," in his edited volume, *The Living Tree: The Changing Meaning of Being Chinese Today* (Stanford, CA: Stanford University Press, 1994), pp. vi–vii.

39. Myron Cohen, "Being Chinese: The Peripheralization of Chinese Identity," in ibid., p. 108.

40. Siu, "Remade in Hong Kong," p. 191.

41. See my "Leaders and Leadership in a New Territories Town," *China Quarterly* 51 (March 1977), pp. 109–125.

42. See Joe C.B. Leung, "Community Participation: Past, Present and Future," in Benjamin K.P. Leung and Teresa Y.C. Wong, eds., *Twenty-five Years of Social and Economic Development in Hong Kong* (Hong Kong: center for Asian Studies, Hong Kong University, 1994), pp. 252–269. The policy statements of the Hong Kong government can be found in the two Hong Kong Government White Papers, *The Further Development of Representative Government in Hong Kong* (Hong Kong: Government Printer, 1984), and *The Development of Representative Government in Hong Kong: The Way Forward* (Hong Kong: Government Printer, 1988).

43. Lee Ming-kwan, "Politicians," in Wong and Cheng, eds., *The Other Hong Kong Report: 1990*, pp. 113–130.

44. See also Lo Chi-kin, "From 'Through Train' to 'Second Stove' " in Joseph Y.S. Cheng and Sonny S.H. Lo., *From Colony to SAR*, pp. 25–38.

45. Wong Siu-lun, "Political Attitudes and Identity" in Ronald Skeldon, ed., *Emigration from Hong Kong*, p. 150.

46. Ibid., p. 152.

47. Yang Dali, "Patterns of China's Regional Development Strategy" *China Quarterly* 122 (June 1990), pp. 230–257; Michael G. Plummer and Manuel F. Montes, "Direct Foreign Investment in China: An Introduction," in Sumner J. La Croix, Michael G. Plummer, and Keun Lee, eds., *Emerging Patterns of East Asian Investment in China* (Armonk, NY: M.E. Sharpe, 1995), pp. 3–20.

48. In 1981, the total value of agriculture and industry in Guangdong was 37 billion yuan, a little under 5 percent of the national total. The province was substantially outranked by Jiangsu, Shanghai, Shandong, Liaoning, and Sichuan, and was at the same level as Hubei and Henan. Even in terms of the value of agricultural production it ranked only sixth. See State Statistical Bureau, *Zhongguo Tongji Nianjian, 1981* (Statistical Yearbook of China, 1981) (Hong Kong: Economic Information Agency, 1982, p. 19). By 1994, Guangdong's GNP of 424.10 billion yuan made up 9.44 percent of the national total, and significantly outperformed its closest rivals, Shandong and Jiangsu. Its agricultural value ranked third, behind Shandong and Sichuan, and its industrial value was second only to Jiangsu. The value of construction and tertiary sector production (transport and commerce) far outranked any other administrative unit. State Statistical Bureau, *Zhongguo Tongji Nianjian, 1995*, pp. 32, 33–35.

49. Zhonggung Dongguan Shiwei, *Cong Nongcun Zhou Xiang Chengshi* (From Village to Municipality) (Beijing: Renmin Chubanshe, 1994).

50. Total labor force numbers for Dongguan are imprecise. Official figures suggest a work force of 795,000 out of a total population of 1.3 million. Interview data indicate an outsider population of 1.1 million, the great bulk of which is of working age. The population of Dongguan, including outsiders, was about 2.3 million in 1993.

6

The Internalization of International Law in Hong Kong

Roda Mushkat

Hong Kong's economic dynamism, resilience, and integration into the global community may be viewed to a certain extent as a product of its historically determined passive posture. The territory has embraced an open-economy model within a flexible common law framework that has allowed it to maximize its comparative advantages in a well-defined institutional environment. This environment has been shaped by a colonial regime guided by a mixture of economically conservative and legally liberal values that have proved conducive to effective external adaptation.

The reason for portraying this configuration as inherently "passive" lies in the fact that the overall institutional structure was imposed from outside and sustained through the hierarchical linkage with the United Kingdom. The "international legal personality" that has thus evolved[1] is embedded in a pattern of dependence underpinned in the final analysis by Britain's international status and the vitality of its parliamentary democracy.

These two factors have helped Hong Kong to establish itself as a respectable player in the international arena—an entity that not merely observes the "rules of the game" in a mechanical fashion, but one that consciously implements them through its domestic channels. As 1997 dawns, therefore, the international legal challenge facing the territory is not "internationalization" per se. Rather, it is the maintenance of the status quo against the backdrop of the decoupling from the United Kingdom. In other words, "internationalization" in this context means—somewhat paradoxically—the effective "internalization" of existing values/arrangements through appropriate support mechanisms.

Successful internalization should ensure continuity by leaving the domestic equilibrium intact and minimizing external friction. It would enable Hong Kong to consolidate its position as a "bridge" between developing China and the global community. By contrast, a failure to internalize present international legal parameters could result in a drift toward parochialism. This, in turn, could undermine socioeconomic stability.

The forces of parochialism are growing progressively stronger, and attempts at internalization in the face of pressure from those forces are in themselves "destabilizing." The tension they beget may nonetheless be regarded as a natural phenomenon in an open society. While it is not certain which side will prevail in practice, and to what extent, there is a reasonably solid international legal basis for attaining the goals toward which the internalization effort is directed. This basis encompasses the notion of a "high degree of autonomy," the principle of (internal) self-determination, the application of international human rights, and an internationally respectable Court of Final Appeal.

A High Degree of Autonomy[2]

The Pledges

There is little doubt that in order to preserve Hong Kong's capacity to exercise its international rights and duties in its relations with other international legal persons, and in order to maintain the recognition it has acquired as a viable and significant international political actor, the territory should be endowed with the necessary attributes to act independently across a wide range of strategic domains. The crucial importance of such a condition was duly acknowledged by the parties to the 1984 Sino-British Joint Declaration,[3] who stipulated that "[t]he Hong Kong Special Administrative Region [HKSAR] will enjoy a high degree of autonomy, except in foreign and defence affairs which are the responsibilities of the Central People's Government."[4] This pledge was further reinforced through its incorporation in the 1990 Basic Law of the HKSAR.[5]

In general, the HKSAR will be vested with "executive, legislative and independent judicial power, including that of final adjudication."[6] More specifically, and in line with accepted minimal prescriptions for autonomy and self-government,[7] the HKSAR will be headed and represented by a chief executive "selected by election or through consultations held locally."[8] The HKSAR legislature—which is to be "constituted by election"[9]—"may on its own authority enact laws in accordance with the provisions of the Basic Law and legal procedures."[10] Judicial power in the HKSAR is to be exercised by the local courts "independently and free from any interference."[11]

In congruence with the objective of facilitating and enhancing the territory's capacity to operate internationally, considerable power is vested in the HKSAR regarding external affairs. The region "may on its own, using the name 'Hong Kong, China' maintain and develop relations and conclude and implement agreements with states, regions and relevant international organizations in the appropriate fields, including the economic, trade, financial and monetary, shipping, communications, touristic, cultural and sporting fields."[12] In addition,

> Representatives of the Hong Kong Special Administrative Region Government may participate, as members of the delegations of the Government of the People's Republic of China, in international organizations or conferences in appropriate fields limited to states and affecting the Hong Kong Special Administrative Region, or may attend in such other capacity as may be permitted by the Central People's Government and the organization or conference concerned, and may express their views in the name of "Hong Kong, China."[13]

In its role as an autonomous entity, the Special Administrative Region may also participate in international organizations and conferences not limited to states. Indeed, the Central People's Government undertakes "to ensure that the Hong Kong Special Administrative Region shall continue to retain its status in an appropriate capacity in those international organizations of which the People's Republic of China is a member and in which Hong Kong participates in one capacity or another."[14] The PRC's undertaking also extends to facilitating the "continued participation of the Hong Kong Special Administrative Region in an appropriate capacity in those international organizations in which Hong Kong is a participant in one capacity or another, but of which the People's Republic of China is not a member."[15]

Consistent with the emphasis on the development of external ties by the territory, the Sino-British Accord stipulates the establishment, with the approval of the Central People's Government, of consular and other official or semi-official missions in the SAR[16]. The accord also provides for official and semi-official SAR economic and trade missions in foreign countries.[17] The SAR's external status is further enhanced by the authority granted to it by the PRC to issue passports and travel documents,[18] as well as to conclude agreements for the mutual abolition of visa requirements.[19]

An attempt has clearly been made to preserve the territory's separate social and economic identity, coupled with a Chinese pledge of noninterference[20] insofar as the socialist system and policies will not be practiced in Hong Kong for fifty years.[21] Basically, the HKSAR will "maintain the capitalist economic and trade systems previously practised in Hong Kong."[22] Accordingly, the HKSAR government is granted almost total control over the economy, including the power to decide its own economic and trade policies,[23] develop its own economic and trade relations with other states and regions,[24] formulate its own monetary and financial policies,[25] and determine its own excise and taxation policies.[26] The HKSAR will retain its status as a free port,[27] continue to pursue its free trade policy, including free movement of goods and capital,[28] and maintain its freely convertible currency.[29] The HKSAR will remain a separate customs territory, capable of participating as such in relevant international organizations and securing its own export quotas, tariff preferences, and other similar arrangements.[30] Hong Kong's separate shipping register[31] and civil aviation management are also to be retained.[32]

In what is considered a somewhat unusual feature in autonomous entity/central authority relationships,[33] there will be essentially no formal financial ties between the HKSAR and the Central People's Government. Rather, the HKSAR will have independent finances to use exclusively for its own purposes. No funds will be channeled to the Central People's Government,[34] nor will the CPG be permitted to levy any taxes in the territory.[35]

Obligations have also been undertaken to preserve Hong Kong's current social system and life-style[36] as well as its self-governing powers and independent decision making in fields such as education, science, culture, sports, religion, labor, and social services.[37]

Potential for Encroachment

Evidently, the "high" degree of autonomy pledged for the territory hinges to a large extent on the insulation of Hong Kong from potential and actual intervention by the PRC. Several concerns have been raised in this regard, identifying conceivable sources of control or interference that range from the specific-legalistic to the more general-ideological.

With respect to the legislative powers with which the HKSAR government is endowed, three potential constraints have been highlighted: (1) laws enacted by the local legislature are subject to invalidation by the Standing Committee of the National People's Congress (SC-NPC); (2) PRC legislation may be applicable in Hong Kong; and (3) the power to amend the region's "constitution" is vested in the NPC.

It appears that the power to invalidate HKSAR legislation assumed by the PRC under Article 17 of the Basic Law goes beyond that which is envisaged in the Sino-British Joint Declaration.[38] Although such power is confined to challenging the "constitutionality" of laws "regarding affairs within the responsibility of the Central Authorities or regarding the relationship between the Central Authorities and the Region," the power of review should more appropriately[39]— and more consistently with a high degree of autonomy[40]—be exercised by the local judiciary.

It has been further argued that the Basic Law expands PRC authority to enact legislation applicable in Hong Kong "in violation of the very limits of autonomy the Basic Law is supposed to preserve."[41] The extension to the territory of PRC laws "relating to defence and foreign affairs as well as other matters outside the limits of the autonomy of the Region as specified by this law,"[42] is incompatible with the notion of Hong Kong's autonomy. Such legislative autonomy is reflected in the negatively phrased provision in the Joint Declaration that [e]xcept for foreign and defence affairs . . . the Hong Kong Special Administrative Region shall be vested with . . . legislative . . . power."[43] The scope for PRC intrusion through legislation is also perceived to have increased by the stipulation in the Basic Law that "[i]n the event that the Standing Committee of the National People's Congress decides to declare a state of war or, by reason of turmoil within the Hong Kong Special Administrative Region which . . . is beyond the control of the government of the Region, decides that the Region is in a state of emergency, the Central People's Government may issue an order applying the relevant national laws in the Region."[44]

A potentially more serious problem, insofar as the threat of PRC "legislative infiltration" is concerned, stems from the fact that the power to amend the Basic Law is vested in the National People's Congress[45] and may be exercised without consulting the HKSAR.[46] Yet, as argued by a comparative constitutional law expert, the "key elements of the autonomy of the Hong Kong SAR are beyond amendment."[47]

> [T]he special circumstances of enactment of the Basic Law—a solemn international treaty and undertaking, the fundamental principle on which Britain transferred responsibility and sovereignty over Hong Kong to China, the assurances given by both to the People of Hong Kong, and their participation in its preparation premised on the principles of the Joint Declaration—all point to an instrument which, though enacted by one party, represents the will of several parties. As such, its unilateral amendment would be contrary to good faith and justice.[48]

A further reassurance is provided under the Basic Law itself to the effect that "[n]o amendment to this Law shall contravene the established basic policies of the People's Republic of China regarding Hong Kong"[49] which "have been elaborated by [the Chinese Government] in the Sino-British Joint Declaration."[50]

With regard to executive powers, fears over PRC interference have focused on the appointment of the chief executive by, and accountability[51] to, the Central People's Government. It has been contended that the power of a chief executive ("with divided loyalties") to dissolve the legislature[52] and appoint/remove judges of the courts,[53] may compromise the independence of the legislative and judicial branches of the HKSAR government.[54]

Arguably, since considerable emphasis is placed on the democratic selection of the chief executive,[55] it may be possible to maintain independence between the branches of government. China's power of "appointment" ought not be interpreted to mean that approval can be withheld at will by the PRC.[56] Certain checks and balances—for example, the chief executive's duty to consult the Executive Council before dissolving the Legislative Council,[57] the Legislative Council's power to impeach the chief executive,[58] and the requirement that judges' appointments be based on the recommendation of an independent commission[59]—should also effectively serve to prevent such unilateral action.

Possibly the most intense debate is over the preservation of independent local judicial power. The central issue of this debate is whether the interpretation of the Basic Law is the " 'linchpin' upon which rests the success or failure of the future system."[60] Specifically, the debate focuses on whether consolidation of power by the NPC will erode the "power of final adjudication" guaranteed to the HKSAR courts under the Sino-British Joint Declaration.

At the same time, it appears that the central government's jurisdiction over certain judicial decisions is not inconsistent with relevant international practice.[61] When appropriately constrained, this jurisdiction "does not inevitably threaten the judiciary's right of final adjudication."[62] Regrettably, no clear delineation of power is offered under the Basic Law. However, some division may be discerned whereby local courts would exercise an incidental, interpretative function, and defer whenever necessary to the SC-NPC's interpretation of the Basic Law provisions "concerning affairs which are the responsibility of the Central People's Government, or concerning the relationship between the Central Authorities and the Region."[63] Although critics correctly highlight the ambiguity of phrases such as "affairs which are the responsibility of the Central People's Government," inherent in the local courts' power to determine the need for referral is also the competence to classify the issues properly.[64]

Perhaps a more serious curtailment in power is the SC-NPC's ability to "disallow" locally enacted legislation. As contended by one writer, the SC-NPC is authorized to "nip errant HKSAR legislation in the bud, thus preempting the courts from exercising the already severely circumscribed interpretive powers granted to them under article 157 by denying them even the very opportunity of reviewing the constitutionality of such legislation."[65] Notwithstanding reassurances by Chinese officials that "the NPC will be unlikely to exercise the power frequently,"[66] judicial review of legislation should reside in SAR courts.[67]

The ousting of the HKSAR's jurisdiction over "acts of state, such as defence and foreign affairs,"[68] may also raise concern as to what other acts of state may be excluded from the purview of the local judiciary. Guided by the present judicial practice—which is to remain unchanged in the HKSAR—it is within the local courts' competence to decide whether the subject matter is beyond their judicial scope. The courts must, however, "obtain a certificate from the chief executive on questions of fact concerning acts of state such as defence and foreign affairs whenever such questions arise in the adjudication of cases. This certificate shall be binding on the courts."[69]

Despite the fact that the reservation of power to the PRC over defense and foreign affairs is a common feature in autonomous arrangements, the absence, from both the Joint Declaration and the Basic Law, of a formal definition of either "foreign affairs" or "defense"—and hence the lack of clear demarcation of the scope and extent of the central government's responsibility[70]—may give rise to fears of potential encroachment. Particular unease is generated by the stationing in the HKSAR of PLA troops. Although charged with "defense" only and constrained by a "noninterference" proscription[71] as well as subject to Hong

Kong law,[72] the forces could presumably be mobilized under the pretext of responding to a "foreign affairs" crisis or upon a declaration of a "state of emergency" by the SC-NPC "by reason of turmoil within the Hong Kong Special Administrative Region which endangers national unity or security and is beyond the control of the government of the Region."[73]

Self-Determination

International Legal Entitlements

The right of peoples to self-determination has been firmly established in both conventional and customary international law.[74] It is in general the right of a people to control its own destiny, "freely determine [its] political status," and "freely pursue [its] economic, social, and cultural development."[75] It has been interpreted as pertaining to two aspects, "external," alluding to the achievement of independence or other appropriate legal status by peoples under colonial and alien domination, and "internal," referring to the right of citizens to "maintain, assure and perfect their full legal, political, economic and cultural sovereignty."[76]

As argued elsewhere,[77] Hong Kong people qualify as a "self" that merits the right to determine its own future, although the task of establishing a legal entitlement to external self-determination based on "colonial or alien domination" may be more problematic.[78] It is also evident that neither party to the Sino-British Joint Declaration has accepted self-determination for Hong Kong as a viable option nor is an international forum likely to collectively sanction any "decolonization" attempt.

On the other hand, the territory's entitlement to internal self-determination should adduce firm support in contemporary international law.[79] Indeed, Hong Kong people would be able to find a strong claim to an "offshoot" "right of democracy." The right of every person to participate in his or her government is recognized and guaranteed in all major human rights instruments. It is enunciated in the Universal Declaration of Human Rights,[80] the International Covenant on Civil and Political Rights,[81] as well as the American,[82] European[83] and African[84] Conventions on Human Rights. It is further affirmed and reinforced in the UN General Assembly Resolution on Enhancing the Effectiveness of the Principle of Periodic and Genuine Elections,[85] which "stresses" member nations' "conviction" that the right of everyone to take part in the government of his or her country is a crucial factor in the effective enjoyment by all of a wide range of human rights and fundamental freedoms, embracing political, economic, social, and cultural rights. Clearly, the most comprehensive prescription of the "democratic entitlement" is contained in the documents[86] generated by the thirty-four members[87] of the Conference on Security and Cooperation in Europe (CSCE).

Internalization

It is apparent that both pre- and post-1997 Hong Kong suffer from a "democratic deficit." Notwithstanding the government's declared objective—to "develop progressively a system of government the authority for which is firmly rooted in Hong Kong, which is able to represent authoritatively the views of the people of Hong Kong, and which is more directly accountable to the people of Hong Kong"[88]—and regardless of the expressed desire of the public for a faster pace of democratization, the British government resolved to open only 18 of the 60 seats in the Legislative Council for direct elections in 1991 and 20 in 1995 (the last elections under British rule).[89]

Although a set of reform proposals[90]—introduced by Hong Kong's governor with the aim of expanding the voting franchise in the territory and broadening other democratic initiatives[91]—has recently (June 30, 1994) been passed (with modifications) into law, this is viewed by democratically inclined observers as a "small and belated steps toward the fully democratic political system for which Hong Kong has long been ready."[92] Indeed, the governor himself has admitted that the fierce row between Britain and China, triggered by the proposals, was not about whether Hong Kong would soon become a democracy but over "greater or lesser degrees of semi-autonomy."[93]

By the same token, these limited reforms are in full accord with the Sino-British Joint Declaration, which provides that the legislature of the HKSAR shall be "constituted by election."[94] Indeed, they should be regarded as a legitimate and reasonable step in the implementation of the obligation imposed on the British government to administer Hong Kong in the transition period (1984–97) toward achieving the common goal agreed by the parties, namely, "maintaining and preserving its economic prosperity and social stability."[95] As elaborated in the white paper entitled *Representative Government in Hong Kong*, "at the heart of this [goal] . . . is the rule of law. . . . It is difficult to envisage the maintenance of the rule of law in a community where the legislative body is neither fairly elected nor free from the possibility of manipulation."[96]

The "constitutional package" is also compatible with the Basic Law, which generally "accepts democracy as a long term principle" (although "does not provide for it").[97] Specifically, no voting system is prescribed under the Basic Law, which nonetheless reaffirms the ultimate agreed aim of electing all of the SAR's legislature through universal suffrage. While approving the creation of new constituencies (up to thirty),[98] the Basic Law does not define "functional constituency" nor does it stipulate who should be included or who should be represented in the functional constituency electorate. The Basic Law is equally silent on the composition of the district boards and municipal councils as well as in respect of the manner of election of the members of these local bodies.

On the other hand, the dismantling of three tiers of government (the last Legislative Council, Urban Council, Regional Council, and district boards) composed of duly elected representatives[99]—and the institution of a selectively appointed legislative body,[100] "provisional" or otherwise—would undoubtedly contravene the Joint Declaration, be at variance with the aspirations of the Hong Kong people, and amount to a clear deviation from established international norms. It would further infringe both letter[101] and spirit of the Basic Law. As forcefully contended by a public law expert, "the purpose of the Basic Law is to provide for a high degree of autonomy for Hong Kong and for the people of Hong Kong to rule themselves."[102] Indeed, "the participation of the Hong Kong people in the autonomous political processes of the SAR immediately on the termination of colonial rule not only underlies the Basic Law, but is central to its success. The denial of that opportunity would confuse and demoralize the community of Hong Kong, sap the vitality of its public life, upset the balance of political forces through outside intervention and destroy the status of the Basic Law. Many other negative consequences would follow, inconsistent with the goal of the stability and prosperity of Hong Kong proclaimed in the Joint Declaration and the Basic Law."

Nor do contentions that the status quo falls short of the democratic ideal mitigate against "internalization" of the entitlement to internal self-determination. In fact, while the process of democracy in Hong Kong might have lagged behind for several reasons,[103] conditions are now in place for its evolution to a more mature phase. As highlighted by one commentator,[104] Hong Kong satisfies all the general requirements for democracy, including an increasingly politicized active population, freedom of speech, potentially capable political leaders, belief in democratic principles and individual rights, a high level of literacy and education, a pluralistic social order, lack of extreme inequalities among the politically relevant strata, an advanced system of law and regulation of executive and administrative action, as well as a political system influenced by a large number of interest groups none of which has absolute control of resources and outcomes.

The development of democratic institutions is essential to progress on the "internalization" front. Such institutions are likely to form a bulwark against influences from across the borders that might render movement in this direction less than smooth. Further, a democratic political milieu should be conducive to the emergence of socioeconomic forces, including a committed elite that draws on grass-roots support, favoring the "internalization" agenda.

A Bill of Rights

Applicability of International Prescriptions

International norms pertaining to human rights apply in Hong Kong by virtue of two main sources. To the extent that certain human rights prescriptions have crystallized into customary international law (i.e., "general practice accepted as law"), they constitute part of English Common Law, and hence of the law of the land in Hong Kong. They should continue to be applicable in the territory beyond 1997 in accordance with the stipulation in the Joint Declaration that "[a]fter the establishment of the Hong Kong Special Administrative Region, the laws previously in force in Hong Kong (i.e., the common law, rules of equity, ordinances, subordinate legislation and customary law) shall be maintained."[105] Arguably, therefore, the so-called "International Bill of Rights," the 1948 Universal Declaration of Human Rights—which, in the light of strong evidence, is regarded as having acquired the status of customary international law[106]—is enforceable in the local courts and/or could be resorted to for the purpose of statutory interpretation.

Several constraints, however, impede an effective utilization of the "customary" source of international human rights law in Hong Kong, including a constitutional convention that in conflict, a rule of common law would yield to an Act of Parliament/Ordinance, and the doctrine of precedent.[107] Of added inhibiting effect is the perception that on matters concerning foreign relations, the state "cannot speak with two voices" and that "sound policy requires that the courts of the King shall act in unison with the Government of the King."[108] Nor would a reliance on a "pioneering spirit" or "reforming zeal" of the local judiciary be likely to generate a more vigorous enforcement of international customary law,[109] given, inter alia, traditional tendencies to stay aloof from political questions and reluctance to rule on questions of international law.

Possibly, a more effective source for the implementation of international human rights law in Hong Kong is the "conventional" one, namely, by means of the legislative incorporation[110] into the domestic law of human rights conventions that have been extended to the territory.[111] Most notable among these treaties are the International Covenant on Civil and Political Rights (ICCPR) and the International Covenant on Economic, Social and Cultural Rights (ICESCR), the continued applicability of which is mandated in the Joint Declaration. The implementation of the two covenants (as well as of "international labor conventions as applied to Hong Kong") in the HKSAR is specifically guaranteed in the Basic Law.

It may, however, be noted that, although ratified and extended[112] to the territory already in 1976, the ICCPR was only formally "incorporated" into the local law—and hence domestically justifiable—with the enactment of the Bill of Rights Ordinance in 1991.[113] No such incorporation has been pursued with respect to the ICESCR. It should nonetheless be emphasized that, while Hong Kong people may be unable to enforce their rights under the ICESCR in the domestic courts, international obligations imposed on the government under the covenant must be discharged. Equally binding are "reporting duties"[114] to the relevant international human rights bodies.

Domestic Implementation

Notwithstanding criticisms leveled at the Bill of Rights Ordinance (BoRO)—concerning its limited scope, temporal restrictions, undue exemptions from its application, and its unmodified incorporation of unwarranted reservations[115]—the enactment of the ordinance clearly reflects an attempt to give effect to mutual pledges made by the parties to the Sino-British Joint Declaration: to enshrine in Hong Kong law provisions of the ICCPR and ICESCR, to preserve Hong Kong's "life-style," and guarantee protection of fundamental rights and freedoms of its people.

Accordingly, legitimate steps have been taken to ensure the entrenchment of the BoRO and its survival beyond 1997. Thus, effected by an amended Letters Patent, "[t]he provisions of the International Covenant on Civil and Political Rights, adopted by the General Assembly of the United Nations on 16 December 1966, as applied to Hong Kong, shall be implemented through the laws of Hong Kong. No law of Hong Kong shall be made after the coming into operation of the Hong Kong Letters Patent 1991 (No. 2) that restricts the rights and freedoms enjoyed in Hong Kong in a manner which is inconsistent with that Covenant as applied to Hong Kong" [Art. VIII (3) Hong Kong Letters Patent 1917–1991 (Nos. 1 and 2)].

The BoRO's "superior status" with respect to subsequent legislation should be maintained after the transfer of sovereignty by virtue of Article 39 of the Basic Law (which in fact "entrenches" the provisions of the ICCPR).[116] As observed by the International Commission of Jurists Mission to Hong Kong, the continued application of BoRO hinges on the willingness of the government of the PRC to abide by the guiding principles and policies it had expressly undertaken to apply to Hong Kong in the Joint Declaration, and which it had repeated in more elaborate terms in Article 39 of the Basic Law.[117]

In a similar vein, despite some divergencies between individual articles in the BoRO and the Basic Law, no fundamental conflict can be said to exist that could render the BoRO invalid by reason of inconsistency with the Basic Law.[118] It is also arguable that the ultimate point of reference is the ICCPR, which is the "facilitator-instrument" for both documents.[119] Consequently, any attempt to repeal or modify the provisions of the BoRO so as to restrict the application of any of those provisions to the HKSAR, would constitute a breach of the Joint Declaration and the Basic Law.

It is of course a trite point that the enumeration of human rights in a Bill of Rights (BoR), entrenched or otherwise, is no guarantee of their implementation. By the same token, apart from focusing attention on the authoritative source and binding nature of the relevant obligations, the incorporation of an international human rights treaty into the domestic law serves to institute respective treaty commitments as mandatory considerations in governmental decision making and policies, to be given judicial effect when necessary. The adoption of a BoR that follows closely the wording of the articles in the international covenant should also make judges feel more secure—with the backing of international jurisprudence and international authoritative interpretation—and less timid to review legislation, develop their own jurisprudence, and, perhaps, assume a more active posture as the guardians of individual rights.[120]

Yet an effective "internalization" of international human rights norms in the territory must be buttressed by what has been described by one commentator as "political entrenchment," namely making the BoR, and the system it creates, a "living reality."[121] Of particular importance in this respect should be the establishment of a human rights commission designed to perform the principal functions of education, standard setting, legislative screening, and dispute resolution. As summarized by the editors of a comparative book of essays on Hong Kong's BoR, such a body "would provide an informal and inexpensive way to resolve disputes and help in the enforcement of standards necessary to give effect to various rights. It can empower groups who are not easily able to obtain access to courts. It can play a particularly useful role in supervising affirmative action policies. It can, through cooperation with nongovernmental organizations, involve the community in the safe-guarding of human rights."[122] Even barring skeptical questions about the effectiveness of the court system to uphold human rights after the transfer of sovereignty,[123] there can be little doubt regarding the potential contribution of a human rights commission toward a more effective realization of the human rights of Hong Kong people.

No less essential is an enduring commitment to report to the relevant international human rights committees on the protection of human rights in the territory. Arguably, Article 13 of the Joint Declaration—providing for the continued application of the ICCPR and ICESCR to the HKSAR—should be construed as covering the international mechanisms available under the covenants that are in force in relation to Hong Kong (i.e., reporting[124]). It is, therefore, incumbent on the parties to arrive at an appropriate arrangement to ensure that a regular submission of reports be maintained beyond 1997. Indeed, despite awareness of some "technical and legal problems"—arising from the fact that the PRC is not a signatory to the covenants—the UN Human Rights Committee has urged China to undertake the reporting process upon resumption of sovereignty.[125]

A Court of Final Appeal

The International Link

While a reflection of constitutional ties with Great Britain, locating the apex of Hong Kong's court system in the Judicial Committee of the Privy Council in London has afforded local aggrieved persons access to an externally based institution that lies at the heart of the international network of common law jurisprudence. Viewed to be of particular importance is the availability of a "forum detached from local interests" in cases with political implications or those concerned with the power of the executive branch of the Hong Kong government, allowing "justice not only to be done but to be seen to be done."[126] The solid sociopolitical foundations upon which the Privy Council rests have lent stability and respectability to the Hong Kong legal system, underpinning the territory's evolution as an international financial and commercial center.

With the transfer of sovereignty under the "one country, two systems" formula, and in conformity with the principle of a highly autonomous Hong Kong, the parties to the Sino-British Joint Declaration have agreed that a Court of Final Appeal, vested with powers of final judgment, be established in the HKSAR. To maintain, however, the current advantages derived from the international judicial link, and to ensure true independence and membership of the highest international standard, provision was made in the Joint Declaration—and reaffirmed in the Basic Law (Article 82)—whereby the court "may as required invite judges from other common law jurisdictions."[127]

Delinking

Given the express stipulations, it is arguable that an arrangement seeking to limit the number of overseas judges to one is contrary to the plain language of both the Joint Declaration and the Basic Law—allowing the court to invite "judges" in the plural—as well as incongruous with a judiciary entitled to exercise its power "independently and free from any interference."[128]

Indeed, applying, as one should,[129] international rules pertaining to the interpretation of treaties, the respective terms in the Joint Declaration must be interpreted "in good faith in accordance with the ordinary meaning to be given to the terms of the treaty in their context and in the light of [the treaty's] object and purpose."[130] Undoubtedly, the "ordinary meaning" to be assigned to the relevant article confers on the Court of Final Appeal discretion to decide *when* a requirement arises to invite judges from other jurisdictions and *whom* to invite. There is no qualification/proviso that could support other than an intention to grant the Court full discretion regarding the exercise of its power. Such an interpretation is also induced by the principle of "institutional effectiveness," favoring wide powers for institutions to perform their functions in the most effective manner.

Further substantiation is equally drawn when the terms are examined "in the light of the object and purpose" of an accord aimed at preserving the stability and prosperity of a region endowed with a high degree of autonomy, including final power of adjudication. As delineated by one commentator,

> The setting up of a Court of Final Appeal in Hong Kong was to provide for continuity in the legal system and the rule of law even while ending the link to the Privy Council, ensuring the territory's stability. The provision for overseas judges to serve on the Court of Final Appeal was clearly intended to lend that court greater stature, so that domestic and foreign investors would continue to have confidence in the judicial system, thus ensuring the territory's prosperity. That being the case, too great a restriction on the court's right to invite overseas judges—both when they might be invited and how many might be invited—would work against giving the court the independence it is meant to enjoy and could, in fact, detract from the territory's stability and prosperity.[131]

Nor should a "deal" reached in a purported "spirit of cooperation"/"attempt to defuse tension"[132] or as "part of a package of compromises"[133] (as distinct from a "subsequent agreement regarding the interpretation of the treaty," which may be taken into account under the Vienna Convention) act to divest the relevant article of an ordinary meaning consistent with the object and purpose of the treaty. Similarly, "subsequent practice" that is contrary to the clear meaning of the treaty provision cannot be considered an amendment or modification of the original accord unless a later treaty is concluded in accordance with applicable rules.

Also of doubtful validity is a line of argument paraphrasing the issue as one not of interpretation but of "subsequent elaboration of a general principle." Specifically, it has been contended that the Joint Declaration and the Basic Law "establish a *general principle* that the CFA is to have *a power* to invite [judges from other common law jurisdictions] to sit on the court, but leave the *precise scope of that power* to be defined in the course of implementation of that general principle." As such, both the Joint Declaration and the Basic Law are said to be "framework provisions which are intended to be fleshed out by more detailed legislative provisions."[134]

Yet the mode of implementation (i.e., through legislative prescription) should not circumvent the primary international obligation to "perform" the treaty in "good faith,"[135] namely in accordance with its letter and spirit (i.e., "ordinary meaning in the light of object and purpose"). An arrangement that denies the Court of Final Appeal flexibility in the choice of judges and unduly inhibits its power to invite overseas judges does not fully comply with one of the Joint Declaration's cornerstone promises of judicial autonomy.[136]

At the same time, pragmatic considerations may point to the "significant advantages"[137] of erecting a Court of Final Appeal before 1997 ("provided it will not be abolished after the transfer of sovereignty"), especially in the interest of avoiding judicial vacuum, legal uncertainty, and community insecurity. One also sympathizes with the administration's desire for an early establishment "to enable the court to gain experience, to build up its reputation, and demonstrate its independence." However, concessions involving deviations from internationally binding pledges are too costly. Nor is it clear that the premises underlying such concessions are correct.[138]

Conclusion

As the analysis offered in the core sections of this chapter demonstrates, Hong Kong does not lack the necessary international legal tools to sustain its status as an autonomous player in the global arena. Thus, by virtue of a legally binding international agreement, as well as general international norms pertaining to "autonomy," the territory has been equipped with the appropriate "international legal personality"; its people possess the right to govern themselves in accordance with generally subscribed democratic principles; they are further guaranteed, under applicable conventions and by customary international law, the enjoyment and protection of universally recognized human rights and fundamental freedoms; finally, assurance, both international and constitutional, has been provided for the maintenance, through an independent and internationally respected final adjudicatory organ, of Hong Kong's rule of law and the integrity of its legal system (which underpin the stability and prosperity of the territory).

At the same time, difficulties in the effective internalization of these international legal tools have been outlined. Attention has been drawn to the potential for encroachment on the pledged autonomy of the HKSAR's legislative, executive and judicial powers; the obstacles in the concretization of the people's right to internal self-determination/right to democracy; the need for further institutional support and procedural safeguards to ensure effective implementation of human rights and fundamental freedoms; and the guarding against compromising indispensable sureties for an autonomous and impartial judiciary.

The balance between the legal imperatives and the forces shaping the behavior of decision makers in Beijing and their representatives in the territory is clearly delicate. The outcome of this historical experiment remains to be seen.

Notes

1. See Roda Mushkat, "Hong Kong as an International Legal Person," *Emory International Law Review* 6 (1992), pp. 105–170. For a more recent discussion see Roda Mushkat, *One Country, Two International Legal Personalities: The Case of Hong Kong* (Hong Kong: Hong Kong University Press, 1997).

2. The discussion in this section is largely based on the author's analysis in ibid.

3. Joint Declaration of the Government of the United Kingdom of Great Britain and Northern Ireland and the Government of the People's Republic of China on the Question of Hong Kong, December 19, 1984, Cmnd 9543, reprinted in *International Legal Materials* 23 (1984): 1366 (hereafter Sino-British Joint Declaration, or JD).

4. JD, Art. 3(2).

5. The Basic Law of the Hong Kong Special Administrative Region of the People's Republic of China, adopted at the Third Session of the Seventh National People's Congress of the PRC on April 4, 1990, to be put into effect as of July 1, 1997, reprinted in International Legal Materials 29 (1990): 1511 (hereafter Basic Law, or BL).

6. JD, Art. 3(3).

7. See Hurst Hannum and Richard B. Lillich, "The Concept of Autonomy in International Law," in Yoram Dinstein, ed., *Models of Autonomy* (New Brunswick, NJ: Transaction Books, 1981), pp. 215–254.

8. JD, Annex I, Art. I, para. 3. To underscore the "local" character of the chief executive, the BL provides that a candidate should be "a Chinese citizen . . . who is a permanent resident of the Region with no right of abode in any foreign country and [one who] has ordinarily resided in Hong Kong for a continuous period of not less than 20 years." BL, Art. 44.

9. JD, Annex I, Art. I, para. 3.

10. JD, Annex I, Art. II, para. 2.

11. JD, Annex I, Art. III, para. 2; BL, Art. 85. To ensure the independence of the judiciary, both the Sino-British Joint Declaration and the Basic Law contain detailed provisions pertaining to appointment, removal from office, and immunity from legal action in respect of

judicial functions: JD, Annex I, Art. III, para. 3; BL, arts. 88, 89, 85.

12. JD, Annex I, Art. XI, para. 1.

13. Ibid.

14. JD, Annex I, Art. XI, para. 2.

15. Ibid.

16. JD, Annex I, Art. XI, para. 3.

17. JD, Annex I, Art. VI, para. 4.

18. JD, Annex I, Art. XIV, para. 2.

19. Ibid., para. 7.

20. See, e.g., BL, pmbl. paras. 2,3.

21. JD, Annex I, Art. I, para. 1; BL, Art. 5.

22. JD, Annex I, Art. VI, para. 1; BL, Art. 5.

23. JD, Annex I, Art. VI, para. 1.

24. Ibid., para. 2.

25. JD, Annex I, Art. VII, para. 2.

26. JD, Annex I, Art. VI, para. 3.

27. Ibid., para. 2.

28. Ibid.

29. JD, Annex I, Art. VII, para. 1.

30. JD, Annex I, Art. VI, para. 3.

31. JD, Annex I, Art. VIII, para. 2.

32. JD, Annex I, Art. IX, para. 1.

33. See Hurst Hannum, "The Foreign Affair Power of Autonomous Regimes," *Nordic Journal of International Law* 57 (1988), pp. 273, 277.

34. JD, Annex I, Art. V, para. 2.

35. Ibid.

36. JD, Art. 3(5).

37. For reaffirmation and details of implementation, see: BL, Chap. VI.

38. JD, Annex I, Art. II, para 2, provides: "The legislature may on its own authority enact laws in accordance with the provisions of the Basic Law and legal procedures, and report them to the Standing Committee of the National People's Congress for the record. Laws enacted by the legislature which are in accordance with the Basic Law and legal procedures shall be regarded as valid."

39. Judicial review would arguably avoid politicization of constitutional issues.

40. See Brian Z. Tamanahah, "Post-1997 Hong Kong: A Comparative Study of the Meaning of 'High Degree of Autonomy,' "*California Western International Law Journal* 20 (1989), pp. 41, 51.

41. Ibid., at pp. 51–52.

42. BL, Art. 18.

43. JD, Annex I, Art. I, para. 2.

44. BL, Art. 18.

45. BL, Art. 159.

46. Note, however, that "[b]efore a bill for amendment [to the Basic Law] is put on the agenda of the National People's Congress, the Committee for the Basic Law of the Hong Kong Special Administrative Region [half of whose membership is to consist of Hong Kong residents] shall study it and submit its views." Ibid.

47. Yash Ghai, "A Comparative Perspective," in Peter Wesley-Smith, ed., *Hong Kong's Basic Law: Problems & Prospects* (Hong Kong: Faculty of Law, University of Hong Kong, 1990), pp. 1–21.

48. Ibid., p. 21.

49. BL, Art. 159.

50. BL, pmbl.

51. BL, Art. 43. Among other duties, the chief executive is to "implement the directives issued by the Central People's Government in respect of the relevant matters provided for in this Law." Ibid., Art. 48(8). It is further pointed out that "there are no institutional mechanisms to enable the Chief Executive of the SAR to challenge the validity of orders or directions issued to him by the PRC State Council even where there are grounds to suspect that such orders or directions may violate the autonomy granted to the SAR by the Basic Law." Albert H.Y. Chen, "Some Reflections on Hong Kong's Autonomy," *Hong Kong Law Journal* 24 (1994): pp. 173,177. But note that the chief executive "shall be accountable to the Central People's Government and the Hong Kong Special Administrative Region *in accordance with the provisions of this Law*'" (emphasis added). BL, Art. 43.

52. BL, Art. 50.

53. BL, Art. 48(6).

54. See Tamanahah, "Post-1997 Hong Kong,", at p. 49.

55. "The Chief Executive of the Hong Kong Special Administrative Region shall be selected by election or through consultations held locally. . . . The method for selecting the Chief Executive shall be specified in the light of the actual situation in the Hong Kong Administrative Region and in accordance with the principle of gradual and orderly progress. The ultimate aim is the selection of the Chief Executive by universal suffrage upon nomination by a broadly representative nominating committee in accordance with democratic procedures." BL, Art. 45. Details of the specific method of selection of the HKSAR's chief executive are provided in Annex I of the BL.

56. A local commentator speculated that the appointment will be a "mere formality" to demonstrate China's sovereignty over Hong Kong. He suggests that if the central government refused to appoint the chief executive elected by the local authorities, a constitutional crisis will follow with a serious adverse impact on the stability and prosperity of the territory. See Joseph Y.S. Cheng, "Looking at the Other Options," *South China Morning Post,* March 2, 1986.

57. BL, Art. 50.

58. BL, Art. 73(9).

59. The commission is to be "composed of local judges, persons from the legal profession, and eminent persons from other sectors." BL, Art. 88.

60. Daniel R. Fung, "The Basic Law of the Hong Kong Special Administrative Region of the People's Republic of China: Problems of Interpretation," *International and Comparative Law Quarterly* 37 (1988), pp. 701, 706.

61. "In virtually all the autonomous entities, the central government has final jurisdiction, whether appellate or original, for judicial decisions regarding the relationship between it and the secondary entity, and exclusively controls decisions relating to its power over foreign affairs and defense matters." Tamanahah, "Post-1997 Hong Kong," pp. 54–55.

62. Ibid., at p. 55.

63. BL, Art. 158. The SC-NPC is obliged to consult the Hong Kong Basic Law Committee before giving an interpretation, and while their interpretation is binding on the courts, "judgments previously rendered shall not be affected." Ibid.

64. See, for example, Liu Che-ning, "The Power of Interpretation of the Hong Kong Special Administrative Region Basic Law—Where Do We Go from Here?" *China Law Reporter* 4 (1989), pp. 185, 193.

65. Liu, Ibid., at p. 195.

66. Quoted in Michael C. Davis, *Constitutional Confrontation in Hong Kong: Issues and Implications of the Basic Law* (Basingstoke: Macmillan, 1989), p. 44.

67. See, for example, a model for constitutional judicial review (combining a "decen-

tralized incidenter system" that permits the local courts to review the acts of the legislative and executive branches for conformity to the Basic Law) proposed by Davis, ibid., at pp. 55–67.

68. BL, Art. 19.

69. Ibid.

70. Distinctions employed in both the Joint Declaration and the Basic Law between foreign and external affairs or defense and public order tend to obscure rather than elucidate the meaning of the two key terms. See, generally, Roda Mushkat, "Foreign, External and Defence Affairs" in Peter Wesley-Smith and Albert H.Y. Chen, eds., *The Basic Law and Hong Kong's Future* (Hong Kong: Butterworths, 1988), pp. 248–267.

71. JD, Annex I, Art. XII: "The maintenance of public order in the Hong Kong Special Administrative Region shall be the responsibility of the Hong Kong Special Administrative Region Government. Military forces sent by the Central People's Government for the purpose of defence shall not interfere in the internal affairs of the Hong Kong Special Administrative Region." See also BL, art 14.

72. Under an agreement signed on June 30, 1994. See "Britain and China Agree to Military Land Transfer," *Financial Times,* July 1, 1994, p. 1.

73. BL, Art. 18.

74. For a recent thorough examination, see Edward A. Laing, "The Norm of Self-Determination, 1941–1991," *California Western International Law Journal* 22 (1991–92), pp. 209–308.

75. See relevant international declarations, agreements, resolutions, and so forth, cited in Roda Mushkat, "Hong Kong's Quest for Autonomy: A Theoretical Reinforcement," in Raymond Wacks, ed., *Hong Kong, China and 1997: Essays in Legal Theory* (Hong Kong: Hong Kong University Press, 1993), pp. 307, 314, 46n.

76. See ibid., pp. 314–315 and accompanying notes.

77. See ibid., pp. 318–321 and accompanying notes.

78. See, however, the conclusion reached by the International Commission of Jurists ("The people of Hong Kong are entitled to the right of self-determination under international law") in *Countdown to 1997: Report of a Mission to Hong Kong* (Cambridge: International Commission of Jurists, 1992), p. 56.

79. See ibid., pp. 320–321 and respective notes.

80. UNGA Res. 217A(III) 1948, Art. 21. That the Universal Declaration has acquired the force of customary international law is amply evidenced by subsequent events and the practice of states during the past forty-six years. See John P. Humphrey, "The Universal Declaration of Human Rights: Its History, Impact and Judicial Character," in B. G. Ramcharan, ed., *Human Rights—Thirty Years after the Universal Declaration* (The Hague: Nijhoff, 1979), p. 33; see also Richard L. Lillich, "Civil Rights," in Theodore Meron, ed., *Human Rights in International Law—Legal and Policy Issues* (Oxford: Clarendon Press, 1984), pp. 116–117; some authors have suggested that the Universal Declaration has in fact the "attributes of jus cogens." See Myres S. McDougal, Harold D. Lasswell and Lung-chu Chen, *Human Rights and World Order* (New Haven, CT: Yale University Press, 1980), p. 274.

81. Reprinted in *International Legal Materials* 6 (1967), p. 368. Article 25 extends to every citizen the right "(a) To take part in the conduct of public affairs directly or through freely chosen representatives; (b) To vote and be elected at genuine elections which shall be by universal and equal suffrage and shall be held by secret ballot, guaranteeing the free expression of the will of the electors; (c) To have access, on general terms of equality, to public service in his country." With a "balance heavily tilting towards the substantial new majority of states actually practicing a reasonable credible version of electoral democracy," the legal obligations contained in the covenant (now binding on more than two-

thirds of all states) may be held to be "stating what is becoming a customary legal norm applicable to all." Thomas M. Franck, "The Emerging Right to Democratic Governance," *American Journal of International Law* 86 (1992), at p. 64.

82. Reprinted in *International Legal Materials* 9 (1970), pp. 673, 682, Art. 23.

83. First Protocol to the European Convention on Human Rights (entered into force on May 18, 1954), *European Treaty Series*, No. 9, Art. 3.

84. African Charter on Human and People's Rights (1981), reprinted in *International Legal Materials* 21 (1982), p. 59, art 13.

85. UNGA Res. 45/150, February 21, 1991.

86. See Document of the Copenhagen Meeting of the Conference on the Human Dimension, reprinted in *International Legal Materials* 29 (1990), pp. 1305, 1308, para. 5; Charter of Paris for a New Europe, reprinted in *International Legal Materials* 30 (1991), pp. 190, 194; Document of the Moscow Meeting of the Conference on the Human Dimension of the CSCE, reprinted in ibid., p. 1670.

87. Including Canada, the United States, and the nations of Eastern Europe.

88. *White Paper on the Further Development of Representative Government in Hong Kong* (Hong Kong: Government Printer, November 1984), para. 2(a).

89. See *White Paper on the Annual Report on Hong Kong 1989 to Parliament* (Hong Kong: Government Printer, April 18, 1990), para. 29. It may be noted that until 1985 all members of the Legislative Council were either government officials or appointed by the governor. In 1985 a system of indirect elections was instituted whereby 12 members (out of 57) were elected by functional constituencies (e.g., commercial, financial, education, and other professions) and another 12 by an electoral college. First direct elections were held in 1991.

90. To lower the voting age from 21 to 18; to replace the 1991 system of double-member constituencies that are directly elected with single-seat constituencies; to replace the corporate voting in existing functional constituencies by individual voters; to propose nine new functional constituencies with wide electorates; to make all district board members elected and to abolish appointed members of municipal councils; to give district boards responsibility for local public work projects and other local activities, and to increase their funding; to establish an independent Boundary and Election Commission; to draw all or most of the members of the 1995 Election Committee (which will select HKSAR's chief executive) from the elected membership of the district boards.

91. See Governor's Address at the Opening of the Hong Kong Legislative Council, *Our Next Five Years, The Agenda For Hong Kong,* October 7, 1992, paras. 101–107 ("The Constitutional Package").

92. Christine Loh, "Not Far Enough," *Far Eastern Economic Review,* April 8, 1993, p. 24.

93. Cited in "Patten's Next Stand," *The Economist,* July 2, 1994, p. 6.

94. JD, Annex I, Art. III, para. 3.

95. JD, Art. 4.

96. *Representative Government in Hong Kong* (Hong Kong: Government Printer, February 1994), para. 83.

97. Yash Ghai, "A Comparative Perspective" in *Hong Kong's Basic Law,* at p. 11. See BL, Art. 45: "The ultimate aim is the selection of the chief executive by universal suffrage upon nomination by a broadly representative nominating committee in accordance with democratic procedures"; Art. 68: "The ultimate aim is the election of all members of the Legislative Council by universal suffrage."

98. See BL, Decision of the National People's Congress on the Method for the Formation of the First Government and the First Legislative Council of the Hong Kong Special Administrative Region, adopted at the Third Session of the Seventh

National People's Congress on April 4, 1990, para. 6.

99. A resolution to terminate Hong Kong's present political structure on July 1, 1997, was adopted by the SC-NPC. See "China to Abolish Hong Kong's Legislature," *International Herald Tribune*, September 1, 1994, p. 1.

100. See proposal by the political subgroup of the China-appointed Preliminary Working Committee (PWC), reported in Linda Choy, Chris Yeung, and So Lai-Fun, "Selected Caretakers to Run SAR for a Year," *South China Morning Post*, October 8, 1994, p. 1.

101. For example, the provision that "the legislature of the HKSAR shall be constituted by elections" and that legislative power for the HKSAR shall be vested only in such legislature.

102. See thorough analysis in Yash Ghai, "Basic Flaws in China's Thinking," *South China Morning Post*, December 14, 1994, p. 21.

103. Including low participation in the political process, the lack of effective political organization geared toward production of strong political leaders (because of "reliance by the colonial system for its stability on the politically unorganised passivity of the masses"), traditional influences (e.g., Confucian philosophy, which regards confrontational politics as bad, and indifference to being ruled by minority), PRC's opposition. See, generally, Norman Miners, "Hong Kong: A Case Study in Political Stability," *Commonwealth and Comparative Politics* 13 (1975), p. 26; Lau Siu-kai, "Institutions Without Leaders: The Hong Kong Chinese View of Political Leadership," *Pacific Affairs* 63 (1990), p. 191; Ming K. Chan, "Democracy Derailed: Realpolitik in the Making of the Hong Kong Basic Law, 1985–90," in Ming K. Chan and David J. Clark, eds., *The Hong Kong Basic Law: Blueprint for "Stability and Prosperity" under Chinese Sovereignty?* (Armonk, NY: M.E. Sharpe, and Hong Kong: Hong Kong University Press, 1991), p. 3.

104. See well-supported discussion in Mason Hills, "The Rule of Law and Democracy in Hong Kong—Comparative Analysis of British Liberalism and Chinese Socialism," in *E-Law—Murdoch University Journal of Law* [online].

105. JD, Annex I, Art. II, para. 1. This provision is duplicated in the BL, Art. 8.

106. See Richard B. Lillich and Frank C. Newman, "The Legal Status of the Universal Declaration of Human Rights," in Richard B. Lillich and Frank C. Newman, eds., *International Human Rights: Problems of Law and Policy* (Boston and Toronto: Little, Brown, 1979), pp. 65–56.

107. For further elaboration see Roda Mushkat, "International Human Rights Law and Domestic Hong Kong Law," in Raymond Wacks, ed., *Hong Kong's Bill of Rights: Problems and Prospects* (Hong Kong: Faculty of Law, University of Hong Kong, 1990), p. 25.

108. See ibid., at p. 27.

109. See Nihal Jayawickrama, "Hong Kong and the International Protection of Human Rights," in Raymond Wacks, ed., ibid. (Hong Kong: Oxford University Press, 1992), pp. 120, 162.

110. Note that in contrast with the position of customary international law, treaties are not directly incorporated into English law and are incapable of constituting a rule of law for the courts in the absence of legislative implementation. For relevant Hong Kong practice, see Mushkat, ibid., at pp. 28–32.

111. Reproduced in Andrew Byrnes and Johannes Chan, eds., *Public Law and Human Rights: A Hong Kong Sourcebook* (Hong Kong, Singapore, Malaysia: Butterworths Asia, 1993).

112. Subject to reservations regarding the right to self-determination, custodial procedures, freedom of movement, immigration restrictions, expulsion of aliens, policies concerning acquisition of nationality or right of abode, and the right to free election.

113. Note, however, the government's contention that "[b]efore the enactment of the

Bill of Rights Ordinance, the two Covenants were implemented in Hong Kong, as in the United Kingdom, through a combination of common law, legislation and administrative measures." *An Introduction to Hong Kong Bill of Rights Ordinance* (Hong Kong: Government Printer, 1992), p. 5.

114. Under the ICCPR and the ICESCR, states-parties "undertake to submit reports [to the UN Committee on Human Rights] on the measures they have adopted which give effect to the rights recognized [in the Covenant] and on the progress made in the enjoyment of these rights." See ICCPR, Art. 40; ICESCR, Art. 16. A reporting duty is also prescribed in the International Convention for the Elimination of Racial Discrimination (Art. 9), the Convention Against Torture and Other Inhuman or Degrading Treatment or Punishment (Art. 19), and in the Convention on the Rights of the Child (Art. 44), which have been extended to Hong Kong in 1969, 1992 and 1994 respectively.

115. See, generally, Johannes Chan and Yash Ghai, eds., *The Bill of Rights: A Comparative Approach* (Hong Kong, Singapore, Malaysia: Butterworths Asia, 1993), pp. 55–69; 71–105; 161–198.

116. Article 39 reads as follows:

> The provisions of the International Covenant on Civil and Political Rights, the International Covenant on Economic, Social and Cultural Rights, and international labor conventions as applied to Hong Kong shall remain in force and shall be implemented through the laws of the Hong Kong Special Administrative Region.
>
> The rights and freedoms enjoyed by Hong Kong residents shall not be restricted unless as prescribed by law. Such restrictions shall not contravene the provisions of the preceding paragraph of this Article.

117. See International Commission of Jurists, *Countdown to 1997,* at p. 99.

118. See Yash Ghai, "The Bill of Rights and the Basic Law: Inconsistent or Complementary?" paper presented at the seminar "Hong Kong's Bill of Rights—1991–1994 and Beyond" organized by the Faculty of Law, University of Hong Kong, June 18, 1994.

119. See ibid.

120. Note, however, the concern expressed by the UN Committee on Economic, Social and Cultural Rights over the "low level of awareness and interest in international human rights law on the part of the judiciary in Hong Kong," cited in Kieron Flynn, "Rights Record Savaged," *Eastern Express,* December 10–11, 1994, p. 1.

121. See David Clark, "Implementing the Bill of Rights: Three Modest Proposals. Or Taking the Bill of Rights Seriously," in Wacks, ed., *Hong Kong's Bill of Rights: Problems and Prospects,* p. 82.

122. Johannes Chan and Yash Ghai, "A Comparative Perspective on the Bill of Rights," in *The Hong Kong Bill of Rights: A Comparative Approach,* at p. 10.

123. See House of Commons, Foreign Affairs Committee, *Relations Between the United Kingdom and China in the Period up to and Beyond 1997* (UK: Government Printer, March 23, 1994), para. 206. The FAC concluded that an independent statutory human rights commission, as well as an independent human rights "watchdog," were "possible, legal and desirable" (para. 207).

For a particularly pessimistic depiction of the prospects for human rights protection beyond 1997, see Michael Kirby, "Human Rights: The Role of the Judge" in Chan and Ghai, eds., *The Hong Kong Bill of Rights: A Comparative Approach,* at pp. 242–251.

124. It may be noted that another mechanism, the individual petition system, contained in the Optional Protocol to the Covenants is not currently accessible to Hong Kong people.

125. See David Wallen, "UN Call to China on Rights Reports," *South China Morning Post,* December 10, 1994, p. 2.

126. See Margaret Ng, "Hong Kong Has Been Cheated over the Rule of Law after 1997," *South China Morning Post,* October 1, 1991, p. 23.

127. JD, Annex I, Art. III, para. 4.

128. JD, Annex I, Art. III, para. 2.

129. Interpretation of treaties is governed by international law as codified in the 1969 *Vienna Convention on the Law of Treaties,* the basic premise being that when two nations speak to each other, they use the language of nations.

130. Article 31, *Vienna Convention on the Law of Treaties.* Note that Art. 31 is considered "customary international law" and as such binding on all states regardless of whether they are parties to the Vienna Convention.

131. Frank Ching, "The Vienna Convention on the Law of Treaties and the Joint Liaison Group's Agreement on Hong Kong's Court of Final Appeal," a paper presented at a Zonta Club Forum on the Court of Final Appeal, October 21, 1994.

132. See Lo Shiu-hing, "The Politics of the Court of Final Appeal Debate in Hong Kong," *Issues and Studies* 29 (1993), pp. 105–131.

133. See Stacy Mosher, "Court of Contention," *Far Eastern Economic Review,* December 19, 1991, p. 10.

134. In a letter dated November 17, 1994, from Attorney General J.F. Mathews to the chairman of the Hong Kong Bar Association, enclosing a British Government's statement on "Hong Kong: Court of Final Appeal."

135. As laid down in Article 26 of the *Vienna Convention on the Law of Treaties.*

136. See the conclusion of the International Commission of Jurists, *Countdown to 1997,* at p. 91 "The agreement reached by the Joint Liaison Group on the composition of the Court of Final Appeal is contrary to the Joint Declaration and the Basic Law and is constitutionally invalid; the Court of Final Appeal itself should be allowed to determine the number and identity of foreign judges to sit as temporary members".

137. See Robert C. Allcock, "Court of Final Appeal," speech delivered at the Zonta Club on October 21, 1994.

138. See So Lai-fun and Linda Choy, "Appeal Court Judges at Risk," *Sunday Morning Post,* December 11, 1994 (referring to a statement by the director of the Hong Kong and Macao Affairs Office that judges appointed to the CFA will not be guaranteed places on the panel when the territory reverts to mainland rule).

7

Labyrinth of Hybridization: The Cultural Internationalization of Hong Kong

Hoiman Chan

Cultural Internationalization as Problematic

At the last juncture of the impending transition toward 1997, the project of cultural internationalization has assumed special irony and impetus. The fortune and trajectory of Hong Kong are even now being decided in a spate of international negotiations and obscure power plays, in which Hong Kong society is not permitted to play an active role. Despite how international and modernized the city's facade has become, it stands as less than a nation able to prescribe its own political destiny. Culture is, however not as unrelenting as politics. While the latter is constrained, maybe the culture field can do better in securing sympathetic hearings and even respect for Hong Kong. Herein lies the more imminent meaning and prerogatives of cultural internationalization—embodying ideals which, moreover, are seemingly within reach with the nascent cultural vision of an alleged "Greater Hong Kong."

As this volume as a whole will address the multifaceted articulation of internationalization, the present chapter can dispense with general discussion on the construct per se.[1] What requires closer delineation is how this project of internationalization is entwined with the cultural formations of Hong Kong. The growth of Hong Kong society—cultural and otherwise—is more often than not fashioned by political and historical vicissitudes from outside of the territory. The different identities that the city incarnated at one time or another—colony, entrepôt, "Little Dragon," soon-to-be SAR—are the unwitting products of changeable international restructuring in alignments of power or in division of labor.[2]

The irony is that with the fateful transition at our doorstep, many in the territory have actively seized on the dynamic nexus of internationalization, and seek to ensure a better future by extending the level of international attention to, and even intervention in, Hong Kong. This endeavor of active internationalization is very much frowned upon by the Chinese side. Yet for the purpose of this essay, these two orientations toward internationalization—from passive to active modes, broadly speaking—set the interpretive parameters for probing the cultural conditions of late-transitional Hong Kong.

The methodological touchstone to this agenda lies first in securing a more pertinent analytical framework regarding the cultural dynamics of internationalization. The following discussions will hence address issues of internationalization not simply as specific problem areas or themes, but rather in terms of the embracing problematic that underlines the often hybridized cultural formations forged in the enigmatic encounter between the local and the international. In this widened horizon of the internationalization problematic, it becomes eminently conceivable that even cultural processes seemingly far removed—such as the formation of local culture and of indigenization—must eventually be understood as embroiling in the same configurations of the forces of internationalization.[3] In other words, the internationalization problematic may well serve as the interpretive pathway into the cultural formation of Hong Kong as a whole. There is no need for the agenda here to invoke the various "post-isms" as perhaps the more far-fetched rubrics for "unpacking" the cultural conjunctures concerned. The purpose of this essay is foremost to make sense of the cultural situation by following through the steps and the momentum of its trajectory. It would be irrelevant and even irreverent to subject the fortunes of Hong Kong to yet another analytical offering of postcoloniality and/or orientalization, to thus deploy the predicament of Hong Kong as an occasion for academic soul searching and/or self-victimization.

The cultural problematic of internationalization, as here postulated, will be charted along three dimensions, denoting plausible cultural scenarios arising from the interface and contestation between the local and outside worlds. Initially, it is helpful to conceive cultural internationalization as a two-way process, with interactions and mutative influences flowing in both directions. If all goes well, there will be a healthy dose of cultural interpenetration between Hong Kong, the adjacent regions, and beyond. There are, of course, wider geographical factors that tend to relegate Hong Kong to the outskirts of global cultural exchange, as, for instance, in relation with the farther away Western world. And there are also time periods in which the input of Hong Kong—if any—on the cultural life of adjacent areas fluctuates. To conceive of internationalization in terms of a two-way street would be instrumental in mapping the resulting variegated scenarios, paving the way for more fine-tuned diagnoses into the problematic as a whole. And to invoke the image of hybridization in the case of Hong Kong is to underscore the ultimately unmistakable imbalance in this two-way process.

Along this vein, the three constitutive dimensions of this problematic can be identified as follows. The guiding rationale has to do with the divergent modes of cultural interpenetration between Hong Kong and the outside regions, and of the extent of repercussions for sociocultural life in Hong Kong. At one end of the spectrum, it is plausible to see outside cultural influences as going through a process of selective assimilation; this would in time come to be considered as part and parcel of the local cultural make-up of Hong Kong society. It is even possible to interpret much of the bulk of Hong Kong culture as, in the final analysis, the hybridized products of original inputs from mainland China or from the West at large. Short of taking the present argument to this extreme, it remains important to underscore the mechanisms of cultural indigenization that define one specific mode of articulation of the internationalization problematic. Indigenization is seen accordingly as not so much countercurrent to internationalization, but rather the integral dimension that would bring the latter to its logical completion. Hence the possible relevance of an agenda of "glocalization" in the study of cultural Hong Kong. It has often been pointed out that during the seventies and the eighties, Hong Kong witnessed the formation of a broadly indigenous culture, even amid simultaneous economic successes. What might have been less obvious is that, alongside and often preceding the growth of indigenous culture, the seemingly contrasting mechanisms of assimilation and indigenization must also be permitted to run their course. The dimension of indigenization attains its primacy because it is the embodiment of the farthest reach of external cultural entwinement, even into the apparent local culture of Hong Kong.[4] This is not to claim that all there is in the indigenous culture of Hong Kong is the wholesale transplant of cultural ideas and artifacts produced elsewhere. There are no doubt elaborate mutative linkages between adaptation, innovation, and originality in the formation of local culture. Yet it is necessary all the same to emphasize the often catalytic role of indigenization in this entire process.

At a more moderate level, the interface of Hong Kong culture with the international scene can be considered in somewhat less holistic, yet nonetheless significant, terms. Thus, even in purely outward appearances, the cultural make-up of Hong Kong displays a dazzling *bricolage* of motifs, style, and artifacts assembled from all over the world. At this more superficial level, the question is not so much one of assimilation and indigenization in the eventual consolidation of an autonomous cultural formation. It is, rather, more a question of the passive and unreflective desire for the exotic, the chic, and fashionable—for the "ins" and "outs" as defined someplace else in the world. That modern Hong Kong society has been acutely fashion-conscious is a common impression. The Hong Kong cultural world—whether seen in consumerist, popular, material, or elitist terms—is as a rule marked by the quick succession of fads and fashions, welding together somewhat arbitrarily the alleged latest trends in some legendary cultural capitals. This is certainly another distinctive mode of articulation in the problematic of internationalization, the mode that in fact endows Hong Kong culture with its prominent international, cosmopolitan outlook. Yet most of the fads and fashions remain just that—they disappear from the cultural formations of Hong Kong as soon as they are phased out in their home countries. In other words, at this level of the internationalization problematic, outside cultural influences in the form of gimmicks, artifacts, style, pastiche, fads, kitsch, and so forth, as a rule do not stay long enough to become indigenized in a more meaningful or lasting way.[5]

This line of thought will have to be further discussed in the following pages. At this point, suffice it to simply contrast this facade of cosmopolitanism against indigenization, as two distinctive vantage points through which Hong Kong culture can take on inputs from the outside world.

In addition to the cultural orientations of indigenization and cosmopolitanism, the other end of the internationalization problematic is marked by the active assertions and impacts that Hong Kong culture is able to project, in particular for the surrounding regions. In a sense, this is probably the facet of internationalization that appeared clearest and most impressive to the local population. It can be defined as internationalization *qua* forces of cultural development and expansion, beyond the limited local geographical and political compass of Hong Kong. It is hence the reversal of indigenization, and may be here designated as a mode of exogenization. That Hong Kong has been able to exert significant cultural impact on the wider world is a development in which the Hong Kong folks can justly take pride. Not only is popular cultural entertainment produced in Hong Kong widely available in Chinese communities all over the world, but ever since the Dengist reform era, Hong Kong has figured among the core resources of cultural imagination and artifacts for mainland China. The situation has in fact become so pervasive in the late 1980s and early 1990s, that observers have variously characterized the expansion of Hong Kong culture as a mode of reversed cultural colonization over China, or in more neutral terms, the spearhead in the shaping of a new South China culture—which in turn may well be the spearhead of the cultural China per se.[6] This is then the active imperative of internationalization that imbued the problematic with its higher raison d'être, by way of which the cultural formation of Hong Kong can secure a much wider level of attention and appreciation. This trend toward cultural exogenization is yet another practical vindication of the achievements and virtues of the Hong Kong folks, over and above the economic miracle that the city has become famous for. Culture has the added aura of creativity and finesse; its diffusion into other regions and communities would no doubt enhance the image of Hong Kong beyond a worldly commercial metropolis.

Programs of Cultural Internationalization

The above discussion thus demarcates a more holistic problematic of cultural internationalization, representing the latter as above all a multifaceted process that reverberates through virtually the entire sociocultural fabric of Hong Kong. It is in this sense that the three interpretive constructs delineated earlier, of indigenization, cosmopolitanism, and of exogenization, together define the comprehensive terrain of cultural internationalization for Hong Kong. Each in its own way constitutes, and is in turn constitutive of, the internationalization problematic. With the stage thus set, deeper insights can be gained into the character of cultural development during the late-transitional phase, by way of these interwoven rubrics of internationalization.

Based on the discussion so far, the unfolding of the internationalization problematic will be formulated in the following as embodying essentially two alternative programs, representing two specific configurations of the internationalization problematic, together with the actual states of cultural development that Hong Kong society correspondingly went through. These two programs of the internationalization problematics are hence of both analytical and historical primacy. On this basis, it would be more viable to further interpret the present cultural conditions of Hong Kong and its future prospects.

The first configuration of the internationalization problematic can be called the normative program, that is, it denotes the scenario when the interaction among all of the three constitutive rubrics of the problematic are deemed in proper operating order. In this normative situation, the cultural problematic of internationalization may be represented as in the following diagram:

Figure 7.1 **The Normative Program of Cultural Internationalization of Hong Kong**

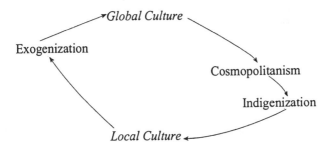

This generally circular movement depicts the unfolding of the normative—the broadly realized program of the internationalization problematics. Several observations can be made in this connection. In the first place, the category of global culture, while it delimits one pole of this cultural circuit, is employed here to indicate the contextual cultural environment extrinsic to Hong Kong. Its referents can and do vary during the historical unfolding of the problematics. At the other pole of the circuit, the category of local culture refers broadly to the internal cultural landscape of Hong Kong, a category that may serve as benchmark for generally assessing changes and magnitudes at different stages of socio-cultural growth. The second point to note is that the right-hand half of the circuit represents the diffusion of external cultural influences into Hong Kong, first at the more immediate level of cosmopolitanism, and then into the more lasting process of indigenization. There is for sure a selective mechanism to the picture such that, as noted before, not every cultural fad and fashion can take root despite their temporary currency. The selectivity is based on a balance among considerations of commensurability, novelty, and competition—to anticipate dis-cussions below. By way of the indigenization process, the formation of local culture can have access to the much wider global horizon of cultural resources. The third point to note in this connection is the elusive linkage between local culture and the active assertion of exogenization. The crux of the situation is that, granted the active imperative of internationalization as the outward expansion of cultural influences and even hegemony, this mandate can be adequately fulfilled only on the groundwork of vibrant, well-consolidated local culture. The ex-ogenization of Hong Kong culture, after all, presupposes that it is the culture of Hong Kong as such that partakes of this great transformation. This explains why the connecting circuits of the problematic are depicted as in the above diagram. It is not plausible to go from cosmopolitanism or even indigenization im-mediately to exogenization. Cosmopolitanism may turn Hong Kong into cultural entrepôt of sorts, while indigenization remains an essentially local-oriented pro-cess. Exogenization, properly speaking, does assume the outward assertion of indigenous, local culture, however it is derived or configured. It is along this specific flow of circuits that the cultural dynamics of Hong Kong may also feed back into global culture, thus completing the normative program of the cultural internationalization problematic.

Yet to depict this framework as being normative is not to say that it is a mere fictive construct. Readers familiar with the cultural conditions of Hong Kong can no doubt perceive the empirical applicability of both the constructs and the circuits as outlined above. What they exemplify is not merely the "completed," analytical version of the normative problematic. Historically speaking, they cor-respond to the pivotal high point in the cultural development of Hong Kong, a stage when this holistic program was to a large extent empirically articulated. This stage is rightly seen as the golden age of Hong Kong culture—namely the decades of the 1970s and early 1980s, when Hong Kong did manage to consoli-date a vibrant spectrum of local culture that was as yet undisturbed by the impending shadow of 1997. And this indigenized culture, with its extravagant configuring of the local and the cosmopolitan, would eventually impress a force-ful cultural style on areas and regions that far outweigh Hong Kong in sheer magnitude and power.[7]

In addition to this normative program of the problematics, there are also variations and exceptions to the norm. This explains the formulation of the second mode of articulation of the cultural internationalization problematic, which in contrast may be designated as the "incomplete" or eclipsed program of cultural internationalization. Taking Figure 7.1 as the point of departure, even in purely analytical terms the problematic can be incomplete in many forms. Each of the constituting categories or circuit can possibly remain unrealized in practice. Yet the present discussion is not of theoretical possibilities. It is one particular mode of incarnation of this partial problematic that is of importance here, because of the dramatic transformation it signifies, and also because it embodies the more current cultural condition of Hong Kong into the 1990s. This version of the incomplete program of the internationalization problematics can be depicted as in the following diagram:

Figure 7.2 **The Eclipsed Program of Cultural Internationalization**

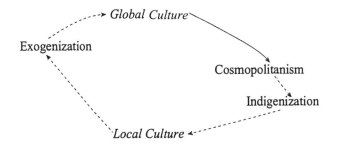

In this diagram, the broken arrows denote, in effect, interactive circuits that have become largely ruptured. Only the fragmented linkage remains that connects global culture with the apparent cosmopolitan facade of society. This is, however, a cosmopolitanism that has generally resisted indigenization, and this resistance contributes further to the demise of the already heavily undermined local cultural formation. Somewhere along the way, for reasons and causes to be specified, the local culture of Hong Kong in the 1990s has outlasted its vitality and creativity, and is too disconcerted to adequately sustain the project of cultural indigenization. The pathways are disrupted that led from cosmopolitanism, as a passive form of internationalization, to exogenization, as its aggressive form. Figure 7.2 is hence a much more shrunken problematic of cultural internationalization, in which only the one-way alley from global culture to cosmopolitanism remains fully in place. At the root of this fragmented problematic are the changing vicissitudes in the external context as well as the failure of nerve in the unfolding of the local cultural project—a failure of nerve that is in turn the result of both a sociopolitical crisis in confidence and the escape into the self-defeating apex of culture industry.

In real terms, the progressive articulation of this eclipsed problematic in the nineties does not appear particularly striking or regrettable to the casual cultural consumers and observers. The exuberance of cultural styles, choices, or artifacts can remain undiminished. The presence of free-floating cosmopolitanism can remain glamorous and endearing all on its own. And in economic terms, the pervasiveness of cosmopolitanism also widens the market and volumes of cultural commodification. Even on the political front, the vibrancy of cosmopolitanism implies that potential streaks of radicalism can become much diluted by the facile abundance of cultural choices and pluralism. The circuit from global culture into cosmopolitanism can in itself serve as the immediate scaffolding of cultural life, whether in Hong Kong or elsewhere. And what society and culture stand to lose is neither obvious nor urgent to the cultural industrialists or the consumers. After all, Hong Kong society seemingly has more pressing issues to worry about than remote pondering on cultural creativity, identity, indigenization, or their combined repercussions on external and internal dynamics.

These two programs of the cultural internationalization problematic can thus have far-reaching analytical and interpretive implications. Above all, they amount to the fact that insofar as the actualities of Hong Kong society are concerned, the internationalization problematic can be taken to mean two very different cultural scenarios. A strong program of cultural internationalization is outlined in Figure 7.1, which depicts the all-around realization of the dynamic circuits that complete the pathway leading from global culture into local culture and eventually feeding back upon the international plane, in the process enriching and deepening the different dimensions, categories, and circuits involved. The eclipsed, partial program of internationalization, in contrast, is charted in the scenario of Figure 7.2, in which the international horizon is restricted to the passive facets of cultural cosmopolitanism. While the latter may yet be sophisticated, wide-ranging, and readily embraced by society, the prime impetus is in any case no longer its assimilation and indigenization to any meaningful extent. Cultural internationalization in this light remains lopsided because it largely stays at the surface of culture industry and commodification and also because its mutative feedback into the outside world has been significantly curtailed.

With this interpretive framework thus in place, a more comprehensive perspective regarding cultural internationalization can be put forth. The following will examine in greater details the historical-empirical articulation of the two programs in question, thereby delineating the morphology of the problematic of cultural internationalization in Hong Kong. These two programs will be unraveled in the page that follows, via the constitutive nexus of categories, dynamics, and circuits as charted above.

Historical Articulations: The Normative Program

Origins

The strong, normative program of the cultural internationalization problematics best describes the general cultural conditions of Hong Kong during the decade of the 1970s and early 1980s. It is unnecessary to claim that this normative program was in any sense 'fully' realized during this golden age of the Hong Kong cultural formation. Yet the period was a time of unprecedented cultural growth all through the development of Hong Kong culture and society. And the articulation of the internationalization problematic therein both exemplified as well as reinforced this cultural high tide.

The epoch concerned unfolded against the backdrop of a much globalized Hong Kong on both economic and cultural fronts. Economically speaking, the take-off into material and financial affluence of Hong Kong was already well launched in the seventies. This marked the beginning of Hong Kong's metamorphosis into an international financial center, progressively displacing its former reliance upon manufacturing and other light industries. In addition, expansion of tourism and communication also strengthened the international connections of Hong Kong, drawing it ever further into the global orbit. All these came to a culmination into the eighties, when the global setting was eventually instrumental in shaping much of the cultural outlook of Hong Kong.[8]

That Hong Kong society has always drawn heavily upon symbolic resources proffered by other regions is, of course, a common observation. The cultural make-up of Hong Kong is widely regarded as the hybridized product of Chinese and Western legacies. Further questions can be raised, however, regarding both the shifting magnitudes and interplay of these legacies, as well as their manner of penetration into the local society. In a nutshell, the main currents during the seventies conjuncture, one may suggest, were that while the horizon of outside cultural influences did greatly expand, what was even more momentous and indicative was the active, conscientious manner whereby extrinsic influences were internalized to become an integral part of cultural Hong Kong. The impetus of foreign impacts in the seventies, in other words, ironically provided one of the key motive forces in the formation of local culture. The internationalization project during this juncture would assume its comprehensive course, first partaking in the formation of an indigenized, local culture, which in turn would exogenize its own cultural imprint elsewhere. This is essentially the master theme that shaped the intricate route leading from the seventies into the eighties, as epitomized in the normative, strong program of cultural internationalization.

At the heart of this newfound imperative of cultural formations is a deepened sense of cultural awareness and identity. The program of cultural internationalization in the eighties, in other words, is both contingent upon, while simultaneously reinforcing of, the prevailing cultural mentality of society. That Hong Kong during the 1970s first saw the genesis and progress of a largely autonomous, local-oriented cultural awareness is a theme that, while still awaiting more in-depth documentation and analysis, is generally acknowledged by interested observers. Many factors can be attributed to the engendering of this heartening scenario: that the traumatic experience of the 1967–68 revolt in turn heightened the senses of unity and belonging of Hong Kong people; that the portents of economic prosperity in the seventies progressively relieved the preoccupation of the population with material survival alone; that the entering into adulthood of the postwar generation signified a cohort that was freed of social memories carrying over from the war-torn mainland; that the politics and ideologies of decolonialization around the world prescribed a more flexible and liberal approach on the part of the government.[9] The purpose here is not to engage in a full-fledged historical unraveling of the seventies watershed. The focus is rather upon the character of the resultant cultural formation itself, both as the outcome of these embedding transformations, and as embodiment of a new, broadly internationalized yet in the main autonomous cultural outlook.

Cosmopolitanism

To cut to the heart of the labyrinthine, cultural matters, the major cultural development in Hong Kong that dominated much of the cityscape of leisure life, mass entertainment, and outlook of the seventies, was no doubt the popularization of television broadcasting. The predominance of Hong Kong popular culture on the cultural scene at large is a phenomenon that must be recognized at the outset. With the establishment of the Television Broadcasting Company (TVB) in 1967, providing free television entertainment in competition against the then more exclusive paid television of Rediffusion (RTV), the institution of television broadcasting made possible for the first time the formation of a strong, spirited institution around which cultural life for the bulk of population could rally and grow. The presence of a core cultural institution was instrumental in consolidating to an unprecedented extent the mental outlook of society within a largely common frame of cultural reference. Other cultural media like movies (both foreign and local), newspapers and magazines, and pop songs (again, both Western and local) were each significant in its own way. Yet it can be plausibly maintained that the overriding popularity of television was the uncontested cultural event of the seventies, an event which, in heightening the centrality of the popular cultural horizon, in fact did much to secure the cultural relevance of these other popular media as well.[10]

As for the question of internationalization, the primacy of television broadcasting is especially pronounced. By its nature, television broadcasting is built upon an assortment, a mosaic of entertainment genres and features. As a "hot," comprehensive medium of entertainment choices, the vitality and popularity of television hinges on senses of variety, novelty, and relevance. The planning of TV programming was hence organized along two axes, namely the promotion of local productions—whether TV drama, variety shows, musical or journalistic programs—as well as the importation of overseas TV productions, mainly in the form of TV series dubbed into Cantonese. In general, local productions were limited in scale and qualities in the earlier years of TVB and RTV. In the late sixties and the early seventies, the main genre of locally produced programs that evoked public enthusiasm were the variety shows, especially the TVB flagship daily gala "Enjoy Yourself Tonight." Locally produced drama series would take some time to grow—even with the early successes of the "Mandarina Duck and Butterfly" styled series—and did not really take off until the waves of family saga and soap opera in the mid-seventies. The importation of foreign TV programs thus played a crucial role in the early years of the TV culture. Many of the more popular foreign series were aired during prime time, and were easily part and parcel of the household culture of the eager audiences. Well-received series such as the U.S.-produced "Charlie's Angels," "It Takes a Thief," "Ironside," "Superman," "Starsky and Hutch," "Tarzan," "The Green Hornet," "Batman," and "Family Affairs," to name a random few, would each be watched as dubbed in the local tongue, and mesmerized Hong Kong audiences in these early years much as they did in the United States. Japanese productions hit even closer to home due to greater ethnic and cultural proximity. The popularity of Japanese TV series went beyond particular productions like the "G-Man," "Ultraman," or various Ninja and Samurai style martial stories. Especially well loved were the uplifting, "strengthening of will dramas," which were often sensationalized stories depicting the struggles and perseverances of protagonists in the face of seemingly insurmountable odds—whether that be hurdles in career, advancement in sports, family tragedies, or the relentless hazards of everyday life in general. The coming of age of the young judo master Sugata Sanshiro, for example, would enchant and inspire the Hong Kong TV viewers much as it did in Japan. While the impact of these foreign-produced TV shows may have varied, the combined effect of these productions made familiar, as well as demystified, the ways of life of the outside world for the Hong Kong audience. The cultural distance between Hong Kong and the outside world would be much shortened. Western culture had hitherto been something of a strong elitist and colonial bent. With the popularization of TV broadcasting, this tantalizing exclusivity would loosen and disperse into even the households of average audiences. In addition, and as a consequence of this broadened horizon, it became more plausible to conceive of a regional and global context as integral to the Hong Kong cultural imaginary. The global context shown through the eyes of TV would be vivid and immediate, far more so than was "objectively" conveyed in books, magazines, and news reports.

Analytically speaking, this development corresponds to what the above discussion referred to as the formation of cosmopolitanism, as a cultural outlook that somewhat randomly takes over artifacts and trends that are of varied sociocultural origins. What gives additional meaning to the development of the 1970s was that the permeation of extrinsic cultural tides would eventually go beyond the mosaic, exciting facade of cosmopolitanism. The latter would in fact come to set the stage for the deeper-rooted and more lasting formation of a distinctive local cultural framework. This subsequent episode also unfolded in connection with the expansion of the cultural horizon brought about by the popularization of television broadcasting in Hong Kong. The mechanism closely tied to this development is the other focal concern of TV programming noted above, namely the endeavor to promote local TV productions. What this effort required were conditions that could not be met easily. Local TV productions in principle would focus upon local concerns, ways of life, and preferably with greater sensitivity regarding social relevance. It was a complex enough goal to identify what these might be, as well as to underline their relevance. And to produce TV programs on these conditions that were moreover of competitive quality and appeal was a different agenda altogether.[11]

Indigenization

The situation in the nascent stage of TV broadcasting was rather complex. To maintain the attraction and diversity of TV programming, foreign productions were brought in for both their novelty and their sophistication. Yet their popular appeal remained remote from local consciousness and relevance. On the other hand, production of programs purportedly with local specificities, to be viable, had to measure up to the craftsmanship of foreign programs in order to maintain satisfactory ratings. What these considerations amount to, then, was a general demand for all-around improvement in the standard of TV broadcasting. One can therefore observe the inner dynamics of localization that would propel the frontier of TV programming forward, and in the process also escalate the level of sophistication of the Hong Kong cultural world.

Thus, in the seventies, in an effort to advance the standard of local production, both TVB and RTV—and even the government-funded RTHK—recruited a number of personnel trained abroad in the fields of television, movies, and drama production. The general climate was geared toward assimilating Western techniques, styles, and standards in the production of local TV programs. The television establishment was hence unwittingly the main experimental venue for a new breed of cultural producers in Hong Kong—those who would be conscientious about local themes and concerns, yet open to modes of expression and craftsmanship originated in the wider world. Insofar as the institution of television was concerned, this development first led to a number of highly Westernized and experimental productions, especially from the film crew of TVB; these productions could be viewed as still shaky attempts to secure a new idiom of expression and of sociocultural themes worth expressing. The culmination of this process was best seen in the raving success of the locally produced, long-running sagas and soap operas, which, within the preset confines of popular cultural products, could well epitomize the coming of age of TV culture in Hong Kong. This coming of age intertwined both local and outside inputs, giving rise to a cultural form that could more justifiably be seen as localized in nature.

The implication here is that the transformation during the golden age of TV production as in the mid-seventies was not limited to the arena of television broadcasting. Rather, the momentum was set for the wider popular cultural world to catch on with this much expanded horizon. The catalytic moment in this broader process was the spillover of creative personnel from the TV establishment into other cultural fields of Hong Kong. This can be interpreted in the following light. On the one hand, the institution of TV production, while serving as a timely experimental arena for innovative cultural projects, was as yet insufficient for the wider-ranging creative ambitions of the new batch of cultural creators. The establishments of TV broadcasting were ultimately limited in terms of both the resources and the intent that could be devoted to carry out cultural and artistic visions. The constitution of TV production, as the bulwark of culture industry in Hong Kong, cannot depart significantly from the logic of cultural commodification. Creative experimentation would be instrumental for upgrading the quality and glamour of TV programs. And yet the eventual target must remain better ratings and commercial support, not the lofty impetus of cultural innovation. This inner strain came to a head in the vicissitudes surrounding the establishment of yet another TV station in 1977—the short-lived Commercial Television, Ltd. (CTV).[12]

The interlude of CTV is noteworthy because it signaled the beginning of the end of television broadcasting as the spearhead for a localized cultural framework. While the process of indigenization cannot be understood apart from the regime of TV culture that spanned the entire decade of the seventies, this monopolistic dominance began to slow down toward the late seventies. And CTV attempted above all at this juncture to break new ground in TV production, by granting even greater creative support for personnel increasingly dissatisfied with the constraints of the other TV establishments. The case of CTV thus became, in retrospect, the field upon which the commercial logic of the culture industry came to a head against the search for cultural breakthrough. For a number of reasons—some institutional, some commercial—the golden age of CTV lasted less than a year, going out with a whimper rather than a bang. And with it began the decline of TV hegemony in the cultural history of Hong Kong. From that point onward, television broadcasting was put in its place, so to speak, as but one cultural medium that must scramble for audience shares and financial gains against other competing media. Many of these cultural media, like movies or pop songs, in fact owed their newfound popularity and vitality to their previous promotion under the umbrella of TV production. In this and other ways, then, the fortunes of the TV industry during the seventies marked the expansion, the exponential opening of the cultural horizon of Hong Kong toward novel attitudes, motifs, and levels of sophistication. All these would not have been possible without the infiltration of wider cultural influences, whether in terms of importation of cultural products, the training of creative personnel, or the shaping of a keener sense of cultural ideal and standard. All these would be part and parcel of the processes of indigenization and indigenous cultural formation that Hong Kong went through during the seventies, even alongside the glittering facets of cosmopolitanism.[13]

In conceptual terms, it can be suggested that the demise of the hegemony of television marked the transition from eclectic cosmopolitanism, by way of indigenization, into the consolidation of local culture. In historical terms, this latter stage of development was best epitomized in the ensuing proliferation of locally produced movies which, in terms of production scale, audience, and public attention, exemplified above all the flourishing of indigenous cultural forms in Hong Kong. Moving into the 1980s then, it was essentially the movie industry that took center stage, though perhaps not to the same hegemonic extent as the highly institutionalized and oligarchical TV industry once did.

Local Cultural Formations

The catalytic episode for this new round of development was a cinematic movement which, echoing the much revered French precedent, became known as the Hong Kong "New Wave." The dramatis personae that took the most active role in this exemplary episode were mainly the same creative talents hitherto associated with the TV establishment. The waning of the TV regime would free many of these cultural workers to become independent movie-makers, or to set up smaller-scale production firms outside of the stronghold of the movie tycoons such as the Shaw Brothers and the Golden Harvest. This was a turning of the tides in the film culture of Hong Kong at large, encompassing the same episode the filmmakers, the audiences, and the critics.[14] The previously existing division between conscientious art movies and popular entertainment films would become much narrowed in the process. Serious art films, mainly Western ones, used to be the somewhat exclusive interests of high-minded critics and sophisticated audiences associated with film clubs such as the prestigious Studio One, or with literary magazines like the *Chinese Students Weekly,* which enchanted the more eager "cultural youths." The New Wave movement of the early 1980s was poised to produce serious, well-crafted films that would also have popular appeal. The source of artistic inspiration was to a large extent drawn from outside Hong Kong, and the film culture at that juncture was beset with references to revered masters like Jean Renoir, Jean-Luc Goddard, Frederico Fellini, Alfred Hitchcock, and the especially endearing Francois Truffaut. These and other acknowledged masters would provide both the creative inspiration and the critical standard for the forging of the new film culture of Hong Kong.[15]

The significance of this movement lies above all in the transition it made possible into the high tide of local movie production in the 1980s. The movie world of the previous decades was dominated by Western—especially Hollywood—productions on the one hand, and the Mandarin language Shaw Brothers productions on the other. Cantonese films, while quite numerous with a stable following, were in general more perfunctory and simplistic, and did not really do justice to the societal context many of them allegedly addressed. There were in addition also cinematic versions of Cantonese operas and fanciful, poorly made martial art movies.[16] The New Wave movies decidedly did not change every-thing in one stroke. What the movement did was to raise the caliber of locally produced movies to a respectable standard, and to demonstrate that locally sensi-tive movies can also be inspiring and well crafted. The success of this move-ment, while still limited in magnitude and market, was a clear indication of the receptivity of the audiences toward movies that were locally oriented. Into the 1980s, not only the cultural producers, but also the population at large, were to become genuinely intrigued regarding the character of the embedding societal context. In this sense, the new movies of the eighties both reflected and rein-forced the emergence of the new sociocultural milieu.[17]

The dramatic opening symbolized by the New Wave films was to continue in somewhat less intense, yet much more pervasive form throughout the 1980s. And if the New Wave films tended to bear more of the personal, creative marks of their producers, the broader development to follow would become more mel-low in temper and more popularly oriented.[18] Even for independent producers, the reality of market mechanisms remained a prime concern. And by the mid-eighties, the movie world would once again see the prevalence of oligarchical domination by major production firms. The net outcome of the New Wave movement for the movie world of the eighties was therefore a multifaceted one. In the first place, the newfound popularity of local movies would supersede the empire of the TV culture and the dominance of foreign films. While in the second place, the exponential development of the horizon for local movies began the new impetus for a more conscientious local film industry. Finally, however, all these developments had to also balance against the variegated demands of the audience and the structure of the culture industry, which prescribed that the more idiosyncratic sides of the New Wave movies be toned down to seek the right mix of conscientiousness and box-office appeal. With the further expansion and con-solidation of filmmaking in the eighties, then, the catalytic episode of the New Wave film was to go through a sea change of sort, into a movie world that was at once entertaining, fanciful, yet unmistakable in its context specificity.[19]

By the eighties, two cinematic genres especially stood out—martial art mov-ies and comedies. Hong Kong would become internationally famous for the proliferation of "Kung Fu movies." For the people of Hong Kong, it was the comedies—heart-warming and fanciful—that stood for more closely to the cul-ture and mentality of the city. The generic distinction cannot be pushed too far, however, for the two generic rubrics regularly permeated other genres—the melodramas, thrillers, detective stories, even ghost stories—while also intertwin-ing with one another. Suffice it to say that local culture, as embodied in the raving popularity of the martial and the comic genres, was generally exhibitionist in form, lighthearted in substance, and increasingly cynical in spirit. At the risk of oversimplification, this was the essential core of what amounts to the local, common culture of Hong Kong society, both as reflected in and accounting for the huge success of the movie industry in the 1980s.

While it is true that for every phase of societal development, distinctive cultural forms and meanings can often be identified, what marked off the 1980s was the fact that Hong Kong was increasingly becoming introspective and self-aware, notwithstanding the parallel persistence of mosaic cosmopolitanism. Cultural productions would aspire for more than passive reflection or imaginative fantasy upon the alleged reality, but rather to the active interpretation and definition of the identity and nature of this entire social and political destiny. For the cultural producers and filmmakers, this would be all part and parcel of finding the right niche or selling pitch for the films involved. Yet even to do just that would prescribe a much closer intertwining between the cultural producers and the consumers. The latter have become far more socially aware and demanding, not least because of their already extensive exposure in the TV culture.

Another factor that heightened local awareness and consolidated social commitment is, of course, the wider political vicissitudes. The social milieu of the eighties was one of impending yet uncertain transformation. The shadow of 1997 began to set in with the rounds of unsettling "Hong Kong talks" between China and Britain. To emigrate or not to emigrate was a question that infused the public consciousness, and its impact for the individuals went far beyond the realistic plausibility of the option. To weight the pros and cons of emigration, it was all but inevitable that the promises and the drawbacks of life in Hong Kong society would be rehearsed in almost everyone's mind. Not that every cultural production must take on such a social motif in an explicit way, but it was a widely recognized leitmotif that confronted the audiences in their everyday lives. The cultural creators cannot but address it in whatever imaginative way they can muster.

Toward the second half of the eighties, the local culture thus experienced an additional metamorphosis, and welded together different genres, themes, and concerns into a highly idiosyncratic and symptomatic cultural style. Thus it began the stage of the absurdist culture of mindlessness—the famous *moleitau*—with all its comic, sarcastic, subversive overtones, which eventually drowned out the colloquial origin of the term.

The culture of mindlessness, with its mode of absurdist realism, is both more and less than is commonly suggested. For one thing, it connotes far more than the alleged unceasing degeneration of comic farce. As well, its popularity indicates more than the spread of colloquial youth culture of Hong Kong. Yet on the other hand, it was also less than the deliberate cultural rebellion it was often made out to be—a kind of cultural weapon of the weak. In all, it might be more accurate to see this absurdist turn as a form of imperfect defiance, of hesitant struggles and inflammatory agony scaled down to fit the joint parameters of popular culture and social vicissitudes in *fin-de-siècle* Hong Kong.[20]

At its logical extreme, even the incompleteness and imperfection of this defiance can become the subject of mockery in the absurdist world view. Yet to mock the limitation and ineffectiveness of defiance is often but a disarming gesture, which paves the way back to compliance and submission. In this connection, it is no accident that real-life hazards occurring in society can often be recast as fanciful targets of mindless laughter in the movie houses. And if defiance and agitation can be thus defused and stopped short, submission to various extents cannot be avoided. Submission and (incomplete) subversiveness can be two sides of the same ironic coin.

For the purpose of this essay, it is unnecessary to go into a detailed chronicle of the cult of mindlessness. It was essentially the culmination of the local cultural dynamics into an exasperating cultural movement that swept over Hong Kong. Never before was Hong Kong society so ingeniously—even fantastically—represented in a cultural mentality that syncretized prevailing cultural motifs and local consciousness into a creative style all its own, and that maintained a rigorous level of technical and dramaturgic craftsmanship in spite of its random, absurdist appearance.[21] The long shadow of real-life crisis is temporarily put off with laughter, sometimes farcical and sometimes inflammatory. In all these respects, it can be surmised that the formation of local culture has reached its epitome at a juncture when the vicissitudes of Hong Kong society are increasingly dictated by economic and political dynamics of the much larger international setting. And this cultural epitome is defined above all by a comic, "absurdist" vision of the world.

In terms of the framework of the present discussion, it may be summed up that in the development of the 1980s, cultural cosmopolitanism was eventually assimilated, crystallized into the formation of the maturing local culture. The endeavors of indigenization were not painless or immediate, yet in the eighties it can no longer be denied that Hong Kong society embodied to a significant extent a cultural milieu that was at once global in frame of reference, indigenized in style and themes, and multifarious in technical resources and inspiration, all these on top of the surface glamour of cosmopolitan consumerism and the associated assortment of cultural commodities. With the conscientiousness, vibrancy, and rootedness of local cultural formation in place, Hong Kong would be able to take on the project of internationalization in an even more active, assertive manner.

Exogenization

The processes of cosmopolitanism, indigenization, and the formation of local culture in Hong Kong culminates in the eventual cultural exertion of Hong Kong upon the wider environment that hitherto furnished much of its symbolic resources and creative standard. This entire process, in a nutshell, represents what is depicted in the above as the completion of the internationalization problematics, embracing both its passive and active poles. While Hong Kong cultural critics would readily allude to John Woo's influence on Hollywood action movies, or Quentin Tarantino's acknowledged indebtedness to Wong Kar-wai, the main sphere of Hong Kong's exogenization takes place closer to home. This exogenous turn of tide began during the dramatic juncture of the 1980s, when cultural ideas, products, and personae of Hong Kong gained unprecedented influence not only in local society but also in neighboring areas, in particular mainland China. Taking shape in the eighties, Hong Kong is not only the coming of age of local culture, but also its ensuing exogenization as a nascent cultural force. This development first took off both as a consequence of the changing cultural conditions of Hong Kong, and of the unveiling of the reform era in Dengist China. Cultural formations in Hong Kong were to provide the most accessible exemplars for a China freshly emergent from the stronghold of socialist dogma. What is more, the model that Hong Kong professed is essentially one of popular culture, which can be readily emulated by the bulk of the Chinese population, particularly in the urban areas and the South China region. Again, one witnesses the same extension of horizon and fumbling for standards, even in addition to direct and unabashed mimesis.

The active outward assertion of Hong Kong culture in the 1980s can be traced via the cultural ideas, events, and personalities instrumental for the genesis of leisure society in mainland China. Hong Kong is not the sole player in this cultural drama, yet the key role that it performed cannot be underestimated either. This development indicates the wider meanings of cultural formation in Hong Kong, going beyond its fragile, contingent sociopolitical existence, beyond its hard-boiled, unrelenting economic pragmatism.

While it is not possible here to detail exhaustively the grandiose northward extension of the Hong Kong cultural horizon, some of the more salient aspects can be underlined. The first important point to note, as mentioned above, is that the cultural impact of Hong Kong is confined generally to the field of popular culture, in terms of both generic media and levels of cultural sophistication. This is at once the strength and the limitations of the cultural exogenization of Hong Kong: that it is in the nature of popular culture to touch a wide spectrum of the populations, and that in the final analysis it cannot exert serious influence on fundamental issues of cultural reorientation.

Of the influx of Hong Kong popular cultural products into mainland China, the situation of the 1980s is nothing short of spectacular. Every facet of the popular cultural world is represented. Canto-pop singers of Hong Kong regularly went on concert tours in the mainland, and TV programs of Hong Kong took up much of the airtime of Chinese TV broadcasting, especially in South China. Nightclubs and karaoke establishments, fast-food franchises, clothing and fashion chains, and other consumer culture setups were in the main either actually owned by Hong Kong entrepreneurs, or closely imitating similar venues in Hong Kong. There were also important cultural joint ventures in the production of movies, CDs, concert tours, and so forth. The Cantonese dialect was even deemed fashionable in the north, and so was Cantonese cuisine by "Hong Kong style" chefs. At its more elated epitome, observers can harp on the reversed cultural dominance of Hong Kong over the mainland, or on the alleged formation of a "South China cultural area" in which Hong Kong is the indispensable leader, or on the emergence of "Greater Hong Kong" as both cultural area and mentality.[22] All these epithets echo the immense exogenized stronghold that can be achieved by way of the popular culture arena. This is the unquestioned niche of Hong Kong culture, and also the much needed anesthetic of sorts for a mainland society worn out by decades of nonstop ideological warfare.

In general, the glamour of Hong Kong culture in the 1980s lay as much in its vitality as in its exogenization. The inherent limitation of the popular culture arena was for the moment still dormant. In any case, neither the cultural producers nor the Hong Kong population at large was too concerned about cultural pursuits beyond the popular arena. The impact and prestige that the Hong Kong cultural world progressively realized toward the second half of the eighties surpassed all expectation and did much to boost the morale of the Hong Kong people. The taunting and slight disdain with which the local population sometimes treated mainlanders is but one of the more unbecoming signs of this simple self-satisfaction. Narrow-minded gloating over forthcoming cultural hegemony is none too commendable. Yet in retrospect, this shallow sense of cultural superiority did much to buffer Hong Kong society against the gathering menace of the 1997 conjuncture. Cultural self-congratulation was perhaps a disguise of strength for a population that recognized its own political vulnerability. It was on this note of a complex sense of celebration and foreboding that the 1980s drew to a close. Whatever political fortune may materialize, at least Hong Kong had its moments of cultural vindication, if not in depth and finesse, then at least in popularity and hegemony. The end of 1980s thus found Hong Kong basking in cultural radiance. Popular cultural formations can be simultaneously fun-filled, profitable, sardonic, and unexpectedly influential. This would be the final completion of the problematic of cultural internationalization for Hong Kong, when the internalization and indigenization of foreign influences not only contributed in important ways to the consolidation of a distinct cultural world, but furthermore to one that proved its vitality in overcoming geographical and cultural boundaries of adjacent political entities.

Historical Articulations: The Eclipsed Program

Background

In historical terms, the fateful year of 1989 marked the turning point in the northward cultural expedition of Hong Kong—as well as in many other facets of Hong Kong–China relation. The Tiananmen incident severely traumatized the fragile goodwill between the two societies. And from that time forward, a state of intensified caution and distancing was to crystallize well into the 1990s. China on the other hand would tighten her control over political and cultural matters, also in reaction to the spring of 1989. Yet even in mainly cultural terms, there are good reasons to suggest that, by the late 1980s, the dynamic exertion of Hong

Kong culture already showed signs of waning. The trauma of 1989 merely placed a more definite benchmark on the as yet incipient decline, which was the joint outcome of the cultural momentum that mainland China in time realized, as well as the failure of nerve—and imagination—that plagued cultural Hong Kong from the late 1980s onward. This would be the juncture that saw the fragmentation of the internationalization problematic of Hong Kong into an eclipsed and partial nexus that prefigured withdrawal and stagnation in a new stage of cultural change.

Thus began the problematics transition, in historical and in analytical terms, from the full-swing of the strong program of cultural internationalization into the eclipsed program locked in the cul-de-sac of facile cosmopolitanism. It is to this second incarnation of cultural internationalization that the following will more briefly turn. This brevity is not the result of instrumental concerns of length or narrative unity, but of the fact that this stage of development is still ongoing; it is a development the final outcome of which cannot be broached with certainty at this point. What can be more plausibly achieved is to map the essential outlook of this new change of tide against the backdrop of the cultural internationalization problematic per se.

As noted earlier, this second incarnation is characterized by the severe weakening of linkages that should lead from the facile formation of cosmopolitanism into more authentic, relevant formations of indigenization and of local culture. The delinking that took place in the late eighties, as well as the state of cultural limbo that entrapped present-day Hong Kong, would form the dual foci for the following discussion. The events of 1989 would seem to suggest that the delinking only took place when local culture of Hong Kong was restricted from its exogenization into China. The argument here is that the crux of the matter lies more in the opposite direction, that with or without the events of 1989, the inner development of local cultural arenas in Hong Kong was not conducive to the upholding of a persistent cultural stamina, and this is effectively undermined the continuation of the indigenization processes. It is the failure of indigenization, not of exogenization, that lies at the root of the problem. In this light, the celebration of international relevance and renown turned out to be but the chance mutation of sociohistorical vicissitudes destined shortly to dissolve.

Transition to the Eclipsed Program

Three different sets of limitations define the paradigmatic constraints of cultural formations of Hong Kong. Together they were the root of Hong Kong's cultural demise even as it was in its most vibrant heyday. As of the present, it can be observed that the cultural failure of nerve—and of creativity—has become virtually overwhelming. In different ways, the three sets of limitations are engendered from the innate, defining attributes of the cultural arenas of Hong Kong: they are mainly localized, popular cultural formations embedded in the market logic of the culture industry.

In this connection, the first deciding limit in the formation of cultural discourse in Hong Kong is that it is a cultural discourse that derived its prominence and impact as popular culture. It is in this particular form and substance that Hong Kong culture enchants and endears, for both the local audience and Chinese communities elsewhere. Yet even at its most creative and vibrant, there is a cultural demand threshold that popular culture itself cannot overstep. China, unlike Hong Kong, is imbued with both the autonomy and the urgency to reconstrue its cultural orientation at a more fundamental—even essential—level. The coloniality of Hong Kong has preempted these fundamental cultural projects even before they can be addressed. As a redress of sort, Hong Kong has been left free to fashion culture as a purely entertaining, mesmerizing pastime, and has in the process produced some stunning results. This cannot be the case with China. There are wider, and higher, demands and questions that Chinese cultural endeavors must address, especially at a time when far-reaching rethinking on the direction of the country is under way. Popular culture will remain just that—entertainment for the people. Yet other cultural problematics and trajectories must be painstakingly construed in order to tackle cultural—even civilizational—dynamics at a more demanding and reflective level. This explains the concurrent development of the so-called "cultural fever" (*wenhuare*) in China, even as alongside the influx of consumer-oriented culture occurred during the eighties. Cultural reconstruction conducted at this level, by intellectuals and other "mental workers," encompassed deadly serious and passionate exercises in the fundamental reconfiguration of ideologies and practices in the post-Mao era.[23] Amid this intellectual pivot of cultural discourse, there is not much that popular culture itself can positively impute or influence. This would be the preset limiting threshold of the cultural impetus of Hong Kong. And should Hong Kong society in turn lose vitality and momentum even in popular cultural creation, there can be little meaningful cultural impact to speak of. Such would be the joint outcomes of the cultural strength and lacunae that Hong Kong must face up to in the northward expansion of its popular cultural world.

Thus, while Chinese audiences may be temporarily mesmerized by the four famous kings of Canto-pop from Hong Kong, or readers enthralled by Hong Kong popular writers of martial art stories, romance, and science fiction, or movie goers delighted by the run-of-the-mill Hong Kong thrillers and comedies, all these forms and more merely lie at the surface of the much more engrossing cultural problematics that China must grapple with. Insofar as Hong Kong popular culture is not likely to exert lasting intervention at this level, it will remain as but passing fads and fashions—forming part of the facile cosmopolitanism of Chinese audiences. And unless the cultural products involved renew themselves also at dazzling speed, there is no particular reason why Hong Kong popular culture should continue to dominate even the Chinese popular cultural scene. This last observation ties in with a second set of limitations of Hong Kong cultural formation: that it derives its vibrancy and appeal primarily from its distinctively indigenized, local character. Its novelty and magnetism escalate at the same time that its concern for local cultural uniqueness becomes all-absorbing. Yet beyond a certain limiting threshold, indigenized culture is bound to lose its generalized appeal for audience outside of the locale.

The second set of limitations thus has to do with the local identity of Hong Kong cultural formation, a source of strength that in time spelled its own constraint. This cultural twist can be observed even in the high tides of local culture in the seventies and early eighties, and its subsequent full-steamed northward advancement. In concrete terms, and as noted earlier, the epitome of this cultural trajectory of Hong Kong is represented in the dramatic growth of the popular cultural world. The height of this development, as in the idiosyncratic current of *moleitau*—mindless comedies—can be seen as taking this localized, self-absorbed sense of life to its carefree, fanciful, and sometimes hysterical extreme.

What needs to be remarked upon, however, is that by its nature, comedy as a genre relies heavily upon the embedding context or scenario that would determine whether certain actions and situations can be seen as comical or even absurd. As is well known in literary theory, while tragic genres appeal to universal principles and values, comedy addresses what is essentially extraordinary, incidental, and unique.[24] The prevalence of comic consciousness in Hong Kong hence marked the progressive integration of the shared, in-group experience of the Hong Kong folks, among whom even a passing allusion to the seemingly idiosyncratic and accidental can trigger a sweeping and hearty response. By this same token, the drumming up of comic consciousness implies that, once beyond a certain threshold of idiosyncrasy—as in the case of the *moleitau*—the capacity for exogenous cultural communication would be greatly curtailed. The symptomatic case of the *moleitau* comedies hence spelled a dilemma for the transformation of Hong Kong culture in its program of localization. New breakthroughs in this direction would require far greater investment of resources and creativity—even the *moleitau* comedies were in fact painstakingly crafted and coordinated pieces of works. Yet any further breakthrough in localization, should it prove possible, would imply taking the required context-specificity to new heights, so much so that audiences unfamiliar with the eclectic Hong Kong ways would hardly see the point. This, then, is the inherent limit of local culture, insofar as the cultural internationalization of Hong Kong is concerned. While Kung Fu movies, melodramas, thrillers, and so forth are more transferrable, comedies and the *moleitau*, as the quaint essential Hong Kong genre, remain in general locally landlocked now that the initial curiosity has died down. And with the sphere of outside popularity—and profit—shrinking, there will be proportionally less motivation to propel Hong Kong culture further into the refinement of local cultural formation.[25] The force of localization, into the nineties, has actually slowed down to accommodate the market logic of popular cultural formations. And this development brings our discussion to the third set of limitations of Hong Kong culture, namely the dynamics of the culture industry as primarily contingent upon unabashed profit motive.

Critique of culture industry is, of course, a recurrent theme in the study of popular culture. In the case of Hong Kong, the same logic of market forces manifests in still other dilemmas of cultural formation. The situation is that expanding the market of cultural consumption would be instrumental in providing resources and support for innovative cultural creations. Yet by the same token, the intensification of market prerogatives makes short-term profits and market shares far more feasible and desirable than long-range and uncertain investment in the progressive renovation of cultural creativity. In addition, the rule of profit motive and market expansion would imply that cultural productions must more and more tilt toward lower socioeducational levels, that the less cultural prerequisites are required, the wider the range of popular appeal for the cultural product concerned. Eventually, there is no intrinsic reason why cultural productions should embrace any localistic themes any more.[26] If for one reason or another the local is no longer a profitable motif, the imperative of culture industry would dictate that other motifs must be adopted and packaged for the fancy of the same local audiences. With the mechanism of the culture industry set in motion, it served both to boost the formation of local culture, when it was appealing and profitable to do so, and also to undermine this same local cultural formation by repeatedly exploiting proven formulas to the point of irredeemable weariness. Even with the resulting stalemate, a breakthrough into a new stage of local cultural innovation would still be too risky and unprofitable in the short run. Hence, a new round of cultural hybridity must begin, in which imported motifs and gimmicks once again configure alongside the surviving localistic cultural idioms, yet are equally detached from their original contexts of meaning, whether foreign or local.

This scenario depicts the popular cultural world of Hong Kong in the current mid-1990s, entrapped in the prison of the impending transition. The popular cultural world is once again decentered, fragmented into arenas of incidental appeal. Market logic has manifested the most unthinking ferocity possible. For every successful movie, there will be opportunistic sequels, spinoffs, and crude imitations. For every popular TV series or program, TVB and ATV will ensure a stream of reruns, tiresome extensions, even simultaneous screening of programs that are either close copies of one another, or actually identical ones.[27] The same pattern applies in broadcasting, Canto-pop, and many other facets of material culture and consumerism. All of these amount to the same street-smart formula of how to be successful and profitable without really trying. When everyone on the bandwagon capitalizes on the successful cases, soon enough they run out of cases to capitalize on. But if local models are exhausted, models can always be sought on the outside. And if outside models are embedded in contextual meanings of their own, models can always be teased out of either meaning or context. In the mid-nineties, once again, hybridized cultural products would be appreciated in their "pure appearance," one ventures to observe, decontextualized and even de-meaning. The mindlessness of *moleitau* turns into panicky frenzy and henceforth loses touch with reality. In its place, a new cosmopolitanism of sorts, in which it is no longer meaningful or particularly necessary to separate the local from the foreign, or creation from imitation.

With these three sets of limiting parameters, several consequences become all but inevitable. In the first place, the cultural impetus of Hong Kong, even at its enchanting best, remained far removed from the fundamental cultural compass of a historic civilization such as China, regardless of how prevalent popular entertainment can become. In the second place, there is a limit to how local culture can be effectively transferable to other cultural contexts, especially if one thinks of such cases as the *moleitau* current at its idiosyncratic best. And in the third place, given the culture industry dynamic that Hong Kong subscribes to, one is tempted to think of cultural creativity as but happy accidents to the norms of profiteering. The real world of Hong Kong popular culture remains, more often than not, heartbreakingly reckless and shallow. With these limiting parameters in place in the nineties, then, Hong Kong once again renounces its cultural assertiveness, and resigns to the earlier state of passive recipient to both external intervention and internal commercial logic.

The New Cosmopolitanism: The Age of Icons

The new cosmopolitanism of the mid-nineties has largely delinked from meaningful processes of indigenization because a new cultural grammar has yet to be sought, upon the ruins of the eighties, that can allow for the integration of cultural products or phenomena into holistic and relevant fabrics. These underlying lacunae also prescribe that the new cosmopolitanism be configured essentially via a hybrid of icons—free-floating symbols that often stand irrelevant to their contexts of interpretation and origins, signifying not much more than their incidental production and possible appeal. In the case of icons, in other words, symbols and meaning stand further apart from one another, because the latter begs references to contexts of interpretation and understanding that are no longer of interest or significance. Instead, icons will be heralded, cheered, worshipped, each for its own sake and for no obvious reason—at least not for any imperative raison d'être of the icon in the first place. In this sense, cultural icons come close to "symbols that stand for themselves," and their prominence would be explained not in terms of what they allegedly do, but in terms of whether a particularly enchanting style, posture, or aura has been manufactured in the process of doing so.[28] The point of this iconography is to catch the fancy of a significant portion of the audience. In this vein, the creation and pandering of cultural icons, even more so than popular cultural productions in general, rely heavily on sophisticated and meticulous packaging, as well as on the fluid sensation of the cultural consumers. And in the elusive art of iconic manufacturing, the cultural world of Hong Kong in the nineties is heavily indebted to Japanese influence. As for the primacy stage upon which this unfolding of iconic construction will be enacted, the focus shifts to the arena of Canto-pop and the emblematic rise of the alleged four kings of Canto-pop in the nineties.

In spite of the fact that the cultural world of the nineties, on the face of it, does not depart significantly from the preceding era—the same popular cultural arenas and media remain in place, the same popularity of all kinds of mass entertainment venues, and so forth—what is really symptomatic of the mode of cultural formation in the last stage of transitional Hong Kong is the centrality of cultural icons. The point is to resort directly to impression, impact, and sensation. In other words, iconic construction is mainly cultic in character. The whole operation hinges on whether enough fanaticism and obsessive euphoria can be generated to keep the momentum going. And fanaticism is not something that can be rationally calculated or designed, is often not proportional to ability or effort.

Two levels of analysis must then be taken into account in this depiction of the new iconography—namely, in terms of iconic objects and personae, and in terms of the iconic attitude as a generalized mode of cultural consciousness. In terms of iconic objects and personae, such emblematic cases as the four kings of Canto-pop are of course particularly exemplary. In the extraordinary following that these singers were able to generate, consideration of singing itself takes a back seat to other general cultic motifs: dashing looks, figure, youthfulness, glamour of excess, radiance of success—all these as packaged in lavish concerts and promotion campaigns carefully rehearsed by major record companies. The flip side of the coin is that musical quality becomes secondary to the group reflex being engineered. While it may be going too far to suggest that many of the popular Canto-pop singers are inept, the fact remains that in terms of both the singers and the music involved, it is the calculated impact upon the fans that matters most. In the process, songs become incantations that bewitch, arouse, and relieve an audience seeking tribal enchantment or postmodern reflex of sort. Thus, it makes little difference if many of the singers are limited in technical skill, or the songs truncated in lyrics, melodies, or orchestration, or that many of the songs are simply imported—primarily from Japan—and dubbed into perfunctory Cantonese. These elements derive their significance simply in being vehicles for iconic figures to achieve further representations and transfigurations before their audiences.

Underlying the iconic cult of specific cultural personae, it is possible to detect a wider terrain of objects, events, fashions, and so forth suggestive of the presence of a general iconographic attitude and consciousness—a cultural euphoria that privileges form and appearance either for their own sake, or for the immediate impression they can assert upon cultural consumers too passive and too incapacitated to reflect or refuse. At a different level, the proliferation of iconographic objects can be most visibly observed in the many small shopping malls that sprang up in the late eighties and the nineties, providing the Hong Kong counterpart to Benjaminian arcades of sort. In these small shopping malls, targeted mainly at youthful consumers, the iconic objects here referred to are not of the same caliber as exclusive brand names in the more up-scale shopping districts. What these modest shopping malls contain are mainly small partitions and kiosks—one hundred or so for each mall—selling bric-a-brac that are allegedly the latest emblems of the ethereal youthful obsession. A large majority of these items are directly associated with Japanese youth culture. The widespread availability of Japanese comics—translated versions—is a prominent case in point. In addition, there are pictorial albums, CDs, posters, and magazines featuring singers and stars, most of which are originals from Japan. And then there is also the proliferation of trading cards and photos of movie stars, comic figures, and singers, both Japanese and local. Even shops selling puzzles, toys, models, and small gifts are an eclectic collection of mostly Japanese motifs, design, and figures. In the well-known 188 Mall of Queen's Road East, for example, up to one hundred shops are peddling Japanese cultural artifacts, out of a total of around one hundred and twenty venues.[29]

By way of a broad nexus of these small shopping malls *cum* Japanese cultural enclaves, the cultural field of Hong Kong is permeated by a source of influence that most of the cultural consumers cannot readily decipher, for only a portion of these artifacts are available in translation. One way of looking at the situation is that given the history of Japanese influence in the form of dubbed TV programs, the audience in general feels sufficiently attached to Japanese culture even without understanding it in any serious depth. Yet this facet is consistent with the prevalence of the iconic attitude—to take something solely in terms of its facile appearance and aura, independent of cultural embeddedness. In this sense, whether or not one understands Japanese lyrics, texts, even way of life, is secondary. These objects and figures are important as they are, stripped of context and signification, to fit in with the sensational and impulsive reflex of youthful intent, for which any fixed foundation of understanding would prove too cumbersome and immobilizing.

In this connection, it can be further maintained that the age of icon of the 1990s, and the iconic attitude as a whole, is not merely something of youthful concern alone. Rather, what took place in youth culture is but a more dramatic manifestation of the iconographic imagination. Into the mid-1990s, currents of popular culture are in general taking an iconic turn. Cultural objects and events are constituted not on the basis of internal meanings or extrinsic functions, but mainly on the sensational impact they can assert. Side by side with the dominance of iconic culture, therefore, is the popularity of exotic spectacles and collective voyeurism, to quench the cultural thirst by taking peeks at generally prohibitive subjects: spectacles that are perhaps too obscene, the violent, the outrageous, or the tragic. To the extent that what is worth observing is only worth observing as icon, icons turn into spectacles for collective voyeurism. It is not surprising, then, that the iconic attitude applies even to such unlikely areas as news reports. The push for exotic spectacles and collective voyeurism reaches an absurd extreme when coverage of entertainment news expends sustained and collective efforts to take "exposed photos" of female stars that allow a glimpse of their underwear. Such infantilism is but part of the collective thirst for voyeuristic spectacles. Special TV tabloid news programs and sleezy magazine coverage are all geared to this same hunt for the exotic and the outrageous, for the ultimate Otherness, one may say, the face of which one is only permitted a peek. And yet in the case of mid-1990s, Hong Kong, the Other, and the Local have become irreparably confused. The iconic attitude, however, is by definition unperturbed by any crisis of meaning.

In the Labyrinth of Hybridization

This depiction of the "age of icon" in the recent development of Hong Kong ties in with the problematic of internationalization in three different ways. First, it signifies the faltering of cultural momentum insofar as local cultural formation is concerned. In the exuberance of cultural icons is the estrangement between meaning, context, and symbols, and all reactions to endeared or coveted icons are largely a function of cultic worship and crowd psychology. Second, the age of icons also stands for the gathering influence of specific outside currents, such as those of Japan. Yet as noted before, this is a decontextualized mode of change, where cultural symbols are turned into icons detached from their original framework. Third, and perhaps most symptomatic of all, even local cultural development has become decontextualized in the same vein—the new cosmopolitanism denotes simultaneously the variegated presence of foreign motifs as well as the de-localization of indigenous cultural development to become part of the un-rooted, free-reined, multifarious cultural scene. Localization, as a quest for rootedness and framework of meaning, inevitably loses out in the face of the iconic attitude. If anything, the only meaningful postures open to the latter would be ambivalence and cynicism. In this way, at the heart of cultural Hong Kong in the nineties are the dual mechanisms of the new cosmopolitanism: that outside influences proliferate, even as indigenous formations become de-localized; that the Local is transfigured into the cosmopolitan Other as well. At this juncture, the logic of hybridization has come full circle, and 1997 may even come as redemption to the vacuous regime of cultural icons.

The mid-1990s once again finds Hong Kong standing at the crossroads of cultural disorientation. The cultural vision of a "Greater Hong Kong" is fast waning, because the cultural stamina of Hong Kong has faltered. China is rapidly developing her own modes of (popular) cultural style and motifs, perhaps also on the shoulders of what Hong Kong has offered. In this way, Hong Kong must pay the penalty for taking the lead. The unfolding of the two programs of cultural internationalization problematics hence amounts to two alternative theatrical stages upon which the cultural drama of Hong Kong is enacted—first came the confident assertion of localized cultural formations born of the winding paths of cosmopolitanism and indigenization, and then came the broken promises of a society no longer able to hold its own in cultural terms, as also in many other aspects of sociopolitical vicissitudes.

In the end, the processes of hybridization were expanded and reasserted and defined as the reconfiguration of forms at the expense of meaning, practice, and context. On the exterior, the cultural scene remains as robust and as multifarious as ever. Yet the looming anarchy persists, as does the decline in cultural preroga-tives and stamina. Hence the haunting allusion to the labyrinth of hybridiza-tion—the labyrinth being the pleasure garden where one enters to have fun, to find fulfillment of the senses, and where, in the process, direction and bearing are inexplicably lost.[30]

Notes

1. There is, in fact, a vast literature that tackles the cultural and theoretical dynamics involved in the encounter of societies and nations, within the broader intellectual rubrics of globalization on the one hand, and of indigenization on the other. For more recent sociological writings in this regard, see, for example, J. Friedman, *Cultural Identity and Global Process* (London: Sage, 1994); and R. Robertson, *Globalization* (London: Sage, 1992).

2. Conversely, the ups and downs of the Hong Kong negotiation would also have a direct impact on Sino-British relations. The complexities of this entire political nexus are well charted in B. Hook, "Political Changes in Hong Kong," *China Quarterly*, no. 136 (December 1993), pp. 840–863.

3. On the interplay between the global, international, and the indigenous, or local, see, for example, J. Friedman, "Being in the World: Globalization and Localization," in M. Featherstone, ed., *Global Culture* (London: Sage, 1990), pp. 311–328.

4. For discussion along these lines, see also P.K. Choi, "From Dependency to Self-Sufficiency: Rise of the Indigenous Culture of Hong Kong, 1945–1989," *Asian Culture*, no. 14 (1990), pp. 161–177.

5. On the dynamics of cosmopolitanism as a sociocultural force, see U. Hannerz, "Cosmopolitans and Locals in World Culture," in Featherstone, ed., *Global Culture,* pp. 237–251.

6. See, for example, discussion in H. Siu, "Cultural Identity and Polities of Difference in South China," *Daedalus* 122, 2 (1993), pp. 19–43; and T. Gold, "Go with Your Feelings: Hong Kong and Taiwan Popular Culture in Greater China," *China Quarterly*, no. 136 (December 1993), pp. 907–925.

7. On the indigenous formations of Hong Kong culture, see, for example, Choi, "From Dependency to Self-Sufficiency." The present writer has also provided his own interpreta-tions on the cultural formation of Hong Kong, cast under a broader intellectual and historical rubric. See especially Hoiman Chan "Culture and Identity," in D. McMillen and S.W. Man, eds., *The Other Hong Kong Report: 1994* (Hong Kong: The Chinese Univer-sity Press, 1994), pp. 443–468.

8. For background on Hong Kong society in the 1980s, the standard treatment would be S.K. Lau, *Society and Politics of Hong Kong* (Hong Kong: The Chinese University Press, 1982); and S.K. Lau and H.C. Kuan, *The Ethos of the Hong Kong Chinese* (Hong Kong: The Chinese University of Hong Kong, 1988). See also the capsule discussion in H. Baker, "Social Change in Hong Kong: Hong Kong Man in Search of Majority," in *China Quarterly*, no. 36 (December 1993), pp. 864–877.

9. For background discussion on culture and social change in Hong Kong, see E. Sinn, ed., *Culture and Society in Hong Kong* (Hong Kong: center of Asian Studies, The Univer-sity of Hong Kong, 1995).

10. As yet, there are few systematic—let alone scholarly—studies on the development and dynamics of the so-called TV culture in Hong Kong. But see the anecdotal accounts by local critics and participants such as Lau Tin Chi and Chow Wah Shan. See also K.C. Chan, "The Role of Television in the Founding of Hong Kong Indigenous Culture," (in Chinese), in ibid., pp. 80–88.

11. On the general development of television broadcasting in the early years, see, for example, the spirited report in W.S. Chow, *Television Is Dead* (in Chinese) (Hong Kong: Chingman Books, 1990). There is also a large volume of TV magazines, newspaper TV sections, as well as TV commentaries, published as part of the supplementary materials to the TV cultural formation in the earlier years. In addition to published materials, it is also fair to say that the "TV lore" in the golden age of television broadcasting in Hong Kong has by now become an important part of the folklore of the city.

12. In all, Commercial Television (CTV) lasted less than three years. Yet the turbulent events surrounding its rise again formed a key component in the "TV lore" of Hong Kong. These events involved the Lam family (a banking family associated with the Heng Seng), which endeavored to establish a third commercial TV station in Hong Kong; the defection of TVB celebrity Selina Chow and her high-power crew to the CTV; the public attention and acclaim that the CTV programs received; the huge deficit of CTV in spite of satisfactory performance; the eventual and inevitable ending of CTV; and even then the subsequent labor movement of former employees in securing reasonable compensations. All these and more made headlines in Hong Kong newspapers during the time period concerned, and were eagerly followed by the population as real-life drama that out-performed even the TV productions themselves.

13. The broader impact of the TV culture in the indigenization process can be seen in a much wider range of events and development. One illustrative case is the contribution of TV broadcasting to the Canto-pop movement of the seventies. In this regard, the impact of television is identical in two directions—i.e., in the promoting of Western popular music, and in developing theme songs for local TV series. Such music programs as the "Star Show" did much to familiarize the local audience with pop music genres then current in the West, as well as providing the arena for local performers, many of whom were to become the backbone of the Canto-pop movement. This development was further propelled by the exceptional popularity of many of the theme songs for local TV series. While improvement in composition and lyrics was certainly important in this regard, such popularity also owed to the fact that these songs were played repeatedly on a daily basis for as long as the series themselves lasted.

14. On the relation between TV broadcasting and the subsequent development of the movie industry, see the account by the senior cultural critic Law Kar, "The 'Shaolin Temple' of the New Hong Kong Cinema," in *A Study of the Hong Kong Cinema in the Seventies*, special catalogue of the 8th Hong Kong International Film Festival (Hong Kong: Hong Kong Urban Council, 1984), pp. 114–117.

15. In addition, and as part of the nascent growth of a more sophisticated film culture, novel conceptual constructs and analytical approaches of Western film theory were regularly applied—sometimes arbitrarily—in the criticism and interpretation of local films. Writings of the more high-minded film critics in those days were hence characteristic in their own right, invoking structuralism, semiotics, film aesthetics, or Marxism of all colors.

16. For background to the movie world of the 1950s to 1960s, see the following special catalogues published at the occasion of the Hong Kong International Festivals: *Cantonese Cinema Retrospective 1950–1959* (Hong Kong: Hong Kong Urban Council, 1978); *Hong Kong Cinema Survey 1946–1968* (Hong Kong: Hong Kong Urban Council, 1979); *Cantonese Cinema Retrospective 1960–1968* (Hong Kong: Hong Kong Urban

Council, 1982). In addition, cf. I.C. Jarvis, *Window on Hong Kong: A Sociological Study of Hong Kong Film Industry and Its Audience* (Hong Kong: center of Asian Studies, University of Hong Kong, 1977).

17. Law Kar, "The 'Shaolin Temple,' " has observed that, between 1977 and 1980, over sixty new filmmakers appeared on the scene and directed their first movies. Benchmark productions at this juncture would include Anne Hui *(The Secret,* 1979; *The Story of Woo Viet,* 1981; *Boat People,* 1982); Patrick Tam *(The Sword,* 1980; *Nomad,* 1982); Yim Ho *(The Extras,* 1978; *The Happenings,* 1980); Tsui Hark *(The Butterfly Murder,* 1979; *Dangerous Encounter—First Kind,* 1980).

18. Tsui Hark, for example, would become highly influential in producing films that in many ways helped to set the agenda of the movie world in the eighties. His works following this popular turn would include: *All the Wrong Clues* (1981), *Aces Go Places* (1984), *A Chinese Ghost Story* (1987), *A Better Tomorrow* (1987), *Swordsman* (1990); all of these films have inspired much of the movie world and occasioned a large number of sequels, spinoffs, and imitations.

19. For general analyses and useful statistics regarding the movie world in the 1980s, see *Hong Kong Cinema in the Eighties,* special catalogue of the 15th Hong Kong International Film Festival (Hong Kong: Hong Kong Urban Council, 1991). The film critic Li Cheuk-to also produced two volumes of often insightful commentaries on individual movies produced in the eighties: Li Cheuk-to, *Notes on Hong Kong Movies in the Eighties* (in Chinese) (Hong Kong: Chong Kin Publisher, 1990).

20. For further study on the nature of Hong Kong comic movies, especially in relation to the *moleitau* current, see Hoiman Chan, "Comedy and Mediation: Charting the Cultural Mentality of Hong Kong," paper presented to the International Conference on Cultural Criticism (Hong Kong: Chinese University of Hong Kong, December 1993).

21. At the peak of success of the *moleitau* tides, the acknowledged hero of *moleitau* film, Chow Sing Chi, was the best-selling star for four consecutive years between 1990 and 1993: *All for the Winner* (1990), *Fight Back to School* (1991), *Justice, My Foot* (1992), and *Flirting Scholar* (1993). In these better years, each of these best-selling pictures could gross more than forty million dollars in ticket sales alone.

22. The Chinese obsession with Hong Kong cultural style and artifacts in the 1980s was reflected on almost a daily basis in the entertainment news of Hong Kong. Reports in newspaper or on TV would detail the newest spate of concert tours, special appearances, joint movie ventures, and so on. The overall outcome was captured in a succinct account by the Chinese writer Lo Fu, see "Epilogue: The Greater Hong Kong Mentality?" in his *A Stroll with Hong Kong Culture* (in Chinese) (Hong Kong: Chung Hwa Publisher, 1993), pp. 209–214, cf. also H. Siu, "Cultural Identity and Politics of Difference"; T. Gold, "Go with Your Feelings."

23. It should also be noted that with culture defined at this high level of aspiration, it is all but inevitable that the movement would cast into doubt the orientation and meaning of popular culture as such. It must hence not be forgotten that there is a subterranean streak of anti–Hong Kong sentiment, even accompanying its northward expansion. The disdain of some Chinese cultural workers—He Yong, Zhiang Wen, and so on—toward the Hong Kong popular cultural world must be seen as more than isolated accidents.

24. On the nature of comedy as a cultural genre, see, for example, M. Silk, "The Autonomy of Comedy," in E. Schaffer, ed., *Comparative Criticism* (Cambridge: Cambridge University Press, 1988, vol. 10), pp. 3–37.

25. The symptomatic event in this regard is the decline of the *moleitau* movies in the mid-nineties. Not even the magic of Chow Sing Chi can secure box-office hits. And a sense of crisis is looming over the local movie industry at this point. This downfall is attributable to many extrinsic factors: overall decline in consumption power, hike in the

price of movie tickets, competition from abroad, and so forth. The discussion here, however, seeks to pinpoint the intrinsic limitation of popular culture in terms of long-range cultural vision and innovation.

26. On perspectives regarding the studying and understanding of popular culture, especially in relation to the case of Hong Kong, see Hoiman Chan, "Popular Culture and Political Society: Prolegomena on Cultural Studies in Hong Kong," in E. Sinn, ed., *Culture and Society in Hong Kong,* pp. 23–50.

27. The most notorious example is, of course, the case of the "Judge Pao" series in television broadcasting. Not only did both TVB and ATV scramble to jump on the unexpectedly successful bandwagon, producing spin-offs and imitations of the Taiwanese original, but through loopholes in contractual arrangements, both TV stations for a time screened the same series simultaneously, thus writing one of the most absurd chapters in the broadcasting history of Hong Kong.

28. While there is no intention here of getting into the more intricate aspects of sign theory, it may suffice to note that an icon may be understood as a sign based on "planned likeness"—that an icon as a sign stands for something either because it is that something or because it is specifically made to resemble that something. The main thing to note, for the present purpose, is the self-reference of an icon—it is self-complete to the point of resisting outward justification or interpretation. As well, as Hodge and Kress maintain, "icons . . . have the modality of direct perception, and hence are the most persuasive of signs." See R. Hodge and G. Kress, *Social Semiotics* (Ithaca, NY: Cornell University Press, 1988), p. 26.

29. Other well-known "shopping arcades" of this nature would include the Sino Center and the Hollywood Center in Mongkok, the New Century in Wan Chai, and the Causeway Bay Plaza in Causeway Bay. In addition, these Japanese gifts shops and curios stores are also found widely in the large-scale neighborhood malls of the many newly established estates in Hong Kong.

30. The labyrinth as literary image and device has been cast in a variety of forms—with or without a center, one passageway or many, with or without an exit, and so forth. It is an image wherein fundamental contradictions are contained, represented, but not resolved—contradictions between the finite and the infinite, the one and the many, man and nature, and so on. Common to all labyrinthine scenarios would be the inevitable and inexplicable loss of bearing. And sometimes even before bearing can be lost, one comes face to face with the monster that, as a rule, always resided in the center. In this light, the labyrinth of hybridization is the labyrinth of the pure and the impure, the self and the other. And in the case of Hong Kong, the monstrous presence of 1997 dominates the center, where, when all sense of direction is lost, the apocalyptic moment of truth will be unveiled. For labyrinth as a literary device, see, e.g., A. Fletcher, "The Image of Lost Direction," in E. Cook et al., eds., *Center and Labyrinth* (Toronto: University of Toronto Press, 1983), pp. 329–346.

8

Globalization of Hong Kong's People: International Migration and the Family

Janet W. Salaff and Wong Siu-lun

Hong Kong's families are a people on the move. From the creation of the colony in 1847, and its massive population increase from China after the Second World War, and through economic outreach starting in the early 1970s, the political and economic globalization of Hong Kong has given rise to local and world-scale movements of people leaving to trade and attend school. Even when they do not physically travel, regional and worldwide decisions shape their daily lives in deep ways. In turn, we expect that the local and international migration of families will contribute further to the internationalization of Hong Kong.

This chapter links international migration to the shifting decisions to remain in Hong Kong or emigrate overseas as 1997 approaches. Writers have been increasingly sensitive to the variety of Hong Kong responses to 1997, and several in this volume differentiate among the demands of sectors of the population. They note the varied paces of actors and agendas in projects that shape the stages on which Hong Kong people enact their responses. We, too, take popular responses to Hong Kong's reversion in the direction of diversity. We find that people interpret the reversion to reflect short- and long-term family histories and fortunes. In many ways they consider emigration as a useful course of action against the backdrop of Hong Kong's globalization. This positioning leads to constant re-evaluations.

As the families we study plan their lives in the face of 1997, they consider three realms of global connectivity. Families' political experiences, their family economies, and kinship networks reveal the importance of the international scene. We find that the move abroad involves long-term plans as well as short-term processes, and each of these three realms incurs long- and short-term shifts.

To understand continuities and contingencies, we describe the emigration decisions of people from different social backgrounds over a recent period of time.

Data Sources

We draw on two sources of information to learn how families decide to remain in or to leave Hong Kong due to the transition to mainland political rule. We began with a representative survey of 1,552 Hong Kong Chinese households in Hong Kong in 1991. Our questionnaire gathered demographic and socioeconomic data from the household head, and asked about the family's plans to emigrate. We divided the survey respondents into four major occupational groups, henceforth referred to as class groups. The affluent class includes managers and professionals. The small businessmen make up the petty bourgeois class. The lower middle class consists mainly of white-collar workers. Finally, the working class is composed of laborers and menial workers. These groupings are consistent with the distribution of families, as recorded in the 1991 Hong Kong census. These families from different social class backgrounds living in Hong Kong reported their perspectives on the approaching political and economic events. They told us whether they intended to emigrate or not and whether their kin were emigrants. We found that social class responses differed broadly, and we decided to pursue this line in a follow-up study.[1]

In 1992, we chose thirty respondents from the survey sample for an in-depth analysis of how social ties affect the emigration decisions of their families. We chose a "purposive" sample of people representing the types of emigration responses and social class of people in the survey.[2] Hence, we do not describe the characteristics of Hong Kong emigrants in general. Rather than a history of recent migration, we link distinctive types of emigration decisions to the family economies and social milieux.

In the qualitative follow up, we sought adequate representation from emigrants and nonemigrants from a range of social class groups in our 1991 study. These are ordinary people, not the elite or very wealthy. The working class included unskilled and skilled laborers, taxi drivers, and others that used their labor power. The lower middle class mainly worked in bureaucracies. The upper middle class were in business and professional jobs. They are of different ages. The youngest two, a businessman and computer technician, have not yet married; the eldest was a retired ivory carver, since deceased.

Our working definition of an emigrant family is one whose member submitted an application form to immigrate to one of the major receiving countries for Hong Kong immigrants: England, Canada, the United States, Australia, and New Zealand. In order to study emigration decisions, we contacted more emigrants than proportionally existed in our 1991 study. Whereas 7 percent in our survey had applied to emigrate, just over half of those we contacted for the qualitative study told us in the 1991 survey that they had applied to emigrate. However, emigration is a process, and emigrant and nonemigrant families are not distinct groups. Applications for visas proceed through several stages and take a number of years. Some respondents did not complete the formalities. Acceptance or rejection by the receiving countries is not clear cut either. Some were accepted, but decided not to emigrate. Others were rejected by one receiving country and applied elsewhere. Finally, some left Hong Kong but have returned. This is not a new phemonenon. Myron Cohen refers to "dispersed" families with members and relatives already living abroad, yet still maintaining a shared economy.[3] These are forerunners to the current "astronaut" families who, divided by the ocean, spend much time jetting back and forth. The family, usually the wife and children, maintain a home in the West to qualify for citizenship, while the breadwinner, usually the husband, returns to Hong Kong to earn a living. In this study, we refer to emigrants as those that went so far as to file an application, regardless of whether they were interviewed, accepted or rejected, or have left or remained in Hong Kong.

Hence we term "emigrants" or "applicants" those still living in Hong Kong who had already applied to emigrate when we chose them. But as time went on, and our intensive study progressed, we learned their plans were greatly in flux. Whereas sixteen households had applied to emigrate when first surveyed in 1991, only five have left Hong Kong five years later. Some applicants were turned down; others changed their minds. Three of the five emigrants still go back and forth between Canada and Hong Kong to improve the family economy.

To compare how people of different settings thought about and dealt with these global issues, we asked the same questions of everyone, including about their family histories, their family economies, and kinship networks. But to avoid imposing our views, we also looked for themes in people's comments, and linked these to their broader family and personal experiences. Our study thus mixes structure with grounded comments.[4]

We can illustrate how we mix structure with grounded comments in gathering information on the social networks of family members that have emigrated. We systematically learned about people's meaningful kin that moved elsewhere. We built up a base of information on people who figured importantly in their lives, to give the wider social context for their views and actions. We think of this information as circles of the respondents' meaningful others. Although the circles are particular to each person, the categories of people we asked about were constant, so that we can compare people. We began with the 30 families, gathered information on both spouses, or 58 respondents, and on their families of origin (parents and siblings). They told us about the emigration decisions of 319 siblings, among whom 98 were emigrants. This allowed us to relate decisions of our contact families to those of their nearest kin. We expanded information on the whereabouts of kin to 403 when we included parents and grown children. By building a data base about our respondents' close kin and friends, we placed the emigration decisions of these couples in the context of their wider, but still meaningful, social world. As we will see, kin that circle the globe have a great impact on Hong Kong families like those we meet here.

Global Connectivities and Migration: Politics and Views Toward Reversion

That Hong Kong was created from global politics, which figures in emigration plans, is our starting point. Hong Kong people have multistranded connections to China. China politics and colonial politics have shaped the views of many toward the 1997 reversion. By China politics we refer here to respondents' families' experiences on the mainland, mainly when our respondents were very young. Two main questions are crucial. Did their families flee China's poverty? Or did they escape certain political discrimination? These alternative scenarios drastically shape the views of many families we met. They worked out plans for their life in Hong Kong after reversion as a result of their family histories, whether they were benign or fraught with terror.

These multistranded connections to China are geopolitically linked. Situated at the mouth of the Pearl River Delta in Southern China, Hong Kong before the Second World War served as the major port for the Chinese living in Guangdong and other provinces to venture abroad. Consequently, the colony became the key economic center for overseas Chinese, handling an intense traffic in people, remittances, and information. Hong Kong has long been a city of migrants with massive outflow and inflow of people to and from all over the world.[5] The ebb and flow of family matters, local unrest, or the search for jobs prompted them to cross the porous border.

Following the Chinese communist victory in 1949, over one million refugees left the mainland and sought shelter in the territory. For the families we met here, Hong Kong's global politics took a decisive turn when authorities newly buttressed the Shenzhen border in the early 1950s. When cross-border traffic grew difficult, migration across the borders became one-way. Hong Kong was closed from its hinterland.

Poverty propelled refugees over the border from the 1950s through the 1970s until the Hong Kong government abolished the "touch base" program permitting those daring illegal immigrants that got across the border to legalize their residency.[6] Although most of these early postwar Chinese immigrants were poor. Those whose property was confiscated by the local Communists joined the flight. But the poor and the disenfranchised not only left for different reasons, they also sought their own niches in Hong Kong. They tended to maintain distinct views toward China, which grandparents and parents passed on to the next generation. These vastly different reasons for arriving in Hong Kong—the flight from poverty or flight from politics—dominate their perceptions about reversion. To paraphrase a well-known sociological statement, "if people take ancestors into account, they are real in their consequences."

We divide our qualitative sample into those with and without personal China experiences, since these critical events polarize current attitudes toward reversion. We shall define those with past experiences as people born in mainland China. In our study, the couple is the base of analysis. At least one spouse in half of the couples in our qualitative sample was born in China. Eleven couples were economic migrants whose parents moved to Hong Kong between the 1950s and the 1970s to improve their family fortunes. The closing of the border in the early 1950s divided many South China families. Some of our respondents came to Hong Kong legally in the 1960s to rejoin parents who had left before the border closed. Others fled village poverty, often illegally. These economic migrants harbor little personal resentment toward their China past. They do not feel they were personally attacked, because they were in the same boat (often literally a "snakeboat") as everyone else.

For these economic migrants, the sharp memory of past poverty is part of their measuring stick for reversion to China in 1997. They maintain their links with China. Recalling the past poverty of their families, they hear and see evidence of China's economic improvement and they think well of China today. They are pleased to reunite with China for family or business reasons. They interact with China through visiting their kin. They want to invest in or find work in China, or retire cheaply in a Chinese town or village. In contrast, they have few global links outside the region.

At the other extreme are "political refugees" whose parents lost their property in China. In our sample of the fifteen couples with one partner born in China, parents of at least one spouse in four couples had property confiscated. These couples are marked by this trauma. These political refugees think of China as the place that made them suffer. Most have planned for years to move further from China's presence by leaving Hong Kong. They maintain few strong personal ties with kin left behind in China. Having been forced apart from their brothers and sisters in the mainland, they led separate lives. Until the 1980s, cross-border kin could not meet because the Hong Kong branch was branded as class enemies. The main contact those in Hong Kong have with China is doing business and training local people. They feel bitter about their treatment by the Chinese Communists. Having lost wealth, they are eager to reassert themselves and to regain the place that was wrested from them. They do not trust a mainland-run political system, however, and want to secure themselves abroad. In contrast to the former economic migrants, political refugees have many global links and seek to use them.

There is a pattern in our sample. Most economic migrants are working and lower middle class. That is, nearly half of the working and lower middle class in our sample were China-born, and most were economic migrants. In contrast, only two affluent couples contained one spouse whose parents reportedly fled poverty. Those that fled politics may be well placed and vocal about their grievances. But those that fled poverty outnumber them.

Both spouses in the remaining half of the respondent couples were born in Hong Kong; we term them "Hong Kong locals." Few Hong Kong locals feel either emotional attraction or antipathy to China. Rather than viewing the reversion through the lens of treatment of their foreparents, they pay most attention to their recent Hong Kong experiences.

The sociology of knowledge stresses that status differences that emerge from work and other social experiences contribute to people's outlooks. For our sample, these differences have to do with politics broadly defined, not electoral politics. In implicit agreement with China, the colonial authorities eschewed democratic politics, creating a political vacuum. The government suppressed political representation and political movements.[7] The belated efforts of the colonial regime that mandated a political voice for the nonelites in the 1990s were a result of international as well as local pressures. Before we began our study, we expected that those new political forums were a response to, and further fueled a demand for, representation. We thought that the new colonial politics would fuel fears among the nascent middle class of losing this voice during reversion to China. If this were the case, explicitly political goals would spur people to seek to leave.

But we did not find that the strong urge to maintain electoral politics prompted people in our study group to leave. Few in our sample expect much of the new right of political representation. While some voted in 1995, few assume greater civic responsibilities. The slogan "give me liberty or give me death" is not grounded in their recent experiences. Political participation ranks low on their list of things they need for a good family life.[8]

Instead, in this apolitical setting, work and other current experiences frame their views toward China and colonial politics. Born and raised in Hong Kong, nearly two-thirds of our qualitative sample assess China largely from their current job status. These frames are based on routines and taken-for-granted ways of life that people wish to maintain after 1997. They tend not to weigh ideology or principle heavily. Some believe that reversion will not alter these routines, whereas others anticipate a challenge.

Some Hong Kong locals without a personal China past are proud to be Hong Kong Chinese and look forward to China's regaining sovereignty. They are family oriented and loath to separate from local kin, whom they visit weekly. They have no economic connections that link them to China or to other countries. Few close kin are currently abroad. Years of work in colonial capitalist Hong Kong commit them to law, order, regularity. All were formed by years of living under British rule, and perceive this regularity of this rule as the ideal. They views politics more generally as a reliable legal framework for property and economic activities than as a means to seek redress. The less change, the less their career lines will suffer.[9]

Some Hong Kong locals we spoke with view reversion with equanimity, expecting communist capitalism to bring few important changes to their work environment. They perceive the colonial government's political moves as challenges to the mainland government, which worries them.

Other Hong Kong locals anxiously expect their current way of life will change greatly after 1997. Most perceive increased corruption.[10] The working class is concerned that 1997 might usher in chaos; the middle class fears the loss of property and freedom.[11] Many seek an environment that upholds this framework, and may move to recover it or avoid change. They fear their property will be insecure and it will be hard to work with legal predictability and regularity. For instance, some whose work is based on contracts and bureaucratic routines are aware of a lack of such legal protections in the mainland work style. Some decide in fact to take advantage of the current risk-taking climate to make short-term profits. These factors affect their evaluation of the new regime. Some of them sought papers to immigrate while others did not. Yet another decision is deciding to leave or to stay.

Differences in family histories of economic migrants, political refugees, and Hong Kong locals are reflected in actual behavior. Those born in China whose parents did not lose property are unlikely to be fleeing China politics. The eleven couples in which there were economic migrants from China attached no negative valence to their China experiences. Only two had applied to emigrate and they were not motivated by 1997 politics.

In contrast, those China-born respondents that knew of their family's deeply negative experiences in China were prompted to apply. Two of the four couples in which at least one spouse had parents with politically charged experiences sought emigration. Their desire to leave was deeply rooted in these early childhood family tales or experiences. And although they cannot emigrate without a substantial economic base and personal support system, the remaining two with such negative experiences worried about reliving such political experiences in 1997.

In sum, half our sample were economic migrants from China who were unlikely to have applied to emigrate. Political migrants, those likely to have applied, were a minority. Consequently, the majority of couples that applied to emigrate were Hong Kong locals.

Why did they apply? Most viewed China politics negatively. Nearly all spoke at different times about their dislike of China politics. They were disturbed by what they had heard about or experienced in China. Job-based contacts with China violated their views of personal rights or contract law. They opposed the June 4 massacre. Under the mainland regime they feared they could not maintain the livelihood they had long enjoyed in Hong Kong. However, these folk did not speak of electoral politics.

Although they readily noted disagreement with China politics, political concerns drove a minority to apply to emigrate. And these political migrants are more likely to be affluent.[12] For the rest, political views were strands in the many other economic and family matters. We thus found that the link between social class and political emigrant backgrounds is social class and emigration. Emigrants that apply to leave, propelled by the China experiences of their families, are in the upper reaches of the class structure in our sample.

Economic Resources

The Hong Kong economy is closely shaped by global forces, which touch the lives of those in our sample in different ways. How people earn money adds an important surface to the crystal that refracts 1997 reunification. The size of family income matters as well, of course, since in order to emigrate, people expect their resources to carry them forward. But the source and nature of earnings also matter. The decisions to emigrate turn on forms of capital. The nature of resources determines whether people can leave, where they will go, and what they expect to do when they get there. As expected, there is much variation in the type of resources members of different occupational classes have.

In a general sense, our 1991 sample survey tested these differences. It showed that Hong Kong folks with funds are most likely to leave for Western lands. By occupational level, 21 percent of those who hold management jobs, 31 percent of the professionals, but only 15 percent of the clerks and 6 percent of the working-class respondents planned to apply to emigrate before 1997. And this was not just empty talk: 15 percent of those in management, 18 percent of the professionals, and 3 percent of the working class had already applied for foreign papers. Those who intended to emigrate had higher educational levels than the rest. Those who had actually submitted applications were the best educated and had the highest status of all.[13] Similarly, the well-off predominate among Hong Kong immigrants to Canada, the major receiving nation. Federal statistics show that from 1986 to 1993, managers and professionals were heavily represented among Hong Kong emigrants. Hong Kong emigrants are more likely to be upper middle class, although a quarter were laborers.

Our qualitative sample explains the differing abilities of our respondent contacts to emigrate. The three distinct classes correspond with forms of capital that people can invest, and bear on their contacts that reach globally.

The international nature of Hong Kong's economy figured from the outset. Britain chose the site for regional trade and production and transshipment of raw materials and processed goods. The American government capitalized on Hong Kong's geographical location, viewing it as a way station for military movements against insurgent forces in Korea and Southeast Asia and the buttress against a buildup of communist forces from China and other nearby Asian countries. The international presence and projects (described in this volume) shaped the local economy. Early post–World War II inhabitants of Hong Kong were migrants from China. Some brought machinery and know-how from Shanghai and other Chinese coastal cities, and formed a local entrepreneurial class that mainly produced textiles and started the industrialization take-off.[14] Others became sources of low-cost labor. With the influx of these immigrants of diverse social backgrounds who were eager to begin their new lives, and the confrontation between communist China and Western capitalist countries during the Cold War, Hong Kong was transformed from an entrepôt into a manufacturing center. A prosperous node in the new Asia-Pacific region, the city-"state" played a key part in the development of flexible and transnational forms of subcontracting and commodity production. With the Chinese mainland isolated from the capitalist world, Hong Kong retained its importance among the overseas Chinese by acting as the sanctuary for their capital and the source for their cultural sustenance through the production of Chinese newspapers, movies, and other forms of popular culture.

The reunification of the two economies, starting in the early 1980s, further developed Hong Kong's trading role, thereby building up its middle class while the blue-collar workers declined in number. Hong Kong became the financier and organizer of manufacturing in China, especially the Southeast. Sandwiched through trading with China and the Asian region and the West, Hong Kong employees feel the pull of both worlds. The entrepôt role of Hong Kong between China and the developed nations has increased the size of the white-collar sector, and reduced or marginalized the working-class sector. The manufacturing structure still figures importantly, but more as tertiary than secondary labor. Hong Kong's other industries also earn it the label "international city": its financial trade makes it a world hub of regional trade, as does tourism, which connects Hong Kong elsewhere. Although many locals remain in family firms, the rapid spread of the tertiary sector has brought with it more chains and branches, and the growth of bureaucratic labor.15

Economic position shapes people's views toward 1997 and emigration in a number of ways. There are questions of location and sources of earnings and place in the local structure. Those that earn money from the China trade as direct employee, trader, or investor leave this region only reluctantly.

Next, the internationalized entrepôt economy is increasingly likely to provide white-collar jobs with the promise of a career. The status and administrative-legal frameworks and culture of these daily jobs give rise to the routine expectations of how the world should be constructed, as discussed above. Working in large British hongs or local establishments that service the housing and living needs of the local populace shapes an orderly view. People in these fields are likely to be worried about the political turmoil around the transition. Such jobs underwrite a structured framework within which employees experience the transition. Freewheelers in small Chinese firms may feel that an orderly transition is less important.

The formal political vacuum of the colonial government, which fostered little political identification with local parties or factions, encouraged economic differentiation in wages and buying power as a main distinguishing feature.16 With liberation politics downplayed, these status differences gained importance. Hence, people tend to state that economics not politics propels them away from Hong Kong.

The size of a family's resources is crucial in emigration. Those who can support themselves in "reluctant exile" will be more likely to apply to emigrate. This turns us to the mobility of resources. Some resources are more mobile than others. A family's evaluation of whether it will profit or lose by emigration affects its application to move abroad.

Finally, since foreign consular officials credit money over credentials and labor power, a sizable family economy paves the way to a successful application. But the overwhelming story to be told is just how family economics work.

The Affluent

The upper middle class in the survey were likely to emigrate, as were the ten affluent class families in our qualitative sample. They include mainly business-men and professionals, nearly all of whom can mobilize enough resources for successful immigration applications. Eight of the ten affluent families had been granted visas that enabled them to exit Hong Kong.

Those with economic capital will follow the logic of comparative advantage. With economic assets of property and the means of production, they can move funds to different countries. Thus, they may send money to different locales, widening their emigration potential. They may not need to accompany the funds themselves if they can find others to partner with them.

Affluent emigrants activate diverse bonds of friendship that help them set up businesses abroad. Their dependence on people is another form of "capital." They tend to seek investment partners among former schoolmates and work-mates. Hence, many sought to immigrate to countries where they had these links. They may have kin abroad as well. Hence networks of people form an important part of their resources.

The affluent had the funds or credentials to seek acceptance. Three husbands thought they could invest their capital outside Hong Kong and work and live abroad on the income. Five other affluent applicants had mainly credentials and valuable work experience, which we call cultural capital. They thought they could use their training and work experience abroad.

Nearly all expected to depend on former coworkers to re-establish them-selves. While several affluent respondents had visas to places where they had kin, they stressed that they were not economically dependent on these relatives. In fact, it was the presence of past and future collaborative colleagues that was decisive in choosing where to immigrate to.

They applied to emigrate under the business or "other independent" catego-ries, or as civil servants under the British Nationality Scheme. Only one, unmar-ried with siblings in Alberta, was granted a visa in the family reunification category. Six applied to a number of locales, and had a range of choices. Only one affluent couple was rejected (by Quebec Province, since they did not speak French), but was accepted elsewhere.

The theme of their applications is self-reliance. Though none of the applicants liked China politics, only two mentioned "1997" as the main reason to leave. Their ideology of independence stresses that they are capable of controlling their family economies under adverse environments. Attributing their exit from Hong Kong to the 1997 reversion might suggest to their friends that they cannot do so. Further, it was fairly easy for these folk to conceive of emigration and making a living in a new land. Given this, it was not just politics that pushed them to apply. It was also the nature of their resources that gave them the needed boost.

The nature of respondents' resources colored whether they followed up their initial forays abroad. Most had to earn money abroad. If their ventures failed, they rarely have the capital to spare. They have to return. The internationalization of the Hong Kong economy connected them abroad. But it is at home that people seek to expand their options, not abroad. Indeed, few have in fact left. Four affluent respondents emigrated, but two have since returned to Hong Kong to work, having gotten a foothold in Canada. Four did not intend to activate their papers unless 1997 precipitated a crisis. Their visas were for "insurance purposes." Their capital can bring greater returns on the home turf.

The Lower Middle Class

The professionals and members of the lower middle class whose livelihoods hinge on bureaucratic careers and wages have a lower emigration propensity. They have knowledge and skills as resources, and these assets have the least global reach. Foreign countries must recognize their credentials, and two educational systems in their own and in the immigrant country are rarely comparable. Consequently, the most popular destinations for the present wave of educated migrants from Hong Kong are English-speaking countries such as Canada, the United States, and Australia. Even here, however, they have trouble transferring their diplomas. Waves of professional protectionism for some professions abroad also means that even those trained in the host country that return to Hong Kong for many years need to requalify. This limits recognition of their cultural capital outside of Hong Kong. Since their capital is not mobile, neither are they.

The lower-middle-class respondents in the 1991 sample survey were less likely to apply and unlikely to qualify. The ten lower-middle-class couples in our intensive study were also unable to qualify. They work in public and private sector bureaucracies, secure their livelihood locally, and have little movable capital. Specifically, these new lower-middle-class employees are not particularly keen to emigrate because, first, they cannot count on getting similar jobs abroad. Some work for the Hong Kong government and other public bodies, and cannot qualify for this kind of work elsewhere. None have the necessary licenses or certification to start again in their lines of work overseas. Second, they earn too little for most investment categories of immigrants. They also lack the higher education or specialized training to qualify as "other independent" immigrants to

Canada and Australia, the countries most Hong Kong people seek to enter. Third, these nurses, technicians, civil servants, assistant engineers, and schoolteachers have enjoyed a spurt of income improvement in recent years, which they fear they cannot match abroad. This is especially true where both spouses work to maintain a dual-income household. They look forward to promotions through fixed steps on career ladders. With few grand economic hopes for themselves, they are not eager to reject the solid living standard they enjoy for an uncertain life abroad.

The four lower-middle-class couples that applied to emigrate in our intensive study are characteristic. The way they applied was distinctive of their class-bound resources. They applied on the basis of cultural capital at their disposal, in the form of achieved qualifications from advanced study and legitimated by diplomas.

Unable to get jobs in their line of work from kin, the new lower middle class use other channels to apply. Civil servant status helps the most. Singapore and England remain options for those with quasi-political civil service jobs. Their main strategy was to take advantage of their jobs, especially civil service status, to apply as special immigrants to Singapore or England. A civil servant, a former policeman, and a teacher pursued this option.

Subsequently, with their immobile capital, they were mainly rejected by the major receiving nations they applied to. While four of the ten in this sector in the qualitative study applied, two were rejected outright. Two were accepted to Singapore and Great Britain, which give special consideration to certain categories of Hong Kong civil servants. Only one has emigrated.

The sole lower-middle-class emigrant in our sample was a clerk in the correctional services, married to a former constable. As a young man, her husband had studied karate in his uncle's martial arts studio. He joined the police force, but continued his avocation. He became proficient under the instructor of the world famous martial artist Bruce Lee, and began to teach in his off hours in a community center. While at a police training course, he met a British constable, also an admirer of Bruce Lee, who had come to Hong Kong to meet Lee's coach and train with him. In early 1989, the British constable invited him to Manchester to teach karate, and arranged for him to have working papers. After the June 4 massacre, the constable became fearful of working in Hong Kong after the handover and tried his hand in England. He joined his colleague and built up a martial arts following. Having firmed his economic base, he split off from his colleague and took his students to his own school. He then took the crucial emigration step through his wife who, as a member of the correctional services, herself qualified for the British Nationality Scheme. This lower-middle-class emigrant family was successful because they combined portable assets—a skill recognized and in demand globally, and colleagual contacts to build a following—with official immigration channels from the government.

The Working Class

Working-class emigrants and those with small family-run firms depend heavily on their labor power. They do not have mobile capital and possess personal employment networks as their main assets. The working class can only look to family and kinship ties to emigrate. They can only move when they find a place to use their labor. Since their working-class kin have slender resources, these people have the fewest network resources, which curtails their ability to emigrate. Finally if they can leave at all, those with low-cost labor to sell can only emigrate to places that need their labor, which greatly limits their choices.

These applicants are mainly motivated to leave Hong Kong for economic reasons. Only one of the four working-class applicants, a correctional worker in the prison system, mentioned political reasons for applying for the Right of Abode. This application in fact cost him little, and in the end he was rejected. The remaining working-class applicants sought to follow family members abroad that might offer them work. None, however, convinced the authorities that their applications gave the host country enough resources, and all were rejected. Having applied only to one country, when the immigration authorities rejected their sole application, they were compelled to give up the idea.

Emigration Decisions and Kinship Networks

The third and most obvious global emigration feature is the international location of kin.[17] It has been argued that Hong Kong's global networks of emigrants draw others to follow them, and we find this to be the case. The networks people have forged globally over the years shape their decisions to emigrate, return to the China land mass, or remain in Hong Kong. How do kin and friends help family members decide? Our study finds that working- and middle-class adults maintain relationships with others abroad and use these contacts to move across the seas. But the global network relations, like other resources, are socially differentiated and link people to overseas in different ways.

Hong Kong emigrants have come from all social classes. As sojourners in their own city, Hong Kong people have moved readily to places where they can find work. The first wave of post–World War II emigrants consisted mainly of unskilled immigrant workers drawn to Britain, which had not yet set up barriers to members of Commonwealth countries. Poorly educated New Territories village men left in large numbers to open and work in restaurants in Great Britain.[18] Gradually, the skills of those who went abroad changed. In the 1970s, Western immigration policies favored young, well-educated, English-speaking professionals, technicians, and managers with financial means. In the 1980s, Hong Kong society developed a strong middle class tied intellectually to Western nations. Parents increasingly sent their children abroad to study. The students often remained there, and these links prompted more people to go back and forth.

Table 8.1

Average Kinship Ties of Survey Respondents by Emigration Status and Class

Social Class	Average Number of Kin Living Abroad		
	Emigrant	Nonemigrant	Average
Working	0.70	0.36	0.38
Lower middle	0.53	0.50	0.50
Petty bourgeois	0.69	0.54	0.56
Affluent	0.61	0.87	0.67

Source: 1991 Emigration Survey.

More recently, Western nations court immigrants with funds. Some countries have opened their immigration doors wider to Hong Kong people. Since 1989, about 60,000 Hong Kong Chinese have emigrated annually, with Canada, the United States, and Australia the main destinations.

Such connections are crucial in determining which people plan to exit and where they go. Emigrants activate their networks to leave Hong Kong. Our survey data found kinship networks to be associated with people's emigration decisions. Many Hong Kong families have emigrant kin. As individuals, the 1,552 respondents in the survey average from 0.67 to 0.38 family members abroad, depending on their class background (Table 8.1). The working class has the fewest family members abroad and the affluent class the most.

Further, most of those that emigrate have more kin overseas than those that do not emigrate. This supports Ronald Skeldon's assertion that immigrants form chains. The 1991 survey could not reveal how network ties actually affect emigration decisions. Further, the survey collected only limited data about the family as a unit, and did not cover friendship and acquaintanceship ties.[19] Our in-depth interviews, which address such questions, found that global emigrant networks especially affect emigration opportunities and choices.

We use the term "network capital" here to refer to access to meaningful circles of emigrant kin. We learned about respondents' brothers and sisters that have emigrated, which in turn deepened opportunities for our respondents to emigrate. As emigrants themselves, our respondents can also provide chances for their kin to emigrate.

We start with the sheer number of kin. We propose that the richer the family in emigrant kin, the easier it is for individual members to emigrate. It should be easier for individuals to find others to help them when they decide to leave. The ways in which family helps may vary, from material aid in the form of money, to a service, to offering a job, or providing a temporary stopover place and offering information on what to expect abroad. We can thus think of families abroad as a

Table 8.2

Emigrant Siblings as Percent of Total Number of Siblings

Social class of respondents	Number of respondents	Number of respondents' siblings	Number of respondents' siblings who are emigrants	Percentage of siblings who are emigrants
Working class	20	113	27	24%
Lower middle class	20	108	26	24%
Affluent class	18	98	45	46%
Total	58	319	98	31%

Source: Interviews 1992–1996.

refuge that can offer concrete help to kin in Hong Kong who wish to join them. A family in which most of the members have emigrated and are planted in different countries may develop an "emigrant culture." With much back-and-forth movement, the family can think of itself at home with diverse locales. While family members may not need to call on kin to help, having kin abroad gives them a choice.

Next, the more diverse the network capital, the easier it is for people to emigrate. In turn, the more diverse their own applications, the easier it is to emigrate. We thus expect that those couples that apply to emigrate should have different kinship ties from the nonapplicants. Almost a third of the brothers and sisters in the two families of husband and wife (30 percent) were emigrants. Table 8.2 further shows that on average there are more emigrant kin among the emigrants in our sample than among the nonemigrants. Each emigrant couple averages 5.1 emigrant siblings. In contrast, nonemigrant respondents average 1.2 emigrant siblings. For all three social class groups we studied in depth, those that emigrated had more emigrants among their brothers and sisters. These kin are likely to become their network capital.

Emigrants in three of the four class groups have more kinship ties overseas than do nonemigrant households. Thus, the most dramatic differences in the number of kinship ties between emigrant and nonemigrant households in the survey are in the working class. Emigrant kin clearly pull their working-class kin along after them. The petty bourgeois businessmen, mainly with family businesses, follow. They, too, need kin to emigrate. The lower middle class shows a small difference, since they mainly emigrate without kin help. The affluent class actually reverses the trend. The affluent not only have more money, property, and education than the rest, but also more kin abroad as resources. In fact, the affluent have many emigrants in their families, regardless of whether they themselves are emigrants (Table 8.3).

Table 8.3

Emigrant Kin of Emigrants and Nonemigrants

Social Class of Respondents	(a) Number of Couples	(b) Number of Respondents' Siblings	(d) Number of Emigrant Siblings as Percentage of Total Siblings
	(a)	(b)	(c)
1. Emigrants			
Working class	4	56	34%
Lower middle class	4	59	37%
Affluent class	8	79	51%
Total	16	206	42%
2. Nonemigrants			
Working class	6	57	12%
Lower middle class	6	49	8%
Affluent class	2	19	26%
Total	14	113	14%

Source: Interviews 1992–1996.

Friends, colleagues, and classmates are other crucial network resources. Having emigrant friends and colleagues they could count for help or tips about life abroad propelled respondents to emigrate. Those with friends applying to exit could also form a reference group of like-minded people, who influence each other about exiting being the right thing to do. Friends were indeed important to future emigrants: 13 of the 16 applicants knew friends, neighbors, or coworkers that had emigrated and with whom they kept in touch. In contrast, nonemigrants did not keep in touch with acquaintances abroad. Indeed, few could think of any close friends who had emigrated.

To better understand the richness of opportunities to emigrate, we looked past the sheer number of emigrant kin to structures of emigration. We expected that the diversity of their options to leave would be a plus for potential emigrants. We measured this within the families we interviewed qualitatively. We believed that the diversity of the opportunities to emigrate in a family should help other family members to emigrate along what we call these "network chains." We took the number of chains of emigration to approximate the number of opportunities people had to emigrate.

We measured chains of emigration by the ways people applied to emigrate. We looked for the proximate person that paved the way for a respondent to apply to emigrate. An independent application was the start of a chain. For those that did not apply independently, the person or opportunity our emigrant sought to follow abroad was the start of their chain. Only if members of a family emigrated under the same narrow conditions would they be counted as a single network, not as part of a choice.

Hong Kong emigrants are mainly family emigrants. They mainly leave as part of family units, rather than being labor migrants or "birds of passage." Consequently, as in our earlier calculations, we defined an emigrant network chain from within the family, and from the perspective of our respondent couple. As before, we based our calculations on our couples and their brothers and sisters.

We wondered would an entire family constitute one chain? How many chains would be contained in a family group? We found that two or even three in one family often shared a network. Typically, husband and wife respondents, both emigrants, belong to a single emigrant network; the husband usually was the applicant and the wife was part of his application. However, if it is true that several people can be part of one network, it is also true that one person can be part of more than one network. Those with several disparate chances to emigrate, in our view, participate in several network chains.

There was considerable variation by social class. Each affluent family in our group averages 4.6 emigrant networks. Lower-middle-class couples average 2.2 emigrant networks. In contrast, the average lower-class family has only 1.6 emigrant networks. The following cases describe the process.

The Affluent

Affluent families have more kin abroad than any other group. Further, their kin are neither spatially nor socially concentrated, but are spread out. Most affluent couples have emigrant kin in many different countries, are widely placed around the globe. They provide a varied set of resources.

Since the affluent mainly depend on their personal resources to emigrate, they are not compelled to rely on these emigrant kin. They also have friends and colleagues that have already gone abroad.

One example of the widely elaborated emigrant networks of the affluent is that of a computer scientist and his civil servant wife, both trained in England. Each spouse has two separate emigrant networks and together they have one joint network, which amounts to five chains between the two. These dramatically describe the wealth of resources of the affluent families that allow them to emigrate with ease. It should not be assumed they actually will emigrate. However, they have the option to so so if they choose.

The affluent families that intend to emigrate all keep in contact with friends abroad. And they have the most extensive circles of friends and colleagues who will emigrate. These loosely textured linkages are most characteristic of the well-to-do because those with more education tend to maintain contact with their classmates years after they have finished school.

A husband and wife recall vividly their family's loss of its property in mainland China. They planned for years to emigrate. Just where and how depended on their global personal resources. Now a site engineer, the husband worked his way through school, getting his training part time in the building trades courses given in the Hong Kong Polytechnic. For six years, he and his classmates went to school several nights a week after work. That grueling stint cemented ties that bind today, a decade later. He was employed by a large Hong Kong construction firm. On the side, he had opened a small interior design firm with his classmates as shareholders. Yet another Polytechnic classmate emigrated to Vancouver: "I bought my Richmond house there with his help. I never even went there; he helped me care for it. My classmate told me not to emigrate because the economy for construction was so bad. But if I do emigrate, I'll probably work with him at the start." Those with more economic resources build up globally based friendship circles. The wife recalled their decision to move to Canada: "Compared with Australia, I have got more friends and some uncles in Canada. But my husband does not welcome people's help. We have cousins in Vancouver and Toronto, but our relatives are not useful. They didn't even answer my fax. They are afraid if they get involved, they can never get rid of us. Friends are more reliable."

Affluent emigrants feel they can depend on their classmates for help. Friends are already established and can give the newcomer a first job. The job can be permanent, or if it does not work out, it provides a temporary shelter while the new immigrant settles in and learns the ropes. Or, a classmate in the same trade can give the newcomer information that leads to a job. The affluent do not feel that this is a form of dependence, for they have their own funds to rely on and many contacts to help them. These emigrant friends are more important than their emigrant kin.

The managing director of a printing company had gotten visas from several countries. As an entrepreneur, he partakes in three networks leading abroad to three countries; his wife shares his networks. His sister was living in Canada, but he excluded that country as an emigration possibility. "It's too far for our children to travel there, and we don't like the weather," his wife said. "If we haven't even bothered to visit her in Toronto, how could we want to live there?" They chose Singapore as their emigration destination, where the managing director had many classmates and business associates. Singapore is also closer than Toronto to their China-based business. They had already bought a house there, as part of their emigration plan. Another of the managing director's brothers would emigrate to Singapore as a teacher, but he claimed he was not influenced by this relation. He chose to apply for Singapore papers because it had more flexible emigration conditions, and because his classmates who were there could help him work out his business arrangements.

When affluent individuals describe how they might work with former classmates, it is clear they are thinking of an egalitarian relationship. They do not feel that by agreeing to work together they are depending on friends. It is understood that each side is ready to put up capital. Classmates know one another's skills and talents. Such a relationship with friends does not make emigrants feel like they are getting a handout. Like those who depend on cultural capital, many potential emigrants from the affluent class prefer to rely on friends than on kin.

Just as the wealthy have more money, so, too, do they join more emigrant chains and have more network capital. That the affluent are "better connected" is reflected in their networks. The affluent had the most emigrant kin networks. As a whole, in the affluent sample, emigrants and nonemigrants alike had 45 emigrant siblings and 46 distinguishable networks. That is, on average, nearly every emigrant was part of a separate network chain.

The Lower Middle Class

There are fewer emigrant respondents and fewer emigrant siblings among the lower middle class in our small sample (as in the larger survey). Nevertheless, lower-middle-class emigrant siblings still emigrate based on their global resources. We measure this as the extent to which their networks are independent. The 26 emigrant siblings in lower-middle-class families have 22 emigrant networks. The near one-to-one ratio demonstrates their network independence.

Only one of the lower-middle-class couples used kinship ties in an application to emigrate, but they also used their qualifications. Their families' loss of property in China had scarred a telecommunications technician and his wife, a nurse who had left her profession at the time of our first interview. The couple was part of a decade-long familywide emigration plan as were their brothers and sisters who had emigrated to Canada and Australia. Before marriage, the wife first applied to join her sisters in Canada, but was rejected. Later, Australia turned the couple down as well. They then tried to emigrate to New Zealand, thinking it would be easier from there to get into Australia. With two of his brothers, the technician organized an investment package for the occasion. But the jerry-built firm did not pass the scrutiny of New Zealand officials, and the couple was compelled to abandon their emigration goal. That this lower-middle-class family did not have enough resources to convince the emigration authorities in three countries strengthens our point that both the economic and the network capital of the lower middle class are likely to be inadequate to help them emigrate. Rejected on all sides, the couple is still trying to increase their cultural capital. The wife has returned to the nursing profession and hopes having a profession in demand will increase their points to enter Canada.

Although they may have kin abroad, those holding modest salaried posts may not join them. They worry that they cannot easily fit into an enterprise that their foreign kin might run. If the work relationship falters, they will be left without a base of their own and will have no economic recourse. Indeed, these lower-middle-class workers pride themselves on being independent.

A land inspector in the Hong Kong civil service, married to factory seamstress, decided not to emigrate even though his sister's daughter asked him and his wife to join her family in moving to Australia. She offered him a job in the drug store her family hoped to open. Since they had not yet opened the firm, he perhaps felt it was a shaky possibility. And in the event it did not work out, he would be without a solid economic base. "I tell my niece 'I won't go.' Her husband is a professor of pharmacy in the United States. But they live in Taiwan. He is doing some research and patented a new medicine. He always goes to different places to deliver lectures. They are very rich. They want to set up a pharmacy shop in Australia, and ask me to go there to do a clerical job. But I don't want to rely on my relatives. I am independent. I never seek help from others. I don't want to depend on them and receive their help. Moreover, I'll lose my pension if I resign. After consideration, I decide not to apply to emigrate."

Working-Class Families

Working-class applicant families depend much more on emigrant kin networks. The 27 emigrants among their brothers and sisters share 16 emigrant networks. This is because there are several family-class emigrants and there is a tendency to emigrate to join family economic enterprises.

This exercise showed us how Hong Kong's global networks shape and encourage its populace to continue the emigration trend. Our in-depth study of specific families shows that while emigrant kin provide an opportunity, they do not determine the exit of Hong Kong–based middle-class families. They are part of the global resources that, taken together, aid the emigration process. The richer people were in emigrant networks, the more likely they were to emigrate. We also found that globalization is a "package": the richer people were in one form of global resources, such as money, the richer they were in other global resources—here, emigrant networks.

Conclusion

Emigration is a selective and transformative process. People mobilize diverse forms of resources to move from place to place. As their assets and endowments vary, so does their proclivity to emigrate. Indeed, people with different resources can be said to make up different types of emigrants. Their motives are different; their opportunities to apply and their successes also differ.

We have drawn out the ways in which these apparently individualistic movements reflect the global position of families. We spoke here of the ways people maximize their resources when they decide to emigrate. Resources of a broad nature including social relationships shape emigration patterns. Clearly, people's access to global resources seems most crucial in determining whether they intend to try to emigrate at all.

The present wave of emigration from Hong Kong has often been characterized as a middle-class phenomenon. By describing the different resources each social class has access to, we have shown that the affluent class has more global resources than the others, which explains their high rate of applications and successes. We have also explained why so few have left Hong Kong, as the global resources they have are more truly usable in the territory than abroad.

While the decision to emigrate is apparently an individual one, it is only superficially so. It is a decision made in the collective context, linking people to others in different manners, with social, and hence diverse, outcomes.

Notes

1. For further details about the 1991 survey and the follow-up interviews, see Eric Fong, Janet Salaff, and Wong Siu-lun, "Kin Networks and the Plan to Leave Hong Kong," in Ronald Skeldon, ed., *Emigration from Hong Kong* (Hong Kong: The Chinese University Press, 1995), pp. 213–233. Henceforth we refer to the 1991 interviews of 1,552 Hong Kong respondents as "the survey," and the follow-up in-depth study of 30 families done in 1992–96 as the in-depth or qualitative interviews.

2. There are several limitations to the sampling for the follow-up qualitative re-interviews: While the families represented the broad range of occupations in the 1991 large-scale survey from which we drew their names, we did not draw the thirty names randomly. One type of respondent is absent in particular: the very wealthy. While we did talk to several of the quite well-off in the large-scale survey, we did not locate them for our small-scale restudy. This was not because they had emigrated between 1991 and 1992. Rather, the well-off had not listed their phone numbers and did not reply to our letters, and thus could not be contacted. Further, our study is circumscribed by time. Although in 1991 we drew a randomized sample of the Hong Kong populace, we could only contact those still living in the colony in 1991. We subsequently could recontact those still in Hong Kong the following year.

3. Myron L. Cohen, "Developmental Process in the Chinese Domestic Group," in Maurice Freedman, ed., *Family and Kinship in Chinese Society* (Stanford, CA: Stanford University Press, 1970), pp. 21–36.

4. We found the qualitative data program Nudist useful in analyzing structures and themes.

5. Elizabeth Sinn, "Emigration from Hong Kong Before 1941: General Trends," in Ronald Skeldon, ed., *Emigration from Hong Kong*, p. 12.

6. Siu Yat-ming, "Population and Immigration: With a Special Account on Chinese Immigrants," in Nyaw Mee-kau and Li Si-ming, *The Other Hong Kong Report: 1996* (Hong Kong: The Chinese University Press, 1996), pp. 325–347.

7. Lau Siu-kai, "Political Order and Democratization in Hong Kong," paper delivered in the University of Hong Kong Lectures (Hong Kong), October 26, 1996. (Department of Sociology, The Chinese University of Hong Kong, typescript).

8. Tai-lok Lui, "The Hong Kong New Middle Class On the Eve of 1997," (Hong Kong: Department of Sociology, The Chinese University of Hong Kong, typescript).

9. Karin Chai, "Export-Oriented Industrialization and Political and Class Development: Hong Kong on the Eve of 1997," In Richard H. Brown and William Liu, eds., *Modernization in East Asia: Political, Economic and Social Perspectives* (Westport, London: Prager, 1992).

10. Lo Shui-hing, "Anti-Corruption and Crime," in Nyaw Mee-kau and Li Si-ming, *The Other Hong Kong Report, 1996*, pp. 152–182.

11. Wong Siu-lun, "Emigration and Stability in Hong Kong," *Asian Survey*, 32, 10 (1992), pp. 918–933; Janet Salaff and Wong Siu-lun, "Exiting Hong Kong: Social Class Experiences and the Adjustment to 1997," in Lau Siu-kai et al., eds., *Inequalities and Development: Social Stratification in Chinese Societies* (Hong Kong: Hong Kong Institute of Asia-Pacific Studies, The Chinese University of Hong Kong, 1994), pp. 205–249.

12. Although they are found throughout the class spectrum, the politically motivated predominate in the affluent group. There are overall six politically motivated emigrants; they include one working-class couple, one lower-middle-class couple, and four affluent couples.

13. The proportions of families in the larger 1991 survey that intended to emigrate at any time were: affluent, 24 percent; petty bourgeois, 15 percent; lower-middle-class, 10 percent; working-class, 11 percent. The correlation coefficients between those desiring to emigrate and higher education are: .2236 (p = 000); and between those applying to emigrate and having received higher education .3040 (p = 000). High-status occupations = 1, low = 6. The mean occupation for all respondents was 4.41 (sd = 1.7). Those who desired to emigrate scored a mean of 3.65 (sd = 1.11); those who did not desire to emigrate had lower-status occupations (they scored above the overall mean, 4.48). Those who applied to emigrate scored 3.55 (sd = 1.85); those who did not submit an application, 4.53 (sd = 1.65) see Eric Fong, Janet Salaff, and Wong Siu-lun, "Kin Networks and the Plan to Leave Hong Kong," p. 219.

14. Wong Siu-lun, *Emigrant Entrepreneurs: Shanghai Industrialists in Hong Kong* (Hong Kong: Oxford University Press, 1988).

15. Stephen W.K. Chiu, K.C. Ho, Tai-Lok Lui, *City-States in the Global Economy: Industrial Restructuring in Hong Kong and Singapore* (Boulder, CO.: Westview, 1997).

16. Tai-lok Lui, "The Hong Kong New Middle Class on the Eve of 1997," forthcoming.

17. Ronald Skeldon, "Hong Kong as an International Migration System," in Ronald Skeldon, ed., *Reluctant Exiles: Migration from Hong Kong and the New Overseas Chinese* (Armonk NY: M.E. Sharpe, and Hong Kong: Hong Kong University Press, 1994), pp. 21–51. Skeldon points out that the sending of people abroad gives Hong Kong's people a unique advantage of being part of chains of related people that span the globe. Indeed, Skeldon defines the globalization of Hong Kong from this emigrant perspective.

18. James L. Watson, *Emigration and the Chinese Lineage: The Mans in Hong Kong and London* (Berkeley: University of California Press, 1975).

19. In the survey, we asked individual respondents which kin lived abroad. This question addressed the respondent alone, not the kin of the respondent's spouse. Hence, it differs from the findings of our qualitative study, which report on kin of both spouses.

9

Media Internationalization in Hong Kong: Patterns, Factors, and Tensions

Joseph Man Chan

Media internationalization is "the process by which the ownership, structure, production, distribution, or content of a country's media is influenced by foreign media interests, culture, and markets."[1] It can be viewed as the diffusion of innovations such as media content, production values, and industrial arrangements across national boundaries. The internationalized and the internationalizing are two sides of the same coin. This chapter will examine Hong Kong from both sides, as an information importer as well as an exporter. As Hong Kong is under British rule and Taiwan is not unified with China, media exchanges among these Chinese societies are not to be viewed as domestic trade but as part of internationalization.

Patterns of Media Internationalization

As a whole, the degrees to which Hong Kong media internationalize and are internationalized are quite high when compared with other East and Southeast Asian countries. On the one hand, Hong Kong is relatively open to foreign media ownership and has easy access to a wide range of foreign media. On the other hand, Hong Kong is an important media exporter of the world, commanding an enviable position that does not seem to match its small size.

Ownership

With the exception of electronic media, which are subject to stricter regulation, mass media in Hong Kong operate primarily within a market environment. This market is open to both internal and external media operators. Foreign media ownership in Hong Kong is often not frowned upon as in many other countries.

The Hong Kong government now rules that individual foreigners cannot own more than 10 percent of the interests in television. As a group, foreigners cannot own more than 49 percent. TVB, for instance, is partly owned by Malaysian tycoon Robert Kwok. It has been a practice for local interest to form consortia with foreign media in bidding for broadcast licenses. The foreign partners are important sources of both capital and expertise. STAR TV and Wharf Cable are examples in this regard.

Hong Kong does not have any restrictions on the foreign ownership of print media. Anyone can register a publication. *South China Morning Post*, the most influential English newspaper, has a long tradition of being owned by foreigners. Regional magazines such as *Far Eastern Economic Review* and *Asiaweek* are also foreign-owned. However, most of the Chinese newspapers and magazines are owned by locals. A few dailies and magazines are owned and controlled by the Chinese Communist Party. In recent years, some media are known to have been bought by pro-China businessmen who can be local as well as foreign by nationality.

Receiving International News

While local news is of primary importance, international news is a routine part of Hong Kong's journalistic diet. About one-third of television news broadcast is dedicated to international news. In off-prime-time hours, the television stations relay unedited newscasts from the United States, China, Taiwan, and Japan. Wharf Cable offers CNN and BBC World services, whose coverage is virtually all foreign to Hong Kong.

Like audiences all over the world, Hong Kong people prefer local news to international news because of social relevancy. Our audience survey in 1990 found that 79.1 percent of the respondents rated local news in newspapers as their favorite content whereas only 63.7 percent rated international news as such.[2] However, it should be noted that over half of the audience is interested in international news. This has to do with the susceptibility of Hong Kong to international development and the extensive global networks that Hong Kong has established.

To identify the sources and actors of international news reported in Hong Kong, I content analyzed *Ming Pao*, a major Chinese-language elite daily, and *Oriental Daily*, the best-selling popular newspaper. The sample includes three constructed weeks from mid-1992 to mid-1993.

Table 9.1 shows that Western wires such as Reuters, Associated Press, Agence France-Press, and United Press International are very influential sources of international news in Hong Kong, accounting for a total of 51.2 percent of international news. In contrast, only 5.5 percent of the international news was derived from the Chinese official Xinhua and China News Agency. While Hong Kong newspapers rely heavily on agencies for events that occur out of Greater

Table 9.1

Sources of International News in Two Leading Newspapers (*Ming Pao* and *Oriental Daily*)

Source	%
Xinhua and China News Agency	5.5
Central News Agency	1.3
Reuters	20.3
Associated Press	8.9
United Press International	1.4
Agence France-Presse	9.5
Combined Western Wires	11.1
Reporters/Correspondents	29.8
Unidentified and other agencies	11.9
Total	100.0

(N = 2,095)

Table 9.2

Sites of International News in Two Chinese Leading Newspapers (*Ming Pao* and *Oriental Daily*)

Country	%
U.S.A.	21.2
Canada	2.7
Mexico, Central and South America	1.3
Great Britain	6.6
Western Europe	11.5
Eastern Europe	4.6
China	24.8
Taiwan	5.4
Japan	4.8
Southeast Asia	2.2
Middle East	2.2
Africa	1.3
Others	6.7
Total	100.0

(N = 2,095)

China, they frequently dispatch correspondents to cover major happenings in China and Taiwan. This makes up 29.8 percent of the international news.

Table 9.2 shows the geographical position of the major actors of international news. China stands out as the single country that commands the greatest attention (24.8 percent). Not far behind is the United States which is one of Hong Kong's top trading partners (21.2 percent). Taiwan (5.4 percent) received about as much attention as Great Britain (6.6 percent) and Japan (4.8 percent). The areas that receive the least coverage include Central and South America (1.3 percent), Africa (1.3 percent), Southeast Asia (2.2 percent) and the Middle East

(2.2 percent). This pattern indicates that Hong Kong tends to cover areas that are close in proximity and are relevant to its political and economic welfare.

Accessibility of Foreign Media

Foreign media fare proliferates in Hong Kong. All television stations—TVB, ATV, Wharf Cable, and STAR TV—carry channels that broadcast primarily foreign programs. Foreign movies with Chinese subtitles are screened throughout the year. Movie videos and popular music from the West are readily available for rental or for sale. Translated versions of Japanese comic books also command a large audience in Hong Kong.

The growing accessibility of foreign media does not necessarily imply the subordination of local media in the Hong Kong market. Domestic media appear to have the ultimate appeal to the local audience as long as they are comparable to foreign rivals in quality and variety. Since the early 1970s, television prime time in Hong Kong has been dominated by domestic soap operas. Table 9.3 shows the sources of programs on terrestrial television on an average week in 1993–94. The English-language channels of TVB Pearl and ATV World broadcast mostly foreign programs (69.4 percent and 54.2 percent, respectively) whereas the Cantonese TVB Jade and ATV Home broadcast many fewer foreign programs (15.3 percent and 17.3 percent, respectively). The ratings are lopsidedly in favor of the Cantonese-speaking channels among the Chinese population of Hong Kong.

A more detailed examination of program sources finds that most of the foreign programs were imported from the United States for the English-language channels (over 40 percent) and from Japan for the Chinese-language channels (over 9 percent). An overwhelming majority of the local programs for the Cantonese-language channels were produced by the stations themselves, and only about one-fifth of their total programming was independent productions.

However, the domination of local programs appears to have suffered some as imported programs from Taiwan and Japan have begun to return during prime time since 1993. The most important event signifying the decline in competitiveness of domestic programs was the success of "Judge Pao," a Taiwanese drama series, during prime time in 1993–94. Since then, programmers have been trying more often than before to test the prime-time market for dubbed drama series imported from Taiwan and Japan.

Although Western movies are among the best-selling movies in Hong Kong, local productions continue to dominate the box office revenue since the early 1980s. Table 9.4 shows that the ratio of box office revenue between local and foreign films was about 1:1 in 1980. But by 1985, this ratio is about 2:1 in favor of local productions. This trend has continued into the early nineties. However, in a survey of the Hong Kong population in 1990, we found that 52.4 percent expressed satisfaction with foreign films but only 19.4 percent did so for local

Table 9.3

Program Sources in an Average Week on Terrestrial Broadcast Television, September 1993–August 1994

Program Source	ATV Home (%)	ATV World (%)	TVB Jade (%)	TVB Pearl (%)
Foreign:				
U.K. and Commonwealth	0.30	9.20	0.10	8.90
United States	2.50	41.10	1.60	51.00
Japan	9.40	1.80	9.60	2.10
China	0.60	0.10	0.40	0.00
Taiwan	3.70	0.00	3.60	0.10
Australia	0.00	0.00	0.00	0.50
Canada	0.00	0.00	0.00	0.10
Others	0.80	2.00	0.00	6.70
Local:				
Station-produced	60.20	27.50	63.30	18.90
Government-produced				
ETV	0.00	10.30	0.00	10.70
RTHK	2.10	0.60	3.20	0.70
API	0.60	1.60	1.00	0.30
Others	0.00	0.00	0.00	0.00
Independent	19.80	5.80	17.20	0.00
Others	0.00	0.00	0.00	0.00
Total	100.00	100.00	100.00	100.00
(Hours)	(159.20)	(125.10)	(167.40)	(120.00)

Source: Broadcasting Authority, *Report of the Broadcasting Authority, September 1993–August 1994* (Hong Kong: Government Printer, 1995).

Table 9.4

Movie and Film Box Office Revenue in Hong Kong

Year	Box Office Revenue of Foreign Films (%)	Box Office Revenue of Local Films (%)	Box Office Revenue of China and Taiwan Films (%)	Total Box Office Revenue (in million HK$)
1980	47.4	46.8	5.8	353
1985	33.7	64.0	2.3	869
1990	20.3	78.7	1.0	1,190

Source: Based on data released in the Motion Picture Industry Association's annual reports.
Note: The box office revenue of soft-porn films is excluded.

movies.³ If the Hong Kong movie industry does not innovate, it will lose its competitive edge to foreign studios.

Making International News

International wire services and media used to set up regional bureaus in Hong Kong that also served as outlooks for China-watching, particularly before China opened its doors in early 1980s. Hong Kong seldom made international headlines before its future became an issue. Hong Kong was covered more as a shopper's paradise, a British colony with junks, rickshaws, taipans, and other exotic oriental customs and foods. If anything, it was mainly the human interest stories about Hong Kong that were dispatched around the world. On other occasions, Hong Kong would make the headlines when it was struck by social disturbances and disasters.

Hong Kong has been receiving more international attention since the early 1980s, when its fate became an item on the global agenda. Political development in the territories often make headlines around the world. Hong Kong has become a popular subject for international documentaries and features. Even CNN features Hong Kong politicians in Larry King's interviews broadcast live from the colony. Hong Kong owes its attraction mainly to the unfolding political drama. Political realignment has resulted in changes in all social realms. It is a rare social experiment in which journalists can monitor all these changes. That explains why issues such as emigration, democratization, press freedom, and confidence in Hong Kong's future make international headlines these days.

In fact, as political transition gathers momentum, more international media make their presence in Hong Kong.⁴ Top American media such as the *New York Times*, the *Washington Post*, CNN, and NBC established their bureaus or regional headquarters in Hong Kong in 1995. As Table 9.5 indicates, journalists from more than 120 foreign media, including 18 news agencies, 53 newspapers, 20 magazines, and 32 television stations, are operating in Hong Kong. Leading the list are American media (31), followed by Japanese media (16), and British media (14). Europe as a whole has 20 media operating in Hong Kong. The crowding of international media in Hong Kong has helped turn the city into a regional hub of communication. Although some journalists may come to Hong Kong primarily for the handover story, there is reason to believe, as argued later, that quite a few international media will continue to run their regional offices in Hong Kong.

Media Exports: Hub of Communication

Hong Kong has earned a reputation as the communication hub of the Asia-Pacific region. Hong Kong has the world's largest Chinese television program library and is an important exporter of audiovisual products. The distributional

Table 9.5

Presence of International Media in Hong Kong

Country	News Agencies	News-papers	Maga-zines	TV	Total
United Kingdom	1	9	1	3	14
United States	6	9	9	7	31
Japan	2	8	—	6	16
Canada	—	2	—	1	3
Europe	5	7	3	5	20
Australia	—	3	—	3	6
Southeast Asia	—	6	—	1	7
Korea	1	4	—	1	6
China	·3	2	—	2	7
Regionals	—	—	7	2	9
Others	—	3	—	1	4
Total	18	53	20	32	123

Source: Fanny Wong, "Press Giants Defy 1997 Fears," *South China Morning Post,* April 10, 1995, p. 6.

channels include videos, cable and satellite television, and piracy. TVB marketed 1,000 hours of its 2,000–3,000 hours of annual production to twenty-five countries, whereas ATV marketed 520 hours overseas around 1987.[5] These exports are estimated to have increased in proportion to the growth in output. TVB produced more than 5,000 hours of programming in 1993. It now owns a library of more than 75,000 hours of Chinese programming that ranges from classic Cantonese films and soap operas to musicals and sports.[6]

With the advent of videocassette recorders in late 1980s, the local TV stations have started exporting video programs. They are particularly popular among overseas Chinese in Southeast Asia and North America. At times, pirates try to beat the television stations by making the programs available by duplicating them right off the air. Hong Kong television programs are bought and broadcast by overseas television stations, which, in some cases, are self-owned subsidiaries.[7] The major markets include Taiwan, China, Southeast Asian countries, and Chinese overseas communities in North America and Europe. The Asian buyers are mostly wireless broadcasters who regard Hong Kong programs as a part of their programming menu. The North American and European buyers are cable operators who specialize in ethnic programming. So far, TVB has subsidiary stations in cities that have sizable Hong Kong immigrant communities and overseas Chinese, such as Los Angeles, San Francisco, New York, and Toronto.

Since the early 1990s, satellite has gained importance as a conduit for exporting Hong Kong programs. The accessibility to STAR TV varies across nations, depending on their regulation regime and other factors.[8] As of late 1993, STAR

TV can reach a total of more than 40 million viewers in all of Asia, with the majority concentrated in China, Taiwan, and India. The most popular STAR TV channel in China and Taiwan is its Chinese-speaking channel, which carries programs from Hong Kong, Taiwan, Japan, and other places. In late 1993, about 30 million Chinese households were capable of receiving STAR TV, often through rudimentary cable networks or reception dishes. STAR TV has reached one-quarter of Taiwanese households.

In 1993, TVB joined with Taiwanese interests to form TVBS in order to broadcast its programs to Taiwan by the Indonesian satellite Palapa, whose signals are redistributed through cable. By 1994, TVB's "Super Channel" (TVBS) had already reached a penetration of more than half of Taiwan's households, or 90 percent of the entire cable audience.[9] While TVB is planning to expand the system to China and other parts of Asia, it has licensed the Chinese Channel to broadcast its programs throughout Europe. Another major satellite television service that originated in Hong Kong is Chinese Television Network (CTN), launched in late 1994. Broadcast in Mandarin, CTN is a twenty-four-hour CNN-like news station that views Taiwan as the initial market and China as the final target.

Hong Kong's television broadcasters also export their programs by spill-over.[10] TVB and ATV can reach a large part of the neighboring Pearl River Delta in Guangdong, covering a mainland population of about 18 million. Surveys in 1993 in the Pearl River Delta show that more than 97 percent of the households in the major cities, with the exception of Guangdong's provincial capital Guangzhou, own at least one television set, and all of these have access to Hong Kong television through cable networks. Some local stations are inserting advertisements of their own.[11] After several failed attempts to stop it, the provincial government has acquiesced to this illegal but widespread practice.

In spite of the introduction of some copyright laws, media piracy is so common in China that it has become an extension of the spillover process.[12] It is also through piracy that videocassette tapes, laser discs, compact discs, and movie videos originating in Hong Kong and Taiwan have made inroads into China in recent years.

Hong Kong has a long history of exporting movies to other countries. As a result of Hong Kong's small domestic market, it has to rely on overseas audiences to make a profit. The scope of its overseas market has expanded rapidly since the 1970s, when action movies popularized by Bruce Lee reached beyond the traditional Southeast Asian market to the United States, Western Europe, Eastern Europe and other parts of the world.[13] Table 9.6 contrasts the imports of movies with exports in the last two decades. It shows that Hong Kong imported more than it exported in 1970. The deficit was reversed by mid-1970s, with Hong Kong exporting its movies to as many as ninety countries. The surplus continues into the 1990s. The most important markets for Hong Kong movies are Asian countries such as Taiwan, Korea, Singapore, Indonesia, Malaysia, and Thailand. In many of these countries, the box office for Hong Kong movies was

Table 9.6

Imports and Exports of Movies, 1970–1990

Year	Import value ($million)	Import quantity (million meters)	Export value ($millions)	Export quantity (million meters)	Number of countries exported to
1970	11.76	7.21	10.25	5.33	24
1975	22.91	13.81	35.34	14.16	86
1980	33.29	17.00	76.03	30.09	90
1985	33.44	12.38	51.33	22.31	68
1990	41.84	23.21	102.91	84.35	49

Source: Adapted from Hong Kong Trade Statistics as complied by Leung, Grace (1993), "Evolution of Hong Kong as a Movie Production and Export Center." Unpublished thesis at the Chinese University of Hong Kong, Hong Kong.

comparable to that of Hollywood productions. Major breakthroughs in exporting Hong Kong movies occurred in 1995 and 1996 when Jackie Chan's movies were widely received in mainland China and the United States.

Hong Kong is an exporter of regional publications such as the *Far Eastern Economic Review, Asiaweek,* and the *Asian Wall Street Journal.* A small circulation of its major newspapers such as *South China Morning Post,* and *Ming Pao* are read in other countries. *Sing Tao Daily* and *Ming Pao* publish separate versions for various overseas Chinese communities. China in general is closed to the distribution of foreign publications. It opens its hotels to *South China Morning Post,* the *Hong Kong Standard,* the communist papers based in Hong Kong, and some regional magazines.

An Explanatory Framework

As the above analysis shows, Hong Kong is outstanding by the degree to which its media internationalize and are being internationalized. The extent of media internationalization in Hong Kong fluctuates over time and varies with media. The competitiveness of domestic movies and television programs ebb and flow over the years. In general, local media fare is spreading to more overseas markets while the market shares of domestic media fare still dominate. The following are the factors that interact to account for why Hong Kong's media is so internationalized and internationalizing at the same time.

Cultural Freedom and the Market Mechanism

Hong Kong has an open cultural policy and a degree of press freedom only second to Japan in Asia.[14] All these favor the free flow of media in and out of

Hong Kong. Only on rare occasions does the government interfere with the exhibition of audiovisual products that are perceived to be detrimental to its relations with China. Otherwise, media fare can be imported from all countries. The newspapers controlled by the Chinese Communist Party are allowed to compete with the rightist newspapers leaning toward Taiwan's Nationalist Party in the marketplace. Freedom as such favors the diffusion of foreign media fare into Hong Kong and the adoption of Western media culture. It also favors the exercise of creativity and imagination, which are essential for the production of attractive media fare.

The absence of prohibitive measures on the media leaves them operating in a market environment. The media in Hong Kong have to compete keenly with both domestic and foreign media. There is constant pressure for them to innovate in order to respond to rapidly changing audience needs. Intensive competition helps generate products that are competitive both at home and abroad. Media operators will import only if there is a profit to be made. The market consequently becomes the mechanism that maintains the balance between localization and internationalization in the media sector.

Small Domestic Market and Large Overseas Chinese Community

With a population of about 6 million, Hong Kong's internal market is too small to sustain an economy of scale, an advantage being enjoyed by media in countries such as the United States and Japan. However, the small domestic market has become the driving force behind Hong Kong's effort to internationalize its media operations. It needs the international market to compensate for its smallness.

Chinese all over the world constitute a potential market for media products that are made in Hong Kong. The most important markets for Hong Kong media are Taiwan and Southeast Asian countries.15 The former has a concentrated population of about 22 million while the latter has a relatively scattered population of 26 million. That this extended market is culturally compatible to Hong Kong gives its media products a competitive edge over Western media fare. Hong Kong's status as a communication center would have been much subdued had it not been for the existence of numerous overseas Chinese communities all over the world.

Strategic Location and Advanced Telecommunications

Hong Kong is attractive to foreign media by virtue of its strategic position. It is located virtually in the heart of Asia, accessible to the major cities in East and Southeast Asia within hours. It is also the gateway to China, the largest and one of the fastest growing countries in the world. Added to its strategic location is the advanced telecommunications facilities it has. One can easily connect to every corner of the world through fiber optics and satellite. All these favor the operation of multinational media and local corporations that have an interest in overseas markets.

Capital and Expertise

Hong Kong has the capital and expertise for media development. The advertising industry has experienced rapid expansion in the last two decades, averaging a growth rate of more than 15 percent per year.[16] This provides the economic basis for media development. In some cases, the mass media derive their capital from entrepreneurs who make their fortune in nonmedia industries or from foreign media interests that have both capital and know-how. Given enough capital, the media can draw on some of the best talents in the local community and the world. Many top media managers are either expatriates or locals who are knowledgeable about both the local situation and Western practices. They serve as natural agents for internationalizing the media of Hong Kong and those of other nations.

Expatriate and English-Speaking Community

Since a century ago, Hong Kong has attracted many foreigners, who work as government officials, traders, businessmen, and professionals. The expatriate community is big enough and powerful enough to support or call for the establishment of English-language channels of information such as the *South China Morning Post*, ATV World, and TVB Pearl. Coupled with expatriates are the English-speaking community of the local population who together constitute the social demands for access to international media. The English-speaking locals are forming a growing portion of the international media's audience. For instance, about 80 percent of the subscribers to *Far Eastern Economic Review (FEER)*, an international publication based in Hong Kong, are Asian natives, up from 20 percent in 1949. The readership of *FEER* overlaps with selected local publications such as *Next* magazine.

Interaction Effects

The above factors do not act alone but in interaction with one another in patterning media internationalization in Hong Kong. For instance, as a result of Hong Kong's policy for free flow of information, the local media have to compete with the best productions of the world. Without market pressures from within and without, it is unlikely that Hong Kong's media products would be so competitive. The small domestic market pressures the local media to search for opportunities overseas. The existence of sizable overseas-Chinese communities in Southeast Asia and other parts of the world in effect extends Hong Kong's markets beyond its borders. Hong Kong also owes its position as a communication center to its strategic location, advanced telecommunications infrastructure, cultural freedom, and availability of capital and expertise that not only attract multinational media to Hong Kong but also help propel the local media overseas.

Tensions

Between localization and internationalization are the forces of nationalization and regionalization. Nationalization, in the case of Hong Kong, represents the pending reunification with China. Technically, reunification at this historical juncture can still be regarded as part of the internationalization process as China and Hong Kong are politically separated. Given that Hong Kong will be returned to China just one year from the time of this writing, reunification is in effect nationalization. Regionalization is by definition part of the internationalization process if it is restricted to the levels of Greater China and Asia. Tensions exist among these processes.

Localization vs. Internationalization

The tendencies to regionalize and internationalize are relatively small for the print media because of their culture-boundedness. However, there is a greater tendency for audiovisual media such as television and film to appeal to a wider audience beyond the national boundaries. This tendency is fueled by the small size of Hong Kong's domestic market. Large media have to expand to overseas markets in order to be profitable. The more a medium is internationalized, the less it is committed to local needs.

Market considerations at the regional and international levels are redirecting the efforts of some media in Hong Kong. For instance, TVB derives about 85 percent of its profits from local broadcasting business and the rest from overseas sales and rentals of TV programs.[17] Realizing that the profit for local programming has surpassed its peak, TVB has to expand overseas to maintain its profit margin. That explains why it is positioning itself as the most resourceful international broadcaster in Chinese-language programs and embarking on satellite television and other overseas ventures.

That mass media should commit to local needs is a principle well accepted around the world. Mass media that deviate too far from this principle run the risk of both losing their appeal among the local audience and inviting government control. They have to strike a balance between localization and internationalization, and to judge when their local audience will find imported media too alienating. Consequently, there is a tendency for mass media to search for the common denominators that appeal to both local and overseas audiences. They sometimes produce different versions of their programs to meet the varying needs in different countries. That explains why Hong Kong's best-selling movie genre is action films, which can be more easily understood by other peoples, and why action movies dominate the movie industry in Hong Kong.

Meanwhile, regional broadcasters such as STAR TV have to make their programming culture-specific or nation-specific in order to penetrate foreign countries.[18] As of now, the domestic market is still the most important source of income for mass media in Hong Kong. It is therefore unlikely that they will stray too far from the tastes of local audiences. This will change, however, as foreign or external markets rise in importance.

Nationalization vs. Internationalization

China is particularly sensitive about Western cultural influence. Haunted by antiforeignism, which ebbs and flows in recent Chinese history, China regards Western media fare as an important source of "spiritual pollution" and "peaceful evolution."[19] Unification with China naturally casts a shadow over the freedom now enjoyed by international media in Hong Kong.

Under the Basic Law, which serves as the miniconstitution for Hong Kong, the foreign affairs of Hong Kong are to be handled by China. Whether international media in Hong Kong fall under the jurisdiction of the Ministry of Foreign Affairs, as is the case in China now, is not yet clear. China will have to show a high level of tolerance if it is to make an exception of Hong Kong's international media. Hong Kong has no specific rules governing foreign journalists' operations. This contrasts with the need for accreditation in China. Foreign correspondents in Hong Kong fear that the same requirement will be imposed on them after 1997.[20] Should that happen, foreign journalists reporting on the mainland will have to seek approval from the Ministry of Foreign Affairs for working away from the base. China's tendency to impose the restriction will be strongest at times of national crisis.

The force of national unification has already posed great pressure on the local communication system in Hong Kong. There are growing signs that journalists and the news media self-censor to avoid being too critical of mainland China. A survey of Hong Kong journalists we conducted in 1990 shows that 23 percent of the journalists polled admitted to self-censorship.[21] An overwhelming majority did not expect the existing press freedom to continue after 1997.

However, the tie between the news media and local interests appears to have a deterring effect on the speed and extent to which they appease China as the new political master. The aforementioned survey indicated that a greater majority of journalists thought that the mass media should strive for the autonomy of Hong Kong during political transition. As many as about one-third of the journalists chose to stand by Hong Kong in the event of Sino–Hong Kong conflicts. This shows that the tension between the media's tendencies to localize and nationalize will grow as China's influence looms in the coming years.

Conclusion

The future of media internationalization in Hong Kong after 1997 depends primarily on China's Hong Kong policy. If Hong Kong is allowed to have a high degree of autonomy as promised in the scheme of "one country, two systems," its communication system will continue to internationalize and be internationalized. If China is to open further to the outside world, Hong Kong media may establish a stronger foothold on the mainland, thereby broadening its "domestic" base for its internationalizing activities.

While the above scenario may apply in the medium run, it seems too optimistic for the near future. Given all the measures that China has taken since the territory's political transition from the mid-1980s to tighten political control in Hong Kong, there is reason to believe that China will at best leave Hong Kong and foreign media operating in a somewhat subdued mode after 1997, particularly on political and foreign affairs issues. It may even seize upon a national crisis to consolidate its controls over media and aversely redefine the rules of media operation. While it is difficult to predict the exact path that media internationalization in Hong Kong will take, one thing for sure is that it will fluctuate as China's policies take sudden turns.

Internationalization in all realms, be it economic or political, represents an increase in social pluralism that favors the continuation of media freedom in Hong Kong. As China is adopting a disjointed approach to development, achieving economic development while restricting political reform, it is natural to expect China to have different orientations toward political and economic internationalization in Hong Kong. The pressure for media freedom will grow if China tries to reduce political internationalization. However, economic internationalization necessitates some level of sociopolitical internationalization. As long as China wants Hong Kong to remain economically internationalized, media freedom in Hong Kong will not be reduced to levels of Beijing or Shanghai.

Media from both Hong Kong and elsewhere want to enter the huge China market. Business opportunities in China are, to a large extent, controlled by the Communist Party and government officials. There is therefore a tendency for Hong Kong and international media that plan to invest in China not to offend the Beijing authorities. Rupert Murdoch, owner of STAR TV, decided to pull BBC world television news from its northern footprint—a good illustration of foreign media's attempt to appease China in order to gain entry to the China market. It has become a textbook case of self-censorship by an international media corporation.

Although the pressure to self-censor applies to all international media, one should not expect all of them to be equally submissive. As evidenced by the diversity of reports produced by international media in Beijing now, there is no reason to believe that their counterparts in Hong Kong will do otherwise after 1997. The greater the number of foreign media in Hong Kong, the greater the likelihood that some media will dare to defy pressure and report what they believe to be true. While the presence of outspoken foreign media will not guarantee press freedom in Hong Kong, it makes it somewhat easier for the local media to speak their minds.

The impending political change in Hong Kong helps draw international journalists to Hong Kong. However, this cannot explain why numerous international media are setting up bureaus and regional headquarters in Hong Kong. This has to be explained by more fundamental factors, such as the strategic geo-economic location of Hong Kong, its advanced communication infrastructure, and its status as a global financial center.

If Hong Kong were not so well located and economically advanced, its political transition would not command so much international attention. For many international media, Hong Kong remains an important gateway to China and other parts of Asia. No global media can afford to miss the story on China as it grows in importance as a political and economic power. Hong Kong itself is a financial and communication center that deserves world attention. All these reasons combine to account for the rise of Hong Kong as a favorite subject in international coverage. Some media operators think that if they can now survive in Beijing, there is no reason to believe that the operating environment in Hong Kong after 1997 will be more hostile.[22] It is unlikely that those media that have invested in Hong Kong now will close their offices and leave Hong Kong right after the handover. Only those journalists who come just for the occasion will do so.

Hong Kong is one of the most internationalized cities of the world. It embraces many cultures, as expressed in the availability of a wide array of media products from foreign countries. Blending the East and the West, Hong Kong has effectively created a culture that fits and constitutes its cosmopolitan nature. Both the local and foreign media play a crucial role in this cultural cross-fertilization. In spite of the great extent to which Hong Kong media are internationalized, they have successfully established a distinct cultural identity for the people of Hong Kong. In fact, the internationalized portion adds color to Hong Kong's cultural mosaic.

If Hong Kong is to continue prospering as a cosmopolitan city after 1997, it should be allowed the freedom to reconstitute a new identity through mediated expression in the cultural market, as it has been done up to now. Tight ideological control imposed by Beijing will only undermine the vitality of Hong Kong's media and its enviable status as a global communication center. It is in the best interests of China that Hong Kong be allowed to serve as a bridge between China and the international community.

Notes

1. Joseph Man Chan, "National Responses and Accessibility to STAR TV in Asia," *Journal of Communication* 44, 3 (1994), pp. 112–131.
2. Joseph Man Chan and Paul S.N. Lee, "Mass Communication: Consumption and

Evaluation," in S.K. Lau et al., eds., *Indicators of Social Development: Hong Kong 1990,* (Hong Kong: The Press of the Hong Kong Institute of Asia-Pacific Studies, Chinese University of Hong Kong, 1993), pp. 79–104.

3. Ibid.

4. Fanny Wong, "Press Giants Defy 1997 Fears," *South China Morning Post,* April 10, 1995, p. 6.

5. Chris Pomery, "Hong Kong," in Manuel Alvarado, ed., *Video World Wide: An International Study* (London: UNESCO, 1988).

6. Y.M. To and T.Y. Lau, "The Sky Is Not the Limit: Hong Kong as a Global Media Exporter," paper presented to the International Communication Association Convention, July 11–15, 1994, Sydney, Australia.

7. Joseph Man Chan, "Television Development in Greater China: Structure, Exports, and Market Formation," in John Sinclair, et al., eds., *New Patterns in Global Television: Peripheral Vision* (Oxford: Oxford University Press, 1996), pp. 126–160.

8. Joseph Man Chan, "Media Internationalization in China: Processes and Tensions," *Journal of Communication* 44, 3 (1994), pp. 70–88.

9. To and Lau, "The Sky Is Not the Limit."

10. Chan, "National Responses and Accessibility to STAR TV in Asia."

11. F.Y. Lee, "Mainland China's Television Is Making a Profit Without Cost," *Next Magazine,* March 26, 1993, pp. 90–94.

12. Chan, "National Responses and Accessibility to STAR TV in Asia."

13. L.K. Grace Leung, "The Evolution of Hong Kong as a Regional Movie Production and Export Center" (an unpublished M.Phil. thesis at the Chinese University of Hong Kong, Hong Kong, 1992).

14. Joseph Man Chan and C.C. Lee, *Mass Media and Political Transition: The Hong Kong Press in China's Orbit* (New York: Guilford Press, 1991).

15. Chan, "Television Development in Greater China: Structure, Exports, and Market Formation."

16. Chan and Lee, "Mass Communication."

17. To and Lau, "The Sky Is Not the Limit."

18. Chan, "Media Internationalization in China: Processes and Tensions."

19. Ibid.

20. Wong, "Press Giants Defy 1997 Fears."

21. Joseph Man Chan, Chin-Chuan Lee, and Paul S.N. Lee, *Hong Kong Journalists in Transition* (Hong Kong: The Press of the Hong Kong Institute of Asia-Pacific Studies, Chinese University of Hong Kong, 1996).

22. Staff, "International Media Competing for the Asian Market," *Yazhou Zhoukan,* 1995, pp. 66–69.

10

Hong Kong's Universities Within the Global Academy

Gerard A. Postiglione

By definition, knowledge has no bounds and thus universities are among the most global of institutions. It is not surprising, then, that Hong Kong higher education is international in character. For many years, until 1990, Hong Kong had sent more of its students overseas for university education, mostly to Australia, Canada, the United Kingdom, and the United States, than were admitted to its local universities. By 1994, the number of students at local universities surpassed that going overseas; however, the international character of Hong Kong's universities remained clearly visible in the composition of their academic staff. Approximately 90 percent of those with doctorates earned them outside of Hong Kong. This ensures Hong Kong's integration into the global academy for a long time to come. This chapter will look at some of the more salient aspects of Hong Kong's membership in the global academy. It will do this by examining the characteristics of its academic staff; their conditions of employment, professional work and attitudes toward governance; and the relationship between education and society. These characteristics will be compared with those of academic staff in other parts of the global academy. Finally, ongoing links with the global academy will be discussed.

Hong Kong's academic profession has much to gain or lose in the coming years as it becomes swallowed up by China. It is more closely bound to Western university traditions and practices than is the case elsewhere in Asia. This gives Hong Kong the potential to influence the academic profession in China by offering a unique model of successful East–West academic integration. In addition, given the status of intellectuals in China, Hong Kong's reincorporation into the People's Republic of China in 1997 could have major implications for its academic freedom and autonomy.[1] The academic profession has the capacity to act as a catalyst for a smooth transition, or as a vehicle of resistance. In the interim, higher education has been greatly expanded, and this growth is accompanied by a greater emphasis on graduate degrees and research capacity. The data in this chapter were collected as part of an international study of the academic profession in higher education coordinated by the Carnegie Foundation for the Advancement of Teaching. The other participating countries were Australia, Brazil, Chile, Germany, Israel, Japan, Korea, Mexico, the Netherlands, Sweden, Russia, the United Kingdom, and the United States.

The Higher Education System

Until the 1990s, the scale of higher education in Hong Kong was modest. A decision to nearly double the number of students admitted to university first-degree studies by 1994–95 was taken in October of 1989. Referred to in some quarters as crisis management and "too little, too late," the sudden expansion acted as a confidence booster in the wake of increased emigration following the Tiananmen crisis. Nevertheless, the move improved the opportunities of secondary school graduates to attend university in Hong Kong.[2] The mean percentage of the relevant age group admitted to degree study increased to 18 percent in 1994–95, when total enrollment reached almost 58,000. An estimated 25,000 or more attend universities overseas (excluding mainland China and Taiwan). The expansion has also been reflected in a drop in the number of overseas student visas issued since 1990.

There are nine degree-granting institutions of higher education in Hong Kong, including six universities, a tertiary institution, the Academy of Performing Arts, and the Open Learning Institute.[3] All but the last of these is fully government funded. Before 1990, most degree courses were offered in two universities. A third university was established in 1991. These three universities may be considered as Hong Kong's top tier or Type I institutions by virtue of their strong research orientation. One polytechnic began offering degree courses in 1983 and the other polytechnic and one tertiary college began to offer degree courses in 1986, representing 42 percent of all first degree enrollments in the University Grants Committee (UGC)–funded institutions by 1988–89. The polytechnics and one of the tertiary institutions earned university titles in 1994. At least one more tertiary institution is expected to be elevated to university status by 1997–98. The three top-tier research universities—the University of Hong Kong, the Chinese University of Hong Kong, and the Hong Kong University of Science and Technology—all provide a range of programs leading to undergraduate and graduate qualifications. They offer research programs in every subject area and provide scope for faculty to undertake consultancy and collaborative projects with industry.[4] The medium of instruction is English except in the Chinese University of Hong Kong, which is a bilingual institution.

The Hong Kong Polytechnic University and the City University of Hong Kong (the former polytechnics) offer a range of courses leading to the awards of diploma, higher certificate, higher diploma, and bachelor's degree. They offer a small number of graduate degrees and have research programs in some areas; emphasize the application of knowledge and vocational training; and maintain strong links with industry and employers. The Hong Kong Baptist University (formerly Baptist College) and Lingnan College together provide undergraduate courses in the arts, sciences, social sciences, business, and communication studies. They plan to or already offer a small number of courses at the graduate level, with research programs in some subject areas that maintain strong links with the community.

The most influential body in higher education is the University Grants Committee (UGC). It was established in 1965 "to advise the government on the facilities, development, and financial needs of the universities."[5] In 1993, the body included eight local Hong Kong Chinese, five members from the United Kingdom, three Americans (including a professor of Hong Kong Chinese origin), and one Australian. It is expected that the future UGC will include members from mainland China. The first chief executive (CE) of the Hong Kong Special Administrative Region (SAR) in 1997 appoints the members of the UGC. The appointment of the CE, to be named by an election committee in Hong Kong, must have the approval of Beijing.[6]

Hong Kong has become the world's eighth largest trading economy, though it ranks ninetieth by population. Its six million plus inhabitants (95 percent Cantonese-speaking Chinese) enjoy a living standard higher than some developed countries, including Britain, Hong Kong's colonial master. With eighty-five of the world's largest banks it is one of the five major global financial centers. Though it supports freedom of speech, and the rule of law, it only gained a fully elected legislature in 1995; this will be lost in 1997. Other features of Hong Kong include its efficient civil service, communications and transport capability, robust textile and electronics industries, a highly skilled and educated populace, and a unique blend of internationalism and neo-Confucianism.

In 1997, the territory will become a Special Administrative Region of the People's Republic of China under a "one country, two systems" arrangement, in which the current education system can be maintained. Embodied in its future constitution, the Basic Law, is a high degree of autonomy and the provision that Hong Kong people will rule Hong Kong.[7] Confidence in its future waxes and wanes depending on events in China and the state of relations between China and the United Kingdom.

The decolonization of higher education has come to mean more frequent contacts with universities in China alongside closer economic and political ties, declining legitimacy of colonial educational policy, localization of the highest administrative positions, efforts to step up as well as resist the pace of democratization, increased emigration of faculty with return migration of those who have

Table 10.1

How Many Years Have You Been Employed In Higher Education?

Faculty country of origin	Mean	Median
Australia	13.3	11
Brazil	14.0	14
Chile	17.5	19
Germany	11.9	7
Hong Kong	10.9	8
Israel	17.8	18
Japan	20.4	21
Korea	12.4	11
Mexico	11.1	10
Netherlands	12.4	10
Russia	23.5	25
Sweden	15.2	15
United Kingdom	14.7	14
United States	16.3	15

Source: The Carnegie Foundation for the Advancement of Teaching, The International Survey of the Academic Profession, 1991–93, Princeton, NJ.

acquired overseas passports, and expanding cultural and human resource linkages with adjacent South China—especially the Pearl River Delta.[8]

Characteristics of Academic Staff

The total number of faculty across the seven institutions in 1993–94 was 3,562.[9] In order to examine the attributes and attitudes of the faculty, an extensive survey was conducted which included questions regarding working conditions, teaching, research, service, governance, the faculty's views of the relation between higher education and society, and the international dimension of their work. Our survey sample constituted over one-third of faculty across academic ranks within all departments and similar academic units of the seven UGC-sponsored degree-granting institutions of higher education. The survey was conducted before the two polytechnics and the Hong Kong Baptist College were conferred university titles. There was a 37 percent response rate from the sample surveyed across departments and academic ranks, accounting for about 13 percent of all faculty across institutions in May 1993.[10]

Less than half the Hong Kong faculty respondents are tenured; within that group, almost two-thirds are at Type I institutions. Hong Kong academics had the lowest mean number of years of employment in higher education (10.9) than any other country in the international study (Table 10.1).

Until 1997 a differentiation was made between overseas and local terms of appointment, the former being entitled to certain travel and accommodation benefits.[11] Four in ten faculty surveyed were appointed on overseas terms with the remainder being on local terms (see Table 10.2). A higher percentage of those on overseas terms are employed at Type I institutions than at Type II institutions. A higher percentage of local than overseas appointees are tenured, though it should be noted that a higher percentage of the latter had doctorates.

Over one-half of the respondents had doctorates; this includes nearly three-quarters of those from Type I institutions, and slightly more than one-third of the younger faculty in Type II institutions (see Table 10.3). Most faculty had earned their highest degree (especially the doctorate) overseas (see Table 10.4). The highest percentage of doctorates were earned in the United States.

Regarding proportions of staff at different academic ranks, Hong Kong academic ranks are bottom heavy compared to their counterparts overseas. For example, at the University of Hong Kong, less than 20 percent of staff are full professors (including professor and reader categories) as compared to 42 percent at the University of British Columbia, 49 percent at the University of Montreal, 59 percent at Brown University, and 56 percent at Harvard University.

Within Type I institutions, 13 percent of respondents are full professors, 27 percent are reader/senior lecturers rank, 55 percent are lecturers, 2 percent are assistant lecturers, and 3 percent are of demonstrator rank. Within Type II institutions, 4 percent of respondents are full professors, 15 percent are reader/senior lecturers, 25 percent are lecturers, 48 percent are assistant lecturers, and 8 percent are of demonstrator rank.[12] There is a near equal balance of faculty between the science/technology and social science/humanities areas. These two groups have nearly the same levels of tenure, but nearly two-thirds of the former and less than one-half of the latter have doctorates.[13]

The average age of the faculty respondents is forty-two years. This is relatively young compared to most countries, including Israel, Japan, and Russia, where the average age was fifty-one. Over 40 percent of faculty are in their thirties, most are on local terms of appointment. Almost three-quarters of those between fifty and sixty-five years of age are on overseas terms. Faculty at Type II institutions are generally younger, and an increasing number are studying for their doctorates at one of the Type I institutions. The number of men exceeds the number of women by four to one. In this respect, Hong Kong is somewhere in the middle of the global rankings. Its proportion of women faculty is less than either Brazil's 39 percent or Australia's 35 percent, but much more than either Korea's 13 percent or Japan's 8 percent. Within Type I institutions, more than four-fifths of the respondents are men, as compared to about two-thirds of respondents at the other institutions. Men are more than twice as likely as women to become university professors.

Hong Kong faculty are among the highest-salaried academics, a situation originally rooted in a colonial system with two small universities, though it came to be maintained due to Hong Kong's high cost of living. Nevertheless, this may very well change if Hong Kong academics are compared to their counterparts on

Table 10.2

Number of Local and Overseas Appointees Employed by UGC Institutions in 1993

Institution	Number of local appointees	Number of overseas appointees	Total number academic staff
CityU	463	181	644
HKBU	218	60	278
PolyU	744	159	903
LC	79	34	113
CUHK	450	265	715
HKUST	137	166	303
UHK	297	309	606
Total	2,388	1,174	3,562

The seven UGC institutions are:
Type I institutions
   CUHK Chinese University of Hong Kong
   HKUST Hong Kong University of Science and Technology
   UHK University of Hong Kong
Type II institutions
   CityU City University of Hong Kong
   HKBU Hong Kong Baptist University
   PolyU Hong Kong Polytechnic University
   LC Lingnan College

Source: University and Polytechnic Grants Committee, March 8, 1994 (See note 9).

Table 10.3

Highest Degree Earned by Faculty (%) (Type I institutions vs. Type II institutions)

	Type I institutions	Type II institutions
Doctorate	73.5	36.2
Master's	25.1	47.3
Bachelor's	1.3	13.2
Associate or Equivalent	0.0	3.3
Total	100.0	100.0

Source: The Carnegie Foundation for the Advancement of Teaching, the International Survey of the Academic Profession, 1991–1993, Princeton, NJ (Survey of Hong Kong).

the mainland rather than their counterparts in other professional sectors of the Hong Kong economy. Only in Hong Kong do more than half of academics say they are satisfied with their salaries. Nevertheless, for a variety of reasons, over 40 percent see themselves as likely to leave their institutions within five years. Moreover, although Hong Kong's vibrant economy provides academics with

Table 10.4

Region Where Highest Degree Was Earned (%)

	Doctorate	Master's	Bachelor's	Associate or equivalent
Hong Kong	10.0	22.5	17.6	37.5
United Kingdom	26.9	37.9	32.4	25.0
United States	39.0	16.0	5.9	—
Other	24.1	23.6	44.1	37.5
Total	100.0	100.0	100.0	100.0
N	(249)	(169)	(34)	(8)

Source: The Carnegie Foundation for the Advancement of Teaching, The International Survey of the Academic Profession, 1991–1993, Princeton, NJ (Survey of Hong Kong).

many opportunities to supplement their salaries, in general, Hong Kong faculty seldom earn income from work outside of their institutions. For example, in answer to the question—"Of your total income, what percentage comes from this institution?"—Hong Kong faculty report a mean of 97 percent and a median of 100 percent—much higher figures than in all other countries surveyed.[14]

Differences between faculty in Type I and II institutions—including the proportion of doctorates, overseas appointees, women, and young faculty—have potential implications for the future of the profession. Type II institutions may become handicapped by the lower percentage of their faculty possessing doctorates. Type I institutions have a role to play in the upgrading of Type II institutions by offering faculty at the latter the opportunity to enroll in doctoral programs locally. Nevertheless, given the expansion of student numbers and the likelihood that they will lose many of their faculty through emigration and retirement, Type I institutions will be tempted to recruit from the cream of the fledgling Type II universities.

In order to minimize the brain drain across types of institutions, a number of measures might be considered, including introducing parity in all aspects of salaries and benefits and across terms of appointment (local and overseas). In addition, mobility of staff between types of institutions, in both directions, could be encouraged by supporting a broader distribution of internationally recognized centers of academic excellence across all institutions in a variety of fields.

The expansion of higher education may also necessitate casting a wider net for recruitment of faculty. That net will surely include China, which will contribute further to the staffing of the universities. At present, however, mainland China has its own shortage of doctorates and doctoral programs. This has created a large market for doctoral programs overseas, something that universities in Hong Kong are also tapping into by increasing the proportion of their doctoral students from mainland China. Hong Kong institutions of higher education have also begun to take advantage of the talents of people from mainland China who have earned doctorates in other countries but have not returned to China.

It is clear from the data that the character of the academic profession in Hong Kong is changing in other ways as well. More doctorates are now earned in the United States than in the United Kingdom or other countries. Rather than following the changing patterns in British higher education, perhaps Hong Kong should draw more upon innovations from other countries as well. Of relevance in this context is the discussion later in this chapter on the ratings given by respondents with doctorates from different countries to the training they received for teaching and research in universities in these countries.

The state of the Hong Kong economy in the coming years may also determine whether Hong Kong decides to increase, decrease, or maintain the degree of internationalization within the profession, especially as it finds a growing pool of talent in China and the surrounding region, where economic links are growing stronger. Other factors will be equally important in the effort to maintain an international profession—factors such as working conditions, the intellectual environment, and the degree of academic freedom, which will be considered in other parts of this chapter.

Conditions of Employment

Having noted that high salaries will not necessarily prevent large numbers of faculty leaving their institutions, the question remains as to how working conditions might influence retention of faculty in the coming years. The data on working conditions might shed some light on the issue. In particular, they will show the sometimes sharp differences in attitudes toward working conditions between faculty in different types of institutions, as well as emphasize differences in work loads between academic ranks.

Hong Kong faculty report high work loads in teaching, research, and service activities—52.4 hours per week when classes are in session and 51.4 when not in session (see Tables 10.5 and 10.6). Time spent on teaching declines as one moves up in rank, although there is little difference between ranks (professor, reader/senior lecturer, lecturer) when it comes to time spent on research (fifteen hours a week when classes are in session). Full professors work the longest hours, with a greater proportion of their time spent on administration (17.1 hours) than on research (14.6 hours).

Hong Kong's tertiary institutions are thought to be well equipped, and this is reflected in the survey. Faculty members, especially those in universities, give very high ratings to the physical resources supporting their work, including classrooms, technology for teaching, computer facilities (highest ranking of all countries), and to a lesser extent research equipment and instruments.

Attitudes toward institutional working conditions are in sharp contrast to those

Table 10.5

Working Hours by Rank (classes in session)

	Teaching	Research	Service	Admini-stration	Other
Professor	10.5	14.6	5.7	17.1	5.3
Senior lecturer/reader	16.8	14.7	4.9	10.0	3.9
Lecturer	18.0	14.5	7.0	8.4	3.8
Assistant lecturer	22.3	11.9	2.9	5.5	3.1
Demonstrator	24.6	9.4	4.3	4.5	3.2

Source: The Carnegie Foundation for the Advancement of Teaching, The International Survey of the Academic Profession, 1991–1993, Princeton, NJ (Survey of Hong Kong).

Table 10.6

Working Hours by Rank (classes not in session)

	Teaching	Research	Service	Admini-stration	Other
Professor	5.2	18.6	6.6	18.1	6.4
Senior lecturer/reader	6.3	23.1	6.0	9.7	4.7
Lecturer	7.4	23.8	5.6	7.9	4.4
Assistant lecturer	9.4	20.6	3.8	5.4	3.9
Demonstrator	11.7	18.5	6.3	4.2	4.0

Source: The Carnegie Foundation for the Advancement of Teaching, The International Survey of the Academic Profession, 1991–1993, Princeton, NJ (Survey of Hong Kong).

toward physical resources. For example, intellectual atmosphere, the relationship between faculty and administration, and faculty morale receive notably low ratings, with Type II institution faculty much less satisfied and more critical of institutional working conditions than their Type I counterparts (see Table 10.7).

Fewer than half of those surveyed consider the intellectual atmosphere at their institutions to be good to excellent (only 4 percent rate it as excellent—a percentage point higher than findings for all but one country in the international study). A look reveals differences among institutions. Fifty-three percent of faculty from Type I institutions describe the intellectual atmosphere as good to excellent as compared to only 30 percent of faculty in other institutions.

Twenty-eight percent judge the relationship between faculty and administration to be good. Most others rate it as fair (46 percent) or poor (22 percent). Of all countries in the international study, only Mexico and Germany have higher percentages of faculty agreeing that communication between faculty and administration is poor. However, while 40 percent of the faculty in Type I institutions rate the relations between faculty and administration as good to excellent, only

Table 10.7

Attitudes Toward Institutional Working Conditions (%)
(Type I vs. Type II institutions)

		Excellent	Good	Fair	Poor	N.A.
Intellectual atmosphere	I	7.2	45.9	35.1	11.7	0.0
	II	0.8	29.0	47.3	22.2	0.4
	T	3.9	37.0	41.5	17.3	0.2
Relations between faculty and administration	I	4.1	35.6	45.0	15.3	0.0
	II	1.2	21.6	47.3	28.6	1.2
	T	2.6	28.3	46.3	22.3	0.6
Faculty morale	I	6.3	34.7	42.3	16.2	0.5
	II	1.2	24.0	37.8	37.0	0.0
	T	3.6	29.1	40.0	27.1	0.2
Clarity of intellectual mission	I	6.8	28.8	41.0	23.0	0.5
	II	1.6	26.9	41.6	29.8	0.0
	T	4.1	27.8	41.3	26.6	0.2
Sense of community	I	5.4	29.7	41.0	23.4	0.5
	II	0.8	27.6	38.6	32.5	0.4
	T	3.0	28.6	39.7	28.2	0.4

Source: The Carnegie Foundation for the Advancement of Teaching, The International Survey of the Academic Profession, 1991–1993, Princeton, NJ (Survey of Hong Kong).
Note:
I = Type I Institutions
II = Type II Institutions
T = Total

23 percent of faculty in Type II institutions rate it as such. The former gave higher ratings to most measures, including faculty morale, clarity of the intellectual mission, relationship with colleagues, satisfaction with courses taught, job security, promotion prospects, opportunities to pursue ideas, and institutional management. This difference may be partly explained by the fact that at the time of the survey, Type II faculty (still within a polytechnic or tertiary college), were being assessed by their institutions according to university-equivalent ranks.

Faculty Mobility

A large number of faculty respondents—37 percent from Type I institutions and 47 percent from Type II institutions—indicated they are likely to leave within five years (see Table 10.8). Respondents were asked to think about their reasons for staying at or leaving their institutions and to rank the relative importance of these considerations on a five-point scale. The reasons given included not only the responses offered on the questionnaire (income, resources for research, aca-

Table 10.8

Likelihood of Leaving the Institution in the Coming Five Years (%)

	Likely	Neutral	Unlikely	Do not know
Type I institutions	37	21	28	14
Type II institutions	47	19	20	14
Overseas appointees	56	15	18	12
Local appointees	33	24	27	16
Science & technology	40	21	26	13
Social science & humanities	45	18	21	16

Source: The Carnegie Foundation for the Advancement of Teaching, The International Survey of the Academic Profession, 1991–1993, Princeton, NJ (Survey of Hong Kong).

demic reputation of the institution, academic cooperation among colleagues, and region in which the institution is located), but a high proportion of write-in reasons as well.[15]

The expressed likelihood of respondents leaving their institutions should be viewed in the context of increased emigration levels prior to 1997, as well as in the context of the generally high mobility rates that exist in Hong Kong across occupations. Finally, a wide gap may exist between expressed likelihood and the probability of making a concrete decision to leave one's institution. Despite the variation in response patterns, there does appear to be a link between dissatisfaction with working conditions and the high proportion of faculty who say they are likely to leave their institutions within five years. Given the expansion of the higher education system and the need for increasing numbers of faculty, this apparent lack of institutional loyalty may be reason for concern. The challenge will be to improve working conditions, and thus to reduce the number of faculty intending to leave their institutions.

How members of the profession view their future prospects might be improved by various reforms of organization and governance, as will be discussed in a later section of this chapter. Given the higher number of doctorates earned in the United States, and to facilitate future recruitment, a change in the system of titles of academic ranks could be given more serious consideration.[16] It is also notable that respondents in the science and technology fields place "resources for research" as the top factors to be considered when deciding whether to leave their institutions. Hong Kong's ability to catch up with its regional rivals in science and technology research would be severely hindered if large numbers of science and technology faculty were to leave their institutions within five years.

Teaching and Research

Hong Kong's institutions of higher education were largely teaching institutions until the mid-1980s, when scholarly publications became an increasingly elevated criterion for promotion and research funding became more readily available. The quality of teaching and research in these institutions can contribute to Hong Kong's future position, both internationally and within China. Hong Kong can become part of the network of universities in southern China, or remain distinct as an international or regional center of higher learning.[17] In this period of rapid institutional expansion, new efforts are under way in Hong Kong to systematically evaluate both research and teaching. The whole issue of upgrading Hong Kong's capacity in the fields of science and technology is linked to its future role locally, nationally, regionally, and internationally.

A high proportion of Hong Kong faculty teach; only two other countries in the international study had a lower percentage of nonteaching faculty. Of those faculty who do teach, over half teach in both undergraduate and graduate or professional programs. Faculty employ a variety of teaching methods, with almost half requiring students to actively participate in class discussions. The survey respondents indicate that on average 56 percent of course time is devoted to lectures, 36 percent to tutorials, 27 percent to laboratory work, and 18 percent to other activities. Faculty at Type I institutions spend more time lecturing and less time on class discussion, laboratory work, and other activities than do their counterparts at Type II institutions. Despite the high proportion of local Chinese appointees, faculty at the latter do not rely to a great extent on traditional didactic methods usually thought of as more in keeping with Chinese culture.

Research has a relatively important impact on teaching. At least 40 percent of respondents say that their research work has a positive effect on their teaching. Yet, about half believe that the availability of research funding has no bearing on their teaching. Almost half (47 percent) say that their administrative work detracts from their teaching.[18] Likewise, there is much agreement that the pressure to publish reduces the quality of teaching (the highest ratings of all countries in the international study), with roughly half the respondents stating that teaching should be the primary criterion for promotion. However, Type I institution faculty and overseas appointees are less likely to hold these views than are local appointees and those in Type II institutions. A shift in orientation is taking place in Type II institutions, away from a singular focus on teaching and toward a more balanced emphasis on both teaching and research. There is reason to believe that those appointed earlier are making this transition with more difficulty than are more recent appointees.

Almost two-thirds of faculty respondents report that their teaching is regularly evaluated (more than most other countries), with little difference in responses between Type I and Type II institutions. Evaluation is slightly more likely to be by students than by department heads. External reviewers, peers, and senior administrators also play a significant role in evaluation. Most respondents believe that student opinion should be used in the evaluation of teaching effectiveness, and almost three-quarters of faculty are of the opinion that better methods are needed for evaluating teaching performance.

Table 10.9

Quality of Training Received for Teaching (%)

	Excellent	Good	Fair	Poor	N.A.
Type I faculty with U.S. doctorate	35.8	43.3	14.9	3.0	3.0
Type I faculty with UK doctorate	4.8	35.7	23.8	16.7	19.0

Source: The Carnegie Foundation for the Advancement of Teaching, The International Survey of the Academic Profession, 1991–1993, Princeton, NJ (Survey of Hong Kong).

Table 10.10

Quality of Training Received for Research (%)

	Excellent	Good	Fair	Poor
Type I faculty with U.S. doctorate	61.2	29.9	6.0	3.0
Type I faculty with UK doctorate	32.4	41.9	16.3	9.3

Source: The Carnegie Foundation for the Advancement of Teaching, The International Survey of the Academic Profession, 1991–1993, Princeton, NJ (Survey of Hong Kong).

Faculty perceptions about the quality of the training they received for teaching vary little across institutions; however, faculty with advanced degrees from the United States rate their training significantly higher than do those who earned advanced degrees in the United Kingdom (see Table 10.9). The same holds true for the perception of faculty about the quality of the training they received for research (see Table 10.0). This is especially apparent in the case of Type I institution faculty with doctorates.

Faculty at Type I institutions express more interest in doing research than in teaching; the opposite is true for faculty at the Type II institutions. While much time is spent doing research, much of this work consists of writing scholarly journal articles or academic book chapters rather than authoring or editing scholarly books. Research funding is still modest by international standards, though increases in recent years have led to more large-scale research projects. Overseas appointees and Type I faculty have higher levels of productivity in research work than do local appointees and those from Type II institutions.

Respondents in science and technology areas are more likely than are those in the social sciences and humanities to have published journal articles or book chapters, as well as to have written more research reports, conference papers, and computer programs. But faculty in the social sciences and humanities are more than twice as likely as those in science and technology to have authored or edited a book. More respondents in science and technology than those in the social sciences and humanities state that regular research activity is expected of them.

This is reflected in the higher levels of research funding they report receiving. Forty-seven percent of academics agreed that research funding is easier to get than five years ago, the highest percentage in the international study. Moreover, 75 percent said they or their research group had received grants or special funding in the last three years, also the highest figure in the international study.

Faculty from Type I institutions are more engaged in research projects and, as individuals or part of an academic group, receiving research grants or special funding over the previous three years than is true of Type II institution faculty. However, the latter received a higher percentage of smaller research grants (those below U.S.$50,000).[19] Moreover, faculty at Type II institutions more frequently feel under pressure to do more research than they would like. More Type II than Type I faculty feel that scholarly publications are "just counted," and not qualitatively evaluated for promotion decisions. Only in Russia did more academics agree with this than in Hong Kong.

Hong Kong's institutions of higher education still appear to be teaching-intensive places, with much attention placed on the evaluation of teaching. However, as mentioned earlier, there is some concern about the pressure to publish and its influence on teaching, as scholarly publications have become the centerpiece of evaluation for promotion. Other countries may have an advantage in that they have a core of researchers free from administrative and teaching duties. This is rare, if not nonexistent, in Hong Kong, but an idea worth considering, especially as Hong Kong moves to establish academic centers of excellence. In the science and technology areas, questionnaire responses do not help to dispel the impression that research funding in these areas is not enough to keep Hong Kong competitive with its regional rivals.

Quality of Students

Hong Kong faculty view their students as adequately prepared in mathematics and quantitative reasoning skills (giving them the highest rating in the international survey), but not in written and oral communication skills (giving them among the lowest ratings). Over half of the faculty do not believe their students would be willing to cheat to obtain good grades; however, over half say that their students do just enough to get by academically.

Less than one-half of faculty at Type I institutions and less than one-third of faculty from the other institutions rate the quality of the students in their departments as good or excellent. Moreover, all indicate that the quality of these students has declined over the past five years; less than 5 percent feel that students currently in their departments are better than those of five years ago. With respect to all undergraduate students in their universities, less than 10 percent agree that the current undergraduates they teach are better than those they taught five years ago.

The views about student quality indicate a considerable decline in standards.

Such a perception is quite logical within the context of the rapid expansion of opportunities in higher education. Moving toward mass higher education requires a consideration of major innovations in almost all aspects of teaching and learning. Yet aside from an increased emphasis on the evaluation of teaching, there are few signs of major efforts to institute the broad range of innovations in teaching that are necessary to deal with a more diverse student population. Hong Kong's traditional reliance on one model of higher education may be partly responsible for this. Mass higher education came late to the United Kingdom. Experience elsewhere could provide valuable lessons as well. In particular, much could be learned from the role that academic culture and governance play in promoting or hindering teaching innovations.

Governance

Given Hong Kong's struggle over representative government and democracy, it is not surprising that institutions of higher education would be expected to take a leading role. A key issue is the degree to which institutional decision making is decentralized, representative, and democratic, and to what extent individual faculty members feel influential in helping to shape key academic policies. Views within the academic profession about such issues can provide an indication of the extent to which the universities will be future beacons of democracy.

Hong Kong faculty generally view decision making in their institutions as relatively centralized, especially in the selection of key administrators, recruiting of new faculty, promotion and tenure decisions, and approving of new academic programs. However, this is less true in decisions having to do with setting faculty teaching loads, budget priorities and admission standards. Faculty at Type I institutions view decision making as much less centralized than do faculty in other institutions. Full professors see the system as being more decentralized than do those in other ranks. The same is true of science and technology faculty when compared to their counterparts in the social sciences and humanities, and of overseas faculty when compared to local appointees.

Only 30 percent of Hong Kong faculty agree that they are kept informed about what is going on at their institutions. Twelve countries ranked higher and only Germany ranked lower than Hong Kong on this question. In Hong Kong, only a small percentage of overseas appointees (22 percent) believe they are being kept informed about what is going on at their institutions.

Compared with faculty at Type I institutions, those at other institutions view themselves as less influential at all levels of decision making (department, school, faculty, or institution) in helping to shape key academic policies (see Table 10.11). This is especially true at the institutional level, where 76 percent of respondents indicate they are not at all influential. The sense of personal influence on the part of faculty at Type II institutions is lower at all levels, but especially so at the department level. Only German and Mexican academics

Table 10.11

Faculty Influence at the Level of Department or Similar Unit in Helping to Shape Key Academic Policies (%)

	Very Influential	Some-what Influential	A Little Influential	Not at All Influential	N.A.
Overall	13.1	34.1	28.0	22.5	2.2
Type I institutions	16.2	41.0	24.3	15.8	2.7
Type II institutions	10.1	27.8	31.2	29.1	1.7
Overseas terms	21.6	41.6	19.5	16.3	1.1
Local terms	7.1	28.8	34.1	27.0	3.0
Type I faculty (U.S. doctorate)	16.7	39.4	24.2	18.2	1.5
Type II faculty (UK doctorate)	23.3	48.8	11.6	14.0	2.3

Source: The Carnegie Foundation for the Advancement of Teaching, The International Survey of the Academic Profession, 1991–1993, Princeton, NJ (Survey of Hong Kong).

Table 10.11A

International Responses to the Question: How Influential Are You, Personally, in Helping to Shape Key Academic Policies at the Level of the Department or Similar Unit? (%)

Faculty country of origin	Very influential	Somewhat influential	A little influential	Not at all influential
Australia	23.5	29.8	25.6	18.1
Brazil	24.6	45.8	18.9	8.1
Chile	19.6	44.1	19.2	14.5
Germany	13.3	27.5	23.3	27.6
Hong Kong	13.1	34.2	27.9	22.7
Israel	28.9	38.8	22.4	8.0
Japan	32.5	37.6	15.6	7.9
Korea	11.8	42.6	38.9	5.6
Mexico	11.6	32.3	23.5	27.9
Russia	31.2	40.6	22.2	6.0
Sweden	25.0	35.5	20.7	16.7
United Kingdom	24.9	34.8	24.5	13.5
United States	28.8	38.4	19.1	10.0

Source: The Carnegie Foundation for the Advancement of Teaching, The International Survey of the Academic Profession, 1991–1993, Princeton, NJ. (Survey of Hong Kong)

indicated a lower sense of personal influence (see Table 10.11A). At the department level, 57 percent of Type I institution faculty indicate they are very or somewhat influential, while only 38 percent of Type II institution faculty express such a belief.

Top-level administrators receive conservative marks from respondents in all sectors of the faculty across institutions. Less than one-quarter agreed that top-level administrators are providing competent leadership. Over half are of the opinion that communication between faculty and administration is poor, and that the lack of staff involvement in management and decision making is a real problem. The leadership in Type I institutions fare somewhat better in matters of management and decision making than do their counterparts in the other institutions.

The data in this section point to a trend toward centralized decision making in Hong Kong's institutions of higher education, with Type II institutions appearing more centralized in character than Type I institutions. This does not bode well for Hong Kong's efforts to promote democratic decision making, and may also help to explain the high levels of dissatisfaction with institutional working conditions cited earlier in this paper.

It is disconcerting that more than three-quarters of Hong Kong faculty feel themselves without influence in shaping academic policies at the institutional level. Even more disturbing is the perception of local appointees that they have less say than overseas appointees. It is difficult to know without further research to what extent this is a reflection of traditional colonial patterns, inflated expectations, or acceptance of a more passive role on the part of local staff, or the fact that overseas staff tend to be more concentrated in the upper ranks. Whatever the reason, this is a key point for further investigation because if the institutions of higher education in Hong Kong are to take a leading role in the democratization of Hong Kong, local academics must first feel themselves to be more involved in academic decision making than is at present the case. Moreover, there can be little doubt that the processes of decision making in the former polytechnics and colleges will have to be modified as their institutional culture evolves along with their new status as universities. The fact that Hong Kong faculty rate the competency of their administrative leadership lower than do faculty of any other country participating in the study is a cause for concern. Finally, the influence exerted by the academic profession within the institutions cannot be decoupled from faculty attitudes about the major issues facing society and their role and influence in society.

Higher Education and Hong Kong Society

This section examines the views of the academic profession about the relationship between higher education and society. Due in part to the fact that Hong Kong is primarily a business and commercial community, academics and intellectuals have not enjoyed the influential role played by scholars within traditional Chinese culture, and this is reflected in the survey data. Despite the influential role reserved for intellectuals in traditional Chinese culture, few Hong Kong faculty agreed that academics are the most influential opinion leaders in society. Academics from Hong Kong's two East Asian neighbors, Japan and Korea, had the highest percentage in the international study agreeing that the academics in those nations were the most influential opinion leaders in society.

Hong Kong came behind Brazil, Sweden, and Mexico. Almost half agreed that respect for academics is declining, though this was far less than in most countries. Also, it is unclear to what extent this may be part of an international as opposed to a local trend. Nevertheless, seven of ten do not view professional service beyond teaching and research as a distraction or as competing with essential academic work, and most agree that they have a professional obligation to apply their knowledge to problems in society.

Only Australian and American academics thought a higher percentage of young people in their countries are capable of completing secondary education than Hong Kong academics, who believe that over three-quarters of their young people are capable of completing secondary education. However, they thought only half should be admitted to higher education, a percentage lower than seven of the countries measured. Seven out of ten faculty say that higher education should be available to all who meet the minimum requirement. Yet there was little support for lowering admission standards to permit disadvantaged students to enroll at their institutions.

Less than one-third of the faculty were in favor of the government providing free tuition for all students. While there was little distinction between Type I and Type II faculty on this issue, major differences exist between the views of local and overseas appointees. Forty-four percent of overseas appointees believe the government should provide free tuition for all students at UGC institutions, while only 24 percent of local appointees take this position.

Eighty-six percent say that individuals and businesses should be encouraged to contribute more to higher education. At the same time, 40 percent were neutral on the subject of whether institutions of higher education are increasingly subject to the interference from special interest groups. Not unlike academics in other countries, more than half of Hong Kong faculty (58 percent) think that the effectiveness of higher education is being threatened by growing bureaucracies.

More than half of the respondents think that academic freedom is strongly protected in Hong Kong (see Table 10.12). Only Mexico and Brazil ranked lower (see Table 10.12A). Three-quarters of the faculty at Type I institutions and less than half of faculty at Type II institutions agree. There is no difference between local and overseas appointees on this question. Yet less than half of Hong Kong faculty feel that administrations in their institutions support academic freedom (see Table 10.13). More Type I faculty and overseas appointees feel that the administrations in their institutions support academic freedom than their counterparts (Type II faculty and local appointees).

Six in ten agree that they are free to determine the content of the courses they teach. Only Russia and Germany ranked lower (see Table 10.13A). This is a view shared by local and overseas appointees, but more in evidence from Type I university faculty than those from other institutions. However, eight in ten state that they are able to focus their research on any topic, with higher levels of agreement by overseas appointees and faculty at Type I institutions than their

Table 10.12

Is Academic Freedom Strongly Protected in Hong Kong? (%)

	Yes	No	N/A
Type I institutions	76	13	11
Type II institutions	47	38	15
Overseas appointees	61	27	12
Local appointees	61	25	14
All faculty	61	26	13

Source: The Carnegie Foundation for the Advancement of Teaching, The International Survey of the Academic Profession, 1991–1993, Princeton, NJ (Survey of Hong Kong).

Table 10.12A

International Survey: Is Academic Freedom Strongly Protected in This Country? (%)

Faculty country of origin	Yes	No	N.A
Australia	74.3	21.7	4.0
Brazil	38.4	61.6	0.0
Chile	63.6	25.4	10.9
Hong Kong	61.4	25.7	13.0
Israel	90.0	7.6	2.3
Japan	68.3	17.8	13.9
Korea	66.3	23.4	10.3
Mexico	62.0	27.8	10.2
Netherlands	58.5	20.3	21.2
Russia	14.3	76.5	9.2
Sweden	79.1	16.2	4.7
United States	78.6	18.5	2.9

Source: The Carnegie Foundation for the Advancement of Teaching, The International Survey of the Academic Profession, 1991–1993, Princeton, NJ.

counterparts. Finally, over two-thirds perceive no political or ideological restrictions on what a scholar may publish; university faculty and overseas appointees had higher levels of agreement.

Fewer than half believe there is far too much government interference in important academic policies, with Type I faculty and local appointees displaying higher levels of agreement. Moreover, almost half the respondents think that government should have the responsibility to define the overall purposes and policies of higher education. These responses need to be viewed in the context of a higher education system that has virtually no private sector. Finally, over half of the respondents indicate that free intellectual inquiry should be of the highest

Table 10.13

The Administration of this Institution Supports Academic Freedom (%)

	Agree	Neutral	Disagree	N.A.
Type I institutions	65	23	12	0.5
Type II institutions	34	30	34	2
Overseas appointees	52	21	26	1
Local appointees	46	31	22	2
All faculty	49	27	23	1

Source: The Carnegie Foundation for the Advancement of Teaching, The International Survey of the Academic Profession, 1991–1993, Princeton, NJ.

Table 10.13A

International Survey: The Administration Supports Academic Freedom (%)

Faculty country of origin	Agree	Neutral	Disagree	N.A.
Australia	43.4	32.1	23.5	1.2
Brazil	52.2	25.4	19.5	2.9
Chile	46.9	29.8	20.4	2.9
Germany	15.3	22.2	49.3	13.2
Hong Kong	48.8	26.5	23.4	1.3
Israel	69.0	16.3	10.5	4.1
Japan	66.8	21.6	6.2	5.4
Korea	34.2	35.7	27.8	2.4
Mexico	46.4	21.8	30.0	1.8
Russia	25.4	53.3	21.0	0.2
Sweden	39.1	36.6	22.7	1.7
United Kingdom	44.7	33.6	20.4	1.3
United States	62.9	22.3	13.6	1.3

Source: The Carnegie Foundation for the Advancement of Teaching, The International Survey of the Academic Profession, 1991–1993, Princeton, NJ.

priority for Hong Kong higher education in the future, also making it the highest ranked of eight selected aims of higher education.

The respondents were asked to rank in importance for Hong Kong eight aims of higher education (see Table 10.14). The ranking, based on the relative percentage of faculty selecting each stated aim, is as follows: promoting free intellectual inquiry; strengthening the society's capacity to compete internationally; promoting scholarship and research; preparing students for work; life-long learning for adults; educating students for leadership; helping to resolve basic social problems; and the preservation of cultural heritage.

Faculty at Type I institutions ranked these concerns as follows: protecting free

Table 10.14

Looking Toward the Future, What Priority Should Higher Education Give to the Following? (%)

	Educating students for leadership	Preparing students for work	Life-long learning for adults	Preserving cultural heritage	Protecting intellectual inquiry	Promoting scholarship and research inter-nationally	Capacity to compete	Helping to resolve social problems	
T	28.0	28.9	28.1	10.3	49.7	39.5	46.2	27.4	Highest priority
I	33.2	27.3	23.6	12.3	52.3	49.8	47.7	22.7	
II	23.2	30.4	32.3	8.4	47.3	30.1	44.8	31.5	
OS	29.4	24.7	33.3	11.8	57.5	43.5	37.4	29.2	
L	27.2	31.6	24.0	9.3	43.9	37.1	52.2	26.3	
T	50.5	48.7	37.5	32.8	35.2	43.6	40.1	47.5	High priority
I	47.7	47.3	35.0	31.5	33.9	43.8	39.1	47.7	
II	53.1	50.0	39.7	34.0	36.4	48.5	41.1	47.3	
OS	51.9	48.4	32.2	30.1	33.3	46.2	40.6	43.8	
L	49.3	49.3	41.3	34.2	36.8	46.7	39.7	50.0	
T	18.9	19.6	30.5	45.7	14.7	13.3	11.7	21.4	Medium priority
I	16.4	21.8	36.4	47.5	13.8	6.4	11.8	25.0	
II	21.2	17.5	25.1	44.1	15.5	19.7	11.6	18.3	
OS	16.0	22.6	31.2	43.5	8.6	10.3	18.2	22.2	
L	21.0	17.3	30.3	47.6	19.0	14.7	7.4	20.7	
T	2.6	2.8	3.9	11.2	0.4	0.9	2.0	3.7	Low priority
I	2.7	3.6	5.0	8.7	0.0	0.0	1.4	4.6	
II	2.5	2.1	2.9	13.4	0.8	1.7	2.5	2.9	
OS	2.7	4.3	3.2	14.5	0.5	0.0	3.7	4.9	
L	2.6	1.8	4.4	8.9	0.4	1.5	0.7	3.0	

Source: The Carnegie Foundation for the Advancement of Teaching, The International Survey of the Academic Profession, 1991–1993, Princeton, NJ.

Note:

T = Total; I = Type I institutions; II = Type II insitutions; OS = Overseas; L = Local intellectual inquiry, promoting scholarship and research, strengthening the society's capacity to compete internationally, educating students for leadership, preparing students for work, life-long learning for adults, helping to solve basic social problems, and preserving the cultural heritage. The rank order for faculty at Type II institutions is as follows: protecting free intellectual inquiry, strengthening the society's capacity to compete internationally, life-long education for adults, helping to solve basic social problems, preparing students for work, promoting scholarship and research, educating students for leadership, and preserving cultural heritage.

From nine selected global issues, faculty were asked to choose which one the government should assign the highest priority. Based on the relative percentage of faculty choosing each one, the issues were ranked as follows: basic education; environmental quality; human rights; world economy; AIDS and other health-related issues; population growth; racial, ethnic, and religious conflict; arms control; and world food supply (see Table 10.15).

A higher percentage of faculty at Type II institutions (36 percent) and overseas appointees (36 percent) believe the government should assign the highest priority to human rights than do Type I institution faculty (30 percent) and local appointees (31 percent). The order of importance according to which local appointees place the issues is as follows: basic education; environmental quality; human rights; world economy; AIDS and other health-related issues; population growth; racial, ethnic, and religious conflicts; world food supply; and arms control. For overseas appointees the order was: environmental quality; basic education; human rights; AIDS and other health-related issues; arms control; population growth; racial, ethnic, and religious conflicts; and world food supply.

The data in this section reveal several trends. Despite a recognition of declining academic standards, the academic profession supports the expansion of higher education provided that there are minimum standards of admission. At the same time, more than two-thirds think that higher education should not be provided free to students, and more than 80 percent say that business should make a contribution. Attitudes concerning goals of higher education and the importance of global issues reflect a commitment to protecting scholarship and the promotion of basic education. However, goals such as preserving the cultural heritage and global issues such as ethnic conflicts were viewed as low priorities.

The position and influence of the academic profession within Hong Kong society pale in comparison to the commercial and financial sectors. Only one in four surveyed describe academics as among the most influential opinion leaders. On the one hand, the expansion of higher education has the potential of enhancing the role of the academic profession. Already academics are becoming better represented in the legislative and executive organs of government. Yet academics that have risen to influential positions do not constitute a homogeneous group that takes a unified position on most issues. Moreover, those academics that have joined the party commanding the most elected seats in the legislative council of

Table 10.15

Looking Beyond the Campus, What Priority Should the Government Assign to the Following Global Issues? (%)

	Human rights	Basic education	World economy	Environment quality	Population growth	World food supply	AIDS and other health-related issues	Racial, ethnic and religious conflicts	Arms control	
T	33.1	54.0	15.4	43.7	13.2	8.8	15.4	11.8	11.5	Highest priority
I	30.4	54.8	18.1	42.9	13.6	8.0	15.4	11.0	11.8	
II	35.6	53.2	12.8	44.5	12.8	9.5	15.3	12.6	11.2	
OS	36.3	53.0	11.5	57.3	18.1	9.9	20.3	16.7	19.2	
L	31.1	54.5	18.0	34.5	9.8	7.6	12.0	8.5	6.2	
T	44.3	38.8	43.4	43.5	33.3	28.4	42.3	24.5	19.6	High priority
I	46.3	37.3	39.1	42.9	31.3	24.9	43.9	24.3	18.5	
II	42.5	40.1	47.4	44.1	35.0	31.6	40.9	24.7	20.7	
OS	49.5	39.5	39.0	34.6	33.5	30.9	48.4	27.8	20.9	
L	40.5	38.4	46.2	49.4	32.8	26.7	38.0	21.9	18.5	
T	17.9	5.9	34.7	11.9	39.7	40.5	35.9	37.9	27.3	Medium priority
I	18.7	6.9	37.7	13.8	38.3	43.2	33.2	36.2	24.6	
II	17.2	5.1	32.1	10.2	41.0	38.1	38.3	39.4	29.7	
OS	10.4	6.5	39.6	8.1	35.2	38.7	26.9	41.1	28.0	
L	23.1	5.6	31.6	14.6	43.0	42.0	42.1	35.8	26.9	
T	4.7	1.3	6.5	0.9	13.8	22.3	6.5	25.8	41.5	Low priority
I	4.7	0.9	5.1	0.5	16.8	23.9	7.5	28.5	45.1	
II	4.7	1.7	7.7	1.3	11.1	20.8	5.5	23.4	38.4	
OS	3.8	1.1	9.9	0.0	13.2	20.4	4.4	14.4	31.9	
L	5.3	1.5	4.1	1.5	14.4	23.7	7.9	33.8	48.5	

Source: The Carnegie Foundation for the Advancement of Teaching, The International Survey of the Academic Profession, 1991–1993, Princeton, NJ.

Note:

T = Total; I = Type I institutions; II = Type II institutions; OS = Overseas; L = Local the Hong Kong government stand a strong chance of being isolated by Beijing after 1997. In short, the academic profession lacks the unity required to become a key player in the future struggle over representative democracy in Hong Kong.

Academic freedom and free intellectual inquiry, while generally well protected in Hong Kong, may face challenges in the future. It is not encouraging that the faculty view academic freedom as generally more highly protected in the broader society than in their own institutions. Dissident academics could be singled out in the years to come. Institutions may only be willing to protect members of their faculty as long as it does not jeopardize the amount of resources they receive from the government. Since the UGC is the major decision maker in resource allocation involving the institutions, the future composition of its membership will be important. The issue of academic freedom will be watched closely in the coming years as an indication of the openness of Hong Kong society, and the vitality of its intellectual life.

Internationalism

The durability of academic freedom will certainly be related to the degree to which the academic profession in Hong Kong maintains a viable international dimension. The extent to which the academic profession in Hong Kong is international in composition has been demonstrated throughout this chapter. Yet the potential of the profession to maintain that international dimension is less certain. This section looks at engagement of the faculty in a variety of international activities that involve teaching, curriculum, research and publications, and membership in professional associations, as well as faculty attitude toward these international activities.

The character of the academic profession in Hong Kong is highly international, not only in terms of its composition but also in terms of the academic activities in which its faculty are engaged. This includes publishing articles or books outside of Hong Kong, and writing them in non-mother-tongue languages. Those who engage in these activities have published an average of 6.5 articles or books outside Hong Kong in the previous three years. Faculty often work collaboratively with academics from outside Hong Kong on research projects, travel outside to study or do research, serve on the faculty of an institution outside Hong Kong, and spend sabbatical leave outside of Hong Kong. Yet the faculty less frequently organize classes for overseas students from outside Hong Kong; of faculty who did, the average number of times over three years was only 2.5.

Overseas faculty and those at Type I institutions are generally more involved in international academic activities, with the exception of publishing in a language other than their mother tongue—an area in which where they are far surpassed by local faculty. Respondents indicate that academics from outside Hong Kong frequently teach courses at Hong Kong institutions, or attend conferences and seminars. However, only 12 percent indicate that overseas students from outside of Hong Kong have frequently been enrolled at their institutions during the previous three years. Only Korean academics indicate they had a lower number of international students enrolled in their universities in the past three years. Hong Kong fares better in the international ratings regarding the frequency of its own students doing study abroad. Fifteen percent of faculty surveyed indicate that students from their own institutions had frequently studied outside of Hong Kong.

Whether over the previous three years or ten years, faculty at Type I institutions published twice as many articles or books outside Hong Kong as did faculty at Type II institutions. This is also true with regard to the number of articles or books written in a language other than their mother tongue during the previous ten years. Faculty at Type I institutions organized almost twice as many classes for overseas students from outside Hong Kong during the previous three years as faculty at Type II institutions.

Faculty belong to an average of two international and two local scientific societies. Eight in ten faculty think that connections with scholars outside Hong Kong are very important to their professional work, and almost all believe that in order to keep up with developments in their disciplines, they must read books and journals published outside Hong Kong. Hong Kong rated high internationally on this measure.

More than eight in ten state that institutions of higher education should do more to promote student and staff mobility from one country to another, and almost two-thirds respond that the curriculum at their institutions should be more international in focus.

The composition of the profession in Hong Kong is clearly international in character, albeit in a selective ways. For example, the highest concentration of international faculty is from the United Kingdom and its Commonwealth countries, and from the United States. Faculty from other European countries and other parts of Asia, as well as the Middle East and Africa, are far fewer in number. Nevertheless, the internationalism that does exist is reflected in the survey data. And this internationalism has served Hong Kong higher education well in many ways, including the maintenance of standards and the amount of international academic interchange. For Hong Kong, the challenge will be maintaining this internationalism. For example, there are differences in attitude between overseas and local appointees on the relevance of international connections. While 72 percent of overseas appointees strongly agree that connections with scholars outside of Hong Kong are very important to their professional work, only 46 percent of local appointees are of this opinion. Thus, as the number of local appointees increases, the profession may become less internationally minded.

Moreover, there are aspects of Hong Kong higher education that are not very international, especially in the area of student exchange programs. The three-year university program, a holdover from colonial education, allows little time for overseas study programs of a year or a half year, which are standard in most universities around the world that have four-year programs. Moreover, the high cost of living accommodations in Hong Kong has been an impediment to attracting foreign students.

Dissemination of research information overseas, the facility to publish in English, and the high degree of international academic interaction and interchange have all contributed to the quality of Hong Kong higher education. It is unclear how deeply localization and nationalization will cut into this internationalism. The meaning of international higher education and the degree to which it should be preserved have yet to be adequately addressed by all institutions of higher education in Hong Kong. Finally, despite the large number of international staff, there is general agreement across higher education that the curriculum at the various institutions needs to be made more international in focus.

Maintaining Global Links

In recovering sovereignty over Hong Kong in 1997, China will acquire at least seven new universities that are very different from those on the mainland. At least five will be larger than the average university in China. More importantly, these universities have different academic traditions and greater autonomy than those on the mainland. Finally, the universities of Hong Kong will be much more integrated into the global academy than China's own top seven universities. As well, they will be staffed by a much higher proportion of non-Chinese as well as overseas Chinese with foreign passports. Not only will these universities have more faculty with doctoral degrees than the top seven universities in China, but most of those doctorates will have been acquired in Australia, Britain, Canada, and the United States. Finally, Hong Kong's strength as a communications hub, coupled with the fact that all academic staff are provided with access to the internet, ensures full participation in global academic discourse. Maintaining these institutions through the SAR government will be a major challenge for Beijing.

At the same time, Hong Kong's universities will also be confronting challenges. The rapid expansion of higher education, the result of confidence-building efforts and the need to replace the outflow of talent, coupled with the complex transition to a "one country, two systems" formula will present the Hong Kong academic profession with a challenging period of change. The data show an emerging profession that will be younger and increasingly localized. However, the dearth of doctorates in the recently elevated institutions, and indications that a large number of faculty, particularly overseas appointees, may leave their institutions, are issues that merit greater attention.[20] Maintaining high salaries will not solve the problem. Dissatisfaction with institutional working conditions, including intellectual atmosphere and relations between faculty and administration as well as with the quality of administrative leadership also need to be addressed, possibly through improved channels of communication between academics and administrators.

The rapid expansion of university enrollments has contributed to the perception that the quality of students has declined.[21] Nevertheless, the profession is supportive of expanding enrollments as long as minimal standards are maintained. At the same time, the traditionally strong emphasis placed on mathematics throughout the Hong Kong educational system was reflected in the perceptions of the respondents. The perceived adequacy of student preparation in mathematics and quantitative reasoning skills was the highest of all the countries in the international study. Yet perceptions of the adequacy of student preparation in written and oral communication skills are less reassuring. This includes skills in both the Chinese and English languages. The former will be increasingly important in the coming years for the image of Hong Kong higher education in the eyes of academics in other parts of China, and the latter will be instrumental in Hong Kong's business with the rest of the world.

The international composition of Hong Kong's academic profession has itself been a major attraction for potential recruits.[22] Quality recruitment and the maintenance of internationalism will depend as much on conducive institutional working conditions such as intellectual atmosphere and good relations between faculty and administration as on salaries and benefits. It is essential to spawn an academic culture that can increase the faculty's sense of influence over the development of key academic policies at the departmental, but also institutional, level.

Within a decade, Hong Kong has moved from a colonial society with two universities serving a small elite to a transitional society with seven universities serving a larger population, and witnessing the modernization of mainland China. Moreover, whether or not they accept the challenge, Hong Kong's universities will continue to be viewed as key institutions for the development of democratic institutions in Hong Kong's future. Finally, given the fact that Hong Kong has long touted its freedom of speech, it is surprising that it ranked below its East Asian neighbors on the question of whether academic freedom is strongly protected in its society.

Notes

Parts of this chapter were published by the Carnegie Foundation for the Advancement of Teaching in Philip Altbach, ed., *The International Academic Profession: Portraits of 14 Countries* (Princeton, NJ: Carnegie Foundation, 1997). The author would like to acknowledge the support of the Carnegie Foundation for the Advancement of Teaching, the Hang Seng Bank Golden Jubilee Education Fund administered by the Centre of Asian Studies of the University of Hong Kong, and the Sik Sik Yuen Education Research Fund. The cooperation of the UGC in provision of related data is gratefully acknowledged, as well as the assistance provided by its secretary-general, Nigel French. Cooperation of the institutional monitors is appreciated: Chinese University of Hong Kong, Leslie Lo; City University of Hong Kong, Agnes K.C. Yeung; Lingnan College, H. Wing Lee; Hong Kong Baptist University, William Wu; Hong Kong Polytechnic University, Lee Ming Kwan; Hong Kong University of Science and Technology, Alfred Hu Ko-wei; University of Hong Kong, Cheng Kai Ming; and John Bacon-Shone of the Social Science Research

Center (HKU). The research assistance of Chan Wai Bo and Chen Xiaoyu is gratefully acknowledged.

1. See, for example, Merle Goldman, Timothy Cheek, and Carol Lee Hamrin, eds., *China's Intellectuals and the State: In Search of a New Relationship,* Harvard Contemporary China Series 3 (Cambridge, MA: The Council on East Asian Studies, Harvard University Press, 1987); also, Richard Madsen, "The Spiritual Crisis of China's Intellectuals," in Deborah Davis and Ezra Vogel, eds., *Chinese Society on the Eve of Tiananmen: The Impact of Reform, Harvard Contemporary China Series 7* (Cambridge, MA: The Council of East Asian Studies, Harvard University Press, 1990); and Merle Goldman, "The Intellectuals in the Deng Xiaoping Era," in Arthur Lewis Rosenbaum, ed., *State and Society in China: The Consequences of Reform* (Boulder, CO: Westview Press, 1992).

2. See the Annual Address by Governor David Wilson to the Legislative Council, October 11, 1989, reprinted in David Roberts, ed., *Hong Kong 1990: A Review of 1989* (Hong Kong: Government Printer, 1990), pp. 4–22; see also University Grants Committee Secretariat, University Grants Committee of Hong Kong, *Facts and Figures 1994* (Hong Kong: University Grants Committee Secretariat, April 1995). The figure of 58,000 refers only to the number of students in the seven institutions of higher education under the University Grants Committee, and includes undergraduate and graduate as well as sub-degree students.

3. Hugh Witt, ed., *Hong Kong Yearbook 1993: A Review of 1992* (Hong Kong: Government Printer, 1993). The six universities and tertiary college are funded through the University Grants Committee, while the Academy of Performing Arts is funded by the Recreation and Culture Branch of the government. Hong Kong also has a postsecondary institution, Shue Yan College, which is privately funded.

4. See University and Polytechnic Grants Committee Secretariat statement of October 1992, entitled "Higher Education in Hong Kong," Ref: UPGC/GEN/222/90.

5. University Grants Committee of Hong Kong, *Facts and Figures 1994.*

6. Basic Law of the Hong Kong Special Administrative Region of the Peoples Republic of China (Hong Kong: The Consultative Committee of the Basic Law, 1990).

7. Ibid.

8. See Gerard A. Postiglione and Ming K. Chan, eds., *Hong Kong Becoming China: The Transition to 1997,* a series of volumes. Among the volumes are Gerard A. Postiglione, ed., with Julian Y.M. Leung, *Education and Society in Hong Kong: Toward One Country and Two Systems* (Armonk, NY: M.E. Sharpe, and Hong Kong: The Hong Kong University Press, 1991); also, Reginald Kwok and Alvin So, eds. *The Hong Kong–Guangdong Economic Nexus: Partnership in Flux* (Armonk, NY: M.E. Sharpe, and Hong Kong: The Hong Kong University Press, 1995).

9. Data supplied by the University Grants Committee in Annex A of a letter from Mr. Brian Lo, for the secretary general, University Grants Committee, March 8, 1994.

10. A staff list from each institution was used. After selection of a random number, every third person was sampled across departmental listings arranged by ranks. The UGC figure for total academic staff across institutions for 1993–94 was 3,562. The sampling process using staff lists yielded 1,247 names, approximately 35 percent of the population. There were 461 respondents for an approximately 37 percent response rate, which accounts for about 13 percent of the total population. Completed surveys were returned either to the General Post Office in Central District or to one of the institutional monitors.

11. Overseas appointees may remain in Hong Kong for less time than it takes to earn tenure. Overseas terms usually include better housing accommodations and travel allowances, along with other benefits in some cases. Eligibility is based on overseas residency. However, because Hong Kong is an emigrant as well as an immigrant society, there are many Chinese—including those originating from Hong Kong, Taiwan, and other parts of

Southeast Asia; Western countries; and mainland Chinese who come via long periods of study in the United States and other places—as well as non-Chinese employed on overseas terms. Moreover, local appointees are not solely comprised of ethnic Chinese; there are also a few "westerners," usually long-term residents of Hong Kong, included in this category. The differences between local and overseas terms gradually disappear with promotion to higher rank. Nevertheless, the appointment itself is still classified as either local or overseas. Since the survey was completed, universities have taken measures to dismantle differences between local and overseas terms.

12. These figures from Type II institutions follow university-equivalent ranks. During the time the survey was conducted, a reclassification of academic staff was being carried out. For example, polytechnics and colleges had some faculty classified as lecturers and others as university lecturers, the latter denoting the conversion to the new system. In the old system of classification, a polytechnic/college senior lecturer rank was roughly equivalent to a university lecturer rank. A principal lecturer in Type II institutions is roughly equivalent to a Type I institution senior lecturer. In short, Type II institution (nonclinical) ranks were used as a standard of measure. Also, see note 26.

13. The largest percentage of departments or units in which faculty were employed are: engineering (15 percent), humanities (14 percent), social science (13 percent), business (11 percent), health sciences (11 percent), and biological sciences (6 percent). If we divide fields of specialization according to two categories: science and technology (S&T), and social sciences and humanities (SS&H), the number of respondents is nearly equal. The universities have a little more than half (54 percent) of the S&T faculty, and less than half (41 percent) of the SS&H faculty. S&T faculty had more advanced degrees. Sixty-four percent had a doctorate while only 45 percent of SS&H faculty had one. Despite this, tenure levels were nearly the same (S&T 45 percent, and SS&H 46 percent). There were also a similar number (61 percent of S&T faculty and 58 percent of SS&H faculty) appointed to overseas and local terms. While overseas appointees are distributed somewhat evenly across fields, higher proportions are found in law and medicine.

14. Hong Kong faculty also had the highest percentage of those responding "no" to the question, "Do you currently hold other paid nonacademic positions outside the institution?" The relatively high salaries also have to be viewed against the cost of living in Hong Kong, where property values are among the highest in the world. Another reason why overseas appointees rate their salaries more highly than local appointees is because the former are earning more buying power in their home society than the latter.

15. The choices offered, with the percentage of respondents indicating a strong reason to leave, were as follows: income (6 percent), resources for research (11 percent), academic reputation of the institution (13 percent), academic cooperation among colleagues (11 percent), region in which the institution is located (10 percent), and other reasons (56 percent). One-third of the respondents indicated "other reason" as their strong reason to leave. Of this group, 79 percent specified the reason by writing it in the space provided. One-third indicated reasons having to do with Hong Kong's post-1997 status. The remainder indicated a variety of factors including retirement, promotion, bureaucracy, administration, management, workload, end of contract, change of career, and personal reasons. The ranking for Type I institutions differed from that for Type II institutions: The rank order of strong reasons (excluding "other reasons") for Type I institutions was: region, resources for research, academic cooperation, academic reputation, and income. For Type II institutions the ranking was: academic reputation, resources for research, academic cooperation, income, and region. Of those in the science and technology areas, resources for research was the strongest reason aside from the category "other reason."

16. A change of titles (from the assistant lecturer, lecturer, senior lecturer, reader, professor categories to a lecturer, associate professor, professor) has been considered by

268 HONG KONG'S REUNION WITH CHINA

the University of Hong Kong Senate. There is little uniformity in the system of academic titles among the seven UGC institutions of higher education. For example, the City University has three systems of titles. It has retained the old polytechnic system of titles (professor, principal lecturer, senior lecturer, lecturer, and assistant lecturer) because it still has subdegree programs. As part of the conversion to a university in 1993–94, the second system of titles (professor, reader/university senior lecturer, university lecturer, university assistant lecturer) was introduced. Since some faculty teach in both subdegree and degree programs, there is an option for those with the old polytechnic titles to apply for the new university titles, though some staff have chosen to maintain their old titles. On May 6, 1995, a third system was introduced to exist alongside of the other two. It permits those in the second system to adopt a more American system of titles (professor, associate professor, assistant professor, lecturer).

17. See the three scenarios in Higher Education 1991–2000: An Interim Report (Hong Kong: University and Polytechnic Grants Committee, November 1993), p. 7.

18. The variance across institutions was relatively small. Research commitments had a slightly more positive influence on teaching in Type I institutions than in Type II institutions, for example. The influence of administrative work had less of a positive influence in the universities than in the other institutions.

19. Below HK$400,000 (U.S.$1 = HK$7.8).

20. The low proportion of doctorates can be partially explained by the fact that three of the Type II institutions still retain some sub-degree courses.

21. Faculty were asked, "On average, how would you compare the quality of students currently enrolled in your department with the quality of students enrolled five years ago?" They answered as follows: 4.3 percent indicted "better now," 13.6 percent indicated "about the same," 47 percent indicated "better five years ago," and 35.1 percent indicated "don't know." A related survey question referred to undergraduate students at their institutions: "They are more studious than students I had five years ago." In response, 8.1 percent agreed, 21.1 percent were neutral, 43.8 percent disagreed, and for 22 percent the question was not applicable.

22. Justin Webster, "Success in Hong Kong: Universities in Hong Kong Attract Top Scholars Despite Concern about Colony's Future after 1997,"Chronicle of Higher Education, October 19, 1994, pp. A58–60.

Appendix 1

Hong Kong's Participation in Multilateral Forums up to March 31, 1996

A. International Organizations in Which Hong Kong's Continued Participation Has Been Agreed in the Sino-British Joint Liaison Group (JLG)

Asian Development Bank (ADB)
Asian and Pacific Development Centre (APDC)
Asia-Pacific Postal Union (APPU)
Asia-Pacific Telecommunity (APT)
Customs Cooperation Council (CCC)
Economic and Social Commission for Asia and the Pacific (ESCAP)
Food and Agriculture Organization (FAO)
General Agreement on Tariffs and Trade (GATT)
Intergovernmental Typhoon Committee (ITC)
International Atomic Energy Agency (IAEA)
International Bank for Reconstruction and Development (IBRD)
International Criminal Police Organization (INTERPOL)
International Development Association (IDA)
International Finance Corporation (IFC)
International Hydrographic Organization (IHO)
International Labor Organization (ILO)
International Maritime Organization (IMO)
International Maritime Satellite Organization (INMARSAT)
International Monetary Fund (IMF)
International Telecommunications Satellite Organization (INTELSAT)

International Telecommunication Union (ITU)
Network of Aquaculture Centres in Asia and the Pacific (NACA)
Statistical Institute for Asia and the Pacific (SIAP)
United Nations Commission on Narcotic Drugs (UNCND)
United Nations Conference on Trade and Development (UNCTAD)
Universal Postal Union (UPU)
World Health Organization (WHO)
World Intellectual Property Organization (WIPO)
World Meteorological Organization (WMO)
World Trade Organization (WTO)

**B. International Organizations in Which Hong Kong
Currently Participates, but JLG Approval for Post-1997
Participation Remains Pending**

Asian Productivity Organization (APO)
International Civil Aviation Organization (ICAO)
Multilateral Investment Guarantee Agency (MIGA)*

**C. Other Organizations in Which Hong Kong Currently
Participates, with JLG Agreement Not Required for
Hong Kong's Continued Participation**

Asia Pacific Economic Cooperation Forum (APEC)
Asia-Pacific Metrology Program (APMP)
International Association of Lighthouse Authorities (IAIA)
International Association of Ports and Harbors (IAPH)
International Organization for Standardization (IOS)
National Conference of Standards Laboratories (NCSL)
United Nations Development Program (UNDP)
United Nations Environment Program (UNEP)
United Nations Fund for Drug Abuse Control
United Nations Fund for Population Activities

D. Organizations in Which the HKSAR Will Be a Full Member

Asian Development Bank (ADB)
Asian Productivity Organization (APO)**
Customs Cooperation Council (CCC)
General Agreements on Tariff and Trade (GATT)

---

*The JLG has agreed that the MIGA Convention will apply to Hong Kong after 1997, but no decision has yet been reached on Hong Kong's participation as a MIGA member after 1997.
**JLG approval for Hong Kong's participation is pending.

Network of Aquaculture Centres in Asia and the Pacific (NACA)
World Meteorological Organization (WMO)
World Trade Organization (WTO)

E. Organizations in Which the HKSAR Will Participate as Part of the PRC Delegation

Asia-Pacific Postal Union (APPU)
Food and Agriculture Organization (FAO)
International Atomic Energy Agency (IAEA)
International Bank for Reconstruction and Development (IBRD)
International Civil Aviation Organization (ICAO)*
International Criminal Police Organization (INTERPOL)
International Development Association (IDA)
International Finance Corporation (IFC)
International Hydrographic Organization (IHO)
International Labor Organization (ILO)
International Maritime Satellite Organization (INMARSAT)
International Telecommunications Satellite Organization (INTELSAT)
International Telecommunication Union (ITU)
United Nations Commission on Narcotic Drugs (UNCND)
United Nations Conference on Trade and Development (UNCTAD)
Universal Postal Union (UPU)
World Intellectual Property Organization (WIPO)

F. Organizations in Which the HKSAR Will Be an Associate Member

Asian and Pacific Development Centre (APDC)
Asia-Pacific Telecommunity (APT)
Economic and Social Commission for Asia and the Pacific (ESCAP)
Intergovernmental Typhoon Committee (ITC)
International Maritime Organization (IMO)
Statistical Institute for Asia and the Pacific (SIAP)
World Health Organization (WHO)

Note: It has not yet been determined in what capacity Hong Kong will participate in organizations listed in Section C.

---

*JLG approval for Hong Kong's participation is pending.

U.S.–Hong Kong Policy Act of 1992

S.1731

One Hundred Second Congress of the United States of America

The Second Session

Begun and held at the City of Washington on Friday, the third day of January, one thousand nine hundred and ninety-two

An Act
To set forth the policy of the United States with respect to Hong Kong, and for other purposes.

Be it enacted by the Senate and House of Representatives of the United States of America in Congress assembled.

Section 1. Short Title

This Act may be cited as the "United States–Hong Kong Policy Act of 1992."

Sec 2. Findings and Declarations.

The Congress makes the following findings and declarations:

(1) The Congress recognizes that under the 1984 Sino-British Joint Declaration:

(A) The People's Republic of China and the United Kingdom of Great Britain and Northern Ireland have agreed that the People's Republic of China will resume the exercise of sovereignty over Hong Kong on July 1,

1997. Until that time, the United Kingdom will be responsible for the administration of Hong Kong.

(B) The Hong Kong Special Administrative Region of the People's Republic of China, beginning on July 1, 1997, will continue to enjoy a high degree of autonomy on all matters other than defense and foreign affairs.

(C) There is provision for implementation of a "one country, two systems" policy, under which Hong Kong will retain its current lifestyle and legal, social, and economic systems until at least the year 2047.

(D) The legislature of the Hong Kong Special Administrative Region will be constituted by elections, and the provisions of the International Covenant on Civil and Political Rights and the International Covenant on Economic, Social and Cultural Rights, as applied to Hong Kong, shall remain in force.

(E) Provision is made for the continuation in force of agreements implemented as of June 30, 1997, and for the ability of the Hong Kong Special Administrative Region to conclude new agreements either on its own or with the assistance of the Government of the People's Republic of China.

(2) The Congress declares its wish to see full implementation of the provisions of the Joint Declaration.

(3) The President has announced his support for the policies and decisions reflected in the Joint Declaration.

(4) Hong Kong plays an important role in today's regional and world economy. This role is reflected in strong economic, cultural, and other ties with the United States that give the United States a strong interest in the continued vitality, prosperity, and stability of Hong Kong.

(5) Support for democratization is a fundamental principle of United States foreign policy. As such, it naturally applies to United States policy toward Hong Kong. This will remain equally true after June 30, 1997.

(6) The human rights of the people of Hong Kong are of great importance to the United States and are directly relevant to United States interests in Hong Kong. A fully successful transition in the exercise of sovereignty over Hong Kong must safeguard human rights in and of themselves. Human rights also serve as a basis for Hong Kong's continued economic prosperity.

Sec. 3. Definitions.

For purposes of this Act—

(1) the term "Hong Kong" means, prior to July 1, 1997, the British Dependent Territory of Hong Kong, and on and after July 1, 1997, the Hong Kong Special Administrative Region of the People's Republic of China;

(2) the term "Joint Declaration" means the Joint Declaration of the Government of the United Kingdom of Great Britain and Northern Ireland and the Government of the People's Republic of China on the Question of Hong Kong, done at Beijing on December 19, 1984; and (3) the term "laws of the United States" means provisions of law enacted by the Congress.

Title I—Policy

Sec. 101. Bilateral Ties between the United States and Hong Kong.

It is the sense of the Congress that the following, which are based in part on the relevant provisions of the Joint Declaration, should be the policy of the United States with respect to its bilateral relationship with Hong Kong:

(1) The United States should play an active role, before, on, and after July 1, 1997, in maintaining Hong Kong's confidence and prosperity, Hong Kong's role as an international financial center, and the mutually beneficial ties between the people of the United States and the people of Hong Kong.

(2) The United States should actively seek to establish and expand direct bilateral ties and agreements with Hong Kong in economic, trade, financial, monetary, aviation, shipping, communications, tourism, cultural, sport, and other appropriate areas.

(3) The United States should seek to maintain, after June 30, 1997, the United States consulate-general in Hong Kong, together with other official and semi-official organizations, such as the United States Information Agency American Library.

(4) The United States should invite Hong Kong to maintain, after June 30, 1997, its official and semi-official missions in the United States, such as the Hong Kong Economic & Trade Office, the Office of the Hong Kong Trade Development Council, and the Hong Kong Tourist Association. The United States should invite Hong Kong to open and maintain other official or semi-official missions to represent Hong Kong in those areas in which Hong Kong is entitled to maintain relations on its own, including economic, trade, financial, monetary, aviation, shipping, communications, tourism, cultural, and sport areas.

(5) The United States should recognize passports and travel documents issued after June 30, 1997, by the Hong Kong Special Administrative Region.

(6) The resumption by the People's Republic of China of the exercise of sovereignty over Hong Kong after June 30, 1997, should not affect treatment of Hong Kong residents who apply for visas to visit or reside permanently in the United States, so long as such treatment is consistent with the Immigration and Nationality Act.

Sec. 102. Participation in Multilateral Organizations, Rights under International Agreements, and Trade Status.

It is the sense of the Congress that the following, which are based in part on the relevant provisions of the Joint Declaration, should be the policy of the United States with respect to Hong Kong after June 30, 1997:

(1) The United States should support Hong Kong's participation in all appropriate multilateral conferences, agreements, and organizations in which Hong Kong is eligible to participate.

(2) The United States should continue to fulfill its obligations to Hong Kong under international agreements, so long as Hong Kong reciprocates, regardless of whether the People's Republic of China is a party to the particular international agreement, unless and until such obligations are modified or terminated in accordance with law.

(3) The United States should respect Hong Kong's status as a separate customs territory, and as a contracting party to the General Agreement on Tariffs and Trade, whether or not the People's Republic of China participates in the latter organization.

Sec. 103. Commerce between the United States and Hong Kong.

It is the sense of the Congress that the following, which are based in part on the relevant provisions of the Joint Declaration, are and should continue after June 30, 1997, to be the policy of the United States with respect to commerce between the United States and Hong Kong:

(1) The United States should seek to maintain and expand economic and trade relations with Hong Kong and should continue to treat Hong Kong as a separate territory in economic and trade matters, such as import quotas and certificates of origin.

(2) The United States should continue to negotiate directly with Hong Kong to conclude bilateral economic agreements.

(3) The United States should continue to treat Hong Kong as a territory which is fully autonomous from the United Kingdom and, after June 30, 1997, should treat Hong Kong as a territory which is fully autonomous from the People's Republic of China with respect to economic and trade matters.

(4) The United States should continue to grant the products of Hong Kong nondiscriminatory trade treatment (commonly referred to as "most-favored-nation status") by virtue of Hong Kong's membership in the General Agreement on Tariffs and Trade.

(5) The United States should recognize certificates of origin for manufactured goods issued by the Hong Kong Special Administrative Region.

(6) The United States should continue to allow the United States dollar to be freely exchanged with the Hong Kong dollar.

(7) United States businesses should be encouraged to continue to operate in Hong Kong, in accordance with applicable United States and Hong Kong law.

(8) The United States should continue to support access by Hong Kong to sensitive technologies controlled under the agreement of the Coordinating Committee for Multilateral Export Controls (commonly referred to as "COCOM") for so long as the United States is satisfied that such technologies are protected from improper use or export.

(9) The United States should encourage Hong Kong to continue its efforts to develop a framework which provides adequate protection for intellectual property rights.

(10) The United States should negotiate a bilateral investment treaty directly with Hong Kong, in consultation with the Government of the People's Republic of China.

(11) The change in the exercise of sovereignty over Hong Kong should not affect ownership in any property, tangible or intangible, held in the United States by any Hong Kong person.

Sec. 104. Transportation.

It is the sense of the Congress that the following, which are based in part on the relevant provisions of the Joint Declaration, should be the policy of the United States after June 30, 1997, with respect to transportation from Hong Kong:

(1) Recognizing Hong Kong's position as an international transport center, the United States should continue to recognize ships and airplanes registered in Hong Kong and should negotiate air service agreements directly with Hong Kong.

(2) The United States should continue to recognize ships registered by Hong Kong.

(3) United States commercial ships, in accordance with applicable United States and Hong Kong law, should remain free to port in Hong Kong.

(4) The United States should continue to recognize airplanes registered by Hong Kong in accordance with applicable laws of the People's Republic of China.

(5) The United States should recognize licenses issued by the Hong Kong to Hong Kong airlines.

(6) The United States should recognize certificates issued by Hong Kong to United States air carriers for air service involving travel to, from, or through Hong Kong which does not involve travel to, from, or through other parts of the People's Republic of China.

(7) The United States should negotiate at the appropriate time directly with

the Hong Kong Special Administrative Region, acting under authorization from the Government of the People's Republic of China, to renew or amend all air service agreements existing on June 30, 1997, and to conclude new air service agreements affecting all flights to, from, or through the Hong Kong Special Administrative Region which do not involve travel to, from, or through other parts of the People's Republic of China.

(8) The United States should make every effort to ensure that the negotiations described in paragraph (7) lead to procompetitive air service agreements.

Sec. 105. Cultural and Educational Exchanges.

It is the sense of the Congress that the following, which are based in part on the relevant provisions of the Joint Declaration, are and should continue after June 30, 1997, to be the policy of the United States with respect to cultural and educational exchanges with Hong Kong:

(1) The United States should seek to maintain and expand United States–Hong Kong relations and exchanges in culture, education, science, and academic research. The United States should encourage American participation in bilateral exchanges with Hong Kong, both official and unofficial.

(2) The United States should actively seek to further United States–Hong Kong cultural relations and promote bilateral exchanges, including the negotiating and concluding of appropriate agreements in these matters.

(3) Hong Kong should be accorded separate status as a full partner under the Fulbright Academic Exchange Program (apart from the United Kingdom before July 1, 1997, and apart from the People's Republic of China thereafter), with the continuation or establishment of a Fulbright Commission or functionally equivalent mechanism.

(4) The United States should actively encourage Hong Kong residents to visit the United States on nonimmigrant visas for such purposes as business, tourism, education, and scientific and academic research, in accordance with applicable United States and Hong Kong laws.

(5) Upon the request of the Legislative Council of Hong Kong, the Librarian of Congress, acting through the Congressional Research Service, should seek to expand educational and informational ties with the Council.

Title II—The Status of Hong Kong in United States Law

Sec. 201. Continued Application of United States Law.

(a) In General.—Notwithstanding any change in the exercise of sovereignty over Hong Kong, the laws of the United States shall continue to apply with respect to Hong Kong, on and after July 1, 1997, in the same manner as the laws of the United States were applied with respect to Hong Kong before such date unless otherwise expressly provided by law or by Executive order under section 202.

(b) International Agreements. — For all purposes, including actions in any court in the United States, the Congress approves the continuation in force on and after July 1, 1997, of all treaties and other international agreements, including multilateral conventions, entered into before such date between the United States and Hong Kong, or entered into before such date between the United States and the United Kingdom and applied to Hong Kong, unless or until terminated in accordance with law. If in carrying out this title, the President determines that Hong Kong is not legally competent to carry out its obligations under any such treaty or other international agreement, or that the continuation of Hong Kong's obligations or rights under any such treaty or other international agreement is not appropriate under the circumstances, such determination shall be reported to the Congress in accordance with section 301.

Sec. 202. Presidential Order.

(a) Presidential Determination.—On or after July 1, 1997, whenever the President determines that Hong Kong is not sufficiently autonomous to justify treatment under a particular law of the United States, or any provision thereof, different from that accorded the People's Republic of China, the President may issue an Executive order suspending the application of section 201(a) to such law or provision of law.

(b) Factor For Consideration.—In making a determination under subsection (a) with respect to the application of a law of the United States, or any provision thereof, to Hong Kong, the President should consider the terms, obligations, and expectations expressed in the Joint Declaration with respect to Hong Kong.

(c) Publication in Federal Register.—Any Executive order issued under subsection (a) shall be published in the Federal Register and shall specify the law or provision of law affected by the order.

(d) Termination of Suspension.—An Executive order issued under subsection (a) may be terminated by the President with respect to a particular law or provision of law whenever the President determines that Hong Kong has regained sufficient autonomy to justify different treatment under the law or provision of law in question. Notice of any such termination shall be published in the Federal Register.

Sec. 203. Rules and Regulations.

The President is authorized to prescribe such rules and regulations as the President may deem appropriate to carry out this Act.

Sec. 204. Consultation with Congress.

In carrying out this title, the President shall consult appropriately with the Congress.

Title III—Reporting Provisions

Sec. 301. Reporting Requirement.

Not later than March 31, 1993, March 31, 1995, March 31, 1997, March 31, 1998, March 31, 1999, and March 31, 2000, the Secretary of State shall transmit to the Speaker of the House of Representatives and the chairman of the Committee on Foreign Relations of the Senate a report on conditions in Hong Kong of interest to the United States. This report shall cover (in the case of the initial report) the period since the date of enactment of this Act or (in the case of subsequent reports) the period since the most recent report pursuant to this section and shall describe—

(1) significant developments in United States relations with Hong Kong, including a description of agreements that have entered into force between the United States and Hong Kong;

(2) other matters, including developments related to the change in the exercise of sovereignty over Hong Kong, affecting United States interests in Hong Kong or United States relations with Hong Kong;

(3) the nature and extent of United States–Hong Kong cultural, education, scientific, and academic exchanges, both official and unofficial;

(4) the laws of the United States with respect to which the application of section 201(a) has been suspended pursuant to section 202(a) or with respect to which such a suspension has been terminated pursuant to section 202(d), and the reasons for the suspension or termination, as the case may be;

(5) treaties and other international agreements with respect to which the President has made a determination described in the last sentence of section 201(b), and the reasons for each such determination;

(6) significant problems in cooperation between Hong Kong and the United States in the area of export controls;

(7) the development of democratic institutions in Hong Kong; and

(8) the nature and extent of Hong Kong's participation in multilateral forums.

Sec. 302. Separate Part of Country Reports.

Whenever a report is transmitted to the Congress on a country-by-country basis there shall be included in such report, where applicable, a separate subreport on

Hong Kong under the heading of the state that exercises sovereignty over Hong Kong. The reports to which this section applies include the reports transmitted under—

(1) sections 116(d) and 502B(b) of the Foreign Assistance Act of 1961 (relating to human rights);

(2) section 181 of the Trade Act of 1974 (relating to trade barriers); and

(3) section 2202 of the Export Enhancement Act of 1988 (relating to economic policy and trade practices).

Speaker of the House of Representatives.

Vice President of the United States and President of the Senate.

Selected References

Amsden, Alice. *Asia's Next Giant: South Korea and Late Industrialization.* New York: Oxford University Press, 1989.

Andersson, Thomas. "The Role of Japanese Foreign Direct Investment," in *The Global Race for Foreign Direct Investment,* ed. Lars Oxelheim. Berlin: Springer-Verlag, 1993, pp. 205–231.

Ariff, Mohamed. "The Prospects for an ASEAN Free Trade Area," *The World Economy* 17 (2), 1995.

———. "The Role of APEC: An Asian Perspective," *Journal of Japanese Trade & Industry* 13 (1), 1994, pp. 46–49.

Arrighi, Giovanni, Ikeda, Satoshi and Irwan, Alex. "The Rise of East Asia: One Miracle or Many?" in *Pacific-Asia and the Future of the World-System,* ed. Ravi A. Palat. Westport: Greenwood, 1993, pp. 41–65.

———. "The Rise of East Asia: World-system and Regional Aspects." Paper prepared for the conference "L'economia mondiale in transformazione," Rome, October 6–8, 1994.

Baker III, James. "America in Asia: Emerging Architecture for a Pacific Community," *Foreign Affairs,* Winter 1991/92.

Baker, Hugh. "Social Change in Hong Kong: Hong Kong Man in Search of Majority," *The China Quarterly,* no. 136, December 1993, pp. 864–877.

Balassa, Bela. "The Lessons of East Asian Development: An Overview," *Economic Development and Cultural Change* 36, 3rd supplement, 1988, S273–S290.

Barnds, William J. "Human Rights and US Policy Towards Asia," in *Human Rights and International Relations in the Asia Pacific,* ed. James T.H. Tang. London and New York: Pinter, 1995, pp. 71–82.

Baum, Richard. *Burying Mao: Chinese Politics in the Age of Deng Xiaoping.* Princeton University Press, 1994.

Bello, Walden, and Rosenfeld, Stephanie. "Dragons in Distress: The Crisis of the NICs," *World Policy Journal* 7, 1990, pp. 431–468.

Berger, Peter L., and Hsiao, Hsin-huang. *In Search of an East Asian Developmental Model.* New Brunswick: Transaction Books, 1988.

Bernard, Mitchell, and Ravenhill, John. "Beyond Product Cycles and Flying Geese: Regionalization, Hierarchy, and the Industrialization of East Asia," *World Politics* 47, 1995, pp. 171–209.

Bienefeld, Michael A. "The International Context for National Development Strategies and Opportunities in a Changing World," in *The Struggle for Development: National Strategies in an International Context,* eds. M.E. Bienefeld and M. Godfrey. Chichester, New York, Brisbane, Toronto, Singapore: John Wiley, 1982, pp. 49–53.

Boissevain, Jeremy. *Friends of Friends: Networks, Manipulators and Coalitions.* Oxford: Basil Blackwell, 1974.

Bottomore, Tom, ed. *A Dictionary of Marxist Thought.* Cambridge: Harvard University Press, 1983.

Bourdieu, Pierre. "The Forms of Capital," in *Handbook of Theory and Research for the Sociology of Education,* ed. J. Richardson. New York: Greenwood Press, 1986.

———. "What Makes a Social Class? On the Theoretical and Practical Existence of Groups," *Berkeley Journal of Sociology,* Vol. 32, 1987.

Bunker, Stephen, and O'Hearn, Denis. "Strategies of Economic Ascendants for Access to Raw Materials: A Comparison of the United States and Japan," in *Pacific-Asia and the Future of the World-System,* ed. Ravi Palat. Westport: Greenwood Press, 1993, pp. 83–102.

Bureau of Investigation, Ministry of Justice (Fawubu Diaochaju). *Zhonggong duitai gongzuo yanxi yu wenjian huibian (A Compendium of Analyses and Documents on the CPC's Taiwan Work)* Taipei, 1984.

Burt, Ronald. *Structural Holes: the Social Structure of Competition.* Cambridge: Harvard University Press, 1992.

Byrnes, Andrew, and Chan, Johannes, eds. *Public Law and Human Rights: A Hong Kong Sourcebook.* Hong Kong/Singapore/Malaysia: Butterworths, 1993.

Castells, M., Goh, L. and Kwok, R. Y. W. *The Shek Kip Mei Syndrome: Economic Development and Public Housing in Hong Kong and Singapore.* London: Pion Press, 1990.

Census and Statistics Department. *Hong Kong Annual Digest of Statistic: 1995 Edition.* Hong Kong: Government Printer, 1955.

———. *Hong Kong Statistics, 1947–67.* Hong Kong: Government Printer, 1969.

———. *Hong Kong 1991 Population Census: Summary Results.* Hong Kong: Government Printer, 1992.

Chan, K.C. "The Role of Television in the Founding of Hong Kong Indigenous Culture," in *Culture and Society in Hong Kong,* ed. Elizabeth Sinn. Hong Kong: Centre of Asian Studies, The University of Hong Kong, 1995. pp. 80–88 (in Chinese).

Chan, Hoiman. "Comedy and Mediation: Charting the Cultural Mentality of Hong Kong," paper presented to the International Conference on Cultural Criticism. Hong Kong: Chinese University of Hong Kong, 1993.

———. "Culture and Identity," in *The Other Hong Kong Report 1994,* eds. D. McMillen and S.W. Man. Hong Kong: The Chinese University Press, 1994. pp. 443–468.

———. "Popular Culture and Political Society: Prolegomena on Cultural Studies in Hong Kong," in *Culture and Society in Hong Kong,* ed. Elizabeth Sinn. Hong Kong: Centre of Asian Studies, The University of Hong Kong, 1995, pp. 23–50.

Chan, Johannes Chan, and Ghai, Yash, eds. *The Bill of Rights: A Comparative Approach.* Hong Kong/Singapore/Malaysia: Butterworths Asia, 1993.

Chan, Joseph Man. "Television Development in Greater China: Structure, Exports, and Market Formation," in *New Patterns in Global Television: Peripheral Vision,* et al, eds. John Sinclair. Oxford: Oxford University Press, 1996, pp. 126-160.

——— and Lee, C.C. *Mass Media and Political Transition: The Hong Kong press in China's orbit.* New York: Guilford Press, 1991.

——— and Lee, Paul S.N. "Mass Communication: Consumption and Evaluation," in *Indicators of Social Development, Hong Kong 1990,* et al, eds. S.K. Lau. Hong Kong: The Press of the Hong Kong Institute of Asia-Pacific Studies, The Chinese University of Hong Kong, 1993.

———. "Communication indicators in Hong Kong: Conceptual Issues and Findings," in *The Development of Social Indicators Research in Chinese Societies,* ed. S.K. Lau. Hong Kong: The Press of the Hong Kong Institute of Asia-Pacific Studies, the Chinese University of Hong Kong, 1993, pp. 175–204.

————. Lee, Chin-Chuan and Lee, S.N. *Hong Kong Journalists in Transition*. Hong Kong: The Press of the Hong Kong Institute of Asia-Pacific Studies, The Chinese University of Hong Kong, 1996.

————. "Media Internationalization in China: Processes and Tensions," *Journal of Communication*, Volume 44, no.3, 1994.

————. "National Responses and Accessibility to STAR TV in Asia," *Journal of Communication*, Volume 44, no. 3, 1994.

Chan, Kam-wing. "Post-Mao China: A Two Class Urban Society in the Making," *International Journal of Urban and Regional Research*, 1996, 20(1), pp. 134–150.

Chan, Ming K. "Hong Kong's Imperfect Transition to 1997: Implications for Chinese Mainland Relations," Paper presented at the International Conference, Taiwan on the Move, Chung-li, Taiwan, April 1996.

————. "Hong Kong in Sino-British Conflict: Mass Mobilization and the Crisis of Legitimacy, 1912–26," in *Precarious Balance: Hong Kong Between China and Britain, 1842–1992*, ed. Ming K. Chan. Armonk, New York: M.E. Sharpe, and Hong Kong: Hong Kong University Press, 1994, pp. 27–58.

————. "Democracy Derailed Realpolitik in the Making of the Hong Kong Basic Law, 1985–90," in *The Hong Kong Basic Law Blueprint for "Stability and Prosperity" Under Chinese Sovereignty?*, eds. Ming K. Chan and David J. Clark. Armonk, New York: M.E. Sharpe and Hong Kong: Hong Kong University Press, 1991.

———— and Clark, David J., eds. *The Hong Kong Basic Law: Blueprint for "Stability and Prosperity" under Chinese Sovereignty?* Armonk, New York: M.E. Sharpe, and Hong Kong: Hong Kong University Press, 1991.

————. "All in the Family: Hong Kong-Guangdong Linkages in Historical Perspective, 1842–1992," in Alvin So and Reginald Kwok, eds., *The Hong Kong-Guangdong Link: Partnership in Flux*. Armonk, New York: M.E. Sharpe, and Hong Kong: Hong Kong University Press, 1995.

————. *The British Sunset in Hong Kong: Historical Challenge in the Wilsonian Era of Transition*. Hong Kong: Hong Kong Economic Journal, 1989.

————, ed. *Precarious Balance: Hong Kong Between China & Britain 1842–1992*. Armonk, New York: M.E. Sharpe, and Hong Kong: Hong Kong University Press, 1994.

Chan, Sau. Y. *Improvisation in a Ritual Context: the Music of Cantonese Opera*. Hong Kong: Chinese University Press, 1991.

Chen, Albert H.Y. "Some Reflections on Hong Kong's Autonomy," *Hong Kong Law Journal* 24 (1994).

Cheng, Joseph Y.S. "Values and Attitudes of the Hong Kong Community" in *Hong Kong Trends 1989–92: Index to The Other Hong Kong Report*, ed. Paul Chun-Kuen Kwong. Hong Kong: Chinese University Press, 1992, pp. 17–46.

————. "Sino-British Negotiations on Hong Kong during Chris Patten's Governorship," *Australian Journal of International Affairs* 48, November 1994, pp. 229–45.

————. "Looking at the Other Options," *South China Morning Post*, March 2, 1986.

Cheng, Z. Y. "Overseas Chinese and Economic Development in China," *World Daily*, 1994.

Ching, Frank. *Hong Kong and China: For Better or Worse*. New York: China Council of the Asia Society and the Foreign Policy Association, 1985.

————. "Towards Colonial Sunset: The Wilson Regime, 1987–92," in *Precarious Balance: Hong Kong Between China and Britain, 1842–1992*, ed. Ming K. Chan. Armonk, New York: M.E. Sharpe, and Hong Kong: Hong Kong University Press, 1994, pp. 173–198.

————. "The Vienna Convention on the Law of Treaties and the Joint Liaison Group's Agreement on Hong Kong's Court of Final Appeal," Paper presented at a Zonta Club Forum on the Court of Final Appeal, October 21, 1994.

Chiu, Hungdah, and Downen, Robert, eds. *Multi-system Nations and International Law: the International Status of Germany, Korea and China*, Proceedings of a Regional Conference of American Society of International Law. University of Maryland Law School, OPRSCAS, 1981, No. 8.

Chiu, Hungdah. "The Hong Kong Agreement and US Foreign Policy," in *Hong Kong: A Chinese and International Concern*, eds. Jürgen Domes and Yu-ming Shaw. Boulder, CO: Westview Press, 1988, pp. 183–95.

Chiu, Stephen W.K. "The Changing World Order and the East Asian Newly Industrializing Countries," in *Old Nations, New World*, ed. David Jacobson. Boulder: Westview Press, 1994, pp. 75–114.

———— and So, Alvin Y. "Will Japan Become the Next Hegemon in the World Economy?" *Contemporary Development Analysis* 1, 1996, pp. 27–51.

————, Ho, C.K. and Lui, Tai-lok. *Economic Restructuring in Hong Kong and Singapore*. Boulder: Westview Press, 1996.

————, Lai, On-Kwok and Lee, Ching-Kwan. A *Study of the Impact of Industrial Restructuring on Women Workers*. Hong Kong: Federation of Women, unpublished paper, 1996.

Choi, P.K. "From Dependency to Self-Sufficiency: Rise of the Indigenous Culture of Hong Kong, 1945–1989," *Asian Culture*, no.14, 1990, pp. 161–177.

Chow, W.S. *Television is Dead*. Hong Kong: Chingman Books, 1990 (in Chinese).

Chu, Godwin C., and Ju, Yanan. *The Great Wall in Ruins: Communication and Cultural Change in China*. Albany: State University of New York Press, 1993.

Chu, Kim-yee. "Transportation," in *The Other Hong Report 1991*, eds. Sung Yun-wing and Lee Ming-kwan. Hong Kong, Chinese University Press, 1991, pp. 389–402.

Clark, David. "Implementing the Bill of Rights: Three Modest Proposals. Or Taking the Bill of Rights Seriously," in *Hong Kong's Bill of Rights Problems & Prospects*, ed. Raymond Wacks, Hong Kong: Faculty of Law, University of Hong Kong, 1990.

Cohen, Jerome A., and Chiu, Hungdah. *People's China and International Law: A Documentary Study*. Princeton: Princeton University Press, 1974.

Cohen, Myron L. "Developmental Process in the Chinese Domestic Group," in *Family and Kinship in Chinese Society*, ed. Maurice Freedman. Stanford: Stanford University Press, 1970.

————. "Being Chinese: The Peripheralization of Chinese Identity," *The Living Tree: The Changing Meaning of Being Chinese Today*, ed. Tu Wei-ming. Stanford: Stanford University Press, 1994.

Coleman, James S. "Social Capital in the Creation of Human Capital," *American Journal of Sociology* 95, 1988, Supplement.

Collis, M. *Foreign Mud*. London: Faber and Faber, 1946.

Copithorne, M.D. "The Canada Hong Kong relationship," *Transactions of the Royal Society of Canada*, 6th series, vol. 1, 1990, pp. 241–48.

Cumings, Bruce. "The Origins and Development of the Northeast Asian Political Economy: Industrial Sectors, Product Cycles, and Political Consequences," in *The Political Economy of the New Asian Industrialism*, ed. Frederic Deyo. Ithaca: Cornell University Press, 1987.

Davis, Michael C. *Constitutional Confrontation in Hong Kong: Issues and Implications of the Basic Law*. Basingstoke: Macmillan, 1989.

de Mesquita, Bruce Bueno, Newman, David and Rabushka, Alvin, *Red Flag over Hong Kong*. Chatham, New Jersey: Chatham House, 1996.

DeGolyer, Michael. "Politics, Politicians and Political Parties," in *The Other Hong Report 1994*, eds. Donald H. McMillan and Man Si-wai. Hong Kong, Chinese University Press, 1994, pp. 75–102.

Deng Xiaoping, *Deng Xiaoping wenxuan* (*Selected Works of Deng Xiaoping*), Vol. 3, Beijing: Renmin Chubanshe, 1993.

Department of Foreign Affairs, Australia. *Australian Foreign Affairs Record 55*, September 1984.

Department of Foreign Affairs and International Trade, Australia. *Australian Foreign Affairs: The Monthly Record*, April 1991, p.134.

Department of Foreign Affairs and Trade, East Asia Analytical Unit, Australia. *Southern China in Transition: The New Regionalism and Australia.* Canberra, 1992.

Domes, Jurgen, and Shaw, Yu-ming. *Hong Kong: A Chinese and International Concern.* Boulder: Westview Press, 1989.

Eckert, Carter J. "Korea's Economic Development in Historical Perspective, 1945–1990," in *Pacific Century*, ed. Mark Borthwick. Boulder: Westview Press, 1992, pp. 289–308.

Erickson, Bonnie, typescript. Manuscript to appear in *American Journal of Sociology*, 1996.

Evans, Gareth, and Grant, Bruce. *Australia's Foreign Relations in the World of the 1990s.* Carlton, Vic: Melbourne University Press, 1991.

Fairbank, John King. *Trade and Diplomacy on the South China Coast.* Cambridge, Mass: Harvard University Press, 1953.

Fewsmith, Joseph. *Dilemmas of Reform in China: Economic Debate and Political Conflict.* Armonk, New York: M.E. Sharpe, 1994.

Fitzgerald, Stephen. "Australia's China," *Australian Journal of Chinese Affairs* 24 1990, pp. 315–35.

Fletcher, A. "The Image of Lost Direction," in *Centre and Labyrinth*, et. al, eds. E. Cook. Toronto: University of Toronto Press, 1983, pp. 329–346.

Flynn, Kieron. "Rights Record Savaged," *Eastern Express*, December10–11, 1994, p.1.

Fong, Eric, Salaff, Janet, and Wong, Siu-lun, "Kin Networks and the Plan to Leave Hong Kong," in *Emigration from Hong Kong*, ed. Ronald Skeldon. Hong Kong: The Chinese University Press, 1995.

Franck, Thomas M. "The Emerging Right to Democratic Governance," *American Journal of International Law* 86, no. 46, 1992.

Frank, Andre Gunder. "Asia's Exclusive Models," *Far Eastern Economic Review*, June 25, 1982, pp. 22–23.

Friedland, Johnathan. "The Regional Challenge," *Far Eastern Economic Review*, June 9, 1994, p.40–42.

Friedman, J. "Being in the world: Globalization and Localization," in *Global Culture*, ed. M. Featherstone. London: Sage Publications, 1990.

———. *Cultural Identity and Global Process.* London: Sage Publication, 1994.

Fujita, Kuniko and Hill, Richard Child. "Global Toyotaism and Local Development," *International Journal of Urban and Regional Research* 19, 1995, pp. 1–22.

Fung, Daniel R. "The Basic Law of the Hong Kong Special Administrative Region of the People's Republic of China: Problems of Interpretation," *International & Comparative Law Quarterly* 37 (1988).

Fung, Rita Mei-ling. "Going Shopping in Chinatown: Hong Kong Immigrant Entrepreneurs and Their Customers." M.Phil. thesis in progress, University of Hong Kong, Department of Sociology.

Garver, John W. *Foreign Relations of the PRC.* Englewood Cliffs, N.J.: Prentice-Hall, 1993.

Gereffi, Gary. "New Realities of Industrial Development in East Asia and Latin America: Global, Regional, and National Trends," in *State and Development in the Asian-Pacific Rim*, eds. Richard Appelbaum and Jeffrey Henderson. Newbury Park: Sage, 1992, pp. 85–112.

Ghai, Yash. "The Bill of Rights and the Basic Law: Inconsistent or Complementary?"

Paper presented at a seminar on "Hong Kong's Bill of Rights - 1991–1994 and Beyond" organised by the Faculty of Law, University of Hong Kong, June 18, 1994.

————."Basic Flaws in China's Thinking," *South China Morning Post*, December 14, 1994, p.21.

————. "A Comparative Perspective," in *Hong Kong's Basic Law: Problems & Prospects*, ed. Peter Wesley-Smith. Hong Kong: Faculty of Law, University of Hong Kong, 1990, pp. 1–21.

Gold, Thomas B. *State and Society in the Taiwan Miracle*. Armonk, New York: M.E. Sharpe, 1986.

————. "Go with Your Feelings: Hong Kong and Taiwan Popular Culture in Greater China," *The China Quarterly*, no. 136, December 1993, pp. 907–925.

Goldman, Merle. "The Intellectuals in the Deng Xiaoping Era," in *State and Society in China: The Consequences of Reform*, ed. Arthur Lewis Rosenbaum. Boulder, Colorado: Westview Press, 1992.

————, Cheek, Timothy and Hamrin, Carol Lee, eds. *China's Intellectuals and the State: In Search of a New Relationship*, Harvard Contemporary China Series 3. Cambridge, Mass.: The Council on East Asian Studies, Harvard University Press, 1987.

Granovetter, Mark. *Getting a Job: A Study of Contacts and Careers*. Cambridge, Mass.: Harvard University Press, 1974.

————. "The Strength of Weak Ties: A Network Theory Revisited," in *Social Structure and Network Analysis*, ed. Peter V. Marsden and Nan Lin. Beverly Hills: Sage, 1982.

Guldin, Gregory E. "Towards a Greater Guangdong: Hong Kong's Socio-cultural Impact on the Pearl River Delta and Beyond," in *The Hong Kong Guangdong Link: Partnership in Flux*, eds. Reginald Y.W. Kwok and Alvin So. Armonk, New York: M.E. Sharpe, and Hong Kong: Hong Kong University Press, 1995, pp. 89–118.

Halliday, Jon. *A Political History of Japanese Capitalism*. New York: Pantheon Books, 1975.

Han, Nian-lung. *Diplomacy of Contemporary China*. Hong Kong: New Horizon Press, 1990.

Hannerz, U. "Cosmopolitans and Locals in World Culture," in *Global Culture*, ed. M. Featherstone. London: Sage Publications, 1990. pp. 237–251.

Hannum, Hurst, and Lillich, Richard B. "The Concept of Autonomy in International Law," in *Models of Autonomy*, ed. Yoram Dinstein. New Brunswick: Transaction Books, 1981, pp. 215–54.

Hannum, Hurst. "The Foreign Affair Power of Autonomous Regimes," *Nordic Journal of International Law* 57, 1988.

Harding, Harry. *A Fragile Relationship: The United States and China since 1972*. Washington: Brookings Institution, 1992.

Harrell, Stevan. "Playing in the Valley: A Metonym of Modernization in Taiwan," *Cultural Change in Post-war Taiwan*, eds. Stevan Harrell and Huang Chun-chieh. Boulder, Westview, 1994, pp. 161–183.

———— and Huang, Chun-chieh. "Introduction: Change and Contention in Taiwan's Cultural Scene," in *Cultural Change in Post-war Taiwan*, eds. Stevan Harrell and Huang Chun-chieh. Boulder, Westview, 1994.

Harris, Stuart. "Australia-China Political Relations: From Fear to Friendly Relations?" *Australian Journal of International Affairs* 49, November 1995, pp. 237–48.

Henders, Susan. "Building Macau's Autonomy under China's Rule," M. Phil Theses, The Chinese University of Hong Kong, 1991.

Henderson, Gregory, Lebow, Richard Ned and Stoessinger, John G. *Divided Nations in a Divided World*. New York: David McKay, 1974.

Hicks, George. *Hong Kong Countdown*. Hong Kong: Writers and Publishers Cooperative, 1989.

Hill, Richard Child, and Lee, Yong Joo. "Japanese Multinationals and East Asian Development," in *Capitalism and Development*, ed. Leslie Sklair. London: Routledge, 1994, pp. 289–315.

Ho, K.C., and So, Alvin Y. "Semi-Periphery and Borderland Integration: Singapore and Hong Kong Experiences," *Political Geography*, V 16, N 3, 1997, 241–259.

Ho, Lok-sang. "Labour and Employment" in *The Other Hong Report 1992*, eds. Joseph Y.S. Cheng and Paul C.K. Kwong. Hong Kong, Chinese University Press, 1992, pp. 197–212.

Hodge, R. and Kress, G. *Social Semiotics*. Ithaca: Cornell University Press, 1988.

Hong Kong Broadcasting Authority. *Report of the Broadcasting Authority, September 1993 - August 1994*. Hong Kong: Government Printer, 1996.

Hong Kong Government. *A Draft Agreement between the Government of the United Kingdom and Britain and Northern Island and the Government of the People's Republic of China on the Future of Hong Kong*. Hong Kong: Government Printer, 1984.

———. *An Introduction to Hong Kong Bill of Rights Ordinance*. Hong Kong: Government Printer, 1992.

———. *Hong Kong 1994: A Review of 1993*. Hong Kong: Government Information Services, 1994.

———. *Hong Kong 1995*. Hong Kong: Government Information Services, 1995.

———. *The Development of Representative Government in Hong Kong: the Way Forward*. Hong Kong: Government Printer, 1988.

———. *The Further Development of Representative Government in Hong Kong* Hong Kong: Government Printer, 1984.

———. *Representative Government in Hong Kong*. Hong Kong: Government Printer, February 1994.

———. *White Paper on the Annual Report on Hong Kong 1989 to Parliament*. Hong Kong: Government Printer, April 18, 1990.

———. *White Paper on the Further Development of Representative Government in Hong Kong*. Hong Kong: Government Printer, November 1984.

Hong Kong Legislative Council. *Reports of the Meetings*, vol 3, 1989–90, May 23, 1990.

Hong Kong Urban Council. *Cantonese Cinema Retrospective 1950–1959*. Hong Kong: Government Printer, 1978.

———. *Cantonese Cinema Retrospective 1960–1968*. Hong Kong: Government Printer, 1982.

———. *Hong Kong Cinema in the Eighties* (special catalogue of the 15th Hong Kong International Film Festival) Hong Kong: Government Printer, 1991.

———. *Hong Kong Cinema Survey 1946–1968*. Hong Kong: Government Printer, 1979.

Hook, Brian. "Political Changes in Hong Kong," *The China Quarterly*, no. 136, December 1993.

House of Commons, Foreign Affairs Committee, United Kingdom. *Relations Between the United Kingdom and China in the Peiod Up to and Beyond 1997*. UK: Government Printer, March 23, 1994.

Hsiao, Michael Hsing-Huang, and So, Alvin Y. "Taiwan-Mainland Economic Nexus: Socio-Political Origins, State-Society Impacts, and Future Prospects," *Bulletin of Concerned Asian Scholars*, V 28, N 1, 1996, 3–12.

———. "Accent Through National Integration: The Chinese Triangle of Mainland-Taiwan-Hong Kong," in *Asia-Pacific and the Future of World-System*, ed. Ravi Palat. Westport: Greenwood, 1993, pp. 133–147.

Humphrey, John P. "The Universal Declaration of Human Rights: Its History, Impact and Judicial Character," in *Human Rights—Thirty Years After the Universal Declaration*, ed, B. G. Ramcharan. The Hague: Nijhoff, 1979.

International Commission of Jurists. *Countdown to 1997: Report of a Mission to Hong*

Kong. Cambridge: International Commission of Jurists, 1992.

Jackson, Robert H. *Quasi-States: Sovereignty, International Relations, and the Third World.* Cambridge: Cambridge University Press, 1990.

Jarvis, I.C. *Window on Hong Kong: A Sociological Study of Hong Kong Film Industry and its Audience.* Hong Kong: Centre of Asian Studies, University of Hong Kong, 1977.

Jayawickrama, Nihal. "Interpreting the Hong Kong Bill of Rights," Paper presented at "Canada and Hong Kong: Legal Issues Workshop," York University, Toronto, October 2, 1992.

————. "Hong Kong and the International Protection of Human Rights," in *Hong Kong's Bill of Rights Problems and Prospects,* ed. Raymond Wacks, Hong Kong: Faculty of Law, University of Hong Kong, 1990.

Johnson, Chalmers. "The Mouse Trapping of Hong Kong: A Game in Which Nobody Wins," *Asian Survey* 9, September 1984, pp. 887–909.

Johnson, Graham E. "1997 and After: Will Hong Kong Survive? A Personal View" *Pacific Affairs* 59, no. 2, Summer 1986, pp. 237–254.

————. "Continuity and Transformation in the Pearl River Delta: Hong Kong's Impact on Its Hinterland," in *The Hong Kong Guangdong Link: Partnership in Flux,* eds. Reginald Y.W. Kwok and Alvin So. Armonk, New York: M.E. Sharpe, and Hong Kong: Hong Kong University Press, 1995, pp. 64–86.

————. "Leaders and Leadership in a New Territories Town," *The China Quarterly* 51, March 1977, pp. 109–125.

Kau, Michael. "The ROC's Diplomatic Impasse and New Policy Initiatives," in *The Role of Taiwan in International Economic Organizations,* ed. Chu Yun-han. Taipei: INPR, 1990, pp. 1–26.

Kent, Ann. *Between Freedom and Subsistence: China and Human Rights.* Hong Kong: Oxford University Press, 1993.

King, Ambrose Yeo-chi. "Kuan-hsi and Network Building: A Sociological Interpretation," *Daedalus,* Vol.120, no. 2, 1991.

Kirby, Michael. "Human Rights: The Role of the Judge," in *Bill of Rights: A Comparative Approach,* eds. Johannes Chan and Yash Ghai. Hong Kong/Singapore/Malaysia: Butterworths Asia, 1993, no.225.

Klintworth, Gary. *New Taiwan, New China: Taiwan's Changing Role in the Asia-Pacific.* New York: St. Martin's Press, 1995.

Kolko, Joyce. *Restructuring the World Economy.* New York: Pantheon, 1988.

Koo, Hagen. "Strong State and Contentious Society," in *State and Society in Contemporary Korea,* ed. Hagen Koo. Ithaca: Cornell University Press, 1993, pp. 231–249.

Kozul-Wright, K. "Transnational Corporations and the Nation State," in *Managing the Global Economy,* eds. J. Michie and J.G. Smith. Oxford: Oxford University Press, 1995.

Kwok, Reginald, and So, Alvin, eds. *The Hong Kong–Guangdong Link: Partnership in Flux.* Armonk, New York: M.E. Sharpe, and Hong Kong: Hong Kong University Press, 1995.

Kwong, Paul C.K. "Emigration and Manpower Shortage," in *The Other Hong Kong Report,* eds. Richard Y.C. Wong and Joseph Y.S. Cheng. Hong Kong: The Chinese University Press, 1990.

————. "Internationalization of Population and Globalization of Families," in *The Other Hong Report 1993,* eds. Choi Po-king and Ho Lok-sang. Hong Kong, Chinese University Press, 1993, pp. 147–174.

Laing, Edward A. "The Norm of Self-Determination, 1941–1991," *California Western International Law Journal* 22, 1991–92, pp. 209–308.

Lam, Willy Wo-lap. *China after Deng Xiaoping: the Power Struggle in Beijing since Tiananmen.* Hong Kong: Professional Consultants, Inc., 1995.

Lam, Danny Kin-Kong. "Hongkong Chinese Emigration and Investment Patterns in Response to the 1997 Problem," *Journal of Northeast Asian Studies* 9, Spring 1990, pp. 63–65.

Lampton, David M. "Hong Kong and the Rise of 'Greater China': Policy Issues for the United States," in *Hong Kong and China in Transition*, ed. John P. Burns. Canada and Hong Kong Papers No. 3, Toronto: Joint Center for Asia-Pacific Studies, 1994, pp. 73–84.

Lands and Works Branch. *Metroplan: The Aims*. Hong Kong: Government Printer, 1988.

———. *Metroplan: The Selected Strategy, an Overview*. Hong Kong: Government Printer, 1988.

Lau, Kwok-yu. "Public Housing," in *The Other Hong Report 1994*, eds. Donald H. McMillan and Man Si-wai. Hong Kong, Chinese University Press, 1994, pp. 265–296.

Lau, Kwok-yu. "Housing," in *The Other Hong Report: 1991*, eds. Sung Yun-wing and Lee Ming-kwan. Hong Kong, Chinese University Press, 1991, pp. 343–388.

Lau, Siu-kai. "Institutions Without Leaders: The Hong Kong Chinese View of Political Leadership," *Pacific Affairs* 63, 1990.

———. *Society and Politics of Hong Kong*. Hong Kong: The Chinese University Press, 1982.

——— and Kuan, H.C. *The Ethos of the Hong Kong Chinese*. Hong Kong: The Chinese University of Hong Kong, 1988.

Law, Kar. "The 'Shaolin Temple' of the New Hong Kong Cinema," in *A Study of the Hong Kong Cinema in the Seventies, Special Catalogue of the 8th Hong Kong International Film Festival*. Hong Kong: Hong Kong Urban Council, 1984, pp. 114–117.

Lee, F.Y. "Mainland China's Television is Making a Profit Without Cost," *The Next Magazine*, March 26, 1993.

Lee, Ming-kwan. "Politicians," in *The Other Hong Report: 1990*, eds. Richard Y.C. Wong and Joseph Y.S. Cheng. Hong Kong, Chinese University Press, 1990, pp. 113–130.

———. "Community and Identity in Transition in Hong Kong," in *The Hong Kong–Guangdong Link: Partnership in Flux*, eds. Reginald Y.W. Kwok and Alvin So. Armonk, New York: M.E. Sharpe, and Hong Kong: Hong Kong University Press, 1995, pp. 119–134.

Leung, Chi-keung, "Transportation," in *The Other Hong Report 1990*, eds. Richard Y.C. Wong and Joseph Y.S. Cheng. Hong Kong, Chinese University Press, 1990, pp. 459–490.

Leung, Joe C.B. "Community Participation: Past, Present and Future," in *25 Years of Social and Economic Development in Hong Kong*, eds. Benjamin K.P. Leung and Teresa Y.C. Wong. Hong Kong: Centre for Asian Studies, Hong Kong University, 1994, pp. 252–269.

——— "Social Welfare," in *The Other Hong Kong Report 1995*, eds. Stephen Y.S. Cheung and Stephen M.H. Sze. Hong Kong, Chinese University Press, 1995.

Leung, K.K. "The Basic Law and the Problem of Political Transition," *The Other Hong Kong Report 1995*, eds. Stephen Y.S. Cheung and Stephen M.H. Sze. Hong Kong, Chinese University Press, 1995, pp. 33–50.

Leung, L.K. Grace. "The Evolution of Hong Kong as a Regional Movie Production and Export Center," An unpublished M.Phil. thesis at the Chinese University of Hong Kong, Hong Kong, 1992.

Lever-Tracy, Constance, et. al. *Asian Entrepreneurs in Australia: Ethnic Small Business in the Indian and Chinese Communities of Brisbane and Sydney*. Canberra: Australian Government Publishing Service, 1991.

Li, Cheuk-to. *Notes on Hong Kong Movies in the Eighties*. Hong Kong: Chong Kin Publisher, 1990 (in Chinese).

Li, Kwok-sing. "The Past, Present and Future of the CPC's Hong Kong Policy," *Yazhou Zhoukan*, No. 9, July 1994, pp. 27–69.

Lilich, Richard L. "Civil Rights," in *Human Rights in International Law—Legal and Policy Issues*, ed. Theodore Meron. Oxford: Clarendon Press, 1984.

Lillich, Richard B., and Newman, Frank C. eds. *International Human Rights: Problems of Law and Policy*. Boston & Toronto: Little, Brown & Co, 1979.

Lin, Ching-yuan. *Industrialization in Taiwan, 1946–72.* New York: Praeger, 1973.

Lin, Zhiling, and Robinson, Thomas W. eds. *The Chinese and Their Future: Beijing, Taipei, and Hong Kong.* Washington, D.C.: AEI Press, 1994.

Liu, Che-ning. "The Power of Interpretation of the Hong Kong Special Administrative Region Basic Law– Where Do We Go From Here?" *China Law Reporter* 4, 1989.

Lo, Chi-kin. "From 'Through Train' to 'Second Stove' " in *From Colony to SAR: Hong Kong's Challenge Ahead*, eds. Joseph Y.S. Cheng and Sonny S.H. Lo. Hong Kong: Chinese University Press, 1995, pp. 25–38.

Lo, Fu. *A Stroll with Hong Kong Culture.* Hong Kong: Chung Hwa Publisher, 1993. pp. 209–214.

Lo, Shiu-hing. "The Politics of the Court of Final Appeal Debate in Hong Kong," *Issues & Studies* 29, 1993, pp. 105–31.

———. *Political Development in Macau.* Hong Kong: Chinese University Press, 1995.

Loh, Christine. "Not Far Enough," *Far Eastern Economic Review*, April 8, 1993, p. 24.

Lui, Tai-Lok, and Wong, Hung. *Disempowerment and Empowerment: An Exploratory Study on Low-IncomeHouseholds in Hong Kong.* Hong Kong: Oxfam Hong Kong, 1995.

Madsen, Richard. "The Spiritual Crisis of China's Intellectuals," in *Chinese Society on the Eve of Tiananmen: The Impact of Reform*, eds. Deborah Davis and Ezra Vogel. Harvard Contemporary China Series 7. Cambridge, Mass.: The Council of East Asian Studies, Harvard University Press, 1990.

Mainland Affairs Commission, *Taihai Liangan Guanxi Shuomingshu (An Explanation of Relations between the Two Sides of the Taiwan Straits)* Taipei: July 1994.

Man, Guida. "The Experience of Women in Middle-Class Hong Kong Chinese Immigrant Famlies in Canada: An Investigation in Institutional and Organizational Processes," Ph.D. thesis in progress, Department of Sociology, OISE, University of Toronto.

Maruya, T. "Economic Relations between Hong Kong and Guangdong Province," in *Guangdong*, ed. T. Maruya. Hong Kong: Centre of Asian Studies, the University of Hong Kong, 1992, pp. 126–147.

McConnell, Mitch. "Hong Kong and the Future of China Three Years After the Tiananmen Square Massacre," *Heitage Lectures*, No. 385. Washington, D.C.: Heritage Foundation, 1992.

McDougal, Myres S., Lasswell, Harold D. and Chen, Lung-chu. *Human Rights and World Order.* New Haven: Yale University Press, 1980.

McGurn, William. *Basic Law, Basic Questions.* Hong Kong: Review Publishing Company, 1988.

———. *Perfidious Albion: The Abandonment of Hong Kong 1997.* Lanham, MD: Ethics and Public Policy Center, 1992.

Miners, Norman. "From Nationalistic Confrontation to Regional Collaboration: China-Hong Kong-Britain, 1926–1941" in *Precarious Balance: Hong Kong Between China and Britain, 1842–1992*, ed. Ming K. Chan. Armonk, New York, M.E. Sharpe, and Hong Kong: Hong Kong University Press, 1994, pp. 59–70.

———. "Hong Kong: A Case Study in Political Stability," *Commonwealth and Comparative Politics* 13, 1975.

Ming Pao, ed. *Daioyutai: Zhongguodi lingtu (The Diaoyutai Islands: China's Territory).* Hong Kong: Ming Pao Publishing, 1996.

Mosher, Stacy. "Court of Contention," *Far Eastern Economic Review*, December 19, 1991.

Mushkat, Roda. "Foreign, External and Defence Affairs" in *The Basic Law and Hong Kong's Future*, eds. Peter Wesley-Smith & Albert H.Y. Chen. Hong Kong: Butterworths, 1988, pp. 248–267.

———. "Hong Kong as an International Legal Person," *Emory International Law Review* 6, 1992, pp. 105–170.

————. "Hong Kong's International Personality: Issues and Implications," in William Angus, ed., *Canada-Hong Kong: Some Legal Considerations*. Toronto: Joint Centre for Asia Pacific Studies, University of Toronto/York University, 1992 (Canada and Hong Kong Papers, No. 2).

————. "Hong Kong's Quest for Autonomy: A Theoretical Reinforcement," in *Hong Kong, China and 1997 Essays in Legal Theory*, ed. Raymond Wacks. Hong Kong: Hong Kong University Press, 1993.

————. "International Human Rights Law and Domestic Hong Kong Law" in *Hong Kong's Bill of Rights Problems and Prospects*, ed. Raymond Wacks, Hong Kong: Faculty of Law, University of Hong Kong, 1990.

————. "The International Legal Status of Hong Kong under Post-transitional Rule," *Houston Journal of International Law*, Vol. 10 (1), Autumn 1987, pp. 1–24.

Myers, Ramon H. ed. *A Unique Relationship: The United States and the Republic of China Under the Taiwan Relations Act*. Stanford: Hoover Institution Press, 1989.

Nadeau, Jules. *Hong Kong 1997: Dans la Gueule du Dragon Rouge*. Montreal: Editions Quebec/Amerique, 1990.

Nathan, Andrew. *China's Crisis*. New York: Columbia University Press, 1990.

Ng, Margaret. "Hong Kong Has Been Cheated Over the Rule of Law After 1997," *South China Morning Post*, October 1, 1991, p.23.

Ng, Mee-kam. "Urban and Regional Planning" in *From Colony to SAR: Hong Kong's Challenge Ahead*, eds. Joseph Y.S. Cheng and Sonny S.H. Lo. Hong Kong: Chinese University Press, 1995, pp. 227–261.

Ng, Norman Y.T. "Population: Growth, Profile, and Redistribution," in *The Other Hong Report 1992*, eds. Joseph Y.S. Cheng and Paul C.K. Kwong. Hong Kong, Chinese University Press, 1992, pp. 229–234.

Ng, Shui-lai. "Social Welfare" in *The Other Hong Report 1992*, eds. Joseph Y.S. Cheng and Paul C.K. Kwong. Hong Kong, Chinese University Press, 1992, pp. 297–308.

————. "Social Welfare," in *The Other Hong Report 1991*, eds. Sung Yun-wing and Lee Ming-kwan. Hong Kong, Chinese University Press, 1991, pp. 329–342.

Niklas, Luhmann. *Trust and Power*. Chichester: John Wiley & Sons, 1979.

Nossal, Kim Richard. "A High Degree of Ambiguity: Hong Kong as an International Actor," in *Hong Kong's International Identity*, ed. Diana Lary. Toronto: York University Joint Centre for Asia-Pacific Studies, 1996.

————. *Rain Dancing: Sanctions in Canadian and Australian Foreign Policy*. Toronto: University of Toronto Press, 1994.

————. *The Beijing Massacre: Australian Responses, Australian Foreign Policy Papers*. Canberra: Department of International Relations, Australian National University, 1993.

Office of Taiwan Affairs and Office of Information, State Council. *Taiwan Wenti yu Zhongguo Tongyi* (*The Taiwan Question and China's Unification*), August 31, 1993. Full text in *Renmin Ribao*, September 1, 1993.

Ogle, George E. *South Korea: Dissent Within the Economic Miracle*. London: Zed Books, 1990, p.37.

Oksenberg, Michel. "What Kind of China Do We Want?" *Newsweek*, April 1, 1996.

Oman, Charles. *New Forms of Investment in Developing Countries*. Paris: OECD, 1989.

Ong, Aihwa. "Limits to Cultural Accumulation: Chinese Capitalists on the American Pacific Rim," *Annals of the New York Academy of Sciences* 645, 1992.

Ovenholt, William H. "Hong Kong and China after 1997: The Real Issues," in Frank J. Macchiavola and Robert B. Oxnam, eds. *The China Challenge: American Policies in East Asia*. New York: The Academy of Political Science in conjunction with the Asia Society, 1991.

Ozawa, Terutomo. "Foreign Direct Investment and Structural Transformation: Japan as a

Recycler of Market and Industry," *Business and the Contemporary World* 5 (2), 1993, pp. 129–130.

Paltiel, Jeremy R. "Negotiating Human Rights with China," in *Canada Among Nations, 1995: Democracy and Foreign Policy*, eds. Maxwell A. Cameron and Maureen Appel Molot. Ottawa: Carleton University Press, 1995, pp. 165–86.

Plummer, Michael G., and Montes, Manuel F. "Direct Foreign Investment in China: An Introduction," in *Emerging Patterns of East Asian Investment in China*, eds. Sumner J. La Croix, Michael G. Plummer and Keun Lee. Armonk, New York: M.E. Sharpe, 1995, pp. 3–20.

Pomerance, Michal. *Self-Determination in Law and Practice. The New Doctrine in the United Nations*. The Hague, Boston, and London: Martinus Nijhoff Publishers, 1982.

Pomery, Chris. "Hong Kong," in *Video World Wide: An International Study*, ed. Manuel Alvarado. London: UNESCO, 1988.

Postiglione, Gerard A., and Leung, Julian Y.M. eds. *Education and Society in Hong Kong: Toward One Country and Two Systems*. Armonk, New York: M.E. Sharpe, and Hong Kong: Hong Kong University Press, 1991.

_____. "From Capitalism to Socialism: Hong Kong Education Within a Transitional Society, *Comparative Education Review*, 35, n.4, November 1991, 627–649.

_____. *Social Change and Educational Development: Mainland China, Taiwan and Hong Kong*. Hong Kong: Centre of Asian Studies, 1995.

_____. "National Minorities and Nationalities Policy in China," in Berch Berberoglu, ed., *The National Question: Nationalism, Ethnic Conflict, and Self-Determination in the Twentieth Century*. Philadelphia: Temple University Press, 1995.

_____. and Chan, Ming K. eds., *The Hong Kong Reader: Passage to Chinese Sovereignty*, Armonk, New York: M.E. Sharpe, 1996.

_____. and Mak, Grace C.L. eds., *Asian Higher Education*, Westport CT: Greenwood Press, 1997.

_____. "The Future of the Hong Kong Academic Profession in a Period of Profound Change," in Altback, Philip G. ed., *The International Academic Profession: Portaits of Fourteen Countries*, Princeton: The Carnegie Foundation fo the Advancement of Teaching, 1997.

_____. "Asian Higher Education: Growth, Diversity, and Change," *in Transforming Higher Education*, Green, Madeleine, F. ed., Washington D.C. and Oryx Press, 1997.

Rabushka, Alvin. "Hong Kong: A Study" in *Economic Freedom*. Chicago: Chicago University Press, 1979.

Riskin, Carl. *China's Political Economy: The Quest for Development Since 1949*. New York: Oxford University Press, 1987.

Ritzer, George. *The McDonaldization of Society: An Investigation into the Changing Character of Contemporary Social Life*. Thousand Oaks, London, New Delhi, 1993.

Roberts, David, ed. *Hong Kong 1990: A Review of 1989*. Hong Kong: Government Printer, 1990.

Robertson, R. *Globalization*. London: Sage Publication, 1992.

Rozman, Gilbert. "The Confucian Faces of Capitalism," in *Pacific Century*, ed. Mark Borthwick. Boulder, CO: Westview Press, 1992, pp. 310–318.

Salaff, Janet, and Wong, Siu-lun. "Exiting Hong Kong: Social Class Experiences and the Adjustment to 1997" in *Inequalities and Development: Social Stratification in Chinese Societies*, eds. Lau Siu-kai, Lee Ming-kwan, Wan Po-san, and Wong Siu-lun. Hong Kong: Hong Kong Institute of Asia-Pacific Studies, 1994. pp. 205–250.

Segal, Gerald. *The Fate of Hong Kong*. London: Simon and Schuster, 1993.

Selden, Mark. "China, Japan, and the Regional Political Economy of East Asia, 1945–1995.

Paper presented to the Japan in Asia Workshop, Cornell University, March 31–April 2, 1995.

Shambaugh, David, and Robinson, Thomas W., eds. *Chinese Foreign Policy*. Oxford: Clarendon, 1994.

Shirk, Susan L. *The Political Logic of Economic Reform in China*. Berkeley and Los Angeles: University of California Press, 1993.

Silk, M. "The Autonomy of Comedy," in *Comparative Criticism*, ed. E. Schaffer. Cambridge: Cambridge University Press, 1988, Vol. 10, pp. 3–37.

Simon, Dennis F. "The Economic Activities of Western Nations in Mainland China. Paper presented to the conference on Trade and Investment in the Mainland, Taipei, June 23–24, 1990.

Sinn, Elizabeth, ed. *Culture and Society in Hong Kong*. Hong Kong: Centre of Asian Studies, The University of Hong Kong, 1995.

———. "Emigration from Hong Kong Before 1941: General Trends," in *Emigration from Hong Kong*, ed. Ronald Skeldon. Hong Kong: The Chinese University Press, 1995, pp. 11–34.

Sit, Victor Fung-shuen. "Industrial Out-Processing—Hong Kong's New Relationship with the Pearl River Delta," *Asian Profile* 17,, 1989, pp. 1–13.

——— and Wong, Siu-lun. *Small and Medium Industries in an Export-Oriented Economy: The Case of Hong Kong*. Hong Kong: Center of Asian Studies, University of Hong Kong, 1989.

Siu, Helen F. "Cultural Identity and Polities of Difference in South China," in *Daedalus* 122, no.2, 1993, pp. 19–43.

———. "Remade in Hong Kong: Weaving into the Chinese Cultural Tapestry," in *Unity and Diversity: Local Cultures and Identities in China*, eds. Tao Tao Liu and David Faure. Hong Kong: Hong Kong University Press, 1996.

Skeldon, Ronald, ed. *Reluctant Exiles: Migration from Hong Kong and the New Overseas Chinese*. Armonk, New York: M.E. Sharpe, and Hong Kong: Hong Kong University Press, 1994.

———. "Emigration and the Future of Hong Kong," *Pacific Affairs* 63, no.4, 1990–91.

———. "Immigration and Population Issues" in *The Other Hong Kong Report 1995*, eds. Stephen Y.L. Cheung and Stephen M.H. Sze. Hong Kong: Chinese University of Hong Kong Press, 1995.

———. "Migration from Hong Kong: current trends and future agendas," in Skeldon, ed., *Reluctant Exiles: Migration from Hong Kong and the New Overseas Chinese*. Armonk, New York: M.E. Sharpe, and Hong Kong: Hong Kong University Press, 1994.

Smart, Alan. "Gifts, Bribes, and Guanxi: A Reconsideration of Bourdieu's Social Capital," *Cultural Anthropology*, Vol. 8, no, 1993.

Smart, Josephine, and Smart, Alan. "Personal Relations and Divergent Economies: A Case Study of Hong Kong Investment in South China," *International Journal of Urban and Regional Research* 15, 1991.

Smith, H. *John Stuart Mill's Other Island: A Study of the Economic Development of Hong Kong*. London: Institute of Economic Affairs, 1966.

So, Alvin Y. "New Middle Class Politics in Hong Kong: 1997 and Democratization," *Asiatische Studien Etudes Asiatiques* (*Swiss Asian Studies*) 1995, XLIX: 91–109.

———. "Political Determinants of Direct Investment in Mainland China," in *Emerging Patterns of East Asian Investment in China*, eds. Sumner La Croix, Michael Plummer and Keun Lee. Armonk, New York: M.E. Sharpe, 1995, pp. 95–112.

———. "The Economic Success of Hong Kong: Insights from a World-System Perspective," *Sociological Perspectives* 29, 1986, pp. 241–258.

————. and Chiu, Stephen W.K. "Modern East Asia in World-Systems Analysis," *Sociological Enquiry*, 66, 4, 1996, 471–485.

————. and Chiu, Stephen W.K. "The Hong Kong Mode of Development: An Exception to the NIEs?" Paper presented at the Annual Meeting of the American Sociological Association, New York, August, 1996.

————. and Chiu, Stephen W.K. *East Asia and the World-Economy*. Newbury Park, CA: Sage, 1995.

State Council Information Office. *Zhongguo de renquan zhuangkuang (Human Rights in China)* Beijing: Zhongyang wenxian chubanshe, 1991.

State Statistical Bureau. *Zhongguo tongji nianjian, 1995 (Statistical Yearbook of China, 1995)* Beijing: State Statistical Bureau, 1995.

Sum, Ngai-Ling. "More than a 'War of Words': Identity, Politics and the Struggles for Dominance during the Recent Political Reform Period in Hong Kong," *Economy and Society* 24(1), 1995, pp. 67–100.

Sung, Yun-Wing. "Economic Integration of Hong Kong and Guangdong in the 1990s," in *The Hong Kong-Guangdong Link: Partnership in Flux*, eds. Reginald Kwok and Alvin Y. So. Armonk, New York: M.E. Sharpe, and Hong Kong: Hong Kong University Press, 1995, pp. 224–250.

————. "Hong Kong's Economic Value to China," in *The Other Hong Kong Report 1991*, eds. Sung Yun-wing and Lee Ming-kwan. Hong Kong: Chinese University Press, 1991.

————. "The Role of Hong Kong and Macau in China's Export Drive," Working paper No. 85/11. Australian National University: National Center for Development Studies, 1985.

————. *The China-Hong Kong Connection*. Cambridge: Cambridge University Press, 1992.

————. *The Economic Integration of Hong Kong with China in the 1990s: The Impact on Hong Kong*, Research Papers no. 1, Canada and Hong King Project. Toronto: Joint Centre for Asia Pacific Studies, 1992.

————. "Non-institutional Economic Integration Via Cultural Affinity: The Case of Mainland China, Taiwan and Hong Kong," Occasional Paper No.13, Hong Kong Institute of Asia-Pacific Studies. Hong Kong: The Chinese University of Hong Kong, 1992.

Sze, Stephen M.H. "Cultural Life in Hong Kong," in *The Other Hong Report 1992*, eds. Joseph Y.S. Cheng and Paul C.K. Kwong. Hong Kong, Chinese University Press, 1992, pp. 447–462.

Tamanahah, Brian Z. "Post-1997 Hong Kong: A Comparative Study of the Meaning of 'High Degree of Autonomy'" *California Western International Law Journal* 20, 1989.

Tang, James T.H. "Hong Kong's Internationasl Status," *Pacific Review*, Vol. 6 (3), 1993, pp. 205–215.

———— "The International Dimension of Mainland China's Unification Policy: The Case of Hong Kong," in Jaushieh Joseph Wu, ed., *Divided Nations: The Experiences of Germany, Korea, and China*, Taipei Institute of International Relations, National Chengchi University, 1995, pp. 149-170.

———— and Ching, Frank. "The MacLehose-Youde Years: Balancing the Three-legged Stool, 1971–86" in *Precarious Balance: Hong Kong Between China and Britain, 1842–1992*, ed. Ming K. Chan. Armonk, New York: M.E. Sharpe, and Hong Kong: Hong Kong University Press, 1994, pp. 131–148.

Tang, Min and That, Myo. *Growth Triangles: Conceptual Issues and Operational Problems.* Economic Staff Paper No.54, Asian Development Bank, Manila, 1994.

Ting Wai, "The External Relations and International Status of Hong Kong." Occasional Papers/Reprint series in Contemporary Asian Studies, University of Maryland School of Law, May 1997.

To, Y. M., and Lau, T. Y. "The Sky Is Not the Limit: Hong Kong as a Global Media Exporter." Paper presented to the International Communication Association Convention, Sydney, Australia, July 11–15, 1994.

Tsai, Jung-Fang. *Hong Kong in Chinese History: Community and Social Unrest in the British Colony 1842–1913.* New York: Columbia University Press, 1993.

———. "From Anti-foreignism to Popular Nationalism: Hong Kong Between China and Britain, 1839–1911," in *Precarious Balance: Hong Kong Between China and Britain, 1842–1992,* ed. Ming K. Chan. Armonk, New York: M.E. Sharpe, and Hong Kong: Hong Kong University Press, 1994, pp. 9–26.

Tu, Wei-ming, ed. *The Living Tree: The Changing Meaning of Being Chinese Today.* Stanford: Stanford University Press, 1994.

United States, Congress. *Congressional Record, 136th Congress,* November 2, 1990, E3704.

———, Senate. *Congressional Record, 137th Congress,* September 20, 1991, S13412–13.

University and Polytechnic Grants Committee Secretariat. "Higher Education in Hong Kong," Hong Kong: Government Printer, October 1992, Ref: UPGC/GEN/222/90.

University and Polytechnic Grants Committee. *Higher Education 1991–2000: An Interim Report.* Hong Kong: Government Printer, November 1993.

University Grants Committee Secretariat. *University Grants Committee of Hong Kong: Facts and Figures 1994.* Hong Kong: Government Printer, April 1995.

Vogel, Ezra. *One Step Ahead in China: Guangdong Under Reform.* Cambridge, Mass.: Harvard University Press, 1989.

Wakeman, Frederick. *Strangers at the Gates.* Berkeley: University of California Press, 1967.

Walker, R.B.J., and Mendlovitz, Saul H., eds. *Contending Sovereignties: Redefining Political Community.* Boulder and London: Lynne Rienner Publishers, 1990.

Wallen, David. "UN Call to China on Rights Reports," *South China Morning Post,* December 10, 1994, p.2.

Watson, James L. *Emigration and the Chinese Lineage.* Berkeley: University of California Press, 1975.

Webster, Justin. "Success in Hong Kong: Universities in Hong Kong Attract Top Scholars Despite Concern About Colony's Future After 1997," *Chronicle of Higher Education,* October 19, 1994.

Wellman, Barry, and Wortley, Scott. "Different Strokes from Different Folks: Community Ties and Social Support," *American Journal of Sociology* 96, 1990.

Weng, Byron S.J. "Taiwan's Mainland Policy Before and After June 4," in *Broken Mirror: China after Tiananmen,* ed. George Hicks. Essex: Longman, 1990.

———. "Beijing's Taiwan Policy: Continuity and Change," *INPR,* forthcoming 1996.

———. "Economic Interactions and Political Altercations: Prospects for Mainland-Taiwan-Hong Kong Relations," in *Sino-American Relations at a Time of Change,* eds. Gerrit W. Gong and Lin Bih-jaw. Washington, D.C.: CSIS, 1994, pp. 181–198.

———. "Taiwan's International Status Today," *The China Quarterly,* No. 99, September 1984, pp. 462–480.

———. "The Evolution of a Divided China," in *The Chinese and Their Future: Beijing, Taipei and Hong Kong,* ed. Lin Zhiling and Thomas W. Robinson. Washington, D.C.: AEI Press, 1994, pp. 345–385.

———. "The Integration of Outlying Areas: the Case of Hong Kong," in *The End of an Isolation: China After Mao,* ed. Harish Kapur. The Hague: Martinus Nijhoff, 1985, pp. 308–361.

Weng, Songran (Byron S.J. Weng), " 'Yiguo liangzhe' chulun: gainian, xingzhi, zhangai han qianjing (A Rustic Theory on 'One Country, Two Systems': Concept, Nature, Content, Obstacles and Prospects)," in *"Taiwan zhi jianglai" dierci xueshu taolunhui lunwenji,* ed. F.Q. Guo and Zhao Fusan. Papers Presented at the 2nd Symposium on "Taiwan's Future."

Beijing: Friendship Publishing Co., 1985, pp. 349–384.

———— "A Preliminary Study on the Relationships Between the Two Sides Across the Taiwan Straits in the Coming Ten Years," *Jiushi Niandai*, (The Nineties) No. 193. February. 1986, pp. 24–31.

Wing, Suen. "Labor and Employment" in *The Other Hong Report 1994*, eds. Donald H. McMillan and Man Si-wai. Hong Kong, Chinese University Press, 1994, pp. 149–164.

Witt, Hugh, ed. *Hong Kong Yearbook 1993: A Review of 1992.* Hong Kong: Government Printer, 1993.

Wong, Fanny. "Press Giants Defy 1997 Fears," *South China Morning Post,* April 10, 1995. p.6.

Wong, Richard Y.C., and Staley, Stanley. "Housing and Land," in *The Other Hong Report 1992,* eds. Joseph Y.S. Cheng and Paul C.K. Kwong. Hong Kong, Chinese University Press, 1992, pp. 308–350.

Wong, Siu-lun. "Business Networks, Cultural Values and The State in Hong Kong and Singapore," in *Chinese Business Enterprise in Asia,* ed. R. A. Brown. London and New York: Routledge, 1995.

————. "Business and Politics in Hong Kong During The Transition," in *25 Years of Social and Economic Development in Hong Kong,* eds. Benjamin K.P. Leung and Teresa Y.C. Wong. Hong Kong: Center of Asian Studies, University of Hong Kong, 1994.

————. "Chinese Entrepreneurs and Business Trust," in *Business Networks and Economic Development in East and Southeast Asia,* ed. Gary Hamilton. Hong Kong: Center of Asian Studies, University of Hong Kong, 1991.

————. "Emigration and Stability in Hong Kong," *Asian Survey* 32, no.10, 1992.

————. *Emigrant Entrepreneurs: Shanghai Industrialists in Hong Kong.* Hong Kong: Oxford University Press, 1988.

————. "Political Attitudes and Identity" in *Emigration from Hong Kong,* ed. Ronald Skeldon. Hong Kong: The Chinese University Press, 1995.

Wong, Thomas W. P. "Inequality, Stratification and Mobility," in *Indicators of Social Development: Hong Kong,* et al. Lau Siu-kai. Hong Kong: Institute of Asia-Pacific Studies, The Chinese University of Hong Kong, 1988.

Wong, Yiu-tim. "Labor and Unemployment" in *The Other Hong Kong Report 1995,* eds. Stephen Y.S. Cheung and Stephen M.H. Sze. Hong Kong: Chinese University Press, 1995, pp. 287–302.

World Bank. *The East Asian Miracle.* Oxford: Oxford University Press, 1993.

Xu, Xueqiang, Kwok, Reginald, Li, Lixun and Yan, Xiaopei. "Production Change in Guangdong," in *Hong Kong-Guangdong Link: Partnership in Flux,* eds. Reginald Kwok and Alvin Y. So. Armonk, New York: M.E. Sharpe, and Hong Kong: Hong Kong University Press, 1995, pp. 135–162.

Yang, Dali. "China Adjusts to the World Economy: The Political Economy of China's Coastal Development Strategy," *Pacific Affairs* 64, 1991, pp. 42–64.

————. "Patterns of China's Regional Development Strategy," *The China Quarterly* 122, June 1990, pp. 230–257.

Yang, Mayfair Mei-hui. *Gifts, Favors and Banquets: The Art of Social Relationships in China.* Ithaca & London: Cornell University Press, 1994.

Yeung, Henry W.C. "The Geography of Hong Kong Transnational Corporations in the ASEAN Region," *Area* 27, 1995, pp. 318–334.

Zhonggong dongguan shiwei. *Cong nongcun zhou xiang chengshi (From Village to Municipality)* Beijing: Renmin Chubanshe, 1994.

Zhongguo gongchandang zhizheng sishinian (*The Communist Party of China in Power 40 Years*) Beijing: Zhonggong dangshi ziliao chubanshe, 1989.

Index